*In Search of the Swan Maiden*

# IN SEARCH OF
# THE SWAN MAIDEN

*A Narrative on*
*Folklore and Gender*

*Barbara Fass Leavy*

New York University Press
NEW YORK AND LONDON

NEW YORK UNIVERSITY PRESS
New York and London

Copyright © 1994 by New York University
All rights reserved

Library of Congress Cataloging-in-Publication Data
Leavy, Barbara Fass
In search of the swan maiden : a narrative on folklore and gender
/ Barbara Fass Leavy.
p.    cm.
Includes bibliographical references (p.        ) and index.
ISBN 0-8147-5068-0 (acid-free paper)
1. Swan maiden (Tale)—History and criticism.   2. Swan maiden
(Tale)—Classification.   3. Women—Folklore.   4. Sex—Folklore.
5. Man-woman relationships—Folklore.   I. Title.
GR75.S8L43     1994
398.21—dc20          93-26313
                        CIP

New York University Press books are printed on acid-free paper,
and their binding materials are chosen for strength and durability.

Manufactured in the United States of America

10  9  8  7  6  5  4  3  2  1

*This book is lovingly dedicated to my husband,*
*Peter B. Leavy.*

# Contents

*In Search of the Swan Maiden*

# Preface

This study was originally intended as a companion to my book on the adoption by many nineteenth-century European writers of the fairy mistress theme *(La Belle Dame sans Merci and the Aesthetics of Romanticism)*. The new work would treat the fairy's male counterpart, a bel homme sans merci, so to speak. But despite Coleridge's woman wailing for her demon lover, the fatal man does not often assume his supernatural form. Scott's Ravenswood, Brontë's Heathcliff, Lermontov's Pechorin are rationalized versions of the demon lover—too human, too much of this world to bear the symbolic weight that emerges from the supernatural in literature. I would later discover the extent of my error in surmising that demon lovers were less prevalent than their female counterparts in the world's narratives, that marriages to fairy women were ubiquitous, unions with fairy men relatively rare. These early speculations, however, focused my attention on gender, and when, eventually, literature moved to the background, folklore to the foreground of my research, I concluded that the stories I was collecting and trying to understand were virtual allegories of gender relations. With surprise I discovered myself in a scholarly otherworld, a literary critic "poaching"[1] on a foreign and not always hospitable territory. The domain of folklore required that I at least make an effort to adapt to a new discipline.

As I began to collect the folklore of the supernatural man, I frequently encountered a figure I already knew but had excluded from my earlier book as seeming to be outside my concerns. She is another kind of belle dame sans merci, one who, despite the many forms she assumes, is generically known as the swan maiden. Her story is that of a being from a supernatural realm who is constrained to marry, keep house for, and bear children to a mortal man because he retains her animal covering, an article of clothing, or some other possession without which she cannot return to the otherworld. When she regains her prized belonging, she flees her husband and children.

The swan maiden story is told in legends, in narratives supposedly depicting real events, their veracity accepted or questioned by those who narrate and listen to the legends,[2] and it is told in fairy tales, assumed to be fictions—which does not mean, however, that the stories exist only to entertain. It is arresting to discover that when the legendary captured fairy bride escapes from woman's traditional role, she rarely comes back to her human family, and that it is mainly in the fairy tale that the swan maiden will be reconciled to her husband or be disenchanted by him in order to live as a human being in his world. The swan maiden story has been interpreted as depicting exogamous marriages, describing "the pitiable lot of a girl from another tribe and territory who has been trapped into an unsuitable union through the guile and strength of a man." That the tale thus focuses on the woman's side of the story has led to the surmise that "its first tellers may have been women."[3] My argument is a more radical and inclusive variation of this speculation: I will propose that the swan maiden tale could at one time be found in virtually every corner of the world because in most of the cultures that retained it and that were reflected in its variants, woman *was* a symbolic outsider, was the *other*,[4] and marriage demanded an intimate involvement in a world never quite her own. The stories' themes depict this estrangement.

This is not to argue that a woman who told the swan maiden's story was necessarily conscious of telling her own. Vincent Crapanzano has pointed out about his work on demon marriages in Morocco that a modern, particularly a Western, listener who hears the folktales of Morocco will be convinced that the storyteller has achieved a contemporary insight that in fact would not be forthcoming if the storyteller were asked to explain the meaning of the folklore material.[5] Even rarer would be a storyteller whose narratives were shaped by a conscious theory concerning the function of folklore. It is one thing for some anthropologists and folklorists to contend that narratives allow a socially approved safety valve for the release of the tensions that arise in conflicts between individuals and their societies,[6] and quite another to find storytellers who could explain that this is what they proposed to do. It is not my purpose here to formulate or even to employ a theory about the relationship of narrative to truth or reality. Nonetheless, I will assume that folktales have meaning, that this meaning is profound, and that since narrators vary greatly with regard to intelligence, perception, and self-consciousness, folktales are often replete with a storyteller's deep insight into significant human concerns. Whether an illiterate as well as unsung genius in some country graveyard would be capable of the psychological depth argued for in the following chapters remains, of course, one of the controversies surrounding folklore studies.

Drawing on the work of David E. Bynum, I will moreover contend that the pattern that emerges from variants of the same basic story reveals often profound meanings not found in a single version.[7] Such a pattern is ultimately an individual creation; and I am quite aware that although I try to bring to this study of the swan maiden the objectivity of one who respects the scholarly requirement of scrupulous research and sound argument, I am nonetheless creating my own narrative. Modern theory would have it that all acts of interpretation involve recreating the text, but I usually resist the most radical forms of this premise. For example, I have never asked myself (nor encouraged my students to ask themselves) how my interpretation of "La Belle Dame sans Merci" is effectively my own (valid) reinscribing of Keats's poem. Rather, I have endeavored to understand how ambiguities in the ballad are reflected in the scholarly debate concerning Keats's work, both text and critics implicated in interpretation. In my search for the swan maiden, however, in my attempt to locate meaning not in one version of her tale but in what what Stith Thompson has called her "kaleidoscopic variations,"[8] I am actively participating in the process of storymaking.

Today, when the once ubiquitous swan maiden is known mainly because Tchaikovsky put a variant of her story on the ballet stage, the tale of the dissatisfied housewife who manages to escape domestic life speaks to one of the persistent problems of contemporary life. Ibsen used the swan maiden as a model for Nora, whose escape from her doll house commences soon after her maid finds the seemingly lost costume in which Nora will dance the tarantella for the delectation and status of that archetypal patriarch, her husband, Torvald Helmer. Nora's irrevocable slamming of the door on her marriage parallels the swan maiden's flight, and Helmer's hope that she may return parallels the usually vain expectancy of folklore husbands who search for their vanished fairy wives (see chapter 8). For contemporary feminists, Nora is the prototype of the liberated woman. From the perspective of folklore, however, the runaway wives and mothers who today are followed not by their husbands but by detectives their spouses hire, may be acting out what was once a widespread and surprisingly well-developed fantasy.[9] Occasionally my reader will be catapulted out of the fairy realm into the contemporary world not only because the stories illuminate modern predicaments often described in terms reminiscent of a long-forgotten folklore tradition but also because the modern situation highlights the ubiquity and age-old nature of the fantasy.

Two of the world's most popular (and interrelated) story groups will thus form the core of this book. Wendy Doniger has described the

simultaneous existence of two . . . paradigms (present in early layers of both the Indo-European and the substratum of non–Indo-European cultures). . . . The myth of the mortal male and immortal female (the king and the mare, the swan maiden and the prince) . . . [and] the myth of the immortal male and the mortal female (the stallion and the queen, Leda and the swan). As the patterns interact, the immortal female often mimics the behavior of the female in the other model —the mortal female.[10]

Insofar as the swan maiden can be distinguished from the imperious enchantress found, for example, in Celtic myth and folklore, and the seductive demon lover can be distinguished from the yearning beast who wants to receive a woman's kiss to become human, there are, in fact, at least four paradigms.[11] The goddess who lures her Tannhäuser into the Venusberg is, again, one about whom I have already written at length, and whom I differentiate from the swan maiden. The Venus-type will not be entirely absent from the following pages, but my focus of attention has shifted. I once invoked Heinrich Heine's ironic account of the goddess's domestication, but at that time "domestication" generally indicated the assimilation of the divine and the imaginative into the mundane.[12] This time, domestic life will be explored as a more literal theme in folklore.

In each narrative group that forms the core of my present study there exists a human wed to or mated with a supernatural being, the human for one reason or another losing and subsequently attempting to recover the immortal spouse. The Cupid and Psyche variant on the demon lover theme (Tale Type 425) has recently claimed the attention of feminist critics, who argue (mistakenly, I will contend) that because Psyche undertakes the difficult trip to find Cupid, she is an active character, a potential role model for contemporary women, a contrast to the passive sleeping beauties who await a prince's kiss to awaken them to life. Be this as it may (see chapter 4), the swan maiden stories (part of Tale Type 400),[13] which depict the husband's comparable attempt to win back his fairy wife, have not received the same kind of attention. As recently as five years ago it was claimed that "modern scholars have not known what to do with the swan maiden."[14]

Folklorists who have juxtaposed or compared the two narrative groups have, moreover, tended to do so in misleading ways. First, they deal with the genders of the otherworldly partners as if no significant thematic changes would follow from the difference. Some have actually said as much, although, admittedly, their work predates the era of women's studies.[15] Second, although Tale Types 400 and 425 are described as though the attempt to win back the lost supernatural spouse were the core episode, scholars either do not note or certainly do not follow the implications of the following: whereas Psyche is usually reconciled to her husband, the mortal man typically cannot recover the swan maiden.[16] His failure is particularly ironic given the insight of Torborg Lundell, who points to a gender-based bias in folklore indexes and types. According to Aarne's and Thompson's accepted classifications, the mortal man *quests* for his lost wife; the mortal woman merely *searches* for her missing husband.[17] A feature of the animal bride tales can, moreover, be added to Lundell's analysis. Frog princes usually receive their liberating kisses from compliant heroines, whereas many a frog princess has been stranded by a reluctant man too cowardly or too repelled to embrace her[18] (see chapter 6). But outside the specialized realm of folklore studies, not many know there are frog princess tales. If Walt Disney Studios really wanted to produce a fairy tale with feminist implications, why did they not adapt one of the many stories that could be designated—if awkwardly—Handsome and the Beastess?

In journeys to find their lost spouses, folklore searchers encounter both adversarial and helpful figures who affect the stories' outcomes. My next chapter will reveal how my quest for the swan maiden placed me in a similar position. I nonetheless owe a debt to almost all the folklorists and critics with whom I directly or indirectly engage in dialogue, even those with whom I do not agree. But I would like especially to acknowledge those whose influence was particularly important, some of whom I have only read, some with whom I have met or corresponded, and some of whom are friends.

It is with deep regret and sorrow that I must posthumously acknowledge the great help and deep influence of the late Bengt Holbek of the department of folklore at the University of Copenhagen. He had been supportive of my endeavors to work with folklore from the time he read the early version of my coauthored book on folklore in Ibsen. He told me he had himself long been fascinated with swan maidens and read an early version of this work, conveying to me his enjoyment but also supplying a long list of "buts" that I have endeavored to take into consideration. I wish that his marginal comments, some of which were his own ruminations on the folktales, others of which were the challenges of a great folklorist to a would-be student of folklore, could be reproduced. Holbek's own treatise *The Interpretation of Fairy Tales* is from my point of view the most important book on the subject ever written as well as one of the finest works on folklore. Since its appearance in 1987, I have been unable to decide whether its earlier publication could have saved me years of trying to work through problems of folklore methodology, or whether I really needed to go through the process itself in order to write this book. I will sorely miss the letters Bengt and I exchanged on how to read folktales and on our lives and interests.

The generous help of Tristram Potter Coffin goes back to our correspondence on Ibsen and Child ballad 243, "The Demon Lover." Coffin has read parts of this book, and although he might not endorse all the liberties I have taken with folklore, he has not wavered in his attempt to be helpful and has encouraged me with his general interest in what I was trying to do. Without his book *The British Traditional Ballad in North America* I could not have so easily consulted the many texts I used for my analysis of the "Demon Lover" ballad. My debt to Alan Dundes goes back to his evaluation of my proposal for a book on folklore in Ibsen's late plays. Since that work grew out of my studies of the swan maiden, I took his positive remarks as encouragement for the longer-term project. Moreover, he is one of those folklorists who is encouraging the *interpretation* of folklore. David E. Bynum has already been cited for his influence, his work helping me to make coherent to myself my own way of constructing the narrative that constitutes this book. William A. Lessa's study of the swan (porpoise) maiden of Oceania contains what I hold to be the best analysis of the story available to those who are interested in meanings. His composite portrait of the swan maiden is one that I have used throughout the following chapters.

Since part of my inquiry has to do with the feminist implications of the swan maiden tale, and since I am a woman writing on this subject, I became particularly sensitive to how other women were treating the subject. I have avoided polemics, however, trying to discern voices from the past without the often ideological filter of feminist criticism. Nevertheless, I would like to acknowledge my debt to three female scholars who had a major impact on my reading of folktales. Annette Kolodny's argument concerning men's failure to create adequate models by which to define themselves (*The Lay of the Land*) influenced, if indirectly, my chapter on Orpheus. My friend Elaine Hoffman Baruch has over the past several years been more directly involved in women's studies than I, and has shared her experiences in that area. My final pages on Ibsen's portrayal of Nora draw on her fine study of *A Doll House*. And I am especially indebted to Wendy Doniger, not only for her enormous scholarly knowledge but also for the example of her willingness to dare to speculate if necessary to illuminate the significance of what she knows. As the quotation above as well as quotations in following chapters reveal, she is very familiar with swan maidens, demon lovers, and animal brides and grooms—a book about which could be gleaned from her work. Wherever I do not cite a specific published source by Holbek, Coffin, and Doniger, the ideas attributed to them were conveyed to me in private correspondence and conversations.

Many people helped me while I worked on this project. Per Schelde (Jacobsen) and I first became acquainted when he translated for me Holmström's monograph on the swan maiden. From that early association came a book on folklore in Ibsen's late plays, which we wrote as I continued to pursue swan maidens, and he read the earliest version of this study in which all I wanted to do was get down on paper what was still only in my mind and on my note cards, when I had little concern for unity and coherence. He has also served as my advisor on anthropological matters. Fred Kaplan took time from his biography of Henry James to help me edit my own big baggy monster; following his advice, I was able to shorten my narrative to manageable proportions. Edward G. Fichtner translated for me and supplied commentary on the Helgi and Kara episode in the Icelandic Edda (see chapter 6). William S. Wilson supplied me with lively conversation and correspondence concerning the social and aesthetic implications of fair and dark ladies, of Odette and Odile, who have come to be characterized as white and black swans. Bette S. Weidman shared with me her interest in and knowledge of the culture and lore of native North American tribes.

David H. Richter persistently encouraged me not to be daunted by methodological problems. For many years, Robert P. Miller and I had lively conversations about loathly ladies: his work on the medieval hag has influenced mine on the romantic shapeshifter. It has also been many years since Charles Dahlberg pointed out to me that "belle dame sans merci" means not only "beautiful lady without pity" but also "beautiful lady without grace." In that duality, I believe, lies the key to the ambiguity that informs so many of the world's supernatural enchantresses, and I have always been grateful for this insight into the double aspects of their character.

Without the vast resources of the New York Public Library, which had the financial luxury of longer hours when I began this project, and without the interlibrary loan section of Queens College's Rosenthal Library, I would not have had such ready access to the uncountable stories I was able to read. I thank Izabella Taler and Suzanne Katz for their efforts to locate esoteric collections of folk and fairy tales. Once again I would like to express my gratitude to editors at New York University Press. Kitty Moore was the first to read my work in progress and express interest in publishing it; Jason Renker and Despina Papazoglou Gimbel were generous in their expertise and their support. And I thank my friend Anastasia Voutsara Friedman for the gift of her enthusiasm for the book at a time when such positive feedback was particularly welcome.

As I sorted through my thousands of note cards accumulated over many years, I recalled my debt to my late father, Joel Widom, who typed and filed and generally kept order for me. Once again I must offer thanks to my mother, Marion Widom, who taught me to read even before I went to school: I owe to her my early immersion in the world of fairy tales. My first book was dedicated to my children, Linda and Steven, for whom tales from many lands were an intrinsic part of early reading. As three generations of us convey our delight in story to a fourth, Abby, Jennifer, Jessica, Julie, Shelley, and Mandy, I think of my work on fairies, mermaids, and disenchanted beasts, and on woman's role in folk and fairy tales, as an important legacy to these beloved granddaughters. Finally, on three previous occasions I have thanked my husband Peter B.

Leavy for patience and assistance as I wrote a book. He deserves to have this one dedicated to him.

My pursuit of the swan maiden involves my search for stories fascinating in their own right, as well as my quest for understanding about how people use story to depict the conflicts that have existed between the sexes, to express the feelings that arise because of these conflicts, and to comprehend their roles and their lives. Many thousands of people in theaters around the globe continue to watch spellbound the swan maiden who expresses through dance her dependence upon a prince's strength to deliver her from evil, usually to be betrayed rather than helped by him. If the lovers triumph over wickedness in the end, it is to dwell in some place other than the social world defined by the prince's court—to bypass, that is, the implications of the prince's taking Odile for Odette. The lovers' leap into the swans' lake is an ominous sign of the difficulty of resolving the conflicts that inform their story.[19] Folklore is replete with similar dualities, substitute brides who reflect the unconscious ambivalence of unsuspecting grooms, and demon lovers who appear to women in the guises of their husbands or lovers. My endeavor is to reconstruct a narrative pattern, to retell, if you will, a story that has acquired special significance for our own time.

# CHAPTER I

# Introduction: The Dangerous Adventure

He would not write with imperfect materials, and to
him the materials were always imperfect.[1]
          —Lord Acton

My subject is the interplay between stories about a fairy captured by a
mortal man and forced into a tedious domestic existence and, obversely,
about a mortal woman courted by a demon lover who offers her escape
from that same mundane world. Other paradigms in the mortal-immor-
tal matings have been discussed in the preface, where the swan maiden
tale was summarized. Its obverse, the demon lover story, frequently
describes a trap the wife stumbles into in her flight from her traditional
role, and the tale is thus more prone than the swan maiden one to be
laden with themes of guilt and retribution. Both story groups contrast
the pleasures of a magic realm with the harder facts of real life, which
for woman include minimal (if any) autonomy in her existence. In folk
narratives the dreams of a magic otherworld are given form. As Peter
Kennedy and Alan Lomax have said about the ballads they collected in
the British Isles, the "past speaks through their lips, but if you listen with
attention you will discover fantasy patterns important to the present as
well."[2]

It is consistent with the fantasy elements in these stories that an
important narrative motif attached to the winning and rewinning of the
supernatural spouse is that of the so-called impossible task.[3] A superhuman effort becomes a prerequisite for the union. Bereft or hopeful
humans undergo arduous trials and attempt herculean feats to prove
themselves: men must climb glass mountains, and Psyche and her sisters

must carry water in sieves or wear out iron shoes to find some vaguely defined place, such as the country of beautiful gardens. In Apuleius, a Venus hostile to her daughter-in-law Psyche "took a great quantity of wheat, barley, millet, poppy-seed, pease, lentils, and beans, and mingled them all together on a heap," ordering Psyche to "separate all these grains one from another, disposing them orderly in their quality" and demanding she complete the task "before night."[4] To win his father's kingdom, a prince must rely on his enchanted frog wife to produce a fine cloth that will encircle the palace seven times.[5]

For the scholarly study of these themes, the motifs themselves become almost parodically autoreferential, for saying anything about the stories that will satisfy all those who have studied them becomes a truly impossible task. The cloth that encircles the palace is a reminder of the culture-specific nature of folklore and the importance of locating a tale in its social context. In contrast, the iron shoes that must be worn out and journeys to castles east of the sun and west of the moon, to what W. M. S. Russell calls an "indeterminate address,"[6] suggest the universality of human predicaments. The stories of supernatural spouses, moreover, seem to be *about* the freedom from cultural necessity as well as about the requirement that such necessity eventually prevail. A collector of Bengali tales, for instance, puzzles over a female folklore character who terrifies her father with her insistence that she choose her own husband. So contrary to custom is her demand that the story collector feels compelled to explain that the prospective bride was a fairy and therefore was not bound by woman's usual constraints.[7] But demon lovers throughout the world seem to have an uncanny ability to single out those women in rebellion against patriarchal restrictions. Psyche's need to separate heaps of grains and legumes seems, in addition, a task very much like that of the folklorist who endeavors to sift through matters of classification and definition. Indeed, Psyche's is the easier task insofar as a lentil can be differentiated from a poppy seed. The problem for folklore studies, writes Holbek, is "not lack of knowledge, but lack of *coherent* knowledge. There are innumerable investigations of the origins, history, diffusion, variation and adaptation of motifs, themes, types and clusters of types, of genres and the relations between genres; of performers and of the art."[8] But even if all of these could be sorted out, the end to which the task should be directed remains a matter of controversy. Holbek has deplored the lack of significant interpretation of folk narratives that would make the prodigious efforts at theoretical clarity meaningful.[9] In short, after years of folklore studies in an academic culture in which I have received, perhaps, my green card but not naturalization, I seem to be proclaiming the impossibility of my venture at the very moment that I begin it. But matters are perhaps not that bad. The husbands and wives who embark on journeys to find and win back lost spouses encounter not only hostile figures intent on thwarting them but also cooperative ones who help the searchers achieve their goals. And so have I.

Anthropologists can be both helpful and obstructionist for literary scholars endeavoring to interpret folk tales. They at least take folklore seriously, and treat folktales as legitimate "texts" for study.[10] Moreover, their ideas about folklore's function is often consistent with literary theories about how art acts as an emotional catharsis for artist, audience, or both. J. L. Fischer argues that folk narratives serve the needs both of the society that pragmatically allows its members outlets for subversive impulses, and also of the individuals who find themselves suffering keenly the discontents of civilization.[11] Anthropologists also have begun to pay close attention to woman's role in the societies they study, and from their work it becomes obvious that terms such as "patriarchy" and "patriarchal culture" need qualification. Woman's status varies from society to society; indeed, it has been argued that where her status is relatively high, she will be more likely to resist a demon lover than where her status is relatively low.[12] Nonetheless, "patriarchy" is a useful designation for male-dominated societies, and male domination was and remains a fact of universal life. Finally, from the commentaries of anthropologists has emerged an essential paradox: believed to be more quickly prone than man to revert to a state of nature, woman is nonetheless entrusted with the task of rooting man in culture and raising her children in such a way as to prevent behavior threatening to the society as a whole.[13] This paradox is useful for interpreting woman's role in swan maiden and demon lover tales.

Anthropologists resist, however, the universalist approach to folklore, focusing instead on its culture-specific elements—especially since, again, folklore can supply data for the study of a particular group. For them, the relationship is reciprocal: the tale helps explain the group, the group the tale. For the stories to be discussed in this book, the work of James M. Taggart—particularly his book *Enchanted Maidens*—stands as an excellent example of an approach to folklore and gender that relies on an ethnological analysis of people and their stories. But as will later be seen, in order to explain some narrative motifs, Taggart is virtually forced to fall back on a generalized view that women per se are better able than men to sustain in marriage the illusion of love, and that this capacity can account for the supernatural strength of the female character who performs extraordinary feats in Tale Type 313 (The Girl as Helper in the Hero's Flight). In chapter 6, it will be clear that I have a vastly different view of this story motif.

There is another, compelling reason to respect the uniqueness of the environment in which a version of a story flourishes. A people's folklore is intrinsically bound to its culture and is therefore part of its identity and self-esteem, which some of the folk may not be ready to surrender to the abstraction of universal human problems. But to concede this is also to run into the theoretical question of what is or who are the folk? Linda Dégh and Alan Dundes have supplied similar answers, the former defining a group of "people united permanently or temporarily by shared common experiences, attitudes, interests, skills, ideas, and aims," the latter invoking "*any group of people whatsoever* who share at least one common factor. It does not matter what the linking factor is—it could be a common occupation, language or religion—but what is important is that a group formed for whatever reason will have some traditions which it calls its own." [14]

Can women per se constitute a group and hence a "folk"? Certainly the concept of uniquely female traditions that are being defined by folklore feminists implies an affirmative answer. [15] Dundes's reference to language and religion, however, is a reminder of how naive it would be to think that ethnic differences do not interfere with the idealistic notion of universal sisterhood. Still, occupation and tradition provide support for the idea of an exclusive as well as inclusive female *folk*. In her novel *Up the Sandbox,* Ann Roiphe's female protagonist abhors her daily drudgery and wonders about the native women who had in earlier ages occupied her New York City neighborhood:

Eat, eliminate, prepare food, clean up, shop, throw out the garbage, a routine clear as a geometric form, a linear pattern that seems almost graceful in its simplicity. Despite computers and digit telephone numbers, nuclear fission, my life hardly differs from that of an Indian squaw settled in a tepee on the same

Manhattan land centuries ago. Pick, clean, prepare, throw out, dig a hole, bury the waste—she was my sister.[16]

The difficult question is whether a native woman would recognize that sisterhood. As Coffin points out, different assumptions about the marital relationship would render different the meanings of tales that appear similar. So would vastly different expectations concerning personal happiness. Some common idiom would be necessary for Roiphe's heroine and the women who narrated or were characters in the widespread star husband tales to share similar fantasies and secure some essential sisterhood.

But as Bynum has noted, human beings do communicate with each other "in a narrative manner": [17] Roiphe's very novel extends the themes of old, widely told tales. One of my premises, arrived at inductively as I gathered these tales, is that folk narratives reveal feminist themes when their subject *is woman's role in culture* and fantasies about escaping that role. And if a story with such a theme is told or heard by a man, it will probably reflect an anxious assumption that his wife does indeed strive to separate from him (see chapters 6, 7). Moreover, I have rarely encountered an anthropological analysis of a swan maiden or demon lover story that was not applicable to societies outside the one being studied.[18] Bynum has criticized those social scientists who confine the interpretation of narrative traditions "to the immediate ethnic context where the traditions are found," as if, for example, the "Oedipal typology of a tale indigenous to New Guinea" bore no relationship to "the import of the Oedipus story anywhere else." There is, he argues, "no necessary contradiction between a comparative and an ethnically delimited approach to the criticism" of folklore.[19]

Originally part of an oral storytelling tradition, swan maiden and demon lover tales were later collected and translated by persons whose knowledge of folklore and fidelity to what they heard varied widely. Today folktales are gathered by rigorously trained fieldworkers whose methodology has become increasingly scientific, while artists unconcerned with methodology continue to render folklore into literature. But literary scholars and even some folklorists have been frustrated by the reluctance of most folklorists to go beyond the data, the "'what'" of folklore, to consider the "'why'" and thus enter "the ever treacherous area of interpretation."[20] The matter goes beyond the clash of methodologies in disciplines that otherwise share interests. Literary critics can often trace their love for story to folk and fairy lore heard from others' lips before the prized gift of reading was acquired. Stories were first read for the sake of story itself, meaning and power perhaps impressing themselves at some unconscious level before—much later—the task of analysis was begun and mastered. That story has meaning, whether that story be part of an oral tradition or written by a known author, is assumed by literary critics, who take for granted that some interpretation is already going on—consciously or otherwise—in any storyteller's retelling of an orally transmitted tale. Fortunately, the gap between folklore studies and literary analysis shows signs of narrowing.

This does not mean, however, that folklore methodology is thereby rendered unimportant for interpretation. But rather than continuing to survey abstractly the problems of imperfect material, I will focus on one story collection to illustrate both the difficulties and the potential insight into a subject that can be gained when one knows what questions are being asked (even if the answers remain subject to debate), and will use that collection as a point of departure for further discussion and other examples. For those unfamiliar with folklore studies, my analysis of this collection is intended as an introduction. For those who need no such introduction, the example is intended to contribute to a developing subject among folklorists—the relationship of folklore to gender.

In the 1930s, Ethel Stefana Drower, daughter of a clergyman, educated at home and in private schools and married to the British adviser to the Iraqi minister of justice,[21] decided that after a residence of more than ten years, she wished to contribute to the world's knowledge of her host country, whose folklore she had long been in the habit of recording. Her *Folk-Tales of Iraq* was published in a scholarly form, including notes and explanations of language and culture, and appeared under the pseudonym E. S. Stevens.[22] Because of her self-consciousness as a woman story gatherer with an ambiguous relationship to the Iraqi women she collected tales from, and because her pseudonym suggests a deliberate vagueness concerning her identity, I will refer to Stevens by her gender-emphatic title, Lady Drower.

For an amateur folklorist, Lady Drower was quite knowledgeable about methods of research, aware, for example, that nuances of language could not survive translation. She assures her readers that she has striven for accuracy even though some Arabic words have no connotative equivalents in English and, in addition, differ in meaning depending on whether they are used by Moslem, Christian, or Jew. She says that when a story was told slowly enough, she took it down verbatim; however, this was not always possible and she was necessarily dependent upon memory. On the subject of editing she remains silent and does not acknowledge that even rendering a story grammatically correct is effectively another kind of translation.

Lady Drower was sensitive to the relation of tales to tellers, providing information about whom she heard each story from as well as brief descriptions of those who supplied variants. As her informants varied from illiterate servants to educated teachers and government officials, she acknowledges that the way they told the same stories might differ according to their position in society. She recognizes, moreover, that some are better tale tellers than others and that gesture, voice intonation, and facial expression are very important. These qualities, of course, are not described or reproduced in her written texts, which as a result cannot include the meanings that narrators can convey through extra-verbal signals. For it is presently acknowledged that even the most scrupulous verbal transcription does not convey a story in its entirety, does not provide the "ideal folklore text," which "must record the aesthetic transaction (manifested through observable behaviors) between the performer and audience."[23]

That performance conveys meaning is not a new idea. More than fifty years ago, a collector of Tibetan folktales described how, "Notebook in hand, I would sit on the ground with my little Tibetan maid [her interpreter] beside me and watch the face of the one who was telling the story. Watch every shade of expression that flitted over his features—'Tell me why he laughs and is amused there. Why does he look sad here? Why does he speak seriously now? What prompted that action? What prompted that thought?'—and so on; and I would make careful notes."[24] To what specific end, however, is not revealed. Roger Abrahams has argued that individual performance is actually a rhetorical tool in the hands of the storyteller, folklore thus able to serve as an instrument of social change instead of a medium through which traditional values are perpetuated.[25] It can be added that the imprint of a unique personality also helps expand a narrative pattern, which enlarges not only by an accretion of story detail but also because of the differing perspectives of individual storytellers. Lady Drower was particularly interested in the relationship between her tales and their culture; she stood, that is, closer to anthropology than to literary criticism. Her introductory material was also influenced by comparative mythology, she being well aware that a tale told by the Iraqis could be found not only in other Middle Eastern countries but also throughout Europe. She notes that it is useful to see how tales can vary from culture to culture, but useful for what she does not say, thereby avoiding some of the knotty issues raised above concerning the culture-specific and internationalist contexts for folklore. Lady Drower's vignettes about her narrators are, moreover, insufficiently detailed to allow her reader to discern an interplay between the culturally determined and individualistic elements in the telling of a story narrated over a wide geographical area.

A significant example of such interplay is supplied by Clementina Todesco, the narrator of a collection of Italian-American folktales. She looks back at herself as a rebellious young woman whose emigration to America fulfilled a dream in which she was freed from poverty as well as the oppressive aspects of Italian village life, part of which may have been the patrilocal marriages in which a woman was "carried like a bundle of logs" to her husband's family, to be taught by her mother-in-law how to behave as wife and mother. But in the United States she had to endure a seven-year separation from her husband (a symbolic number in fairy tales) and also missed the strong connections with other women she enjoyed in Italy. She compensated for these lacks by forming attachments to adoptive sisters in America. In her swan maiden tale, a young man leaves his poor mother to make his economic way in the world; his swan maiden bride is an enchanted being awaiting the man who will free her from tyranny and provide a better life; but as his wife she must adapt to her mother-in-law's household; and when she runs away, it is not to flee her husband's world but to fulfill promises to her sister swan maidens, other women to whom her ties are very strong. There is a tight fit between Clementina Todesco, whose biography is told in detail, and her tale. It is noted, moreover, that she moves among folklore genres, frequently employing narratives to relate personal experiences, thus shifting "from a communal experience represented in traditional tales to an individual experience represented by personal memories." In her retelling of the swan maiden tale, she has indeed combined two essential patterns: the story of the captured fairy wife who escapes bondage as soon as she can; and the enchanted human who awaits a prince to release her from her swan form, from her captivity by some evil enchanter. It has already been noted that some scholars attribute these variations to differences in genre.[26]

Genre criticism is playing an increasingly important role in folklore studies, but as Alan Dundes has argued, "not so much as one genre has been completely defined,"[27] Dégh and Vázsonyi also conceding that this may be particularly true of the *legend*, a "capricious genre" that is not easily delimited "from other forms of folk prose." Like myths, legends are deeply rooted in the "social reality" of specific cultures;[28] as Jan Brunvand has described legends, they are a "unique, unselfconscious reflection of major concerns of individuals in the societies in which the legends circulate," and the stories people believe to be true "hold an important place in their worldview."[29] But Wendy Doniger has dismissed what she deems false distinctions among genres, in this case between myth and folktale, arguing that the "most one could hope to do would be to postulate a kind of continuum, with stories located all along the line, some more 'folk' than 'myth,' some the reverse."[30] Swan maiden stories seem to appear all along that continuum, but, again, one feature of the story strongly differentiates versions in legends and myths from the fictions of fairy tales. As Christiansen describes it,

The essential difference between such legends and the folktale is that according to the latter the husband, having lost his wife, succeeds in finding his way to her castle and in winning her back, while the legends end on a tragic note with her disappearing for ever. Both folktale and legend are, undoubtedly, very old, and even though the question of the relative antiquity of each type can never be determined satisfactorily, the most reasonable explanation would appear to be that the international folktale has its origin in local legend.[31]

But the implications of tracing the historical development of the story and defining its genres are nowhere near as arresting as the point made by Christiansen and Hartland about the connection between the presumed truth of the swan maiden tale and the way the story ends: *veracity* is related to the wife's resistance to resuming her role in the domestic realm. And this feature of the story crosses international boundaries.

Lady Drower, both recognizing an international family of folklore characters[32] and also acknowledging the importance of individual cultures and even individual narrators, does not speculate about the conflict inherent in these two approaches to folk narratives. What she argues for is the historical importance of Iraqi tales in terms of how a narrative develops and is transmitted. In this she is influenced by a now-discarded theory expressed, for example, by John A. MacCulloch, who writes in *The Childhood of Fiction* that folktales "are the earliest form of romantic and imaginative literature, the unwritten fiction of early man and primitive people" seeking to "clothe their impressions of the universe, their ideas and beliefs" in the form of a story.[33] While not specifically engaging in a hunt for the origins of individual folktales, Lady Drower implies that since the country she is living in is the cradle of civilization, the Iraqi stories she is collecting must be, if not the originals, close to the first versions told.

This evolutionary theory is no longer held by folklorists, the theory itself having been relegated to the history of the discipline. Yet this book will invoke the views of the evolutionists. The writings of MacCulloch, Hartland, Lang, and others are replete with fascinating discussions of the fairy otherworld and its inhabitants. And even if their theories can be discredited, their insights are often significant, and, even when incorrect, more provocative for the discovery of meaning in folk and fairy tales than many of the scientific studies that succeeded theirs. Some folklore, moreover, has been traced to real (rather than hypothesized) cultural practices, and these have illuminated the stories. And finally, it is difficult to dismiss Hartland's conception of how the swan maiden story *changes* over time: "We might expect to find that as advances are made in civilization, and marriage becomes more regarded, the reason for separation would become more and more complex and cogent."[34] It is Hartland who focuses attention on the relationship between reality and the conclusion to the swan maiden story, on the husband's characteristic failure to win back his wife.

In any event, from the purist's standpoint, Lady Drower's theories are either antiquated or incompletely developed, and her tales contaminated. They are, first of all, translated, and despite assurance that she has aimed at fidelity to her sources, grammatical correctness alone belies her claim. But as Stith Thompson has written in *The Folktale*, it "is impossible to make a complete separation of the written and the oral tradition."[35] The Italian-American swan maiden tale described above comes from a collection in which stories were orally related by mother to daughter, and hence followed traditional lines of folktale transmission. But the daughter who transcribed the tales for a published collection made "stylistic changes and additions which transformed the natural cadences and tones of the folk artist into something more closely resembling a literary text (in the familiar fashion of the Brothers Grimm)."[36]

Whether this is to be deplored is a matter that will be taken up again at the end of this introduction. Meanwhile, it can be noted that Richard Dorson's description of the methods followed by the Irish collector T. C. Croker is probably at least partially true of many from whom folklorists must recapture the folk narratives of the past: at that

early date [1860s] Croker did not, as his accusers make plain, observe the precise methods of the modern folklorist. He inflates a kernel of spoken legend into a full story. Hence the sighting of a mermaid by a country fellow, which could be related in a few sentences, becomes a sketch of the stage Irishman sportively conversing with the sea beauty and plighting his troth before a perplexed priest.[37]

Dorson's use of the word "accusers" reveals how seriously the folklorist takes such contamination of the original oral rendition (which itself may be suspect because it is often impossible to know whether it has been corrupted by literary analogues transmitted, for example, by missionaries or teachers who worked among the "folk"). But his argument may be tinged here as elsewhere with irony: "the purist approach to defining and collecting folk tales by the touchstone of oral currency is gradually being refuted by poaching literary historians."[38] Rigorously applied, the purist approach would insist that Lady Drower's Iraqi tales border on "fakelore"[39] despite her scrupulous intentions. Like countless other collections, hers would be consigned to some netherworld, excluded from serious study as neither true folklore nor created literature.

Moreover, fakelore—often the product of a literary imagination schooled in folklore—does a great deal to elucidate a complex folklore pattern studied in its variety and multiplicity. The literary scholar who turns to folklore may wish to reverse the inquiry's direction, to move from supposedly sophisticated literature back to folk tales, acquiring an increased respect for the folk's insight, to discover in early, anonymous narratives the complexity and ambiguity in human motives that later writers would consciously recognize and draw upon.[40] Without dissenting from Bengt Holbek's distinction between genuine folklore and collections such as *The Arabian Nights*,[41] I will frequently move among different fields of story for the mutual illumination they supply. Again, folklore characters and narrative motifs constitute an idiom that many unschooled storytellers understood as well as their literary successors.

Lady Drower was a self-conscious folklorist when she put together

her collection of tales. Moreover, despite her considerable talent and education, she was keenly aware of being a woman in a country where the separation of the sexes was extreme, and of being identified as the wife of an important man—that is, a woman who did not find it easy to feel productive in her own right. The first of these awarenesses is explicit, the second implicit in the very opening of her introduction:

Realizing one day that I was in the second decade of my sojourn in 'Iraq, I asked myself if I could make any useful contribution, however slight, to the sum of knowledge about the country. I have an advantage in being a woman, since my countrymen in 'Iraq are for the most part workers employed in official or commercial activities, and therefore with limited time and often little opportunity, to devote themselves to matters not vital to politics, business, history, or science. Moreover, as men, they are shut off from the family life of a large part of the community. As a woman I can enter where they could not, and so am free to study the country from an aspect denied to them.

She thus turns to advantage what must have been the irritating disadvantage in which, as an educated, energetic woman, she found herself. Almost half a century later, a female anthropologist married to a diplomat would analyze a similar situation: "unlike the housewife (which she often is as well) the diplomat's wife experiences the presumption that she is committed to an institution from whose central operations she is necessarily excluded." [42] In the realm of folklore collection, however, the disadvantage would attach to the man, who would be as excluded from the world from which Lady Drower gathered stories as she was from the world in which he worked. Nonetheless, her pseudonym, E. S. Stevens, seems to indicate not only the attempt to mask her identity but also the need to infer a male persona.

The folklorist Linda Dégh has noted that "researchers are split in their opinions about which sex is prevalent among storytellers." [43] And in an early and theoretically influential collection, Ruth Benedict described how different a story may appear when told according to a male or female point of view, especially when, among her subjects the Zuñis, the tale had to do with marriage or sex roles in general. [44] In addition, Marie-Louise von Franz, who has written widely on fairy tales from a Jungian perspective, has contended that it is difficult to distinguish between a genuinely female point of view and that of a man expressing some aspect of his personality traditionally deemed feminine: the mere existence of a female character does not prove either. [45] Such considerations may be joined to recent concerns about women and language. It is known that in some societies, women and men literally speak different languages, and that in some cultures, folklore genres themselves are divided between the sexes, men relating tales in verse, women in prose, for example.[46] But even when men and women speak the same language, this in itself is not "sufficient evidence that both sexes stand in the same relationship to that language."[47] And it remains possible that some female narrators may have so thoroughly internalized male views of reality that they transmit them as if they were the only possible views.

Ingrid Bengis has written eloquently about the impossibility for women to separate themselves from considerations of their role *as* women:

All men's understanding of the "female condition" is separated from the condition itself, separated from the daily monotonous and repetitious occurrences which reinforce that condition. And as soon as they stop talking to the woman they "understand," they are able to go about their business thinking about something *other* than the condition of women, whereas the moment I attempt to go about *my* business, I am obstructed in some way and am forced to deal with that condition simply because I am a woman.[48]

If it has indeed always been true that even in woman's seemingly exclusive space, her otherness and relationship to man cannot be evaded in any self-awareness, then this might explain the narrative phenomenon Holbek reveals about the Danish tales he has studied: that men tell stories with male protagonists, whereas women tell stories with both female and male protagonists.[49] In the next chapter the question will be raised of whether the focus of interest in the swan maiden's tale is on the captured wife or on the husband who, having lost her, undertakes the search to bring her back to his world. Unfortunately, most variants came into print without any knowledge of the storyteller, without the kind of biographical information supplied about Clementina Todesco. It will, nonetheless, be possible to make generalizations about how the story's basic outlines would appeal differently to male and female interests— both as constituted in the world and as imagined in fantasy.

Lady Drower's consciousness of *being* a woman and of how her otherness in male-dominated Iraq benefited her endeavors as a folklorist coincides with her very attempt to go beyond the role of a woman as British and Iraqi society would define it (if to varying degrees). She is very explicit on this point. But she does not extend such self-consciousness to a consideration of how her very collection of stories—her choices as well as the stories themselves—might reflect the conditions under which she gathered them.

In contrast to Lady Drower, who was admitted as folklore gatherer into a female world closed to her husband, C. G. Campbell took his stories from Iraqi tribesmen. They are replete with overtly sexual themes not made explicit in Lady Drower's collection. Would the tribesmen have told her different stories, no stories, the same stories transformed? It is difficult to know. For the vicarious expression permitted by story-telling may tear down conventional inhibitions that adhere to social discourse. Some early collectors admitted to being troubled by what they perceived as indelicacy on the part of both male and female storytellers. William McCulloch, gathering Bengali folktales from what he calls "a very intelligent young Brahman," notes that he "found no reason to doubt his often repeated assertion that he told me the stories exactly as he had heard them. For one thing, his stories varied widely in quality, some of them being both coarse and dull, whereas he, himself, was of a decidedly refined and distinguished type of mind, and was, besides, quite competent, when he let himself go, to make a good story of almost anything by his way of telling it." [50] Alice Dracott, who also collected Indian tales, relates how in "one or two instances I was asked if I would allow a Paharee man, well versed in local folk-lore, to relate a few stories to me; but, for obvious reasons, I was obliged to decline the offer, for many Simla Village tales related to me by women, and *not* included in this book, were grotesquely unfit for publications." [51] How much worse, she implies, if told by a man. Perhaps the only hypothesis to be drawn from these scattered samples is that gender is an important factor down the line, from the telling of the tale to the reading of the book that the gatherer creates out of what she or he hears—that gender supplies keys for the interpretation of folktales, but that no single key fits all locks.

One way to approach the matter of gender is to consider the inclusion or exclusion from Stevens's and Campbell's collections of the swan maiden and demon lover stories. Campbell's volumes include no ex-ample of the Cupid and Psyche tale, whereas Lady Drower includes two variants of this story, which is claimed by folklorists to be favored by women. The story of the swan maiden, attached to a narrative group presumably favored by men since its main narrative line (at least accord-ing to folklorists) depicts the husband's search for his lost wife (see my chapter 7), can be found in neither collection. Lady Drower at least feels the need to explain the omission: the well-known tale of Hasan el Basorah (from *The Arabian Nights*) was too long for her purposes. Campbell, in contrast, does not mention the swan maiden story but his collection includes tales that reflect one of its most widespread and erotic motifs. The swan maiden is frequently captured while bathing, her magic skin or garment left on shore and stolen by the man who then lays claim to her. For some scholars, this motif links the universally told swan maiden story to one of the most popular Hindu myths, the love between Krishna and Raidha, Krishna having seduced the cowherd women by taking their clothes while they bathed and by forcing them to reveal their nakedness. C. G. Campbell, who, again, either did not hear from Iraqi tribesmen or did not choose to include in his collection a variant of the swan maiden tale widely told in Moslem countries, nonetheless does recount more than one tale in which a man spies on bathing naked women, or pays a woman to remove her clothing or the veils on her face.[52] I am not suggesting that these story motifs have been lifted from the swan maiden tale by a lascivious male imagination that chooses to dispense with the other, more problematic motifs in the story, those in which a man holds his woman through coercion and then loses her in the end, although I am not rejecting the possibility either. Rather, I am pursuing the idea that gender both affects and reflects the relationship between the informant and the gatherer of tales, and between the gatherer of tales and the audience for which collections are prepared. For some folklorists, this shifting relationship can end in the intrusion of an alien element into a pure folklore tradition;[53] I will treat the relationship as paralleling some of the story motifs themselves.

There is, for example, an interesting correlation between what Lady Drower has revealed about herself and how she came to collect her Iraqi tales, on the one hand, and certain elements within the Cupid and Psyche tales she retells, on the other. In the basic form of the story, a mortal woman enters into a union with a mysterious supernatural man, who imposes on her a prohibition whose defying means the termination of the relationship: for example, she may not see him or ask any questions about who he is or where he comes from. The reason why the Psyche character commits the forbidden act varies from story to story. In the versions collected by Lady Drower, "Psyche" is prodded by idle townswomen, whose gossip not only reflects their curiosity about the heroine's lover but also their malevolent intentions as well.[54]

The issue here does not concern what the reader may learn about the specific culture that retains such variants, although such knowledge is interesting in itself and may aid interpretation as well. Rather, as Raymond Jameson has argued, universal folklore themes present "the lowest common denominator of human nature, the nuclei of human aspirations and human terror," and once the material is collected, the task of the comparative folklorist is "to examine the variations of symbol and to determine the reasons for these variations."[55] It is the common denominator itself that brings variants into sharp relief, and the reasons why Psyche characters break the taboo, although differing from tale to tale, combine to increase understanding of the significance of the act. But there may have been a reason why the Iraqi Psyche, pushed into betraying her mate by idle townswomen (rather than the envious sisters of Apuleius's famous version), might have impressed herself on Lady Drower's particular imagination.

The nature of Psyche's revolt may vary according to the degree of passivity expected of her in her strange union. Such passivity may itself be highlighted in her relations with others, these relationships impinging on any assessment of her character. Do the troublemaking, gossiping women of Iraqi versions mirror a social hierarchy in which a certain portion of the population has the leisure in which to cause trouble? Does the enforced isolation of Arab women foster envy and dissension rather than bonds among them, or is their mischief making the view of a lower-class narrator critical of a privileged group she remains outside of? Does the storyteller disapprove of these gossiping females, and would her voice and gesture have made her contempt clearer than the text itself? Or do the trouble-making women reflect a male view of woman's behavior, her propensity to gossip and thus cause trouble, transforming the Cupid and Psyche story into a nasty version of the Pandora theme, any subsequent narration by a woman indicating just how capable women are of internalizing negative images of themselves?

Lady Drower's motivation for selecting this tale may illustrate Henry Glassie's argument that in gathering tales, the gatherer will of necessity experience the distance that "opens between the writer [collector] and the storyteller" and that "confusions arise from the different motives that writers and storytellers have for telling their tales to others."[56] Once again, the question is whether among women some kind of basic sisterhood will transcend such confusion. Reporting on his work in

Morocco, Crapanzano describes how one of his informants, Mohammed, "preferred to keep [himself] aloof" in order to function as an
informant on his culture, whereas Mohammed's wife Dawia "looked for
the similar in [Crapanzano's] wife—in their common womanhood. Theirs
was a relationship of sharing." [57] Lady Drower seems to have both
identified with and differentiated herself from her female informants,
thus perhaps from the female characters in the stories they told. Biographical information suggests that she might be particularly sensitive to
the provocation that causes the Iraqi Psyche to defy the taboo. The
daughter of a clergyman would have been encouraged to be industrious,
if not necessarily in the areas she turned to. Her need in her second
decade in the Middle East to make some "useful contribution" to the
world would contrast her with the idle and gossiping townswomen of
the story she collects. It is striking to contemplate the layers of complexity that have been added to the story through but one variant in it.
Claimed by folklorists to be a favorite among women (see chapter 4),
the Cupid-Psyche tale recounts its heroine's rebellion against her passive
role, although the rebellion in this instance is instigated by other women
who wish her ill. These idle mischief makers, in turn, appeal to the
storytelling impulses of one who fights against idleness, while, at the
same time, as a collector of tales Lady Drower shares with Iraqi women
a self-conscious awareness of their basic sisterhood, of the boundaries
between man's and woman's space.

And to add another layer to these relationships, I am a woman trying
to analyze women's importance in the narrating and collecting of stories.
Not unlike the diplomat's wife, I am married to a businessman and
attend many social gatherings at which I meet women most of whom are
not employed outside the home. Almost invariably they ask me if I am
still working, as if it is some insufficiency on my husband's part or some
oddity on mine that makes me want to earn a living. And when the
tensions that arise from my attempt to balance family and other domestic responsibilities with my teaching, research, and writing overwhelm
me, I sometimes think longingly of what appears to me other women's
leisurely existence. I supply this brief biographical information because
of my awareness that this book, more than the others I have written, is
in part my own narrative; that my speculations about Lady Drower's
collection arise in part from my own self-consciousness; that I am, as I
claimed in my preface, participating in the storytelling process, not

merely recording others' stories; that fantasies of an otherworld that promises relief from woman's role are ones I sometimes share rather than observe from a scholarly distance.

In the following pages, it will not always be possible to identify whose fantasies and whose fears—the man's, the woman's, the storyteller's, or the collector's—are the most operative in a story. Active fieldwork is helpful in such identifications, as folklorist Dov Noy has pointed out, for the folktale gatherer can talk to women informants about where they learned their stories and can trace the genealogy of tales and the genders of the storytellers who passed them down from generation to generation.[58] Moreover, swan maiden and demon lover tales involve wish-fulfillment, often invoking forbidden fantasies; but they also lay bare the down-to-earth issues upon which the relationships between men and women are based. Gender relations themselves are crucial elements in their themes, and to consider (if not always to know) how gender affects the transmission of narrative from storyteller to listener to collector to reader is to achieve increasing insight into the very meaning of the stories in question. If the patterns that emerge from multiple variants of written folklore texts do not substitute for fieldwork and the ability to question the informant, such patterns nonetheless supply such an extraordinarily rich and multilayered depiction of the relations between the sexes as to make possible an almost inexhaustible study.

In this regard I have, as I noted earlier, borrowed from Bynum's theories, from his argument that single variants of a tale belong to a larger narrative pattern that is rarely completed in one version. What he calls generic and nominal motifs make up the pattern, and

story-tellers know what plantings or substitutions of motifs are possible, because they know what . . . motifs have thriven before on a given tract of story, and they make their choices accordingly. Distributed in separate stories, their choices complement each other in such a way that a single narrative pattern may have much greater power to organize logically the diverse data of a people's real world . . . than any one text of a story alone would suggest.[59]

Following this argument, one thinks of the collecting of variants as the reconstruction of a narrative pattern that becomes clearer as stories are added to it. In this way, the process could be likened to the assembling of a jigsaw puzzle when no box cover exists to reveal what the completed picture should look like. Such a metaphor can help explain how this book has been assembled. First, the more pieces are added to the puzzle, the clearer the emerging pattern will become. At the same time, the same picture could be cut into fewer or more pieces. This book was originally about twice its present length, and even then I had omitted intriguing story variations. But the practicalities of book publishing as well as the tolerance of my readers obviously necessitated cutting. My readers will hopefully take my word for the existence of unmentioned tales that support my interpretations. They may also take up my search for the swan maiden by pursuing more examples of tales that catch interest or pique curiosity. Indeed, stories that challenge my reading may emerge: I am only too conscious that the pieces of my puzzle are almost infinite and realize that even the vast number I have thought about must constitute but a fraction of what is available for study. The patterns that have emerged from my reading are, nonetheless, persistent and contribute to what I consider a clear picture.

The absence of a puzzle piece or the dull shadings of others will not drastically alter the emerging picture. As I noted in the preface, storytellers vary widely in narrative ability and intelligence, and this is also true for collectors of tales. It was often obvious that a version I chose to cite because it contained an important motif was either badly told or was narrated with the literary embellishments of the collector. But because I have merged collectors and informants as participants with me in the construction of a narrative pattern, my choices were not based on the quality of tale telling. And, again, in published collections of folktales, genres are rarely kept distinct: myth, legend, and fairy tale combine as pieces of the same overarching narrative.

Puzzle pieces are constructed so that a single piece links more than one other piece. Sometimes I had to decide whether a story should be discussed in one or another chapter: for example, a male horse lover belongs to the animal groom stories but also merges with the female horse to play an important role in incubus tales, the "mare" in "nightmare" having become embroiled in etymological as well as folkloristic confusion (see chapter 5). And I have sometimes had to repeat in one chapter a story already discussed in another, because the narrative motifs could not be neatly separated; but I have tried to keep such repetitions to a minimum. For the same reason, I have also not attempted a subject index for this book. Despite my efforts at separation, classification, and organization, the items such an index might contain involve narrative themes that weave themselves through all the stories in this book. A subject index would virtually duplicate the notes.

My analogy is of course not exact: obviously a real jigsaw puzzle can only be correctly assembled in one way, and the presence of the cover picture is only an aid to the assembler. But the idea of reconstructing a large narrative pattern from pieces found in variants has the additional advantage of complementing the premises of reader response theorists. Holbek has claimed that, ultimately, the meaning of a story resides in the mind of the person who receives it; and Susan Suleiman has noted a problem that is easily applicable to the audiences of tales originally transmitted orally: "Obviously it is not easy to study variations within audiences and their reception of literary works in the distant past."[60] But the variations within a narrative pattern, reflective of choices among motifs made by individual narrators, have the benefit of revealing the ways that different tales *could be received.* Most of this book involves prose narratives with occasional references to ballads, whose development and transmission involve special considerations, such as how individual variations must meet (or can be explained by) the requirements of song, including rhyme and rhythm, such requirements also being dependent upon a singer's memory, which could fail at any given moment. But I have engaged in an analysis of Child ballad 243, "The Demon Lover," for two reasons. For a book in which demon lovers play so important a role, it seemed unthinkable to omit this very popular ballad. Also, because of the many variants that exist in the British Isles, and because "The Demon Lover" was, of the ballads brought to America, one of the most widely sung and disseminated, thus being available in many versions, it forms by itself a potential jigsaw puzzle and therefore a microcosm of the effort to reconstruct an overarching swan maiden/demon lover tale. Even allowing for Tristram Coffin's caution about the random lyrics and themes that float among ballads,[61] and even admitting that I may be attributing to an individual singer more insight than that singer deserves, I discovered in collecting versions of Child 243 that I eventually located every version of the story that I could imagine, every variation in plot and human motivation that my own mind began to conceive of as I read.

Jameson wrote nearly half a century ago that the "study of folklore is a dangerous adventure." [62] It appears particularly hazardous when one comes to it as a lover of narrative itself rather than as a trained folklorist. One way to undertake the perilous journey is to carry the most scientific equipment available, treading cautiously. Another way is fearlessly to plunge into the territory to be explored, transforming the terrain if necessary. In his *Grandfather Tales* Richard Chase describes how in his collection he has "taken a free hand in the re-telling." He describes how he "put each tale together from different versions" as well as from his own experience in telling them. "I have," he writes," told the tales to all kinds of listeners, old and young; and only then, after many tellings, written them down. This spontaneous telling process is really important for you, too, the reader. After you have read these tales, put the book away and try telling one." [63] It is arguable that Chase is still perpetuating an oral tradition, but is it really the case that to commit the tale told to print is to destroy the integrity of the folk tradition? Italo Calvino invokes and explains a Tuscan proverb—the tale is not beautiful if nothing is added to it—to explain how he put together his collection of Italian folktales. "In other words," argues Calvino, the story's "value consists in what is woven and rewoven into it," and he unabashedly announces his willingness to recreate his material without admitting for a moment that he had violated its spirit: "I selected from mountains of narratives [and] enriched the text selected from other versions and whenever possible did so without altering its character or unity, and at the same time filled it out and made it more plastic. I touched up as delicately as possible those portions that were either missing or too sketchy." [64]

This book, too, will tell a story—or rather, retell it in chapters that represent parts of a complex narrative, which overall depicts the enforced capture of the fairy wife, her husband's lonely search for her when she has escaped him, the woman who elopes with her demon lover, and the one who willingly spurns him to live, like Damayanti or Etain, in the world of domestic relations. Woven of countless tales, the story tells of Psyche, who first rebels against and then accepts her role, and the animal groom whose humanization is dependent upon her doing so, as well as the animal bride whose disenchantment depends upon a male strength that too often fails her. These tales, thematically unified, tell of weary drudgery and of erotic dreams, of relationships that tragically are more often thwarted than fulfilled, or partially fulfilled at a price that modern interpreters of the tales have yet to fully evaluate. To conceive of a unified narrative may involve an audacious act of interpretation, but despite the dangers involved, it will be clear that the tales are so fraught with significance that what astonishes most is the extraordinary degree to which their meanings have been neglected in commentaries upon them.

# CHAPTER 2

# Urvaśī and the Swan Maidens: The Runaway Wife

Not all swan maidens are swans; some are doves, or ungainly geese, ducks, or cranes.[1] Seal maidens abound in Scottish and Scandinavian tales, and in Russia the stolen wolf's skin evokes werewolf legends.[2] Other swan maidens have no animal form, and are bound to their mortal captors because some other significant possession, such as a dress or secret name, has been stolen or discovered. The graceful swan has nonetheless characterized what has been called "one of the most beautiful stories ever evolved from the mind of man,"[3] a story so affective that attempts to find meaning in the tale have no "power to detract from, but ... serve only to enhance its elusive and poetic" appeal.[4] These are romantic but hardly satisfactory explanations for the story's wide popularity. Moreover, the swan is not an entirely attractive bird: it is frequently aggressive; its trumpetlike voice is raucous; and its snakelike neck can suggest evil or threatening sexuality. The ballerina who must dance the roles of both Odette and Odile in *Swan Lake* need only transform the submissive flutterings of the swan maiden into the sensuous undulations of a serpentine imposter to demonstrate the ease with which one animal can become the other.[5] In an exotically strange short story, "The Enchantress," a woman with a pet swan tests her lovers by daring them to make love to her while she is entwined by a serpent.[6]

Looked at closely, the swan maiden tale is only deceptively romantic, its power residing not in a love story but in its depiction of a fierce marital struggle. Its themes can be traced back to those attached to the story of what Doniger has called the "quintessential swan maiden,"[7] Urvaśī, who, in the Sanskrit *Rig Veda*, lives on earth with the mortal Purūravas, returning to her home among the demigods when he betrays the terms of their relationship, impervious to his entreaties that she come back. Only in later renditions of this ancient tale is the couple reunited, Purūravas joining Urvaśī in the divine realm. Whether or not Urvaśī is, as some claim, the original swan maiden,[8] from the story of her union with a mortal radiate virtually all the motifs found in the world's animal bride and demon lover tales. For this reason Purūravas and Urvaśī will supply a point of reference for each chapter in this book. The mortal and his supernatural mistress are featured in what has been called the world's first love story, one full of "deep feeling and real pathos,"[9] in which the pair suffer deeply over their separation. The truth is, however, that the Sanskrit story, like the swan maiden tales that may have descended from it, requires the disconnecting of the superficially sentimental elements in the narrative from the deep and bitter conflicts actually portrayed.

Because no single source tells the whole story, a summary must be pieced together from different accounts:

(1) [Urvaśī] had to come down to the earth from the heavenly world on account of a curse and then on certain conditions [that she never see her husband naked] she agrees to stay with the king [Purūravas]. (2) On account of the breach in the promise to observe the conditions, [Urvaśī] leaves the king. (3) After a long search, the king turns mad in her absence, finds [Urvaśī] first in her transformed condition [swan], and then in the original form. (4) She refuses to go back with the king who requests her to return with him. (5) The king obtains a son born of her after some period. (6) The king is elevated to the position of a Gandharva after performing the sacrifice and enjoys [Urvaśī's] company for ever, in the land of the Gandharvas, he himself being a Gandharva then.[10]

Purūravas's inadvertent breach of his promise is the result of a plot concocted by the Gandharvas, demigods in the Hindu pantheon who want Urvaśī to resume her place among the heavenly nymphs who are their consorts. To this end, they arrange for the late-night theft of Urvaśī's prized pet sheep, and when she laments their loss, Purūravas leaps out of bed to retrieve them, at which point the Gandharvas send to earth a bolt of lightning that illuminates his naked form.

That Purūravas and Urvaśī pine over their separation is not, however, obvious from either the *Rig Veda* or the *Satapatha Brahmana*, the main sources for the story. The Vedic hymn begins with Purūravas's having located his lost wife, their dialogue consisting of his entreaties that she return and her resistance, of his reproaches and threat of suicide and her refusal to be swayed. If love is to be read into their exchange, it is a very different love from that espoused by romantically inclined readers of the tale.

To begin with, the Vedic hymn is ambiguous on the subject of why Urvaśī lived with Purūravas for four years. He reproaches her for having once been willing enough to accept his advances, for unlike the usually reluctant swan maiden, Urvaśī had (according to him) made a sexual game of his courtship.[11]

[Purūravas] When I, a mortal man, courted these immortal women who had laid aside their veils, they shied away from me like excited gazelles, like horses grazed by the chariot.

[Urvaśī] When a mortal man, wooing these immortal women, unites with their group as they wish, make your bodies beautiful, like water birds, like horses biting in their love-play.

[Purūravas] She of the waters flashed lightning like a falling lightning-bolt and brought me the pleasures of love.

Urvaśī does not deny that she was receptive to his love-making. But the relationship between mortal and immortal is tenuous, and Purūravas's invocation of lightning as an image of passion may foreshadow the later dissolution of their relationship.

It is the *Brahmana* that highlights the taboo motif, the prohibition that must be respected if the mortal lover is to retain the supernatural spouse. For Urvaśī imposes two, not merely one stipulation concerning their union. When she weds him, she says, "Thrice a day shalt thou embrace me; but do not lie with me against my will, and let me not see thee naked, for such is the way to behave to us women."[12] This passage, which expresses Urvaśī's demand for autonomy in their sexual relations, can be compared with a corresponding section of the *Rig Veda*, which suggests that despite Purūravas's assertion that Urvaśī "came to his home across from her dwelling-place and took her pleasure in him," she has been less compliant than he believes.

[Urvaśī] Indeed, you pierced me with your rod three times a day, and filled me even when I had no desire. I followed your will, Purūravas; you were my man, king of my body.

Even more discord emerges when Urvaśī, seemingly taken aback at Purūravas's threat of suicide, intimates that he has misunderstood their relationship:

[Urvaśī] Purūravas, do not die; do not vanish; do not let the vicious wolves eat you. There are no friendships with women; they have the hearts of jackals.

Part of the obscurity in the Vedic hymn, and therefore part of the difficulty in interpreting it, has to do with questions of whether or not all lines have been assigned to the correct speaker.[13] The antifeminism in Urvaśī's words would seem to indicate a masculine point of view, although she may also be mocking Purūravas with the negative stereotype of woman created by mortal men. In any event, these words are somewhat softened when she compares herself to the wind, "hard to catch and hold." Her portrait of herself is both winning and ominous, provocative and threatening. But such duality has been intrinsic to their relationship.

For however much Urvaśī feigns subservience to Purūravas, she employs feminine wiles to gain her way. After the Gandharvas steal her sheep, she goads her lover into action: if Purūravas were truly a man, she need not lose her pets. She appears, that is, to manipulate his image of his own masculinity, turning against him the power man ordinarily uses against woman. Urvaśī's wiliness, however, sustains notions of woman's cunning. Significantly, when Purūravas is provoked into proving his manhood, the Gandharvas are given their opportunity to reclaim Urvaśī. Tensions between the couple indicate that Urvaśī is ready to return to the otherworld, and she appears to have incited Purūravas to defy the very terms that she imposed on their union. Role playing more than love appears to inform this ancient story, less a romantic tale than the portrayal of a gender-based struggle for power within the love relationship and subversive of it—the woman yielding, at times reluctantly, to the man, but paying him back when he has lost her and she now holds the cards.[14]

In theoretical terms like those employed by evolutionary folklorists, the argument has been made that the enigmatic hymn in the *Rig Veda* can be explained by reference to a time when men were ritually sacrificed as the sequel to "some kinds of primitive sacred marriage." Urvaśī would represent the powerful, unyielding woman to whom Purūravas futilely appeals for pity.[15] The interest in this theory is not in its probably dubious claim, but in its rendering the hymn understandable in terms of a power struggle. For no interpretation could more effectively subvert the basis for a romantic explanation for the stories of Urvaśī or the swan maiden. Male dominance inverts matriarchal power, but, as will be seen, it is impossible to rid the swan maiden tale of the real and symbolic dependencies that underlie the struggle between man and woman.

Clearly, however, the story of Purūravas and Urvaśī could not be interpreted as a love story at all were there not more in it than a contest for power between man and woman. Purūravas is not entirely wrong in locating a contradiction in Urvaśī's attitude, in their push-pull relationship, in her seductiveness toward and retreat from him. Urvaśī conforms to—indeed she may be the best example of—the composite portrait of the swan maiden drawn by William Lessa in his study of the porpoise maiden of Oceania. Lessa says that the swan maiden is essentially "hyperfeminine, being shy and submissive, delicate and sensitive, loyal and affectionate, patient and dutiful," but that even though she is a good wife and mother, she never gives herself entirely to her family. Being out of place in a world of aggressive and misunderstanding humans, she is "often ready to abandon both her children and her spouse without too much remorse as soon as she finds a way to escape from her forced detention." Lessa describes the fairy wife as "slightly hebephrenic—torn between the mundane and the superphysical" life.[16] Comparably, David Thomson reports on the Scottish folk for whom the seal maiden is a living legend: "it is given to them that their sea-longing shall be land-longing and their land-longing shall be sea-longing."[17]

Similar conflicts are implied in the *Volundarkvida*, an ancient Nordic work of literature also held to be the source of the swan maiden tale.[18] Three women fly up from the south and spin fine linen on a beach, and three men take them home as wives. But after seven years, the women long to fight in battle, and when the husbands return from a year's hunting, their wives are gone. The activities in which these supernatural wives engage reflect a significant duality. Their spinning suggests both the magic powers traditionally associated with some goddesses as well as stereotypical female tasks. As female warriors (swan maidens are often likened to Valkyries),[19] they differ from ordinary women, assuming a traditionally masculine role and intruding into space ordinarily occupied by men. Yet they had for years been wives to hunters. In this oscillation between subservience and dominance, they reveal the ambiguity of the seal maidens torn between land- and sea-longing.

To create his model of swan maiden and to emphasize the ubiquitous components of her personality, Lessa must confront a problem in folklore methodology. Ordinarily, he contends, basic elements in a folk narrative blur as they pick up local variants in the process of dispersion. Since Oceanic porpoise maiden tales do not essentially differ from swan maiden stories told elsewhere, Lessa suggests that rules governing folklore cannot be as precise as, for example, chemical reactions.[20] Swan maiden stories appear to rest more on constant elements than on variations, and Holbek wonders if this reflects a constancy in the narrative pattern or if the narrative is forever generated anew in a similar fashion because it reflects persistent human conditions. The matter is not subject to proof, but the themes in the swan maiden tale and the essential marital relationship portrayed in it support the latter position. Whatever its cause, the stability of the swan maiden tale allows Lessa to divide it into a series of recurrent motifs.

On the other side, Bynum contends that variants in a narrative are not departures from some otherwise constant pattern but pieces of the pattern itself. Bynum employs the term "complementarity" to describe the way in which a "given pattern may govern the composition of many individual tales without necessarily being complete" in any one of them, arguing that the "purpose in comparing variants of fables and extracting generic motifs from them is precisely to lighten the otherwise heavy work of deciphering variants, which, if taken one by one and without reference to each other, constitutes a truly insurmountable labor of decipherment." The grandeur of an isolated tale would be "often bought at the expense of complementarity, whereby in oral fable multiforms of the same story-pattern are playfully combined with other patterns to demonstrate or explore the patterns' logical possibilities."[21]

To combine Lessa's view, in which the meaning of the swan maiden story inheres in its stable elements, and Bynum's, which suggests that variants are constituent parts of a narrative pattern that illuminate the constant features, is also to counter the idea of the so-called one-dimensionality of folk narratives as compared to literature.[22] Folktales are only one dimensional when taken one at a time (and not always then); once the stable elements and variants of a folktale or related group of tales are understood to interact, they form layers of meaning that imbue the narrative pattern with complex significance. Even seemingly contradictory versions of the same story are enlightening, since the contradiction is likely to reflect the strife depicted in the narrative situation.

The following discussion will be organized along the lines suggested by Lessa, emphasizing stable elements in the swan maiden tale: the isolation of the swan maiden from her sisters as she is forced into domesticity by a mortal man, and her escape when she regains her prized possession or he violates some taboo. Her usually unambivalent relief in getting away challenges the romanticized view of love and marriage held by those who extol the tragic beauty of the tale. But beyond this basic story is Lessa's portrait of a woman in conflict with herself, as well as the tension between two realms—this world and the otherworld from which the swan maiden comes. Variations in the tale make possible a deepening perception of her dilemma. Thus a Japanese swan maiden who barely pauses as she makes her escape[23] is complemented by an Icelandic seal maiden, who oscillates between earthly home and sea, until the call of the ocean proves irresistible and she plunges into her native element.[24] Different still is a Greek swan maiden who cleans house and cooks her family's meal when members of her family are not at home, stealing away before they return in order to take up each night a carefree existence that contrasts sharply with her domestic life.[25] But Bynum's emphasis on the variations that constitute a large narrative pattern leads to the realization that the more swan maiden stories known, the more rich Lessa's portrait appears—less a composite than a multi-leveled creation at once stable and alterable. And as other narrative patterns attach themselves to the swan maiden story, stories of other animal brides and grooms, the complex themes in the swan maiden tale themselves proliferate, the growth not arithmetic but geometric.

To be aware of gender as a significant part of folklore narration is to become cognizant of the irony that the swan maiden is not ordinarily held to be the main character in her own story, usually considered a variant of Tale Type 400, which involves a man's attempt to regain his lost wife. In elevating his search for her to a "quest" and making the husband's journey the central point of the narrative, folklorists actually reenact the husband's attempt to make his supernatural wife subservient to him. True, the meeting between the mortal man and the swan maiden frequently takes place well into the narrative,[26] which may begin with the man's adventures, his fairy wife often being a prize for success in earlier exploits. In such versions of the swan maiden story, the initial winning and subsequent recapturing of the wife (if she is recaptured) appear to chart the husband's progress toward maturity, at least as a male-dominated society would define maturity, and his domesticating the swan maiden is part of a rite of passage by which he proves his manhood. Still, the way the swan maiden is captured and the kind of life she leads in the domestic realm are hardly mere introductory elements in the tale; rather, they illuminate her escape and the tale's denouement by defining the mundane world in which she is trapped and the ensuing struggle between her and her husband. If anything, the swan maiden tale proves a particularly difficult one to classify as a predominantly man's or woman's story. (Holbek points out that most folktales have two central characters.)

The scholars who study the swan maiden sometimes compare her with another kind of supernatural mate, the imperious Celtic fairy who traditionally demands a mortal man's subservience as the price of consorting with her. Swan maiden and Celtic fairy are said to represent the "two different types of women found in real life in different stages of the development of the human race." An extremely ancient social system is posited, in which "women exercised an astonishing freedom in the choice or abandonment of their mates" and from which came the domineering fairy of Irish folktale and myth. But under a "different social system, where marriage by capture was practiced or where marital bonds, once formed, were less easily severed, other-worldly maidens (like their mortal prototypes) were more skittish and could be induced to join their fortunes to those of mortal lovers only by guile."[27] The theft of the swan maiden's possession thus becomes a claim against her person; only when she retrieves what was lost can she assert autonomy.[28] But the theme can be inverted, highlighting the contrast between the different worlds inhabited by the hostile parties. An Eskimo story tells how, by means of alien human clothing, a man captures an *ugruk:* the man's protective parka becomes his imprisoned mate's straitjacket, human clothing constituting not only a trap for this swan maiden but also an explicit symbol of culture's triumph over nature, here explicitly expressed as man's control of woman.[29]

The swan maiden's stolen possession is a link not only to her freedom but also to her sisters, from whom she is separated precisely because they retain the outward signs of their precious identity while she loses hers. And thus her encounter with her mortal mate thematically links the war between the sexes with the controversial subject of female bonding. Relatively few stories depict the capture of a single fairy; usually swan maidens form groups, the kidnapping and isolation of the fairy invoking her despair and the helpless pity of her companions. In a story from Assam, the youngest of the sun's six daughters must marry Harata after he steals her clothes and must confront a hard life whose most painful feature may be the absence of female companionship. She burst into helpless tears. She is being left alone by her sisters with an unknown man in an unknown place. The sisters are also in tears as they console her. The eldest sister says to her captor, "Harata, because you are so much eager to marry one of us, we are leaving our youngest sister with you. But she is the most beloved to us all. Never ill-treat her. Never tell her to cook. Never touch her hands and feet."[30] Similarly, with more resignation than grief the sisters of a Philippine swan maiden abandon the search for her stolen garment: "We will have to leave you here because you are no longer able to go alone."[31] In contrast, a group of Japanese swan maidens seek in panic their own safety, peremptorily leaving behind the sister who has lost her freedom.[32]

Female groups play more than one role in these stories, for women are also entrusted with the task of socializing their sisters and daughters, encouraging them to adapt to man's world. Sometimes it is a rebellious woman's chosen isolation from other women that marks her as a target for the unwelcome advances of an alien, predatory lover. An Australian aboriginal story of a female water bird that is not quite a swan maiden tale but that contains themes common to the captured bride motif tells how a young duck "used to swim away by herself in the creek. Her tribe told her that Mulloka, the water devil, would catch her some day if she were so venturesome."[33] A Malagasy tale similarly relates how a mortal is undeterred by the wariness of three swan maidens afraid to swim near him because they perceive danger, eventually catching the one who carelessly moves away from her sisters' protection.[34]

Although such stories were probably cautionary, intended to discourage female independence or exogamous relationships, their depiction of female solidarity is also paradoxical: what the woman's female companions prepare her for is her eventual separation from them, for after she passes into her husband's control, their influence becomes potentially subversive. This pattern is ritually literalized in Morocco: Daisy Dwyer describes how a bride is no longer permitted to associate with her unmarried female friends, and their companionship during her wedding week is a prelude to a final farewell. Should the new wife persist in these relations, condemnation from her husband and mother-in-law will be harsh. "As in other things the route from virginity to adulthood is made irreversible, which breeds its sadness among those women."[35] In the swan maiden story, marriage is characteristically a literal or symbolic capture, and the world to which the fairy wife later escapes is frequently depicted as one where she can recreate former ties to female companions.

In English, the word "rape" denotes either the kidnap or the forceful sexual violation of a woman, or both. And perhaps it is the rupture of female bonds as the swan maiden is torn from her sisters as much as the literal act of defloration that creates the essential image of rape in many swan maiden narratives. The inherent violence in the capture is rendered explicit in *The Arabian Nights* when Hasan of Basorah is instructed that when the swan maiden's sisters see that her dress has been stolen, they will fly away, at which point he will be able to drag her by the hair to that subterranean place that is his private chamber.[36] Even more explicit is a native Iowan tale that combines elements of swan maiden and demon lover stories to depict a woman's rape during which her helpless companions flee:

One day Ishji'nki [a trickster] was travelling [and] some of his playmates told him that there were some girls swimming down by the river bank. Ishji'nki went to the spot and saw a party of women swimming on the other side. He unwrapped his organ and thrust it under the water for a long way and finally captured the prettiest girl. The others cried and ran out of the water but the one that Ishji'nki had selected could not escape, but could only stand there and weep.[37]

In a Ten'as origins myth, the capture and symbolically depicted rape becomes a necessary condition for marriage itself. A man dwelling in a society without women "went up quietly [in his canoe] and launched his spear, which passed through the parka of one of [the water women]. The rest turned into geese and flew away; but he captured this one and took her home. The rest of the men began to get women in the same way."[38] As Doniger has noted, the "organ" of one story and its counterpart, the "spear" of the other, suggest an interesting symbolic transformation of nature into culture.

A male camaraderie predicated on the brutal overpowering of women supplies a theme in a Mikhail Lermontov poem. A prince captures a sea princess; pulling at her braid,

Strongly he holds her—her fingers are tight—
Letting her writhe on his saddle and fight.

Back to his friends he returns through the spray,
Eager to show his companions the prey.[39]

Occasionally brutal drives for sex and for power are transformed by the
rhetoric of romantic love, as in the florid prose of a Tibetan swan maiden
tale, rendered by a narrator apparently unaware of the essential contradiction in imagery: "No sooner had the youth set eyes on [the swan
maiden] than he was suddenly enchained by the bonds of passion—
passion which, like the pure and spotless moon reflected in water, is, on
account of its unstable nature, not easily to be grasped, and like a sea-
monster in a billowy torrent, is not easily to be distinguished."[40]

These stories, then, not only raise questions about relationships between men and women but also about groups differentiated according
to gender, relations to a same-sex person also being reflective of how
men and women interact.[41] An ideal of female bonding may itself depict
a fantasy based on a harsher reality. Frequently woman's role in male-
dominated societies breeds discord and competition; or a bitter situation
forces a woman—such as the Algonquin mother of a swan maiden—to
send her runaway daughter back to the husband she had fled from.[42]
Women may live physically together because of the different occupations
that isolate them from men, but occupying the same space does not
guarantee spiritual togetherness. Stories about the captured bride's separation from her sisters or companions may express some desired communion, even the depicted helplessness of swan maidens unable to protect their captured sister perhaps speaking to some longed-for emotional
attachment.

This analysis of female bonding as a motif in the swan maiden tale
presupposes that it is a woman's story, the narrator identifying with the
main character. But, again, the search for the lost wife after the swan
maiden escapes her husband focuses on his plight and assigns to him the
active role of adventurer in pursuit of a difficult-to-achieve goal. If the
swan maiden's husband is held to be the focus of the tale's interest, then
even female solidarity will be viewed from a male vantage point. For
such communion has traditionally been viewed by men with distrust,
and it is an ironic aftermath of discouraging women from bonding that
it has come to be believed that they are not capable of doing so. Madonna Kolbenschlag, who has studied fairy tales from a feminist point
of view, explains that "women are not so comfortable in groups—
chiefly because it confirms and accentuates their identity as females, a

class excluded from the dominant caste in our society. In part, these feelings are introjections of a traditional male paranoia about women in groups."[43] If indeed such a paranoia exists and is traditional, it is reflected when swan maiden stories combine the capture motif with the separation theme, the maiden responding in desperation to a double catastrophe.

A dual perspective permeates swan maiden narratives, whose themes can reverberate in the conscious and unconscious awareness of both men and women. But so long as male and female needs are entangled, man's are more likely to be met in reality if not in fantasy. That some people recognize that fantasy can serve social reality[44] is strikingly evidenced in the description by anthropologist Edwin Ardener of a Cameroon ritual in which woman's rebellion against her role leads to "therapy" in the form of her experiencing exclusive female solidarity, after which she returns to what she has recognized all along as an essentially man's world. What makes Ardener's study illuminating for swan maiden tales is that during her short period of female togetherness, the rebellious woman is initiated into a group of mermaids, and mermaid tales frequently form subgroups among swan maiden narratives.

The rebel enjoys with her fellow mermaids a life from which all male interests are excluded, even to the point of her learning a mermaid language that the men do not know. The initiate is secluded among women, participating in activities that act out symbolic defiance of masculinity. Her initial protest against female domesticity is recognized by her people when she symbolically kicks over a hearthstone. In effect, they acknowledge that only by allowing her to act out her discontent will they be able to reclaim her as an active member of society. It is striking that when in the *Brahmana* Purūravas finds Urvaśī after his search for her, she appears among a group of female companions (swans or water birds) from whom he cannot again separate her. For although it was the Gandharvas who conspired for her return to the divine realm, it is other divine nymphs who witness her obduracy in the face Purūravas's pleas that she return to the world. A Cameroon man is, in effect, both Purūravas and a Gandharva in reverse, hoping to reclaim his mortal wife from the otherworld, tolerating her visit there and her pretense that it is her true realm because allowing her to enact such a fantasy may be the only way to get her back. As Ardener explains it, the men "feel a danger has been averted" because the woman "has been rescued from the wild," that is, the natural world beyond the confines of village life, associated with such beings as mermaids, and is thus now "fitted for marriage with men." There is, of course, a central paradox in the Cameroon ritual, one that Ardener acknowledges, but it is also a paradox intrinsic to woman's relationship to her own sex. Men may distrust the influence of other women on their wives, but they also must rely on women to socialize children, particularly young female children, in accordance with the social structures men have created.[45]

The implicit acknowledgment that women are strong, not weak, may account for versions of the swan maiden tale in which the captured maiden's companions rescue their sister rather than abandon her to her fate. In a Siberian story, a bird woman's mother-in-law defends her son's interests by scolding his wife for joining other women to collect leaves (that is, for moving away from patriarchal culture). The older woman becomes a reason the captured woman "pined to return to her own land," and went with her children behind the tent as some geese passed by.

"How would it be," she [asked them], "for me to carry away my children?" The geese plucked their wings and stuck feathers on the children's sleeves, and the wife and her children flew away together.[46]

This is not the only mother-in-law who plays the swan maiden's adversary, either by representing masculine concerns, by enslaving the younger woman out of spite for her own earlier bondage, or by viewing the younger woman as her rival.[47]

The mother-in-law's role in the story, furthermore, highlights a question concerning a so-called woman's folklore: a female voice does not guarantee a feminist voice, any more than a woman can be counted on by another woman for protection. For example, in societies that practice female circumcision, it is usually a close female relative who comes to fetch the young girl, forcing her to submit not only to pain but also to a loss of capacity to experience sexual pleasure. By ensuring her fidelity to her husband, the older women, of course, may be realistically acting in what they perceive to be the young girl's own long-range interests; the uncircumcised woman may not be able to marry or assume any other status among her people. With equal plausibility, a female storyteller may instruct a female audience in how to conform to patriarchy. The mother of an Algonquin swan maiden has already been cited in this regard:

[A] hunter, returning [from the hunt] saw a very beautiful girl sitting on a rock by a river, making a moccasin. And being in a canoe he paddled up softly and silently to capture her; but she, seeing him coming, jumped into the water and disappeared. On returning to her mother, who lived at the bottom of the river, she was told to go back to the hunter and be his wife; "for now," said the mother, "you belong to that man."[48]

No wonder, then, that the captured swan maiden may utter wails of despair or may in tears lament her bondage. A hunter in an Icelandic story steals a sealskin because it is valuable, but, economic needs met, he returns for the woman whom he finds "stark naked, and weeping bitterly."[49] This hunter's greed is paralleled in one of the best-known of the Japanese Noh dramas, *The Robe of Feathers,* in which a swan maiden deplores her union with the mortal whose avaricious coveting of her garment stands in sharp contrast to the spirituality of the dance she performs when she wears the robe. In a Japanese folktale, the swan maiden similarly descends from a spiritual to a grossly material world: "she felt the cold because her clothes were thin, and she also felt pangs of hunger. So she had to go down the mountain to the village and ask a farmer for some food."[50] He becomes her husband because she has little choice but to depend on him for protection.

Not that all male captors are indifferent to the swan maiden's grief. Keightley recounts a "Mermaid Wife" story from the Shetland Islands, in which the hunter who has stolen the seal skin returns to find his prospective bride lamenting "in most piteous tones" not only the "loss of her sealskin robe" but also the result of that loss. She never could "hope to rejoin her family and friends below the waters, but must remain an unwilling inhabitant of the region enlightened by the sun." In Western thought, it was once traditional to draw parallels according to which the sun dominates the earth, rationality controls instinct, and patriarchy triumphs over matriarchy, an ordering the romantic age often deliberately strove to invert. No wonder then that the mermaid recoils from the upper regions of the earth. But her captor has steeled his heart, representing to her the impossibility of her return to the waters, convincing her of what she probably suspects, that "her friends would soon give her up." After these coercions, he softens and offers her "his heart, hand,

and fortune," indulging in a courtship that barely conceals the force behind it. The sea maiden is not deceived, however, but "finding she had no alternative, [she] at length consented to become his wife."[51]

Keightley's version infers an erotic pleasure to be derived from the swan maiden's resistance. Not even a hint of such perverse enjoyment can be found in Thomas Croker's analogous tale of a sea wife, in which one Dick Fitzgerald needs someone to clean his house and mother the children she will bear him. The storyteller's sympathy lies entirely with the man left bereft when she escapes him. Ironically, the narrator elicits pity for the destitute man by establishing from the outset a soft heart that shrinks from the necessity of capturing his bride by stealing the cap that sustains her in water:

When the merrow [mermaid] saw that her little diving cap was gone, the salt tears—doubly salt, no doubt, from her—came trickling down her cheeks, and she began a low mournful cry, with just the tender voice of a newborn infant. Dick, although he knew well enough what she was crying for, determined to keep the *cohuleen driuth*, let her cry never so much, to see what luck would come of it. Yet he could not help pitying her; and when the dumb thing looked up in his face, and her cheeks all moist with tears, 'twas enough to make anyone feel, let alone Dick, who had ever and always, like most of his countrymen, a tender heart of his own.[52]

In the Malagasy story discussed above, one Adrianoro forthrightly asks his swan maiden what it is about him and his world that repels her, and she has two responses. First she doubts her husband can match her father in power and ability to protect her, "for if father speaks the thunder-bolt darts forth"; second, she seems to fear abuse: "I do not drink spirits," for if "spirits even touch my mouth I die."[53] This swan maiden is not rejecting the dominance of man so much as expressing doubt that the man's obligation to care for her will be honored, especially if he is under the influence of alcohol. It will be seen later that a frequent constraint placed upon men in animal groom and animal bride tales is that women not be in some way mistreated. When she accepts Adrianoro's assurances, this swan maiden willingly consents to be his bride.

Frequently the swan maiden can anticipate new pleasures and security in marriage, and these benefits will soften the capture motif. In a Welsh tale, the Lady of the Van Pools agrees to wed the man who had tossed her gifts of cheese and bread (images of genuine sustenance), and in return she brings to him her own dower of flocks and herd,[54] an exchange that symbolizes her acceptance not only of his culture but also of culture itself. Sometimes the swan maiden's husband coaxes the fairy into submission, or she allows herself to be seduced—although, again, by concealing what is often force, romantic courtship remains a symbolic capture, the stories reflecting a modern predicament. For, the lies of individuals aside, the line between consensual sex and rape has become a legal conundrum. In one story, the aggression and violence intrinsic to a male hunter cannot be separated from the affectionate blandishments of one who would rather court than capture the swan maiden, and it is difficult to distinguish the vulnerable woman from his animal prey.

> The happy hunter now exerted himself to assuage the terror of his beloved prize. Gently leading her toward his lodge, he recounted his adventures in the chase, dwelling at the same time, with many endearing words upon the charms of life upon earth. His incessant kindness so won upon her delicate nature that she consented to become his bride.[55]

In a tale from Australia, a man uses rhetoric rather than weapons to lure fairy bathers out of the water, but the capture motif concealed by his method is finally unmasked.

> A little persuasion succeeded in causing them to listen, each moment lessened their dread, and admiration of the stranger so quickly succeeded fear that they seemed all at once to have forgotten their life-long hatred of men, and to yield to the witchcraft young eyes possess over their fellows. . . . And when he took out a large soft rug of emu skin for each of the girls, and threw them on their shoulder over the dreaded wings, there did not remain one thought of flight in their hearts.[56]

The stolen clothing motif has once again been inverted: human garments, possessing the power of culture, are contrasted to the wings that later in the story promise the wife her chance for freedom. Once again, the love motif has yielded to the practical requirement that the man be able to restrain his bride.

If swan maidens are portrayed as having sexual desires, these merely provide their would-be husbands with another opportunity to capture their brides. In a story from Assam, the swan maiden at first hides in a cave, resisting an apparent symbol of her natural inclinations:

> But she could not hide herself for long. There was a very clever man called Nongriji Kongor. He decided to catch the mysterious girl. So he took a flower

with him called "U tiew-jalyng Kteng," and stood in front of the cave. The flower bears a very strong and charming scent. The girl was attracted by the scent and she came out to take it. But Nongriji Kongor was not such a fool that the flower could be snatched away from him. The girl tried to catch the flower but she could not. It was always at a distance from her. She could no longer resist the desire to have the flower. She came out in the open from her cave. That is what Nongriji Kongor wanted. As soon as she came out in the open he caught her. He brought her to his house and married her.[57]

That surrendering to her own desires may prove the swan maiden's undoing is a theme highlighted in a tale from Sutherlandshire that juxtaposes the submissive swan maiden type character with the traditionally treacherous siren, the former actually being defined by the male character as the latter:

A mermaid fell in love with a fisherman of Lochinver. Her lover was enamoured, but he had heard how youths ensnared by mermaids had found a watery grave. It became necessary then to make his own terms, and to arrange matters so as to assure himself. To rule a mermaid it is necessary to possess yourself, not of her person, but of the pouch and belt which mermaids wear.[58]

Some swan maidens even take the initiative in courtship, again embodying both the aggressive and submissive fairy. Lessa has pointed to this feature in some Oceanic tales, which distinguishes them from what he calls the "classic version." Rather than being transformed into a helpless and hapless being when her clothing is stolen, the supernatural woman "comes to the man of her own free will and makes amatory advances toward him, although she is seized by force." Appearing to long for the usually mundane features of earthly life—to "disport themselves like human beings"[59]—such swan maidens may desire integration into the imperfect mortal world. Such a theme makes it only that much more tragic that a debacle rather than a happy ending is characteristic of what Lessa calls the classic swan maiden tale. As Holbek points out about the versions of the stories he knows, they are more likely to end happily if the swan maiden is lost before marriage takes place and children are born; once domestic life has been firmly established, the otherworld becomes that much more threatening to the union, and the supernatural wife is unlikely to be won back.

But there has been a recent shift in how "woman's work," despised alike by most swan maidens and feminists, is perceived: once seen as the slave labor wives must engage in, domestic tasks (for example, the weaving done by swan maidens in the *Volundarkvida*) can be exalted as being among the few surviving skills that get passed from parent to child. Moreover, the domestic realm has provided space separate from that dominated by men and thus supplies women an opportunity to participate in an exclusive female community (quilting bees are an example). Thus women can "celebrate the unstoried pattern of Hestia, goddess of the hearth." [60] This celebration of the mundane characterizes the Oceanic swan maidens singled out by Lessa, who freely choose human life; and they find their counterpart in mortal women who rebuff demon lovers who promise freedom from domesticity or those who choose a mortal husband when a divine mate is theirs for the asking. But these examples will have to await the concluding chapter of this book. Most swan maiden tales paint a dreary picture of domestic life, one that makes readily understandable the reluctance of the escaped wife to return to her husband's world.

The Cameroon rituals described by Ardener tie the discord between man and woman to the mundane conditions of their everyday lives. The Bakweri world is divided into the village that represents their agriculturally based society, and an area outside of this fenced-in enclosure, which for them is nature and thus the "wild." This is the natural realm of their "mermaids," as it is the natural habitat of the swan maidens. It is into the wild that the Bakweri women venture each day to labor, "returning at evening with their back-breaking loads of wood and cocoyams, streaming with rain, odds and ends tied up with bark strips and fronds, and screaming with fatigue at their husbands." They have returned to face additional chores, for the "Bakweri men wait in their leaking huts for the evening meal." It is no wonder, adds Ardener, that "the women seem to be forest creatures, who might vanish one day for ever." [61] Man's security traditionally lies in restricting his woman's space if he can, and where he cannot, increased tension between them will result. Ironically, however, the natural world that to the swan maiden (e.g., Bakweri "forest creatures") often spells freedom, spells to the Bakweri women only more drudgery as they forage for wood. In their exclusively female mermaid rites, during which the rebellious woman is freed from the hearth whose stone she had symbolically kicked over, Bakweri women may be invoking a more symbolic female relationship to the natural world, separating nature from culture more definitively than their lives actually allow.

But swan maiden tales raise questions concerning why men render themselves vulnerable by taking supernatural wives in the first place—even if only in their imaginations. Perhaps it is because of man's acknowledged tendency to split the female image, attaching himself symbolically to two kinds of women inhabiting different worlds, in this way participating in a generally human rather than gender-based conflict between life as it is and life as it can only be imagined. Keeping conflicting realms separate may represent a pragmatic approach to the ensuing conflict, and some people encourage customs in which men at least have this privilege.[62] But to marry a swan maiden and then try to domesticate her may be to set up what Hartland calls the catastrophe inherent in the swan maiden story. As will be seen, swan maidens venture or are dragged protesting into the mundane world, and then are trapped in or driven from it. Perhaps this is what Hartland implies, if not necessarily intends, when he says that the swan maiden *must* return to her own domain.[63] Yet it is difficult to believe there is not a deep meaning to the Faroese proverb reported by Thomson—"She could no more hold herself back than the seal wife could when she found her skin."[64]

Swan maiden narratives depict the tension between the wild with which woman is traditionally associated and the domestic space to which she is nonetheless assigned—in part to subdue nature. But usually the narratives leap from the capture of the wife over years to the time just before her escape, and details about the intervening years are rare. Enough variants, however, depict this time period to make it possible to recognize an emerging pattern of female drudgery and anger on the wife's side, and sullen fear and vulnerability on the husband's—the very situation Ardener described as the roots of the Bakweri mermaid rites.

Sometimes the swan maiden initially adapts to the mundane world and is for a time even ambivalently content in it, her children binding her to a person she will come to perceive as their father rather than her husband. A gypsy folktale poignantly tells how Russalka, the wind maiden, is captured by a mortal whom she later leaves to follow the wind, only to be recaptured when she returns for her son. Resigned, she remains with her family: "And so she Russalka, the Wood-nymph, forgot the forest for the sake of her fine son; she forgot the forest, Russalka utterly forgot the forest."[65] Forgetfulness, virtually bordering on amnesia, is often the only means by which the captured maiden can adapt. After her clothing is stolen, a Japanese swan maiden "forgot all about the heavenly world where she had lived, and became an ordinary human girl."[66] But not all captured brides experience such fortuitous losses of memory. An Eskimo husband is not confident that if he leaves his swan maiden wife in order to ride his kayak, she will be there at his return: "and thus it happened that he gave up kayaking altogether, until one day she declared, 'Now thou mayest leave me without fear, for I do really love thee, and thou mayest depend on me.' "[67] Some storytellers interpret the swan maiden's assurance as wiliness, a way of disarming the vigilant man. Her feigned contentment within the marriage is held to conceal a mere waiting period during which she calculates her means of escape:

The Finn [seal] women were said to make good housewives. Yet there was generally a longing after some previous attachment; if ever a chance occurred of recovering the essential dress, no newly formed ties of kindred could prevent escape and return to . . . former pleasures. This was assiduously guarded against on the one [man's] side [and] watched on the other [woman's].[68]

Other versions are related by narrators who sympathetically recognize genuine conflict or the sad plights of swan maidens unable to adapt to the mortal realm. In a Lithuanian tale, even marriage to royalty does not assuage the swan maiden's distress, for her husband's world is fundamentally alienating: "Even in the king's palace the young woman would not cheer up. She kept walking up and down, wringing her hands and weeping. She would not smile even when her daughter was born."[69] An Icelandic seal maiden comes genuinely to care for her husband, "but did not get on so well with other people." Often she would sit alone and stare out to sea.[70]

Some mortal husbands mistakenly believe their children are guarantees that the swan maiden will not leave. A Korean man is advised that if she has at least three children, his wife "can't fly away whereas with two she can take one under each arm."[71] It is, of course, a classic feature of the swan maiden stories that children rarely, in fact, deter the fairy's flight. In a Visayan tale, it is precisely as she is swinging her child in a hammock that a swan maiden accidentally discovers her stolen magic wings and flies off without the infant. The narrator wonders at this flight, for she apparently had no reason to complain about her life. While she had rocked her child, her husband had been making rice soup, and thus child care is implied to be her only responsibility.[72] In another version, a specified male narrator not only minimizes but also idealizes the swan maiden's responsibilities: "It wasn't many years when this wife gave birth. The baby was a girl. Indeed the child was the image of her mother. And now the mother is busy sewing and embroidering dresses for her child." When she escapes, her husband succeeds in winning her back through a test common in folklore, picking her out from a group of seemingly identical women. The characteristic that allows him to recognize her is a sign of her mundane and domestic life: "This one, Chief, is my wife because I recognize the tiny mark of a needle here in the center of her smallest finger." "You can take her," says the chief, "for she is indeed your wife."[73]

To think that swan maidens can be content in the mundane world points to male insensitivity or obtuseness—or so a Bulgarian story suggests. The Samodiva—as the swan maiden is called—escapes from the very party that celebrates the birth of her son. When she retrieves her magic clothing, she taunts her husband:

Hear my words, O Stoian; seek not
For thy wife a Samodiva—
Samodivas are not thrifty,
Know not how to tend the children.
Said I not to thee, O Stoian,
Samodivas are not housewives?[74]

Nor will heaping praise on his fairy wife for her housewifely duties keep her content, as the aforementioned Dick Fitzgerald learns, dumbfounded when his wife departs in spite of her customary way of busying "herself about the house," nursing the two boys and girls she had given birth to.[75]

In choosing one swan maiden bride from among her companions, the men in these stories characteristically pick the youngest or most beautiful, an erotic motive triumphing over practical considerations. But this is not always the case. A Welsh swan maiden's domestic skills attract the mortal's attention, for he seeks not so much a sexual partner as a convenient maid: "And such a servant she turned out to be! Why, she was wont to milk the cows thrice a day, and to have the usual quantity of milk each time, so that the butter was so plentiful." Although she "was so charmingly pretty," he stresses that it was because she was "so industrious, so skilled in every work" that he offered to make her his wife.[76] That wife equals servant is a reiterated theme when the narrator chooses to depict the couple's domestic life. Few existences, however, are as bleak as that of the swan maiden trapped in Sutherlandshire, and those commentators who have found great beauty in the swan maiden tale could hardly have stumbled over this version. It relates how a young man "by fair means or foul" gets hold of a mermaid's pouch and she became his "bride and bondswoman."

There was little happiness in such a union for the poor little wife. She wearied of a husband, who, to tell the truth, thought more of himself than of her. He never took her out in his boat when the sun danced on the sea, but left her at home with the cows, and on a croft which was to her a sort of prison. Her silky hair grew tangled. The dogs teased her. Her tail was really in the way. She wept incessantly while rude people mocked at her. Nor was there any prospect of escape after nine months of this wretched life. Her powers of swimming depended on her pouch, and that was lost. What was more, she now suspected the fisherman of having cozened her out of it.[77]

This was the mermaid whose captor perceived her to be a dangerous siren—that is, endowed her with traditional qualities of feminine evil and used his perceptions as an excuse for retaining power over her. The symbolism of the pouch in the context of nine months of wretchedness is hardly subtle, but it is an ambiguous symbol, for it denotes not only a female but also an individual identity that is lost with the swan maiden's capture. The specific details in this narrative emphasize the connection between the swan maiden and ordinary housewives. The loss of beauty, moreover, points out what is dreamed of about fairyland, for there women's lives do not degenerate into pedestrian misery. In the story of Hiawatha, it is said that in the spirit world every woman "shall also change her state and looks, and no longer be doomed to laborious tasks. She shall put on the beauty of the starlight, and become a shining bird of the air. She shall dance, and not work. She shall sing, and not cry."[78]

Essential to the otherworld's appeal, then, is that it allows the wife to retain or somehow preserve her youthful beauty and to enjoy freedom from onerous chores—the supernatural realm, in short, reflects a life that might have been and thus once was. In "Lady Featherflight" a fairy wife hides in a tree over a spring to observe the life she sees enacted there:

Now this spring was used by all the wives of the townspeople to draw water for breakfast. No water was so sweet anywhere else; and early in the morning, they all came with pitchers and pails for a gossip, and to draw water for the kettle. The first who came was a carpenter's wife, and as she bent over the clear spring she saw, not herself, but Featherflight's lovely face reflected in the water. She looks at it with astonishment and cries, "What! I, a carpenter's wife and I so handsome? No, that I won't," and down she threw the pitcher and off she went.[79]

The townsmen, who first miss their breakfast and then their wives, want to hang Featherflight as a witch. Quickly, however, they reject the value of their wives and bid them good riddance—a comic but hardly adequate response to the situation. It has often been claimed of American folklore that it naturalizes the supernatural elements of the narratives brought over from the old world. Rather than being a mournful captured bride, Lady Featherflight represents the ordinary discontented and complaining housewife. To reduce the story to one of bickering spouses is also, however, to minimize a larger symbolic conflict, and the men whose point of view is so well represented in this tale do not have to confront a metaphysical anxiety harder to deal with than domestic squabbles.

The depiction of a magic world in which a woman need never experience drudgery leads to significant ambiguities about how these essentially human fantasies affect the telling of swan maiden stories. Is woman's plight being sympathetically portrayed, or is her supposedly tenuous hold on cultural reality being criticized? Are men who themselves entertain erotic fantasies splitting the female image into the housewifely and maternal on one side, and the erotic on the other, experiencing their own dissatisfaction with reality but projecting their disillusionment onto the wives they do not satisfy? The disappearing swan maiden can symbolize the fleeting nature of male visions of the perfect domestic life. In the *Dravidian Nights*, a male storyteller uses narrative to instruct his wives about how to create a bower of bliss in their home. He relates how a young man has the ambition to be emperor of the world so that he can realize his dream of reclining on a "sofa with the daughter of Indra giving [him] betel-leaf rolls to chew, the daughter of Agni shampooing [his] legs, the daughter of Varuna singing [him] sweet songs, and the daughter of Adiseshna fanning [him] with white chauries." Indra's daughter is explicitly portrayed in this story as a swan maiden who must be convinced of the advantages of marriage to him, but it is difficult to perceive what benefits she would receive beyond the satisfaction of serving him. Through his divine mate, the man wins great fortune and, moreover, secures her acquiescence and help in attaining as other wives the daughters of the gods of fire, the seas, and the serpent world.[80] In this pleasure dome, there is no need to transform his female partners into household drudges.

But even in the practical world of mundane marriages, the advantages in the union appear to remain with the man. In the United States it is forthrightly argued that "married men and single women [are] much better off than married women."[81] Husbands of a growing number of runaway wives[82]—contemporary swan maidens—prove surprisingly obtuse when asked by detectives to describe the runaway, revealing how long it had been since they had truly looked at their wives as persons, "really seen" them. One wife reported that she felt like nobody, only a "service station."[83] Yet an abandoned man will usually perceive himself as his wife's victim rather than a contributor to her unhappiness. One version of the swan maiden tale highlights this masculine point of view: a Shetlander who marries a seal maiden loves her but finds that "she made but a cold return to his affection."[84] Here it is the man who is portrayed as suffering in the marriage, and suffering even more when his wife runs away.

Swan maiden stories supply a wide range in depicting the life of the mismatched couple: if the fairy appears content, her mortal husband will be suspicious; if she is obviously discontented, he will remain wary; if she evidences conflict, he will try to ignore her plight until the final catastrophe. As a woman's story, the tales reflect women's conscious awareness of why they married, and at the same time reveal that a central feature of female fantasy is that a wife has options, since few societies have allowed women choice in their roles. Indeed swan maiden tales suggest that romantic love constitutes not only a literary tradition but also a universal dream resulting from the human imagination's capacity to imagine a better life. Woman's supposedly greater capacity to love than man's has been argued to be one of her strengths,[85] but it is a capacity that often redounds to man's benefit more than her own. It has been argued, moreover, that cultures "use their myths of love in much the same way as do individuals their central sexual fantasy: to express their deeper wishes which are utterly at odds with the accepted ideologies of the man-woman relationship."[86]

Rather than *being* a love story, the swan maiden tale exposes such myths of love to uncover cultural reality. The fairy bride's abandonment of her mortal husband parallels a real woman's abandonment of expectations for happiness. But her husband will be convinced that in her search for happiness, his wife is insatiable, too unstable to ground herself in reality. For as a man's story, the swan maiden tale speaks to a deeply rooted male fear, perhaps going back to a young boy's separation from his mother, that his wife will leave him and that his hold on her is precarious. What these stories also portray is the man's incapacity to distinguish among and then integrate the motives that led him to desire a swan maiden wife, because to confront his own dependencies would subvert his position as the dominant partner in the relationship. Ultimately, rather mundane concerns prove overwhelming, and he seems incapable of grasping the possibility that merely providing for them is not enough to satisfy his spouse.

It sometimes happens, though, that swan maiden tales reflect a human fantasy that goes beyond gender differences. It is implied that the conflicts that beset the mismatched pair could be evaded altogether if the couple lived in the swan maiden's world. Thus in the *Brahmana* Purūravas ascends to dwell with Urvaśī among the demigods; and swans that can soar above the mortal world evoke what Kinsley describes as a metaphor for the complete transcendence of the "limitations and imperfections of the phenomenal world."[87] It is not unusual for the swan maiden's husband to join her in the otherworld. Such versions have been explained as survivals of matrilocal cultures,[88] the bride's unhappiness on earth being an expression of her anguish at being plucked from a protective family and thrust into the essentially alien environment of her husband's people. The story can thus be read as a protest against the supplanting of matrilocal by patrilocal structures. Putting evolutionary theories aside, what may have survived is essentially human and timeless: a symbolic regression from the reality principle to pure wish fulfillment may account for the married pair's escape to the swan maiden's world. For if hers is a place where people are freed from the pains of both the human condition and their socially defined roles, it would not be illogical to conceive of the swan maiden's husband as a potential Tannhäuser who follows his goddess to some fantasized realm.

In a story from South America, the supernatural otherworld offers release from the greed and injustice of the human world. One Juan Martin hears how once a year seven beautiful ducks appear on a lake, capable of being caught with a rosary. This admixture of paganism and Christianity suggests that worldly and unworldly paradises have combined to offer a sanctioned escape from the mundane. As one of the enchanted water birds explains,

Once there was a great temple here where the Indians worship their god. But when the white men came and wanted our gold and emeralds, and even our lives, my father put a powerful magic on us, and we went under the water. We come up only once a year, for one day, as golden ducks. Then we go back down to our palace at the bottom of this lake. But now that you have broken our magic with your rosary, we cannot go back. We will all be unhappy.

Instead of retaining the water bird by force, converting her to the values of his world, Martin follows her into the lake. The story ends with a suggestion that such a magic realm might entice anyone who could gain access to it: "Where is that lake? I mustn't tell you. It's not good for you to know. [Too] many boys and girls, and even grownups, might leave their homes" to find it.[89]

Puzzled commentators on the swan maiden story wonder why swan maidens leave, and among their answers lies a conviction that the fairy wives are just obeying their nature[90] as supernatural beings—as if the laws governing narrative were self-referential and had no basis in actual life. Again, Hartland contends that as civilizations advance, marriage itself becomes more complex, as does the reason for the separation. Yet he can think of no other cause for the star maiden to return to the sky except that she is homesick, adding that "homesick heroines are not very interesting."[91] In fact they are quite interesting, being the antithesis of those occasional swan maidens who are drawn by the human world rather than imprisoned by it, and homesickness figures as part of a significant conflict. The resulting tension seems to have appealed to the ironic imagination of some storytellers, who have conceived of the very life that restricts the swan maiden as providing the means for her escape.

In a Melanesian version, Tagoro takes the swan maiden to weed his people's garden, a symbol of culture and social communality that renders threatening the swan maiden's essential rootedness in the natural, that is, asocial, world. (One manifestation of the supernatural is, paradoxically, nature conceived of as totally untouched by human culture.) Her husband's people remain guarded and hostile, ever ready to protect themselves against this perceived intrusion into their lives: as she weeds and touches the yam vines, ripe tubers come into her hand. Tagoro's brothers think she is digging the yams before their time and scold her; she goes into the house and sits weeping at the foot of the pillar, and as she weeps her tears fall, wearing away the earth pattered down upon her buried wings. She hears the sound, takes up her wings, and flies back to heaven.[92] The Jesup of North America similarly relate how a people who benefit from the swan maiden nonetheless destroy their good luck: a man "lived with his Goose wife for some time; and when the people were starving, her father sent them food. But one day something was said that offended her, and she flew away."[93]

An equally foolish husband from Java ignores the swan maiden's prohibition that he never look into the pot where their rice is boiling. One day, while she is at the river washing clothes (perhaps a variation on the bathing woman's stolen garments), he

accordingly . . . raised the lid, but saw nothing in the pot except boiling water and a single grain of rice; and so, replacing the cover, he awaited his wife's return. When she came, she hurried to the pot and looked in, only to find the single grain of rice, since the magic power by which she had hitherto been able to produce food miraculously had been destroyed by her husband's curiosity. This, of course, made her angry, because henceforth she was obliged to labour and to prepare rice for every meal in the usual manner.[94]

It is when she comes to the bottom of their food store that she finds her missing garment and escapes her husband's world.

Sometimes the swan maiden's husband appears more careless than heedless. In an Icelandic story, he goes to church alone (that she does not accompany him is a sign not only of *her* resistance to society but also of the essential threat the seal maiden's origins in nature pose to a Christian world), leaving in his everyday clothing the key to the place where he had hidden her animal skin.[95] That the husband of another swan maiden had not thought to destroy his wife's feather robe is treated as equal carelessness—if the "foolish man" had burned or otherwise destroyed the wife's skin, she could never have fled[96] (the destruction of the animal mate's skin is an important motif that will be taken up again in later chapters). But other husbands are portrayed as merely naive, such as the Eskimo husband who takes his wife at her word that it is all right to leave her alone in their house,[97] or the Polish husband who trustingly returns the swan maiden's wings after their church wedding.[98] In a Korean tale, the husband remorsefully contemplates his wife's capture: "I stole her person and I stole her heart. See how sometimes her rosy cheeks turn pale with sad thoughts about her dress. I must tell her about it now. Perhaps it will bring peace to her mind."[99] All of these men discover their swan maidens have fled, and such outcomes might reinforce for a male audience the need to maintain a forceful grip on an ever potentially faithless wife.

When a husband is obtuse or insensitive to his wife's needs, less sympathy is evoked for him than when he blunders—however stupidly. A significant example is the Polynesian legendary hero Tawhaki, whose offense highlights the role gender itself plays in the tension between the fairy wife and her mortal husband. Tawhaki forfeits his entire family when he is repulsed by the birth of a female child, for he had promised his fairy wife that a daughter would be treated exactly as a son. It is common for male children to be valued over female, and some societies actually mourn the birth of a girl. But Tawhaki's disappointment is so offensively expressed that both spouse and child flee to the otherworld. His search is in fact for his daughter, not his wife, his ability to win back his spouse perhaps being the result of his new ability to value woman.[100]

For a man to devalue woman is also to give himself permission to be unfaithful to her. A man's mistress follows him home in one story, confirming his fairy wife's fears that he has broken an essential taboo in their marital relationship.[101] But the wife's vulnerability in the face of a rival also illuminates a striking feature in some versions of the swan maiden tale, which often makes clear that in entering the human realm, the fairy is as subject to mutability as any human woman. The Sutherlandshire mermaid is not the only captured bride to lose her beauty in marriage or to worry about her fading looks. The stolen garment or skin can symbolically represent a youth sacrificed in the service of a man. A seal maiden extracts from her husband an agreement that although he may hide her skin, he must keep it in good condition, wet and supple. On the day she makes her escape, she finds it as fresh as the day he took it from her on the beach.[102] A goose girl who "dried [her] goose-skin and put it away" after being captured cannot prevent her husband from hiding it; but when she later finds it, "she chewed it till it was soft as when first removed."[103] In contrast, a runaway porpoise wife throws herself into the sea, frustrated, however, because her tail has become so dried out it has lost its buoyancy and she cannot maneuver as she once could in her natural element.[104]

In short, the swan maiden concerned to regain some previous attractiveness or power can be conceived of as middle aged by the time she manages to free herself from her mortal ties, and it would appear that part of the fantasy embodied in at least some of these tales is that even in her stay on earth, the effects of time have been evaded. This theme suggests another way to read a swan maiden story from Greenland: "the woman does not recover her original feather-dress, but she collects feathers and makes new feather-dresses for herself," after which she flies away.[105] Doubtless, her skill and ingenuity in escaping her husband reflect the important role Eskimo women play in the survival of their group, especially in fashioning protective clothing, but the *new* feather dress seems analogous to the well-preserved sealskin or the renewed gooseskin. But probably no swan maiden goes as far as the Bulgarian Samodiva, who, having exercised her ingenuity by tricking her husband into returning her stolen dress, returns to her own land, where her virginity is restored during a ritual bath and the birth of her child is quite literally canceled out.[106]

Still another way that a man undermines his marriage to a swan maiden is to manifest the violent aggression that subdued her in the first place. An Algonquin story relates how two captured water fairies witness the hostility between their mortal husbands and resolve to escape the murderous behavior of human beings.[107] A Musquakie bird wife is similarly frightened by her human husband, and her concern extends not only to herself but also to her people. Although North American tribes frequently tell stories that link the acquisition of an animal wife with success in hunting or special luck in acquiring a seemingly endless food supply, in this case a hunter's brutal destruction of a duck wife's people is mirrored in the way her husband commands her to obey him:

The girl was a good wife. She could not talk. He said: "Don't go to the river." She did not go. One day a hunter went there. He had many dead ducks. He said: "Cook these ducks." She was scared, and ran to the river and swam away. The young man could not find her. He never liked any wife he had as well as that duck-girl.[108]

In this version, hunter and husband are at first separate characters, but they merge to form a generalized aggressive male figure who first prevents the woman's contact with water, her native element, and then commands her to turn against her kind. In this combined persona, he comes to represent a particularly brutal form of patriarchy.

Whatever the source of the husband's blunder, his wife gains the opportunity she has awaited to escape the marriage. Ancient folklore motifs are frequently reflected in contemporary accounts of runaway wives, such as the one who develops an aversion for the husband who refers to her only as " 'the wife,' " and who uses the car he buys for her convenience as a vehicle in which she can embark on another life.[109] Feminine duplicity is a given in some swan maiden tales, such as the one that describes how "female curiosity and cunning were always more than a match for male care and caution; and the [seal] woman always got the slip."[110] Greek swan maidens are depicted as equally wily, and men are enjoined not to think that it is sufficient to capture them. The sequel to the Greek swan maiden narratives is held to be discouraging, for although the fairy is a good wife in the "commonplace estimation,"

though her skill in domestic duties be as proverbial as her beauty, she either turns her charms and her cunning to such account as to discover the hiding-place of her stolen kerchief, or, failing this, so mopes and pines over her work that her husband worn down by her sullenness and persistent silence decides to risk all if he can restore her lightheartedness.[111]

A Chinese husband is similarly manipulated: the swan maiden "often asked him where he had hidden her fairy dress. He would never tell her, until one day she asked so often and so caressingly that he eventually betrayed his secret. Then she seized the dress, jumped onto a cloud, and flew away."[112]

Not all swan maidens count on wearing their husbands down. Again, an Eskimo wife uses the time when her husband is away to fashion new wings to replace her hidden ones;[113] others trick their husbands or other members of the family who have access to the stolen garment or animal skin. It is possible to compare versions in which the swan maiden plays an active part in retrieving her clothing with those in which her discovery is purely accidental. Sometimes there is a correlation between woman's status in a society and the swan maiden's exercise of ingenuity in effecting her escape. Bulgarian Turkish women may supply an example, for according to Lucy Garnett, their work in the fields makes them valuable to their fathers, and they marry later in life, leading a "freer life, not only than that led by the Bulgarian townswomen, but by the generality of Greek peasant women."[114] It is not surprising, then, that their swan maiden, the Samodiva, takes the initiative to secure her own release by exploiting the egotistical weakness of a husband who treats her like a mere possession. It will be remembered that the Samodiva escapes the day he celebrates the birth of their son. Carousing with his male companions, he boasts of his wife's ability to dance and, like Ibsen's Torvald

Helmer, offers her performance as entertainment for his friends' pleasure.[115] When the Samodiva argues that she dances best with her magic
dress, he unwittingly or perhaps dull-wittedly returns it, and she leaves
him with the taunt that she had warned him Samodivas are neither good
housewives nor mothers.[116]

It has already been noted that for some folklorists, the wife's flight
from her family is actually the beginning of the story, the capture and
the couple's life together constituting introductory elements even when
lengthy. And it is true that some swan maidens leave hints or even clear
instructions about how they may be found, virtually guaranteeing a
reunion with their human spouses, the reconciliation eliminating what
some storytellers find the most disturbing element in the tale, that the
runaway wife usually leaves behind not only her husband but also their
children. Her return to her family allays concerns about what will happen to the children, or to the man who cannot care for them without
her, or to a society undermined by runaway wives. The problems surrounding the runaway are also features of complementary stories about
mortal women who enter the swan maiden's domain by eloping with
what is often the consort she left in the otherworld—a demon lover.

# CHAPTER 3

# The Devil's Bride

As their story develops in Sanskrit literature, the matter of why Purūra-vas and Urvaśī separate becomes ambiguous. The *Rig Veda* reveals an underlying and apparently gender-based hostility that splits the pair; the *Brahmana* emphasizes the Gandharvas' plot to reclaim the nymph who dared to prefer a mortal. That triangular relationships may objectify internal strife can be seen in the development of a theme in three seal maiden tales. In the first, the captured wife escapes her mortal husband, after which she plunges into the sea "where a male seal came up by her side—he had all the time been lying out there waiting for her."[1] A Shetland tale forges a stronger link between her discontent on land and the irresistible pull of the sea: the "lady would often steal alone to the desert strand, and, on a signal being given, a large seal would make his appearance, with whom she would hold, in an unknown tongue, an anxious conference." Escape, however, does not fully resolve her dilemma and lingering conflict follows her to the otherworld: "before she dived to unknown depth, she cast a parting glance at the wretched Shetlander, whose despairing looks excited in her breast a few transient feelings of commiseration. 'Farewell,' said she to him: 'I loved you very well when I resided upon earth, but I always loved my first husband much better.' "[2]

The third story dramatizes her conflict in a battle between her husband and the bull seal. Sensitive to his wife's unhappiness, the man would take her to the sea, hoping she would derive solace from her natural element. On one such occasion he fights the seal, and after he staggers home weak with loss of blood, his wife confesses that although she left her seal mate for love of him, she often experiences an impulse to "return to her own kith and kin among the Seal-folk." At such times the bull seal would seek her human spouse in order to kill him.[3] Two important themes have been introduced in this version: that the other-worldly lover appears in response to an unvoiced signal from the troubled wife; but also that when she runs away, she does not so much desert her present family as return to an earlier existence she conceives of as *rightfully hers*.[4]

Ruth Benedict has argued that among the Zuñi it is believed that union with a supernatural being prepares a human for marriage. In Indian mythology, the Gandharvas are traditionally one of the "three immortal husbands of [a] bride before she marries a mortal."[5] But the return of Urvaśī to the Gandharvas and the seal maiden to her seal lover reverses the direction according to which unions with an otherworldly mate yield to the necessity of human marriage. The universal popularity of demon lovers in folklore and myth suggests the dialectical interaction between a fantasized transcendence of the mundane and the descent to reality. But triangular relationships produce guilt, the woman's anxious dread being revealed when the supernatural mate is associated with the hellish. One of his ghastlier forms is the revenant, a specter returned from the dead.

In Cornwall, where there are many legends of drowned sailors who return to visit their lovers, one story depicts the protracted grief of a woman whose fiancé has perished in a storm. Rather than finding another man to wed, she instead cries night and day for her lover's return. "Nothing would pacify her, until one night, when a storm swept the coast, she was aroused from her bed, believing that she could hear her name being called above the screaming of the wind." Beholding the figure of her betrothed standing below, "soaking wet, with seaweed hanging from his boots and hair and his facing shining deathly white," she runs out into the night to follow this specter, "no man of flesh and blood but a ghost returned from the sea." No further word of her is heard in the area.[6] In some of its narrative motifs, this story evokes one of the most widespread of the demon lover narratives, the ballad "James Harris (The Daemon Lover)" (Child 243). The number of versions, both in England and in the United States, where it is one of the most popular of the ballads brought from the British Isles,[7] offers a rare opportunity to discern what Bynum calls the many logical possibilities contained in a narrative pattern constructed from multiple variants.

The ballad appears to have originated first in a printed broadside (Child A), subsequently giving rise to an oral tradition.[8] Two major strains seem to have developed. As Burrison describes it, Child A crossed the border into Scotland where the revenant became a demon lover. In Child B, "The Distressed Ship Carpenter," the seducer is not described in supernatural terms, and all that is reported is that the runaway wife and the mariner were drowned and never again heard of. It was usually version B, appearing more than a century after the broadside, that emigrated with settlers to America. Whether the supernatural elements of A combined with version B before or after the emigration is, according to Burrison, not clear. But in the United States the naturalized explanations for the wife's flight and fate prevailed. The history of the ballad is significant because it supplies another example of how this world and the supernatural realm interact (even if the supernatural elements are expunged, their very absence remains significant by way of contrast with the supernatural versions) in the life of a woman who seeks elsewhere the satisfaction lacking in her domestic life.

The broadside was published as "A Warning for Married Women." One Mrs. Jane Reynolds behaves in an exemplary fashion while her sailor fiancé is at sea and for many years after he is reported dead, but finally marries a carpenter. When her seaman reappears as a "spirit in the night," but speaking "like to a man," she follows him, to disappear as did the bereaved Cornwall woman:

> And so together away they went
>    From off the English shore,
> And since that time the woman-kind
>    Was never seen no more.

Her distraught husband commits suicide, and the ballad concludes by voicing concern for the fatherless (not motherless) children, suggesting a pervasive masculine point of view whether or not the broadside singer was a man. Jane Reynolds is a cautionary example of the havoc wreaked when women abandon their responsibilities in order to pursue their own pleasures. Still, the ballad allows its singers the possibility of following the thread of her fantasy in perceiving of her *marriage* rather than her flight as *an act of infidelity*—if not to her former lover then to a self-realization that domestic life denies her. The British Isles variants of "The Demon Lover" will from here on be referred to as the Child versions; there are eight of them. In the United States can be found hundreds of published versions, usually entitled "The House Carpenter."[9] Much has been made by commentators of the so-called rationalization of most American versions, in which a promiscuous seaman rather than a revenant lures the housewife away.[10] Similarly, the ship on which the pair elopes sinks, a completely plausible event, even if implying some kind of divine retribution. In Child E, which introduces some of the most famous lines in the ballad, the so-called hills of heaven and hell stanzas, the woman's damnation is made explicit. After she elopes, the runaway wife asks her lover to identify bright, shining hills in the distance. He replies that they are the hills of heaven, where she "shall never be." And when she asks him about a black hill that looks "so dark" to her, he taunts her with, " 'O it is the hill of hell' " where " 'you and I shall be,' " thereupon sinking the ship in a flash of fire. The exchange reflects both religious and popular beliefs concerning the devil, but the woman's inquiry also suggests that subjective and objective reality war with each other, both being reflected in the runaway's uncertain perceptions of the landscape.

Whether the wife elopes with a sailor or the devil, the love triangle still places her between two modes of existence. Sailors, after all, represent that which is remote from the day-to-day life: they travel, journeying to exotic places, and are for long periods free of domestic ties. A restless wife could project onto the sailor's life her own longings. Both natural and supernatural versions of Child 243, then, warn that wives are at peril if they act on their discontent. But the ballad may owe its power less to its threat of death or the runaway wife's damnation than to its realistic depiction of her conflict and torment.

The ballad usually begins when the seaman appears, sometimes claiming to have sacrificed an advantageous marriage in order to return to his former love. The housewife at first proclaims her attachment to her good husband, but is unable to resist asking what her lover might offer to tempt her away. When he describes the ship luxuriously appointed to receive her, she kisses her children goodbye, instructs them to look after their father, dresses in her most splendid attire, and departs. Soon, however, she regrets what she has left behind, but her remorse comes too late and the boat sinks. What happens to her abandoned spouse and children provides the conclusion to the Child broadside but is only occasionally the concern of later balladeers. When codas do exist, they add a significant layer of meaning to an already complex story.

The demon lover often appears when the wife is particularly vulnerablc to his appeal. The broadside relates that the carpenter is on a three-day journey from home, and that a "spirit in the night / Came to the window of his wife." The link between her husband's absence and the sudden appearance of the demon is more than a plot detail. For the broadside emphasizes the woman's good character; she has never been known the "wanton for to play." If, after she is married, mundane reality causes her to idealize her dead fiancé, it would seem that her fantasies have been ordinarily repressed. But without the presence of her husband, she is likely to give in to subversive impulses. Thus this warning to married women may be extended to husbands and perhaps entire societies, which seem to be enjoined to control their women.

That the demon lover subverts the wife's good intentions is suggested in two versions from Virginia. In one, she admits to pent-up yearnings:

> "Come in, come in, my own true love,
>     Come in, come in," said she,
> "I haven't spoken a word to my own true love
>     In five or seven years.
> I haven't spoken a word to my own true love,
>     In five or seven years."

In the other, "come in" is not so emphatically repeated, and the time of separation is shortened, but the effect is heightened urgency: " 'For it's been over three quarters of a year, / Since I spoke one word to thee.' "[11]

Other wives are less receptive and must be cajoled, the ballads depicting stereotypes of female weaknesses. In a version from New Hampshire, the lover exploits a seemingly peculiar female sentimentality, comparing himself to a bird mourning for the absence of its true mate.[12] And from Virginia comes a variant that depicts woman's supposed propensity to lust:

> "When I was a-lying across my bed,
>     And his hand across my breast,
> He made me believe by the faults of his tongue,
>     That the sun rose in the west."[13]

Here, physiological detail combines with metonymy to create an erotically ambiguous image of the demon's lovemaking. Ordinarily, however, the seduction *is* more verbal than physical, pitched to latent discontent rather than sexual desire.

Whatever the sources of temptation, the housewife ordinarily remains concerned with practical matters: in Child B she asks what her lover could "maintain" her on if she leaves with him, and similar questions are posed in C, E, and F. Typically, he offers splendid ships and mariners to protect and amuse her. Although some narrators believe she is taken in by promises of prosperity, in one variant, as Tristram Coffin has noted, she tells her seducer she has no need of his wealth. This may be the variant in which she proudly proclaims, "Rest assured, I'm not so poor, / As to have to marry for clothes."[14] Her reasons for eloping are not simple and what it is that she *does* want has to be perceived across the ballad's wide tradition.

For economic deprivation is insufficient to explain the runaway's motives or the wide appeal of "The Demon Lover." Nonetheless, promises of luxury do play an important part in the ballad, for such enticements have symbolic as well as literal meanings. Both British and American variants employ imagery that links the woman to the ship that carries her away, an association possibly influenced in part by the convention that assigns to boats a feminine gender. Sometimes the vessel and sometimes the wife is splendidly decked out. In Child F, the ship's finery, sails "o the taffetie" and "masts of the beaten gold," promise the fulfillment of the wife's dreams. But they do not connect her inner and outer states as fully as do American versions that create out of *her* fine adornments not only a metaphor for what she seeks but also a moral judgment.

Perhaps these American variants are influenced by Child E, in which the ship's luxury is paralleled by the portrait of the woman succumbing to the demon's spells.

> As they were walking up the street,
>   Most beautiful for to behold,
> He cast a glamour oer her face,
>   And it shone like the brightest gold.

To cast a glamour is deceptively to allure, and the wife's very appearance speaks to the fantasy that grips her.

In other versions, how she looks reveals her disregard for the society that will judge her: dressed in her very best, she "glistened and glittered" as "proudly she walked" to the banks of the sea.[15] In one variant, she "dressed up all so gay, / Just to leave her house carpenter,"[16] while yet another ballad makes clear that her ostentatious "richery" reveals how improper a wife she is: as she "shined and she glittered," she boldly walked the "streets of Purity." While "richery" has been explained as a contraction of "rich array,"[17] this does not contradict the singer's possible intention to contrast purity with greed and corruption.

Colors often denote the wife's fall from decency. One housewife dons a "scarlet robe" to walk "the downward road."[18] But other narrators soften this judgment: from Arkansas comes a ballad in which the color green is associated with the wife's dressing herself "all neat and clean."[19] In another version, however, color is used to signify the runaway's and perhaps the balladeer's ambivalence.

> She dressed herself in scarlet red,
>     Her waist with maiden green.

The contradictory colors are joined in a version from Missouri:

> She whirled herself all in her room,
>     And she dressed herself in scarlet-green.
> She shone as bright as a morning star
>     As she walked the streets alone.[20]

Coffin has noted that as a ballad's narrative tradition develops, plot details are diminished in importance, yielding to lyric intensity.[21] As the woman dresses in colors that contrast purity with hedonistic impulses, her very isolation emphasizes how, in her conflict, she has placed herself outside the boundaries of her society. Alone, she is rendered thus both deviant and pitiful. Even the vessel that carries her away has become less a symbolic wonderland than a vehicle that conveys her towards freedom; but what it is she longs to be free of must be discerned in other versions of the ballad.

Some clues to what the runaway wife seeks can be found in the destination to which she believes herself bound. The hills of heaven and hell stanzas depict her error in confusing an earthly with a heavenly paradise. But the eloping lovers' destination varies from ballad to ballad. Often local geography or the requirements of rhyme will convey a promise that the wife will be taken to, for example, the banks of Tennessee or Maree.[22] Maree, evoking a more generalized word for the sea,[23] begins to substitute symbolism for geography. When in another version the demon lover promises that they will go to " 'where the grass grows green, / On the banks of Italy,' "[24] the ballad moves closer to the real point of the wife's departure from her husband and babies. Italy implies a journey to a more remote and exotic land than localized rivers could suggest, heightening the contrast between what is imagined and what is left behind. A perceptive narrator from Maine bypasses geography altogether and gets to the heart of the matter, describing no particular place but rather the "isle of sweet liberty,"[25] and another singer tells how the wife is promised she will reach the "banks of sweet relief."

What she seeks relief from may be suggested by another version in the same collection in which the wife asks not how her lover will keep her from poverty, but rather how he will protect her "from hard slavery,"[26] a word that denotes enforced labor but at the same time connotes a personal identity swallowed up by a role not necessarily of her choosing, the woman's drudgery being matched perhaps only by monotony. For in Child F the wife is promised not only luxury but diversion by "four-and-twenty bold mariners, / And music on every hand." A narrator from the Southwest similarly depicts a respite from tedium and seems willing to sacrifice the ballad's logic to make the point. For the wife asks not what her lover will "maintain" her on, but what he will "entertain" her on, to keep her from slavery.[27] Perhaps the singer's memory was faulty; the linking of "entertain" and "slavery" is nonetheless not so illogical.

Her desire to escape home conflicts, however, with the security the wife is often reluctant to give up, and she may seek assurances from her demon lover that she will be safe with him. He understands her very well and in Child B, as well as in a version from Maine, the demon promises that his mariners will not only row her along in the ship but "keep [her] from overthrow"[28]—a pledge that implies not only physical but also spiritual safety. In Child E the demon manipulatively conveys the false assurance that the need for both luxury and security will be met:

> "I'll build my love a bridge of steel,
>    All for to help her oer;
> Likewise webs of silk down by her side,
>    To keep my love from the cold."

And in a ploy to keep her quiet when she repents her flight with him, the seducer in an American ballad offers the ultimate deception, that her elopement is revocable, and that she will soon enjoy the comfort of her "own happy home, / On the banks of old Tennessee."[29] As a point of destination Tennessee may not be compelling; as a place to return to, it may be very much so.

For the runaway wife's essential attachment to the mundane is reflected in the broadside and in subsequent versions by her concern for her family, almost always her children: in the broadside (Child A) she asks, "If I should leave my children small, / Alas! what would they do?" She also expresses guilt over her husband's disgrace. A "carpenter of great fame," he would experience a loss of status (she does not infer any emotional loss, any tie to herself). Although the wife cries "for the man [she] left behind" in Child E, and in other variants asks her children to look after their father, it is rare that she regrets the loss of her spouse. When asked by her seducer if she weeps for her husband, she corrects him and expresses remorse over her deserted baby.[30] Atypical, then, is a ballad from North Carolina in which the lover asks if she weeps for her children and learns that she misses her house carpenter.[31] Perhaps an error in memory has caused this reversal, but it is more likely that different balladeers have varying conceptions of what first drives the woman to flight and then to repentance.

Sometimes, the remorseful runaways of "The Demon Lover" ballads drown themselves or otherwise express despair. Their dismay is comparable to the expressed ruefulness of women who in recent years perceive that in a man's world, their husbands fare better than they do when they leave their homes.[32] From North Carolina comes a ballad that could speak to their predicament:

"Well, my house carpenter is still at home,
    And living very well,
While my poor body is drowning in the sea,
    And my soul is bound for hell."[33]

The husband's importance is heightened when the ballad singer's attention turns to what happens to him after his wife departs. For ironically enough, despite the ballad's various titles, "James Harris or the Demon Lover" and "The House Carpenter," neither the husband nor his devilish rival is the ballad's focus of attention.

If the argument holds true that when the ballad came to America, both old world signifiers—"Demon Lover" and "James Harris"—were inappropriate, since the latter is not mentioned in the ballads and the former is based on supernatural motifs,[34] so might it be contended that

"The House Carpenter" is also a misleading title, since the husband is more often talked *about* than active in the narrative. Moreover, all of these titles obscure the ballad's real interest, the conflicted wife whose neglect in the ballads' titles parallels her lack of personal identity in the domestic realm. In the broadside, the four concluding stanzas emphasize her diminished importance, being given over instead to her husband's suicide and the plight of the children left, significantly, *without a father*. But usually the husband and father survives, to curse (as in Child B) all seafaring men: "They ruined me, a ship-carpenter, / By deluding away my wife." The husband thus remains oblivious to his wife's discontent and, in a piece of psychological realism, evades any responsibility for the catastrophe. It may be asking more than even a vast ballad tradition could yield that the husband evidence any self-awareness of shortcomings that would cause his wife's flight, but his lack of insight heightens his wife's predicament.

Two variants from West Virginia provide sharp contrasts about the husband's life after his wife's elopement. In one, she is drowned, her baby is dead, and its "father roams all over the world," unable to foresee any "pleasure" in his existence. In the other, however, he and his children easily get on with their lives:

> O now her child is growing up,
>     Her husband doing well,
> While this fair lady lies in the bottom of the sea,
>     And her soul is doomed to hell.[35]

The husband's role becomes truly problematic, however, when the question arises of just *what that role is*. For although the ballads remain fairly stable from version to version, borrowings from other ballads have been noted, and one of these suggests that some ballad singers were interested in developing themes surrounding the father left alone to care for his children. In order to do so while remaining within a ballad tradition, they drew on other songs for additional material.[36]

In one version, the runaway wife pauses at home to wonder about her child's well-being.

> "But who will shoe your pretty little feet,
>     And who will glove your hand,
> And who will kiss your sweet little lips,
>     When I'm in a foreign land?"[37]

Her question proves no less than an inquiry into the relative importance of mothers and fathers in their children's lives, into the extent to which women are necessary to their children's welfare.

In four versions that contain the borrowed stanzas, there is a crucial difference in response to this inquiry, and, significantly it is a difference related to just who is answering the wife's query. In two instances her child replies to the question, and the mother alone is conceived of as supplying its emotional needs. The father is credited only with the economic welfare of his family, shoeing his baby's feet and gloving its hand. In one instance, the child tells its mother that "no one shall kiss my sweet little lips, / When you're in a foreign land,"[38] and in the other version her baby looks forward to her kisses when she returns, perhaps indicating some disbelief that she plans to be gone forever.[39] Each time, the child makes a blatant appeal to its mother's love as well as to her conscience, but these are the very ties to her old existence that she seeks to break.

When, in the other two versions, the demon lover picks up the question, he assures the mother that her husband can supply all the child's needs, that he "will kiss its rosy little lips"[40] when the woman is gone. The father, that is, can adequately supply both economic and emotional sustenance:

> Papa will kiss its little cheek,
> And also shoe its feet,
> And also sleep in its lily-white arms
> While we're sailing for dry land.[41]

The seducer's assurance that her family as well as she will be safe is part of his deception, or so the ballad's audience could probably be counted on to understand. But a listener would need to pay close attention to perceive that it is the lover, *not the narrator,* who responds to the critical question. Like the wife, the ballad's audience must confront this challenge to the traditional belief that only a mother could adequately raise a child.

Whose voice is heard in the "The Demon Lover" ballad significantly affects its themes. Again, the husband's imprecations concerning the bad morals of sailors reflects his lack of self-awareness, as well as his inability to comprehend his wife. In a profound sense, he does not know who she is. Frequently, however, the wife herself speaks the final curse, either as she and the boat sink or as a voice from the dead. In such versions, it is possible to distinguish between wives who are as deficient in insight as their husbands, and those who recognize that their fate reflects their choices. One wife damns "all sea men" who have robbed her of her family and taken away her life,[42] whereas another identifies a curse on all women who "would their baby leave / And sail the raging sea."[43] The turbulent ocean provides an apt metaphor for the woman's plight: as suggested earlier, the ballad's power lies less in the outcome of its plot than in its depiction of the wife's conflict, the two men who lend the ballad tradition its names being symbolic projections of the worlds she must choose between. In delivering the ballad's final lines, some narrators perceive this essential dilemma, others are more obtuse. A singer from Maine cautions mothers against selling their babies "for gold,"[44] and one from Virginia warns young girls not to leave their house carpenters to "go with a man on sea,"[45] portraying the popular stereotype of the sailor with women in every port. A survey of the ballad's endings suggests that where the conclusion picks up complexity, it is because the narrator grants wife and/or husband some self-awareness.

Commentary on "The Demon Lover" ranges from the rather naive view that it depicts "man's errant way with women,"[46] or that it portrays a "foolish, faithless wife,"[47] to Lomax's complex analysis of the ballad. He contends that the folk songs most popular in the backwoods were "a selection from that lore of vehicles for fantasies, wishes, and norms of behaviour" that corresponded "to the emotional needs of pioneer women in America." For, says Lomax, "no fantasy could have been better calculated to reinforce the Calvinist sexual morality of our ancestors" than this story of the demon lover who leads a wife to temptation, transgression, and punishment for sin. He contends (without documentation, however) that "The Demon Lover" is among those ballads that were "women's songs, attached to the household and the fireside."[48] Significantly, a collector of Texas folklore has described how he recognized Scott's version of "The Daemon Lover" because as a child he had heard his mother sing it so often,[49] and it is fascinating to speculate about the psychological impact on young men of such an early exposure to "The Demon Lover" ballad—sung not only by the first woman in their lives but also the symbol of secure hearth and home.

In both "The Demon Lover" ballads and swan maiden tales, a woman marries reluctantly. The swan maiden is constrained by the loss of her feathers, by the symbolic absence of choice in her life; the wife of the ballads marries after the death of a lover who in her dreams comes to represent a paradisal alternative to her actual existence. In both instances the woman runs away when the opportunity presents itself, and in both both the ballad and some versions of the swan maiden tale, a former lover speaks not to the woman's infidelity but instead to her *fidelity*. That the swan maiden is returning "home" rather than running away from it suggests an even higher level of fantasy than exists in "The Demon Lover"; in any event, children as well as husband are left behind. The swan maiden usually (but not always) lacks remorse for her abandoned children. In contrast, guilt supplies an important phase in "The Demon Lover," where the discontented wife has internalized and thus cannot easily discard her society's values. But the stories are alike in that both provide examples of Ethel Person's "imaginative split-object triangle";[50] a longed-for existence is realized in a realm outside woman's usual domestic space, a lover rather than sanctioned spouse promising relief from the mundane. And in both stories psychological reality wars with fantasy. Some earlier hopes and dreams have been thwarted or at least not realized within the marriage, and the runaway is attempting to find what has been taken from her. Like all humans she can imagine life better than it actually is, only one more step being needed to imagine that that is how it *once was*.

Admittedly, there are corresponding stories that tell how a fairy summons a mortal man to the otherworld and similarly offers him freedom from responsibilities to the world. (I have written before on this subject.[51]) But such stories not only resemble but also differ sharply from tales that tell of women who leave their homes for the promised pleasures of an otherworld. Both men and women dream of bowers of bliss in which they may evade the human condition, but women flee not only the plight of generalized humanity but also a specific gender-based predicament as the second sex in a world dominated by men. Still, like men, women are firmly rooted in their societies, and it is more than guilt that causes the runaway to regret her elopement. Frequently the wife in "The Demon Lover" desires not so much to evade reality as to transform the one she knows. Her demon lover is then not so much a separate character as a symbolic personification of her fantasy concerning what her husband *might be*.

In Child A, the wife goes with the demon because there is something essentially comforting and familiar about him:

When he had told her [his] fair tales,
   To love him she began,
Because he was in human shape,
   Much like unto a man.

It is indeed the revenant's origin in and connection to the mundane that provides the seeming reassurance that what is safe in her life will be retained after she runs away. In the New Hampshire variant, the wife in a similar spirit not only admits to missing both husband and children but also rejects the demon: "I am tired of thee!" There is a wide body of folklore and myth into which these ballad versions fit, stories of women (they will be met again in later chapters) who prefer mortal husbands to otherworldly suitors. Their demon lovers sometimes masquerade as their real-life suitors or spouses in order to seduce them. In the Western tradition, Zeus's seduction of Alcmena is perhaps the most renowned version of this story pattern.

Once again, the titles of the ballad can supply a clue to its meaning. If "demon lover" evokes images of forbidden desires and exotic realms, the enticer's name, James Harris, is inconsistent with his promise. For it would be difficult to find a name more comfortably familiar than James Harris, and if the anonymous house carpenter, who stands for the stolid comfort of a secure place in society, were given a name in the ballad, it might very well be that of his devilish rival.

The paradoxical juxtaposition of "James Harris" and "demon lover" informs Shirley Jackson's fictional adaptations of Child 243. The seducers in those stories she based on "The Demon Lover" ballad are the seemingly ordinary Jim or Jimmy or Mr. Harris, shadowy figures who touch the lives of Jackson's female protagonists, both married women trapped and helpless in wedlock, and single women yearning to be brides in a world of couples. James Harris tempts them with the realization of their hopes and then cruelly abandons them to their desperation.

In "Elizabeth," a young woman comes to the city to find herself eleven years later with faded looks and prospects, her hopes sustained only by fantasies of one "Jim Harris," a "gallant dark man with knowing eyes who watched her across a room," a stranger but nonetheless someone who loved her, "a quiet troubled man who needed sunlight, a warm garden, green lawns." Like Elizabeth, the female protagonist of Jackson's story "The Demon Lover" is a woman in her thirties with a monotonous job and a bleak life. She is jilted by James Harris on their wedding day and begins the frantic search for him throughout the city that is a commentary on her life, not her love. With sardonic irony, Jackson seems to be warning young wives to be content with their house carpenters if they are lucky enough to get them.[52]

However, her wives fare no better, terrified as they are and desperate to escape what they perceive as a domestic prison. Their very panic probably reflects the rage of women in what can now be recognized as a preliberation era in the United States.[53] In one story, a wife loathes her husband, and when he forgets to read a letter from someone named Jimmy, who never appears in the tale, she gives vent to an unexplained fury and imagines bashing in her spouse's head and leaving him under the cellar steps: "and it's worth it, she thought, oh it's worth it."[54] In "A Day in the Jungle," a wife leaves her husband while he is at work, thinking back to the humiliation of her wedding and the ensuing "hideous" intimacy. Checking into a hotel, she is drawn to a quite ordinary man around whom she spins fantasies that echo the "Demon Lover" ballad; he becomes "some vaguely glimpsed stranger" asking her "to dine, to dance, to go off to Italy." But like the runaway wife of the ballad, she has second thoughts and experiences "a convulsive, brain-splitting terror," which drives her back in relief to the man she had married.[55] In "The Tooth," a housewife's life appears symbolized by her excruciating toothache, and after the anesthesia is administered so that the tooth can be extracted, reality is no longer separable from fantasy. Jim Harris is a stranger she meets on a train, and she does not find it strange that he offers her another destination than her home, one " 'farther than Samarkand,' " with " 'the waves ringing on the shore like bells,' " with flutes playing all night and stars " 'as big as the moon and the moon . . . as big as a lake.' " Like the carpenter's wife, she gives up her domestic life as she had already given up the aching tooth and follows Harris to an unspecified future.[56]

The story that most exploits the seeming ordinariness of James Harris is Jackson's "The Beautiful Stranger," in which the revenant motif from the "Demon Lover" ballad finds its deepest thematic significance. The narration begins with a quite ordinary scene of a young woman and her children waiting at a train station for the man of the house, who, the story later suggests, may be dead (a revenant), a reality she may be vehemently denying by meeting the train. But what she feels when he arrives is less relief than resentment over a now lost independence: "when Margaret got in beside him she felt a little chill of animosity at the sight of his hands on the wheel; I can't bear to relinquish even this much, she thought; for a week no one has driven the car except me." But soon her resentment gives way to wonder, for she decides that this man is not her husband but rather a stranger who is impersonating him, restoring to her existence the passion that had given way to the tedium of ordinary life.

Once Margaret has transformed her husband into a demon lover, she becomes content with the routines of her life. "She laughed while she did her housework and dressed the baby. She took satisfaction in un-packing his suitcase, which he had abandoned and forgotten in a corner of the bedroom, as though prepared to take it up and leave again if she had not been as he thought her, had not wanted him to stay." But as her fantasy takes a deeper hold on Margaret, she cannot maintain her al-ready fragile equilibrium, and the familiar has become so strange that after leaving her house one day, she cannot find her own home among the many in her suburban neighborhood. "The evening was very dark, and she could see only the houses going in rows, with more rows beyond them and more rows beyond that, and somewhere a house which was hers, with the beautiful stranger inside, and she lost out here."[57] Like the wife in the "Demon Lover" ballad who cries to return to land and to home, Margaret's imagined existence has become the source of her exile, and she is trapped by her own unreality. The woman in the ballad who follows her demon lover because he is so very like a man—that is, a husband—and Margaret, who can only bear her husband if she pretends he is a demon lover, reflect the same impulse. Reality and fantasy are irrevocably split, and what each woman longs for is a reconciliation of conflicts raging within. Jackson's drawing on "The Demon Lover" as a source for her fiction lays bare the complex meanings already in the ballad, which speaks to more than a wife's economic deprivation or the narrow conventions of a Calvinist ethic: the runaway wife longs to be free of cultural reality itself, and it sometimes hardly seems to matter what the specific details of that reality are.

The themes in the "Demon Lover" ballad recur in folktales found throughout the world. Women are haunted by their imagination's ability to create a better existence than the one they actually have. In an African tale, the children of the Thunder Spirit and his mortal bride are taught "how to travel through the air on flashes of lightning, and they had a much more exciting life than the children of the earth, who could only walk and run."[58] In contrast, both wife and children in a Norwegian folktale suffer after she rejects a demon suitor to marry a cotter: the couple "had lots of children, so it was hard for them to make ends meet." One night, when she is working in the fields, she is taunted by the demon: "You could have chosen me, you could! Then you wouldn't have had to toil and struggle the way you're doing now!"[59]

But swan maidens who need do no more than embroider their children's clothing are as anxious to escape their earthly homes as captured brides turned into household drudges. What women want from their demon lovers is universal and timeless, as the novelist Gail Godwin recognized when she drew on folklore to portray a woman artist, *Violet Clay*, whose very name evokes the tension between ethereal beauty and the mundane. Violet is engaged in an affair with a fellow artist—by her description, a parodic "demon lover who went flapping through the daylight world disguised in his funny-fitting clothes." When Violet refuses her lover's "practical offer of a 'real life,' "[60] she becomes in effect a Psyche who refuses to turn on the light to look directly at her situation. For marriage in the daylight world seems to have little to offer women.

There have always been women who refuse such a life, writes Germaine Greer, who describes "the most notorious" of the devil's brides, the witches, who "withdrew from 'normal' human intercourse to commune with their pets or familiars," making their own living by exploiting their knowledge of "herbal medicine and the credulity of the peasantry."[61] Greer's witch (who may be as much Greer's conception as a figure from history) is not a victim of a vengeful society intent on eradicating the devil, but rather the self-chosen exile, the adventurer, actively choosing Satan rather than passively being chosen by him for perhaps no less reason than Faust entered into his infamous pact. But there are scholars who reject such a romanticized portrait of the witch because it suggests that female identity could be chosen and thus denies the misery visited on many vulnerable women who hardly understood what was happening as they were tried and punished for sorcery: "For whatever witches might have been, one things is certain; they always lost."[62] And they lost because a strong antifeminist tradition usually demanded that women live under male control and because few women who chose to defy this cultural imperative had the power to protect themselves from retribution.

The discussion of the devil's bride here and of the incubus visitation in chapter 5 will invoke the complex world of debate surrounding the European witchcraft craze that began in the Middle Ages and reached its height in the sixteenth and seventeenth centuries. For feminist critics, recent historical accounts have been welcome, for they expose the plight of women likely to be tried as witches, and focus on often rabidly misogynistic witch hunters prone to exploit age-old traditions of feminine evil, making use of the fantasies of disturbed or just unhappy women to prove that they worshiped the devil at unholy sabbaths. Women (just how many is not clear, but some historians argue for female genocide) were subject to psychological force or were the agonized victims of torture, their confessions constituting attempts to pacify their persecutors. But strong qualifications to this approach have exposed the absence of attention paid to the accused. Because they focus on the misogyny and paranoia of the inquisitors, argues Carlo Ginzburg, contemporary historians ironically duplicate (if inversely) the tendencies of the witches' accusers: the inquisitors turned fantasies and popular beliefs into real events; most historians not only dismiss the witches' confessions as lies or fantasies, but as a result also ignore what the witches actually believed about themselves (or, Hans Peter Duerr would add, what they actually practiced).

Ginzburg notes that it is now generally accepted that folklore and learned beliefs combined to create the demonologists' conception of the diabolical sabbath. But, he argues, the rich symbolism of the witches' admissions cannot be accounted for solely by the pressures exerted on the accused, who acknowledged practices deemed heretical; these confessions, "made by male and female witches [remain] shrouded in darkness." It is Ginzburg's exploration of elements of shamanistic origin that unites his work with Duerr, the latter arguing that some persons could through drugs (the witches' salve) experience the passage beyond the boundary between civilization and wilderness. Both of them analyze what Ginzburg calls the "deep resemblance that binds the myths that later merged in the witches' Sabbath. All of them work a common theme; going into the beyond, returning from the beyond." For Duerr the trip is essential to human adaptation to culture, and he conceptualizes a complex therapy (akin to deep psychoanalysis) undergone by those who understood that members of society who "wanted to live *consciously* within the fence [that delimited culture] had to leave the enclosure at least once in their lives":

> In contrast to our own culture, the societies possessing what we called "archaic" cultures have a much clearer idea about the fact that we can *be* only what we are if at the same time, we are also what we are *not,* and that we can only know who we are if we experience our boundaries and, as Hegel would put it, if we thus cross over them.

For Ginzburg there is an essential story embedded in the myths that describe such a passage: it is "not one narrative, but the matrix of all possible narratives."[63]

Folktales, to repeat Darnton's emphatic assertion, are historical documents. As such they can supply a bridge between analyses such as Ginzburg's and Duerr's and feminist-oriented studies of witchcraft. Shapeshifting animal brides and grooms, fairy emissaries from another world, and demon lovers are about nothing if not about the boundary between culture and that which lies outside it. The image of the wild man and the wild woman is embedded in fairy lore and demonology, and appears in other folklore characters that pervade the world's narratives.[64] Like Shirley Jackson's short stories, folktales about the devil's paramour are, moreover, about woman's role, about her dissatisfaction with domesticity, or, conversely, about her desperate attempt to find a place within the narrow sphere allowed her in society. Folktales, in short, portray just what kind of woman is likely to become the devil's bride.

A commonplace assumption is that woman is more "natural" than man. And so long as the "natural" in human beings is denigrated, so will woman be seen as more irrational than man, more ready to succumb to basic drives. As Nicholas Remy wrote in his notoriously antifeminist *Demonolotry,* it was "much easier for the Demon to impose his deceits upon" women.[65] It has even been argued that the connection between woman's natural baseness and witchcraft extended to woman's failure in etiquette at a time when refinement was increasingly valued as a triumph of culture.[66] If women are, as Bruce Kapferer argues, the "linch pins of culture," occupying a central position in the "nature/culture dialectic and in the cultural order,"[67] it is paradoxical but not surprising that as culture begins to prevail over nature, there is more, not less, stress on keeping woman in her place.

And her place was in the domestic sphere where she lived as someone's daughter, wife, mother. Some historians thus contend that witchcraft was likely to flourish wherever marriage patterns left a large number of women unmarried, the argument being that "witchcraft accusations can best be understood as projections of patriarchal social fears onto atypical women, those who lived apart from the direct male control of husbands or fathers. These defenseless and very isolated women became the group most often exposed to charges of witchcraft."[68] John Lindow has said of the importance of marriage in Swedish folktales that because "marriage implied economic respectability and a measure of independence, it was regarded positively, and bachelordom or spinsterhood were regarded negatively," and the "strongest symptom of this point of view concerns witchcraft, which tended to be laid at the door of unmarried or widowed older women."[69] This view is essentially echoed in Kinsley's description of goddesses' place in Hindu mythology. Marriage not only completes a woman but tames her, "channeling her dangerous sexual energy in acceptable ways." Human men as well as gods constitute a "civilizing, calming, ordering presence," whereas alone, not only women but also goddesses are "perceived as powerful and dangerous."[70] Folklore can help address the historians' query about why it was that so many women paid with their lives for what can be described as a transformation of popular belief into demonology (see chapter 5).

Swan maidens are often likened to witches, as in the Polish gypsy tale in which the swan maiden is a sorceress's daughter.[71] And the Passamaquoddy tell a story in which to be a swan maiden *is* to be a witch.[72] Similarly, women who consort with demon lovers are likened to witches, whose sabbaths are made to resemble the otherworldly revels at which folklore husbands discover their kidnapped or runaway wives. Monter argues a less psychologically complex variation on Duerr's thesis, speculating that some accused witches used drugs, and hence acquired from a "fund of arcane knowledge of herbs and special formulae which could be used to cure as well as to harm" the means to achieve "in a drugged sleep, some excitement into their monotonous and wretched lives."[73] Effectively, if the nightly visit of a woman to her demon lover's revels were not just a dream, drugs were deliberately used to convey her to the swan maiden's realm of magic delights.

However it happened, folklore and demonology merged, and the fairies of popular belief were identified as agents of evil. Katharine Briggs tells how in many of the witch trials of northern England, Scotland, and the Isle of Man, "fairies and witches were believed to work together," how in the seventeenth century "the fairy ladies of Holinshed turned into witches," but also how when "the witch fever abated," the "fairies went back to their old places in the popular regard."[74] Jules Michelet similarly marks the end of the belief in witches: "The Sorceress has perished for ever, but not so the fairy. She will appear afresh under this form, which is immortal." She would have to, according to Michelet, for when the bourgeois housewife finds her life unrewarding or harsh, it will be of the fairies' life that she dreams.[75] Such a sanguine view does not prevail everywhere. Wentworth Webster contemplates why "witches and fairies are so often confounded," why in Basque legends the witch is often a fairy, and the fairy a witch. He concludes that the reason for such confusion "is not that the belief in witchcraft is extinct among the Basques, but because it is so rife."[76]

Not only are witches and fairies confused in folklore, but so also are two kinds of witches, those who practice magic for diabolical reasons, and those who practice magic as a healing art that nonetheless makes them suspect,[77] perhaps because such white witches, as they are sometimes called, were also self-sufficient and therefore as threatening to a male-dominated order as their more malevolent sisters. Moreover, it has been argued that magic spells were often used as a means of revenge by those incapable of using ordinary forms (physical violence or litigation), and thus any group that had reason to feel vengeful would fall under suspicion.[78] Among such groups would be those who lived only on the fringes of society, frequently older women beyond childbearing who posed potential economic burdens or women who placed themselves outside society by not marrying, or by defying the authority under which they should have placed themselves.[79] Folklore depicts all of these female types as consorting with or forming erotic liaisons with the devil.

Folklore motifs concerning the devil's paramour correspond to almost all the theories of witches advanced by contemporary historical, sociological, and psychological investigation. The popular narratives appear to vary widely in their purposes, although in most instances gender relations form significant themes. Sometimes antifeminism is presented humorously (if with questionable benignity) in stories that play a variation on the song about the devil who stole a man's shrewish wife, only to return her in dismay, complaining that although he had been a devil all of his life, he had never known hell until he met the man's wife. Straparola tells such a tale of how the devil tries marriage to test accusations against women, finding them true: "rather than set eyes on [my wife] again," cries the demon, "I prefer to depart for the nethermost hell."[80] But most stories about marriages to demons are anything but funny.

Some are clearly intended as cautionary exempla for young women. In a Mexican tale, a young woman defies her mother to attend a dance, and on her way meets a demonic character whose ominous warnings prove accurate when two young men at the festivities quarrel and accidentally kill the disobedient daughter.[81] This didactic story narrated by a fifty-year-old woman conceivably harkening back to her own rebellious youth has thematic ties to widespread legends of a demon dancer,[82] or the tale type of the "Danced-out Shoes," a famous literary version being Hans Christian Andersen's "The Red Shoes."[83] In Norwegian lore, the young women often die of their folly, and a French version tells how some frivolous girls actually invite the devil to a party, their compulsive dancing being described in horrific detail:

And still they must dance, and dance, higher and faster, though they were foaming like spent horses. Someone held them by their hands, their waist, their neck, drove them, flung them hither and thither—someone who was either laughing or grinding his teeth, and both were terrible. They spun about, their hair clung to their wet cheeks, their eyes stood out of their heads, faster and still faster, turning like a wheel.

They are given a second chance when the demon's power is temporarily exorcised by a priest, but one of the young women has not learned her lesson and her fate is a a macabre one. Seizing her by the wrist, the demon drags her to "deep roaring waters," and on a flat rock in the middle of a stream, he strangles her. "The water runs rusty by there, as though it were stained with blood. You can still see the marks, graven upon the stone—those of her head, her body, her heels. On each side of her there are the marks left by the demon, and they are those of hooves, those of a beast."[84]

Sometimes spiritual or medical healing proves successful. But the question of why women are more often than men the subject of exorcism rites[85] is closely allied to the one concerning why it is that more women than men were executed for witchcraft. Even the relatively enlightened societies that attempted to rescue their deviant members would appear to have assumed from the outset that women were more prone than men to fall under the devil's influence. There are, however, folktales in which women resist the demon lover with their own remarkable strength, needing no assistance from men. An example is the Magyar story of "The Lover's Ghost," in which a revenant who seeks to drag his fiancée to the grave fails in his attempt (the "Lenore" type story).[86] But attention to such self-sufficient heroines will be postponed to the last chapter of this book.

Folktales not only treat what happens to a woman who consorts with the devil but also reveal *why* a woman may become the devil's bride. A distinction can be drawn between women who cannot win ordinary, earthly husbands, and those who choose not to marry. The latter prefer a life outside the sanctioned domesticity that offers them the security of occupying a designated and sometimes protected place among their people but that exacts a price for such security: terrible drudgery and the psychological pain of being the "other," essentially alien in their own world. The argument may appear misconceived that invokes modern conceptions of selfhood to explain the stories of peoples whose societies taught them to prize values such as loyalty over the quest for personal fulfillment. But most cultures have recognized individual differences among their people and have made more accommodations to them than might be thought. This recognition is consistent with the theories of folklore narration advanced by Benedict, Bascom, and Fischer, for example. It is possible to add another point to the argument that stories supply outlets for discontent not otherwise capable of being vented. The human imagination is capable of conceiving life very different from what it actually is, and to dream of a paradisal existence is also to quest for a personal happiness not sanctioned as a valid goal until the quite recent past. But folktales reveal that the dream of self-fulfillment remains a persistent component of human desire. Both women who cannot marry and also those who prefer not to wed enter into fantasized relationships with beings who are frequently but not always defined as devils.

Stories from Eastern Europe tell of women who fall short of some feminine ideal and turn in desperation to the devil. The narrator of a Czech tale describes a woman whose shrewish personality turns away potential suitors and adds that to make matters worse, she is not pretty, the story betraying no inkling that the young woman's awareness that she would not be desirable to men might have affected her personality. In another version, a servant desperate to marry attends every dance her village has, although nobody ever asks her to dance. "So at last she said: 'I'd dance with Old Nick if only he'd come.' "[87] These stories support the contention that changing marriage patterns left more young women unmarried in Europe during the sixteenth and seventeenth centuries, and that the women were likely to be perceived as witches.[88] In a Hungarian tale, being pretty is not enough to insure that a woman will marry. A couple is heartbroken because the other girls in the village "all had their lovers who kissed and embraced them," but no one ever kissed or embraced their own "beautiful marriageable daughter." She is industrious and always fasts on appropriate holy days, but in vain the poor girl frets, for no lover comes her way. One day, in great despair, she utters these words: "Almighty God, let me too have a lover! I care not whether he be the devil himself!"[89] In a British tale, a similarly frustrated "Christina Murray, or 'Kirstie' they used to call her, was always fair rampageous for a man, and used to try Halowe'en spells and all they things." Kirstie almost elopes with the devil, but avoids her fate with the help of the town doctor; she finally marries an old sweetheart conveniently returned from India—a happy ending perhaps needed to reinforce a moral point.[90]

What such tales really teach is that to be unmarried is for a woman a dreadful state, and that invoking the devil is less a sin than a sign of despair. Witches are not only old widows or aging spinsters, but young women excluded from the lives they are raised to lead. Old witches thus become almost symbolic portraits of young women, for, as Baroja has argued, a woman may "become a witch after the initial failure of her life as a woman"; in old age, "perhaps her only satisfaction is to see younger women go the same way as she, living a life of false or inverted values."[91] The juxtaposition of loathly hag and beautiful young woman is common to both folklore and literature: behind Dickens's Estella and Miss Havisham is a long narrative tradition. The seemingly arbitrary presence of an old woman in a gypsy tale of a young woman who acquires a demon lover in default of a human husband indicates how persistent the tradition is and also how forceful is its symbolism:

There was an old woman in a village. And grown-up maidens met and span, and made a "bee." And the young sparks came and laid hold of the girls, and pulled them about and kissed them. But one girl had no sweetheart to lay hold of her and kiss her. And she was a strapping lass, the daughter of wealthy peasants; but three whole days no one came near her. And she looked at the big girls, her comrades. And no one troubled himself with her. Yet she was a pretty girl, a prettier one was not to be found.[92]

Since the appropriateness of a woman's life is defined by her relationships to men, it is not surprising that single or widowed witches also exist without those other men who should "share their domestic space —fathers, brothers, husbands, sons."[93] Lacking men, they experience an "especially tenuous role within society,"[94] and it is not surprising that they are disaffected. From folklore emerges the idea that women are subject to diabolical unions not only because they are supposedly the weaker sex and thus more subject than men to delusive fantasies but also because their roles make them more prone to unhappiness. It has been said that "women became devils' brides whenever they were not content with sitting at home with the distaff and the child";[95] they must find in dreams and nocturnal visions the satisfactions denied them in life. And if they are unmarried or old, they must create some space of their own, their people offering them so little. The devil's realm becomes theirs by default, whether they in reality indulge in occult practices or condemned ancient rituals, invoke fantasies that are often, tragically, mistaken for reality, or use drugs to transport themselves out of their misery.

But folktales also tell of young women whose *choose* not to marry, becoming the devil's bride not in default of a mortal lover but because the devil becomes implicated in the reasons they do not wed. Frequently such stories tell how young women spurn numerous suitors before they meet the demon. Sometimes, parents will consider no one good enough for their daughter, as is the case with an English couple who were so "loath" to give up their daughter that "they finally said she should never marry unless she could view her suitor ten thousand miles down the road."[96] The figure she eventually glimpses in the distance is the devil. More typical, however, is the daughter who scorns her parents' entreaty that she wed. A story pattern popular throughout Latin America is typified by a Mexican version of "an old woman who had a vain daughter":

And since the woman was old and poor, she said to the daughter one day, "*Hijita*, I believe it would be well for you to get married." "The idea!" laughed the proud young lady. "Just as if there were a man in the whole world fit for me."[97]

She agrees to wed a man whose golden tooth attracts her; he, again, proves to be a demon.

The Salishan depict a young woman who marries a crow, because although her "parents and the chief of the village were angry with her," she would not accept a suitor. Under their pressure, "she became sad, and would have committed suicide had not her brothers talked kindly to her." One morning, "when she had gone to the river to bathe and to draw water for the house, she thought, 'I wish a man from far away would come and take me.' "[98] The chief of her tribe represents the highest level of patriarchy, and her brothers' kindness only highlights her dependence on men, their offer of protection being a façade for control over her. The wish for a husband from far away suggests her need for distance from her people and expresses her desire for autonomy. The Arapaho portray a similar situation to explain how a woman acquires a dog lover. The tale supplies the woman's point of view, and she minces no words about the relative benefits of working at her own crafts, which are profitable, or losing her independence in marriage: "I know my little brother has a right to say about myself, but I can't help it, just simply because I don't want to get married and become a servant. So please leave me alone." Part of her defiance is aimed at the "old women" of her tribe, who ought to know that she has "no desire for a husband,"[99] but nonetheless support societal values that even a little brother may enforce.

In a German tale, however, a "lovely but finicky" young woman decides only after marriage to a demon that she should have heeded her mother's counsel and accepted an ordinary suitor, and proclaims, "Mother you were right!" Another German story tells how a woman married death itself because she found no ordinary man "good enough for matrimony."[100] Examples of such rebellious women could easily be multiplied by versions drawn throughout the world, for typical is the Spanish story from the Philippines that tells of one who spurns all suitors with the defiant claim that "she would rather have a devil for a husband than such a man."[101] Such narratives illustrate the adage that one ought to be careful of one's wishes, for they might come true. The devil's bride, however, may not be so much rebellious as different from most women. Sometimes she is simply more beautiful, but since beauty is a component in man's definition of ideal femininity, some other quality must place her in conflict with her people. One young woman is "more quick-witted than most of the women of her region, so that she received much attention from the young men," whom she rejects with an undisguised contempt. Only after she escapes the devil's snare does she settle for the life of a bourgeois housewife.[102] Such stories are not only studies in female deviance, but they also provide negative portraits of gifted but sometimes vain or haughty women most likely to protest against woman's traditional role.

Their extraordinary gifts are thus perceived to be a curse, as in the case of Nancy, the main character in an English tale. Her own mother might at some other time and in some less enlightened locale have suffered the fate of a witch, for she had "exerted over the villagers around her considerable power. They did not exactly fear her," for she was free of evil, but they "were conscious of [her] mental superiority, and yielded without complaining to her sway." Her daughter Nancy is aware "that her mother was a superior woman to any around her," and decides that her natural inheritance entitles her to a better existence than her station in life would allow. After she bears an illegitimate child to her employer's son, he dies, only to return as a revenant and carry her away.[103]

One way to cut a woman down to conventional size is to reduce her special qualities to pride, which is implicated in the ambition to go beyond one's position in life, and to make pride her fall—her punishment for the transgression of boundaries. A folklore character particularly smitten with a strong opinion of herself appears in a Breton folktale that bears a strong resemblance to the Danish ballads that inspired Matthew Arnold's "The Forsaken Merman." Like Nancy, Mona belongs to a lower economic class than she aspires to, and announces that she will never marry a fisherman, that her beauty makes her worthy of a prince, or the son of a powerful and rich aristocrat, or, failing those, a merman.[104] As Kierkegaard would say of her folklore sister, Agnete, she seeks the interesting, and when the merman kidnaps her, it is because he recognizes an ideal victim.[105] Calvino relates with stark realism the folktale about a widow with four daughters who "worked their fingers to the bone." Seeing no happiness in her future, the oldest proclaims, "I intend to leave home, even if I have to go and work for the Devil."[106] A sadder version of this tale involves an Icelandic young woman whose husband would spare her "working her fingers to the bone," but who for other, unspecified reasons takes an elf for a lover and bears his child. The foster-daughter of a priest, she resists her father's entreaties that she wed, for "she had no fancy for such things, and was very happy as she was," there being no "luck in marriage." When she finally succumbs to pressure and takes a husband, "she was never cheerful or happy-looking," and, unable to forget her elf lover, she dies brokenhearted.[107]

Similar folklore from Ireland inspired George Moore's short story, "Julia Cahill's Curse," in which the priest who sermonizes that a "disobedient daughter would have the worst devil in hell to attend on her" conspires with Julia's father to force her into marriage. Julia strives to preserve her personal integrity, and what most angers the priest is her contention that "the boy that would marry her would be marrying herself and not the money that would be paid" as a bride price. Turned out of her father's house for disobedience, she disappears (where to remains a mystery), and her departure bodes ill for the community, repeated catastrophes forcing emigration to America. In this romantic rendering of popular folklore motifs, society is depicted as not only at fault but also as paying a high price for its inability to accept Julia's difference from other women:

"Didn't she go into the mountains every night to meet the fairies, and who else could've given her the power to put a curse on the village. . . . [She] was as tall as I'm myself, and as straight as a poplar. She walked with a little swing in her walk, so that all the boys used to be looking after her, and she had fine black eyes, sir, and she was nearly always laughing."[108]

Because of woman's supposed potential for disrupting the social order, she is even more threatening when she is a superior woman rather than a weak one who justifies the male control that will prevent her straying into the devil's domain: thus the stories often give with one hand what they take back with the other. Folktales often reveal a potentially feminist consciousness, the narrators treating with ambiguity the special qualities in a woman that a story can neither wholly condemn nor wholly approve. Usually the tale of the devil's bride is a cautionary one, warning young women to accept their traditional roles. For, as Kapferer argues, the social instability brought about by female rebellion mirrors a cosmic disorder that is greatly feared.[109] Nonetheless, the folktales also imply that there are some whose superior talents and intelligence, or emotional sensitivities, may make them unfit for the ordinary life, and that demon lovers embody aspirations that cannot be satisfied in the usual ways open to women.

As is true in some swan maiden tales, the conflict in demon lover narratives is not so much resolved as transcended. Two tales in which the supernatural lover takes a bird's shape, one from Tibet and the other from Mexico, depict a striking contrast between the kinds of women who spurn mortal suitors and acquire supernatural lovers. In the Tibetan story, a young woman is portrayed as dangerously spoiled from birth, a child who has not known what it is to be denied any pleasure she glimpses and demands. "As she grew up her tastes changed; she craved more costly gifts—baubles and fine clothes. Her father, who was well-to-do and, therefore, able to indulge his daughter's whims, gave her everything she asked for."[110] What she finally demands is a magic bird who is actually a demon from whom she can only free herself by a simultaneous act of murder and suicide. Such sacrifice is averted because she learns in time the meaning of virtue; that is, she is finally socialized after an upbringing in which her drives toward self-gratification are never curbed.

It is her materialism that highlights by way of contrast the unworldly young Mexican woman too sensitive to conform to her society. A "delicious little princess, of unexampled beauty," her "life was all love."

She loved the clear skies of her country, which smiled to see her, and the burnished mirror surface of the lakes. She loved the flowers and the songs of birds. Thus, loving always and always loved, the most beautiful maiden of the Mexican lands saw her existence glide on.

In her semi–dream state, she "rested no thoughts on the elegance and gallantry of kings and princes who lay siege to her," and indeed their courtship of one so ethereal *is* a virtual siege. But those around the princess are "impatient that she accept some one of the advantageous alliances that were proposed," and they are "disquieted" by the "uncommon nature" of the woman. She, in turn, remains oblivious to their demands, secluding herself in the hidden recesses of her garden, until a small point in space draws her attention, growing into a large imperial eagle that descends to take its place beside her. When a jealous and rejected suitor kills the maiden and her bird lover, he seems to be enacting society's vengeance on those who remain outside it.[111] But the lovers' romantic negation of worldly reality survives in a picture of the

two of them pierced by a common arrow, their love not only aestheti-
cized but rendered religious—her lover not demonic but godlike.

The discontent that accompanies civilization supplies a central theme
in the Mexican tale, as it does in one of the most widely distributed
groups of folktales related by North American Indians, who tell many
stories of star wives and husbands. One of the former depicts the star
maidens who descend to earth in a wicker basket and dance to celestial
music. A hunter triumphantly captures one of them, and while they
remain together, she bears a son. But the fairy is not content with her
life on earth: "her heart was filled with longing to revisit her native
home" (this is Hartland's homesick swan maiden).[112] This narrative has
been described as a reversal of the star husband tales "in which two
[human] girls marry stars and successfully escape back to earth." [113] It is
a story with many variations, but the basic synopsis provided by Stith
Thompson is as follows:

Two girls are sleeping in the open at night and see two stars. They make wishes
that they may be married to these stars. In the morning they find themselves in
the upper world, each married to a star—one of them a young man and the
other an old man. The women are usually warned against digging but eventually
disobey and make a hole in the sky through which they see their old home
below. They are seized with a longing to return and secure help in making a long
rope. On this they eventually succeed in reaching home.[114]

The existence of both star wife and star husband tales suggests a keen
awareness by the peoples who narrate them that the mortal wife of a
demon lover and the swan maiden wife of a mortal man signify two
sides of the same narrative coin. That the star girl trapped in the mortal
world longs to return to the otherworld, whereas the human woman
comes to long for the secure reality of her earthly existence, has to do
with a virtually unresolvable oscillation between a pleasure and a reality
principle.

The traditional swan maiden tale as well as familiar motifs from it are
also narrated by the tribes who relate star girl and star husband stories.[115] The story of "The Girl Who Married an Elk" portrays a young
woman, who, upon discovering an inviting body of cool water, "determined to bathe, and . . . threw off her skirt and plunged in. While
sporting in the water she noticed that a man had come and sat down on
her skirt." Because he possesses her clothing, she must go with him.[116]
A similar theme shows up in the Salish tale of how Crow Man appears

in the shape of a bird that sits down on the clothes of a bathing woman: "If you become my wife, I will release your clothes," he tells her. She agrees, saying, "You must be my husband, for you have seen my naked body."[117] And the Wishosk tell of how the "raven went to get a woman for another man. She was bathing and did not see him coming. While she swam he went on the sand and took her dress. [He refuses to return it] but he would pull it away and she would follow him to get it."[118]

In telling stories about women unable or unwilling to enter into ordinary marriages, some narrators seem to have perceived the thematic connection between the swan maiden and star husband tales, thereby combining them into a single narrative. The Passamaquoddy of Maine tell of "The Indian Devil, the Mischief Maker," portraying Moose, a clever fellow who hunts well, and Marten, who is lazy but cunning, and who depends on Moose for food. When Marten spies on some fairy women bathing, he hides their clothes and captures one of them with a slight tap on the head. "Thus," say the Passamaquoddy, "the ancient Indians conquer the witches." Moose tries to emulate Marten's success, but he strikes his swan maiden so violently that she dies. Marten then acquires a second swan maiden wife. And although Moose provides food for all of them, Marten refuses to reciprocate by providing a fairy wife for Moose. The latter becomes intensely jealous, enmity develops between them, and during a fight they endeavor to kill each other, frightening the swan maidens, who take flight from this spectacle of human aggression and perfidy. It is at this point that the star husband tale enters the narrative.[119]

The disaffected fairy brides of Marten lie in the woods and look up at the stars and are finally transported to the heavens. This version of the story is not consistent, for when they later look back at earth, they remember their childhood and miss the lakes, woods, and rivers, as if they were originally mortal women. This confusion may have resulted from the imperfect combination of what were originally independent stories, perceived to be thematically similar, but the result (even if inadvertent) is to illuminate a larger narrative pattern by paralleling confused story detail with the essential confusion experienced by a wife torn between two worlds, conceiving of herself either as a transcendent being from another realm trapped in the world, or as a human aspiring toward some transcendent place. A similar story of fairy wives tells how women complain about their irksome earthly husbands and are as a result transported to sky land: "This was the work of an Indian spirit, whose duty it is to punish unfaithful wives, and who had overheard their remarks on the previous night. Knowing that the fulfillment of their wishes [to escape their marriages] would be the best punishment, he transported them to the Star-country, where they were wedded to the stars of their choice."[120]

The star husband tales have been widely studied although, typically, rarely interpreted. Ironically, one attempt at interpretation leads to the explanation that the narrative deals "with the life-arc of women, beginning with adolescence and moving on to adult life, symbolized by the sky world, including marriage and childbirth, and ending with death, symbolized by descent from the sky world"[121] (the woman often dies in her attempt to get back to earth). To the contrary, the stories themselves, which are quite stable in terms of basic plot, join other demon lover stories to depict women whose motives are precisely to avoid the life for which they are destined.

The Caddo begin their narration of the star husband by describing a family and a young girl that threatens its stability:

Long ago there lived a large family—father, mother, and eight children, four girls and four boys. They were all beautiful children, especially one of the girls, who was exceptionally beautiful. The time came when three of the girls were married, but the youngest and most beautiful would not receive the attention of any one. The girl was peculiar in her tastes and roamed around alone. She wished to go away somewhere, for she was tired of her home.[122]

Her defiance of her family is by now, of course, familiar, as is the particularly explicit Micmac version, which tells how the two prettiest girls of an encampment engage in a conversation in which the older warns, " 'We better go away. Many boys are coming after you and you don't want to get married. We better go.' "[123]

To switch back to the star girl story for a moment, it has been studied in Panama as expressive of the "essential difference and *otherness* of women."[124] In star husband tales the rebellious woman often seems anxious to preserve this difference because it distances her from her people and ironically supplies at least the potential for some kind of self-realization. It is significant that she often obtains a star husband when she secludes herself to sleep outside the confines of the encampment or in some other fashion goes off by herself. In some versions, two young women cannot follow their people as they move their camp because the

straps on their backpack break and as they fix them, the distance between them and the others widen.[125] Possibly their difficulty is itself
meaningful, and their failure to keep their equipment in good condition
can be construed as a symbolic rebellion. A Shuswap variant depicts this
conflict in terms of a dual quest, for self-sufficiency and for a choice of
mates. "Two young women could not get along with the people, so they
said they would leave, and live by themselves. They agreed to train
themselves, and then to wander over the country in search of husbands."[126]

Sometimes such isolation is depicted as romantic yearning reminiscent
of the Mexican eagle lover story. A longing for some ideal characterizes
a young woman in a Blackfoot tale:

The Morning Star was just rising from the prairie. He was very beautiful, shining
through the clear air of early morning. She lay gazing at this wonderful star,
until he seemed very close to her, and she imagined that he was her lover. Finally
she awoke her sister, exclaiming, "Look at the Morning Star! He is beautiful
and must be very wise. Many of the young men have wanted to marry me, but I
love only the Morning Star."[127]

Such romanticism will often distinguish one of two women from her
companion, who also wishes for a star husband but retains more practi-
cality in her vision. Their differing personalities often result in the acquisition of different kinds of star husbands. The Otoe of Kansas, for
example, tell how one of two women yearns after a "dim star" that
seemed to be vanishing behind the clouds, winning as husband a handsome young man. The other finds that star too ephemeral and prefers a
larger, more brilliant star, acquiring an aged star husband. The narrative
explains that the dim star, who proves to be a brave young chief, only
appeared that way while the young woman "was yet upon the earth,"
because "it was so far, far away that she could not see its glorious
light."[128] Perhaps, as Holbek suggests, her wish reveals her modesty
(just as some heroines in the Beauty and Beast type stories request
modest gifts—see next chapter); but another possible reading is that she
prefers the dim star because of its remoteness from the familiar world.
In any event, the story rewards this romantic and punishes her more
aggressively worldly sister.

Other star husband narratives are less concerned to depict the spiritual yearnings of women who wish for star husbands. They tell instead

of the overwhelming drudgery necessary for the tribe's survival as well as a division of labor that makes woman's job an arduous one:

At seasons when the fern roots were good for food these sisters would dig them to store for other times. When evening came they built a fire in camp, dried their roots and made their bed as comfortable as they could with the scanty means at their command. At early dawn they would return to work and repeat this for several days.

This version is from Puget Sound; another from the same place depicts the women's dependence on men for the most important part of the food supply. The younger of two sisters asks, " 'Where can we find men?'—'We want fisherman so that we can eat fish with our fern roots' [replied the older]. 'We don't want fishermen, we want hunters; then we can eat meat.' "[129] They may well resent the hard labor imposed on them, while at the same time they are deprived of free access to the fish and animals more satisfying and nourishing than the roots they collect. In a Washo story two women offer their grandfather flour in return for fish, but he contemptuously refuses this bargain. One of them becomes "angry and did not go to him, but went a little way to a big tree and cried. Then she went home and told her elder sister." They decide to go away and eventually become star wives. Only when they disappear from the tribe does the grandfather repent his treatment of them.[130]

Such variations emphasize not the elevated sensibility of the star's romantic bride, but rather her economic inferiority on earth, where she is subject to the control of men, who also control the distribution of the best food supply. Significantly, in the star world as well as on earth, the wives often dig for roots, and digging itself results in their glimpse of their homes on earth. Usually they have been specifically prohibited from doing in the sky world just what it is that they wanted to escape from on earth, but their insistence on digging nonetheless is an important feature of the tale. It is difficult to interpret the prohibition the stars' brides are intent on defying, unless it suggests that activities familiar from their earthly lives will draw them back to their former existence. The sky people may not want them actually to glimpse or symbolically to recall their homes any more than the demon lover of the Child ballad wants the runaway wife to long for what she left behind (unless her regret is conceived of as part of some diabolical torture). In any event, both on earth and in the sky world the stars' wives seek an autonomy that is denied them.

Gladys Reichard's early study of the literary motifs in the star husband tales distinguishes among three groups into which the story may fall. In the one that is being considered here, the story ordinarily ends with the women's successful return to earth, where they choose to pick up their lives once more after discovering that their dreams have not yielded what they had hoped. Their successful escape from their demon lovers suggests some kind of growth that they have achieved on their own—that is, without male intervention (sometimes an older woman helps them get away). The second story complex identified by Reichard often involves the death of the woman as she descends from the sky, a child surviving to become the hero of the popular star boy group of tales. Many swan maidens and other fairy wives are the mothers of heros, and the death of the star's wife may suggest that once she is a mother, she has fulfilled her purpose. But Reichard's third complex involves the Indian trickster figures with whom the star wives enter into usually successful contests when they return to earth, out-tricking the tricksters.[131] Overall, what a woman's role is conceived to be in contrast to what she may achieve on her own seems very much a part of these stories. The star girl tale has been described as a man's story, told by the fathers and leaders of tribes who express the need to keep the family together and society cohesive.[132] But both star girl and star husband tales depict woman's rebellion. And while the stories may be intended to subvert woman's attempt at independence (the Ojibwa call the star husband narratives stories of "Foolish Maidens"),[133] they nonetheless express female vulnerability, protest, cunning, and, sometimes, triumph.

Because of the centrality of woman's role per se in star husband tales, many of them depict a female rite of passage, although negatively portrayed. The young women's rebellious behavior is often associated with puberty and thus the onset of female sexuality. The Arikara version explains the separateness of the women that usually precedes their wishing for star husbands by reference to menstruation: "One night two pretty young maidens were sleeping on top of a summer arbor. They were ill with monthly sickness."[134] Many cultures segregated women during their periods to avoid the pollution of their blood; implied here is that young women are also in an unstable emotion condition at such a time, and it is in these circumstances that they are likely to be irrational and yearn for supernatural lovers.

The otherness of women is particularly marked in a Tahltan story of "two adolescent sisters who were living together [and] were staying apart from the other people," playing and joking with each other. In their amusement they indulge in fantasies of supernatural husbands and find themselves among the stars.[135] As in other versions, games and other play motifs, some of them incorporated into ritual, supply important themes where it comes to describing the supposedly erratic behavior of women not yet mature enough to assume their proper roles:

Two girls who were of an age to dance the puberty dance, were dancing it. And having stopped dancing just at dawn, they both slept. Toward morning the two girls, who were sleeping, arising, went off to dig roots. When they returned at night, the people all danced the round-dance.

When these girls dream of demon lovers, they do not heed their mothers' instructions about how to dispel bad dreams (that is, forbidden desires): "They dreamed of Star-Men, but did not blow the evil away from themselves."[136]

That young girls are particularly vulnerable to such fancies is explicit in another version that is ambiguous because of the way it deals with the play element; it is unclear whether a young girl is not yet ready to give up the fancies of her youth or not yet ready for the sexual "games" that will mark her initiation into womanhood:

At Kodoi a girl was being kept in the house during her adolescence. After two days her playmates came and wanted her to play. . . . Her mother said she was not yet ready. They kept calling her; then the girl went out to them. Soon Ha'kudu't, the Whirlwind, came, whirled her around and up, and took her to the sky.[137]

A similar tale from the New Hebrides describes how two older women and a young girl are burning dry leaves, the youngster having been warned not to go near the fire. Curious, she disobeys, "and was caught into the draught and carried up, with the smoke," to the sky world.[138]

A lack of respect for adult authority, indicating an inadequate internalization of the tribe's values, is a feature of a Bella Bella "Sun Husband" story. Significantly, this theme is once again attached to the isolation of a young girl from the rest of the tribe, a dangerous condition prevalent in the emergence of womanhood:

[A chief's] daughter was named Welx. She had a younger sister. Welx had almost reached puberty. Still she liked to play with the younger girls outside of her father's house. One time the girls built small houses large enough for four or five of them and they played inside. Sometimes they stayed there until late at night and their parents came to call them home, but they did not pay attention to their orders. Then all the people found fault with the girls because they made such noise late at night so that they could not sleep. Very often they stayed in the play houses overnight. One night the people heard the girls talking about the stars and the sun and the moon.[139]

The parents warn the young women not to speak of such matters, but their offspring do not obey this injunction, and one night they disappear. The story is particularly charming, and it is difficult to see in the mischievous girls the deviance often intrinsic to demon lover themes. And yet the conflict with adult authority is a serious matter, and the noise that keeps the tribe awake is but a sign of general disruption. The girls' failure to obey, their separateness, both literal and symbolic, is a genuine threat to their people, as, in their clinging to play, they resist the adult female roles that they must fulfill.

The final group of star husband stories to be introduced here forms a prelude to the next chapter of this book. In some versions the unhappiness of the women is not attributable to their homesickness in an alien realm but to an essential ignorance about their supernatural mates:

Two stars, large and bright, married two sisters. The girls were very unhappy, however, since they only saw their husbands at night and never in the day time.[140]

The Wishram similarly tell of how star lovers regularly visit five young women. One of these supernatural beings is older than the rest and hence unable to depart with the swiftness of the others. As a result the girls' people find out about these nightly visitors and the men do not come again.[141] Whether such motifs are part of tales that are indigenous narratives or are borrowings from other folktale traditions,[142] it is clear that the star husband story has strong affinities to the Cupid and Psyche type tale, which depicts, first, woman's rebellion against her role, then her subsequent loss of her demon lover, and, finally, her adaptation to mundane reality, the outcome of the story being capable of erasing the feminist themes commentators on Cupid and Psyche are fond of locating in the tales.

CHAPTER 4

# The Animal Groom

Urvaśī may be the quintessential swan maiden, but her union with Purūravas is more often situated among the Cupid and Psyche tales, which tell of the human wife of a supernatural being who is "forbidden to see or name her husband,"[1] the obverse of the motif in which the human husband, Purūravas, is bound never to appear naked before his supernatural wife. The Cupid and Psyche tale type forms what has been called one of the "oldest, most studied, and most widely distributed folktales in the world," the most extensive treatment of them being based on over a thousand versions.[2] Folklorists who study only their own countries' variants have shown how easily that number could be multiplied.[3] But just what stories can be classified under Tale Type 425 (is the classic fairy tale of "Beauty and the Beast" justifiably included?) and just which incidents belong to the basic narrative are questions that have provoked controversy.[4]

The supernatural mate is frequently a beast, often a human being suffering from an evil spell or punished for some transgression against a powerful witch—hence the general designation of animal groom cycle borrowed here from Bruno Bettelheim, in part because an animal bride cycle complements the Cupid and Psyche type tale. This complementarity has been neglected,[5] unfortunately so, because each group of stories illuminates the other (see my chapter 6 on the animal bride). For now, it will be useful to survey the kinds of beings who appear as supernatural husbands. Sometimes the animal mate is a human being enduring a spell from which he must be released; at other times he is the beast offspring a desperately childless couple will accept in place of no child at all, such a husband not being restored to his human form but being made human. But other supernatural lovers are not animals at all. Young women may pluck flowers that prove human or marry trees. And black men in predominantly white societies, lepers, and hideous men are sometimes portrayed as if they were beasts. Supernatural lovers may also be demons or tricksters, or deities whose seduction of human women betokens an amorality only the gods may enjoy. A demon lover may also be benign, a savior, for example, such as Elsa's Lohengrin. In rarer instances, he may even be the artfully contrived model of a human being magically brought to life, the male counterpart to Pygmalion's Galatea.

It is the search for the lost supernatural husband that has usually defined the Cupid and Psyche narrative: Swahn, for example, distinguishes the essential feature of Type 425 tales, that is, the search motif, from the "animal marriage motif."[6] The centrality of the search underscores what feminists applaud in Cupid and Psyche narratives, since Psyche's journey involves her in an active pursuit that contrasts her with such fairy tale characters as Snow White or Sleeping Beauty, who lie in deep sleep or virtual coma until awakened by brave and adventurous princes. Psyche has become a feminist folklore heroine[7] (from here on, the human wife of a supernatural or animal husband in the folktales will frequently be generalized as "Psyche"). This reading of the tales will, however, be challenged. In the meantime, so long as Psyche's search for her husband defines the narrative, all details concerning how the couple meet and eventually separate will be designated mere introductory elements.[8] But it has been argued that Cupid and Psyche tales enjoy wide popularity because their imagery reflects "so much of the relations of man and wife,"[9] a premise that can only be maintained if the conditions of the relationship before the catastrophic separation are acknowledged to be significant. The story would virtually make no sense without its so-called introductory elements, an example existing to make the point. A New Mexican tale describes how a woman is for no apparent reason abandoned by her supernatural husband, who leaves her golden slippers, which she must wear out searching for him. Perhaps she should be seen as Patient Griselda, who replaces Psyche in many versions of Type 425. Still, the search motif makes little sense unless attached to a more complete story or to other pieces of the narrative by someone who knows the rest of the tale.[10]

The story may, conversely, be both popular and thematically significant when no ensuing search for the lost husband is conducted. Sometimes the supernatural lover is a demon and the woman who outwits him demonstrates her superiority over not only him but also women less strong and resolute than she.[11] The broken taboo, moreover, sometimes has irrevocably tragic results. Purūravas and Urvaśī, Zeus and Semele, Lohengrin and Elsa are well-known examples of couples who cannot be reconciled,[12] and folklore supplies other examples. Does the Japanese woman who thrusts a needle and thread into the clothing of her mysterious nightly lover to follow him and discover his serpent identity outwit a demon or destroy her own chance for happiness? The Japanese tales suggest that these are not mutually exclusive possibilities.[13] And some very compelling versions of the lost supernatural husband reveal that the woman must pay a high price to win back her spouse or disenchant her beast.

Animal groom tales have long been recognized as being connected to the swan maiden type tale,[14] the most obvious similarity being that the brute exterior of the beast can be at times discarded, just as the swan maiden can take off the feather dress that makes her a bird or lay her animal skin aside to take human form.[15] An obvious parallel to the swan maiden story exists in a Russian tale that relates how a young woman joins her friends to bathe in a pond.

They all stripped off their shifts, and went into the water. Then there came a snake out of the water, and glided on to the daughter's shift. . . . She tried to drive him away, but there he stuck and would not move

until she promised to marry him.[16] The story of a marriage to an elk depicts a girl who had reached puberty and was prohibited from visiting a lake. Her curiosity aroused, she defies the prohibition and "threw off her skirt and plunged in." When she notices that a man has come and sat down on her skirt, she becomes frightened and wishes he would go away.[17] Her propensity to strike out on her own, her independence, marks her as being as much a fit object for an animal's attention as the disobedient daughters of the last chapter were for the devil's.

A star girl tale similarly combines the swan maiden pattern with elements of the animal groom narrative. The star girls who descend from the heavens to the natural world are in a symbolically appropriate fashion captured by a hunter who takes an animal shape.[18] From Ceylon comes a story of how a king and his chief minister pledge their yet unborn children to each other. The minister's wife bears a turtle instead of a human son. His betrothed nonetheless agrees to marry him if he brings her an exotic flower she longs to possess. To find it, he must first locate the sun maidens' pool and steal their clothing, exchanging it for a rare plant.[19] When the mother in a similar story becomes convinced that no woman would marry her monkey son, not because he is an animal but because he cannot speak, she orders him to find his own wife.

> One day he set off to look for a wife and came to a tank in which some girls were bathing, and took up the cloth belonging to one of them and ran up a tree with it, and when the girl missed it and saw it hanging down from the tree she borrowed a cloth from her friends and went down and asked the monkey boy for her own; he told her that she could only have it back if she consented to marry him; she was surprised to find that he could talk and as he conversed she was bewitched by him and let him pull her up into the tree by her hair, and she called out to her friends to go home and leave her where she was.[20]

In possessing language, the monkey husband comes close to being human; in being captured, the woman becomes more like an animal. Rarely, however, does the exchange between nature and culture take place so effortlessly.

Bird mates in a subgroup of animal groom tales have an obvious affinity to bird maidens. In an Iraqi tale, a woman is visited each night by a bird who doffs his feather cloak to become a man. She breaks the taboo against speaking of him, loses him, and embarks on a search that leads to an underwater realm where forty doves take off their feather robes and are transformed into forty handsome youths.[21] In other variants, the bird man is wounded when the lovers' enemies discover the clandestine meetings and plot against the pair, often sprinkling broken glass on the place where the bird lands and assumes human shape. His physical injury corresponds to the broken taboo.[22]

The donning of human clothing (rather than shedding of the beast covering) is sometimes necessary for the animal to assume human form,[23] as in the popular story of the swan children who fall under the spell of an evil woman. Because their sister fails to sew enough shirts to disenchant them, one young man retains a wing, a remnant of the evil visited on him.[24] In a version of this story invoked to explain the origins of the swan knight or Lohengrin, the mother of the enchanted children is herself a swan maiden.[25] Thus the swan knight legend ties together motifs that frequently overlap in popular narratives: the knight's origins point back to the swan maiden tale; his subsequent adventures form part of the Cupid and Psyche tale.

Another instance of close ties between the story groups is that of the tale of the Irish swan maiden who bears a son to the Earl of Desmond. He fails to heed her warning that he must never betray surprise about their extraordinary son, and the boy disappears: "Up to that instant [the son] had the shape of an ordinary man, but when he touched the water he was transformed into a goose, and in that form away he swam before their eyes." Legends sprang up about the reappearance of the lost son, Geroid, and one of these involves the Patient Griselda theme, which describes how a wife is cruelly tested when her children are taken from her at birth but nonetheless obeys her husband's prohibition against revealing pain over their loss (probably the most brutal taboo imposed on the Psyche character in the entire narrative group).[26] Usually, Griselda's resolve breaks down at the loss of the third child, and she sheds the forbidden tears. Geroid's similar testing of his own wife places his story in the Cupid and Psyche group; that he himself is son of a swan maiden and that his son has affinities with the swan knight indicate that at least one storyteller saw the narrative possibilities inherent in combining these diverse yet closely related stories.

These few examples from among many have been gathered to reiterate the centrality of the swan maiden story as other narratives cluster about or overlap with it, and also to introduce some essential similarities between Psyche and the swan maiden. It may be useful to put aside for a moment the question of whether the female character is supernatural (swan maiden) or human (Psyche) in order to consider their shared plight. The swan maiden lives on earth by enduring conditions uncongenial to her nature, and her imposition of some taboo on her husband seems to be her attempt to redress the power balance that weighs so heavily on his side. Similarly, Psyche's initial disobedience of her supernatural spouse involves a striving toward some independence within the relationship. Her subsequent search for her lost spouse may indeed engage her in an active quest, but it is difficult to argue that the reconciliation between the pair is her just reward, for control is restored to her husband as she resumes her place in his world. Since it is this chapter's purpose to explore the ramifications of these themes, little more need be said now beyond pointing out that Psyche's so-called victory places her at the end of her story where the swan maiden is near the beginning of hers—a dutiful wife.[27]

This is not to argue that the dutiful wife is without benefits, given her alternatives. (I am reminded of the female student who recently explained "The Gypsie Laddie" ballad by contending that the runaway wife left her husband to explore other options in her life.) The wife who wins back her husband is assured of his protection, support, loyalty, and perhaps his affection, as well as the security of her children (as Holbek points out). And she maintains her status within a community that offers her few if any other choices. The matter is just more complicated than either the happy endings to the search or the feminist argument would suggest. Psyche and Semele are given a place in the divine realm, which is symbolically tantamount to telling women that their life on earth does not matter in comparison with the rewards to come in the hereafter—or to placing woman on a pedestal as the so-called civilizer of the male beast, keeping her in her place for her own sake as well as that of society. The rich symbolism of Cupid and Psyche narratives, in short, makes it difficult to ignore the price Psyche may have to pay for her good fortune, ceding to her husband the very active role that had won him back.

It is easy to romanticize the separation of the human wife from her supernatural spouse, to think that the "loss of the mate through disobedience or by some misunderstanding or lack of sympathy" reflects nothing more than the "quarrels of lovers and their alienation," and that eventual reconciliation, "but only after toil and sacrifice," results in some kind of equitable relationship.[28] It is equally romantic to claim that lovers can only truly unite at the moment when the bond between them is ruptured.[29] The gender-neutral language of such interpretations of the Cupid and Psyche tale bypasses the essential struggle that is usually resolved in female surrender or adaptation to reality, which is often the same thing. In his Jungian analysis of Apuleius, Erich Neumann at least acknowledges the paradox of the story's ending. Psyche had initially turned on the light to see who her husband really was. But in acquiring knowledge of (and implicitly power over) him in order to love him truly, she must enter into a struggle with him that is resolved when he rescues her from the outcome of her failing at the last task set her as she searches for him. For she defies the prohibition that she not open a box whose contents will make her forever beautiful to her beloved, and only then does she become really feminine and worthy of the rewards awaiting her. Moreover, in her failure, in her sacrifice for him, the divine lover is changed from a wounded boy to a man and savior, because in Psyche he finds something that exists only in the earthly human middle zone between heaven and underworld: the feminine mystery of rebirth through love.

Paradoxically, then, Psyche's first disobedience is canceled out by her last, and if Neumann's argument could be succinctly summarized, it could be said that in his analysis, Psyche's role in her marriage rests on a gender-based version of the principle enunciated by the Gospel of Matthew: she who would win her life must lose it.

Neumann's analysis of Apuleius's tale is compelling because of the way in which gender is essential to it. But male and female function in his work on many levels and the way Neumann must accommodate Psyche's initial rebellion, which he approves of, and her final defeat, which he says is necessary, effectively places woman in a place subservient to man even if his argument is correct that this place exists on a higher level than Psyche first occupies in Apuleius's tale. His Cupid and Psyche reflect many paradigms. They represent the relationship between man and woman that must transcend the solely sexual union to become one based on true love. They also symbolize the inherent war of the sexes that came about when the "patriarchate" succeeded the "matriarchate" and women came to be essentially hostile toward men, a hostility destructive both to individuals and civilization. Psyche, however, is also *the psyche*, the archetypically feminine element in human beings. Initially, psychic life exists in a "phase" of darkness, but Psyche's striving toward consciousness—the onset of her own spiritual development—is a promise of the integration within the human personality of conscious and unconscious forces. For Neumann, such "totality" is the object of Psyche's search. If she fails at the last task set her in that search, says Neumann, it is because "she must fail, because she is a feminine psyche. But though she does not know it, it is precisely this failure that brings her victory." Moreover, such personality integration is paralleled on a cultural level as civilization develops (as Neumann's book on *The Great Mother* reiterates). Psyche's real battle is not with her supernatural husband so much as with her mother-in-law, Aphrodite, who represents a regressive element within the feminine, "anonymous lust and the dark embrace of the mere drive." Nature's accommodation to culture is figured in Psyche's becoming truly "feminine," developing beyond her bondage to the solely natural and instinctual.[30]

Neumann's developmental theories have elements in common with

those of the evolutionary folklorists, whose bases for the interpretation
of folk narratives were discredited for several reasons. Rather naively
the evolutionists assumed that story motifs reflected actual customs: if
the bride in an animal groom story had her eyes sealed during marriage
to a beast, it must have been because at one time actual brides in that
society married with blindfolds.[31] Not only was the assumption un-
proven and often simplistic, but, as noted in the introduction, a very
important element in the fantasy at the heart of animal groom and
animal bride stories is freedom from cultural necessity, the tension between an attachment to reality, which involves roots in society, and an
imagined flight from it. But it was also the idea of the *childhood* of
fiction, with its concomitant idea of a childish culture that was eventually rejected, although later folklorists often threw the baby out with the
bathwater. Certainly with regard to fairy tales, and particularly the
folklore of animal brides and grooms, these early critics supplied insights
that should not be ignored. Their attempt to match a story to the people
who told it, moreover, was a move in the direction of the cultural
specificity demanded by many folklorists today, although—again—animal bride and groom tales often reflect a symbolic rejection of life as
actually lived. Still, a brief look at some specifically described practices
that closely match features of the Cupid and Psyche tales suggests correc-
tives not only to Neumann's analysis but also to one that is today even
better known, the interpretation of the animal groom cycle in Bruno
Bettelheim's *The Uses of Enchantment.*

In notes to a poem based on American Indian lore, Henry Whiting
describes a supposedly "common form of courtship," in which

the inamorato goes at the hour of midnight, and lights a small torch by the
embers of the wigwam fire. With this he approaches the spot where the object of
his visit lies slumbering, or seems to be so. If she blows it out, it is a sign that his
visit is agreeable; if not, he takes the hint, and retires.[32]

With greater authority, Keigo Seki invokes a similar custom to explain
the widely told Japanese serpent bridegroom story, in which a mysterious lover's nightly visits to a woman end in a catastrophe when she
attaches a thread to his clothing and follows it to his daytime abode,
often to find a snake dead of the needle that she unwittingly had thrust
into his skin. According to Seki, a young Japanese man could at one
time steal at night into a girl's room without her parents being aware of

his presence. But at some point the family's knowledge or the girl's pregnancy would force a marriage to take place.[33] Another study reveals that this custom persisted until relatively modern times: "All-night trysts in the village dormitory, the custom of *yobai*—whereby a young man sneaked into a young girl's room at night—and even forms of trial marriage were familiar customs in parts of rural Japan until at least the end of the 1920's."[34]

Actual practices may also illuminate a frequent story element in animal groom tales, the woman's visit home after dwelling for a time with her strange lover. Permission is granted with conditions that ensure her return. In the "Beauty and the Beast" fairy tale, the animal narrowly escapes death when the woman remains away too long. Such stories may reflect exogamous marriages in which the bride is sent away to join her spouse among alien people. Interesting in this folklore context is Kinsley's account of a celebration of the Hindu goddess Durga, who violates "the model of Hindu woman" by not being submissive or subordinate to a male deity, not fulfilling household duties, excelling instead at a traditionally male function, fighting in battle. In North India the festival of Durga Puja has to do with the arrival home of married daughters who customarily "married at an early age and [left] their parents' home when quite young," to live with in-laws.[35]

In Bulgaria, where it has been said that wedlock puts "an end to a maiden's freedom under the indulgent care of her loving family,"[36] a marriage custom itself reveals how difficult it would be for the wedded pair to achieve a close relationship:

When the newly married couple, accompanied by singing and shouting, come to the threshold of their house, they are met by the bridegroom's father, holding a pair of reins in his hand. These he places round their two heads, just as one does to a beast of burden, and thus he drags them into the house. The manifest meaning of all this is that henceforth the newly wedded beasts of burden are under the yoke of their choice—the most inexorable yoke in the world.[37]

Although the ritual suggests that bride and groom share this burden, the husband assuming new duties and responsibilities, it is the bride who has been symbolically captured, like the swan maiden plucked from an earlier and easier existence. Another part of the wedding has been described as its most dramatic moment: when the bride is taken from her parents' home, her "mother-in-law meets her with bread, water, and a distaff of wool."[38]

No wonder the defiant Bulgarian Samodiva (met with in chapter 2) escapes her husband with the reminder that her kind were not meant to be housewives. In another version, she is described as mournfully beseeching her husband to restore her fairy robe as "before her shining eyes / A veil of darkness seemed to hang."[39] In other Bulgarian folklore, marriage to a dragon depicts a bride "who reluctantly submits to the unhappy prospect of life away from loved ones and friends," and the song, "A Dragon Loves Me," is a marriage lament in which a daughter reproaches her mother: "you never have asked me, / Whether I wish to be married."[40]

In Africa, the Basuto bride "must not say good-bye to her parents, nor must she speak or look back until she reaches her husband," with whose family she remains on probation for a month, after which she runs back to her parents after symbolically breaking a pitcher at the well (much as Cameroon women kick over the hearthstone to begin their initiation into the mermaid world). The Basutos may extend such symbolism into their animal groom tales. In one, parents wed their horrified daughter to a serpent, ignoring her entreaties. After the crawling beast follows her to a hut, "it darted its body through the door, and so terrified her that she ran to the other end of the hut. The snake followed and began lashing her with its tail"—an obvious piece of imagery.[41] Both Bulgarian and Basuto brides outwit and destroy their animal demons, but in actual life the bride who comes back to her parents will be allowed her ritual visit only as prelude to being returned to her new existence. Chapter 2 introduced the Algonquin swan maiden who escapes her human husband only to be sent back to him by her mother. (Even today many women who seek shelter with their family from bad marriages are told that having made their beds, they must sleep in them.)

What specifically women resist in marriage will vary from culture to culture and story to story. The rite of passage by which the bride moves from parents' to husband's home involves significant changes in her life. That she must surrender to her sexual partner and that this is but the first of many submissions to her husband is reflected in much folklore. An African story tells how a prospective groom assumes a snake's form to intimidate the people from whom he will take his wife. When he crawls into the girl's bed, she asks her father to kill him, but the male parent recognizes that the serpent is human (perhaps recognizes himself in the beast) and insists his daughter marry despite her entreaties for his protection.

When she saw that she would soon be past the boundary of her tribe, she could not resist singing a song of reproach to her parents. "You are my parents," she said, "and when the snake came to my house you did not kill him. Instead of that, you have given me to him, and now he must be my husband."[42]

Similar resentment develops into fury when a Korean bride discovers that her father has married her to a frog. Since she will not see him until "she meets him in the bridal chamber,"[43] it is little wonder that such a groom will appear the loathsome beast to whom she must yield although she has had no say in choosing him and had had no previous contact with him.

A South African tale similarly depicts a bride's separation from her family to meet an unhappy fate. She is rejected by her in-laws as a witch and is sent with her marriage gifts back to her own people—not entirely to her or even their dismay (she is a good worker): "Lungile took her old place in the kraal again and worked as hard and as well as ever." But no more suitors come, and it appears that her kilt of black ox-skins, her marriage garment, might never be worn. The story reveals that an animal had incited her in-laws' hostility so that he could wed her. When he assumes a human shape, she is much happier with him than she could have been with her first husband.[44] A similarly benign serpent lover follows a young French girl into her bedroom and she is horrified to "find herself without relatives, without friends, and a serpent beside her." She fares better, however, than her Bulgarian or Basuto sisters. The serpent reassures her that he can become a man when he chooses and asks whether she prefers him in human form by day or by night. "His wife replied that she preferred him to be a man at night, for thus she would be less terrified; by day she would have less fear than by night to have a beast near her."[45]

In analyzing the meaning of the choice presented by the beast to the woman, Joseph Warren Beach has argued its connection to the bestiality theme in the animal groom and bride cycles: because civilized people shrank from the notion of literal bestiality, the story pattern underwent a change over time, at the end of which the animal took on human form whenever the sexual intercourse of the couple was involved.[46] Whether such a development in the narrative actually occurred is hardly clear; but it will be seen that the bestiality motif in the story is problematic. Meanwhile, the bride in the French story also seems to be asking for tenderness from the man because it is during their sexual relations that his "humanity" will be most important to her: she will not merely be submitting to the beast. The really provocative element in such story patterns occurs not when she welcomes her human lover but—as will be seen below—when she prefers the beast.

In a tale from St. Maarten, the realities of wedded life under harsh conditions result in a less happy outcome. The bride who had refused a beast's offer of marriage agrees to marry him in his human shape. But after he is married to the lady, he goes back to being a dumb beast tied to a tree. When his wife realizes this transformation, she dies of a broken heart.[47] When man is socially and economically a veritable beast of burden, or so the story suggests, he may revert to behavior deemed bestial and shatter his wife's hopes of happiness. But of course, it is the plaint of many women that after marriage, their husbands treat them very differently than they had during courtship—assuming there had been a courtship.

Marriage customs that reflect exogamy or inherent male dominance against which the Psyche character usually protests in vain, and the realities of married life under harsh social and economic conditions will thus affect the way storytellers understand the Cupid and Psyche type tale. But the connections between a culture and the versions it tells need not be exact. Individual narrators may understand how longing or anxiety will prevail over a realistic depiction of life, and fantasies of loss or escape may influence the story's outcome. Moreover, isolated comparisons between specific customs and motifs from the Cupid and Psyche tale, however close the connections, are inadequate to explain the universal hold such stories appear to have on the human imagination. The tales themselves provide better glosses on each other than any explanations derived from factors outside them.

Unlike most social historians and anthropologists, psychologists take the universality of folktale motifs as a given. Bruno Bettelheim's is among the best-known psychological approach to the animal groom stories, and he supplies provocative insights into the tales. To study him, however, particularly to study him from the perspective of the vast folklore tradition that makes up the Cupid and Psyche type tale, is to discover significant weaknesses in his arguments. The purpose of his work is to encourage parents and educators to make the *so-called classic Western fairy tales* part of children's early exposure to literature so that children may thereby unconsciously work through childhood problems and achieve a healthier adulthood. But although Bettelheim goes outside the limited fairy tales to folklore when he needs to, he does not know enough folktales to recognize a need to qualify assertions about the narrative patterns to which they belong. His essential thesis, for example, that the animal groom tales reveal the necessity for the female character to undo the repression of sex[48] is contradicted by versions in which she apparently likes sex and her animal mate too well and must learn to repress. In addition, mothers play a more important role in the world's animal groom tales than they do in the collections Bettelheim studies. Finally, a most glaring error is the claim that although there are animal bride as well as animal groom tales, the animal bride is characteristically a charming beast, such as a swan,[49] whereas the animal groom is a more repellent creature, such as a frog. In the world's folklore there are many male swan lovers and frog princesses, and chapter 6, on the animal bride tales, will treat not only their themes but also the implications of their neglect and of errors such as Bettelheim's.

The sheer vastness of the Cupid and Psyche narrative pattern resists any single explanation of all of them, although gender supplies persistent contextual elements, however different perceptions of them may be from culture to culture, or storyteller to storyteller. Using Bettelheim's study as a reference point, however, will provide a starting point for considering some widespread story motifs in the animal groom cycle.

Folk narratives are known to be often extraordinarily violent and sadistic[50] (that is why Bettelheim had to make an argument for their place in children's early exposure to story), and in some animal groom stories, the symbolic defloration of the woman is depicted in extremely brutal terms. In the Grimm's "Hans the Hedgehog," for example, the animal avenges himself on a false bride and her father by piercing her "with his hedgehog's spikes until she bled all over."[51] Calvino tells a similar tale about sisters substituted for a favored daughter whom the animal desires; the unfortunate young women come to an even more gruesome end when the snake bites them on the neck until they die.[52] In many of these tales, seemingly unfeeling or helpless fathers turn their daughters over to such brutes, and even more helpless mothers cannot protect female offspring from their fate. In their more active and destructive aspect, these older women are also the witches who enchant the animal; as Bettelheim explains, since "our mothers—or nurses—were our earliest educators, it is likely that they first tabooed sex in some fashion; hence it is a female who turns the future groom into an animal."[53]

An example of an older woman who teaches her daughter to repress sexual desires can be found when a young African girl is the paramour of a snake, whom she caresses with great enthusiasm until her female parent persuades her that he is dangerous.[54] In an Eskimo story, a girl tends a snail in her bed, treating it in what she thinks is a maternal fashion until it grows to the proportions of a serpent. When she arrives at puberty, her mother becomes alarmed about this pet and arranges to kill it.[55] A Haida tale involves a woman who "suckled a woodworm" until it grew to enormous proportions (a significant commingling of sexual and maternal themes); in this instance, however, the daughter is frustrated because her father will not give her in marriage.[56] Such narratives explain why and how the repression occurs, not how it is to be undone. Mothers must be entrusted with the socialization of their daughters, and these mothers appear in the stories as themselves, not disguised as witches. Nor do they recede from the story to allow the relationship between the girl and her father to prevail, as—according to Bettelheim—she must transfer her affection from the parent who promises her to the beast (that is, arranges the marriage) to the beast itself.[57]

But in some variants, not the father but the mother—frequently driven by economic desperation—promises her daughter to a monster. In a Greek tale of a girl who marries an animal, there is, in fact, no mention of a father. Mother and daughter are enmeshed in tedious labor, and when the mother is delayed in gathering brushwood, her child eats an unbaked cake. In exasperation perhaps born of her essential helplessness, the mother utters the fateful curse: "Away with you, my daughter, and may the kerchief on your head fly away to the house of the ogres."[58] Neither is there mention of a father in the Chippewa story of a marriage to an ox, in which the mother of three girls is described as an old lady who gives her daughter to an animal to avoid eviction from the place they live. That the owner of the property is unknown may suggest an absent male figure intended to stand in for the father who fails to provide for the desperate four women.[59] And, as a final example, a frog husband tale popular in both England and Germany relates how a poor mother and daughter must labor for sustenance, and here too the old woman's temper is sorely tried so that the beautiful maiden "led but an ill life with her."[60]

It is such underlying social reality that may account for a wicked stepmother version in which a stepdaughter is wed to an animal in order to get her out of the way (the tale will be discussed shortly). Whether the evil stepmother involves what has been designated the family romance —the child's fantasy that the real, loving parent has died and has been superseded by the evil substitute—or whether frequent death in child-birth created many actual stepmothers in most societies would have to be determined tale by tale. The two ways of reading the stories, more-over, are not mutually exclusive. On some symbolic level, a bride forced to wed against her will might very well invent a family romance ex-pressed in the folkloristic marriage lament. The Bulgarian maiden who reproaches her mother for marrying her to a dragon reminds her female parent that she, her daughter, was not asked how she wished to live her life or whether she desired marriage to this beast.[61]

Often it is a mother, not envious siblings, who persuades the bride to break the taboo imposed by her mysterious husband. In three animal groom stories from Mykonos, not only is the mother-daughter relation-ship paramount, but in one case it is highlighted when the taboo involves the injunction against shedding tears. A young wife wishing to visit her dying mother is permitted to do so provided that her grief does not cause her to weep.[62] The importance of a mother appears as well in another Greek variant, where the bride of a crab can only disenchant him if she can keep his secret (that he has a human form) for only three weeks. But her mother is so appalled that her daughter must give herself to so loathsome a husband that her daughter fears for her mother's life and tells her the forbidden truth.[63] In another Greek tale, the mother threat-ens suicide if she does not have the truth about her daughter's strange marriage.[64]

Some folktales indicate that it is the mother-daughter relationship that must be altered if the marriage is to succeed. In the well-known Norwegian story, "East o' the Sun and West o' the Moon," the bear husband agrees to his wife's visit home, warning her, however, "not to talk alone with your mother, but only when the rest are by to hear; for she'll take you by the hand and try to lead you into a room alone to talk; but you must mind and not do that, else you'll bring bad luck on both of us." [65] And in the fourth story of the *Dravidian Nights,* a mother and not, as is more usual, a bride, destroys her son's animal covering, his tortoise shell. [66] If the destruction of the animal skin, a common motif in which the beast covering is burned or in some other way demolished so that the husband cannot revert to his animal shape, is symbolic of an adaptation to culture, this mother is true to her role as socializer. But to the extent that she does what it is ordinarily given the bride to do in such stories, she points up the conflict as well as the important link in a man's life between his mother and his wife. In short, not only mother-daughter but also mother-son relationships are important in animal groom tales.

Sometimes both parents in concert persuade their daughter to break the taboo, as in an Israeli Cupid and Psyche tale. Having wed their child to a serpent, a man and his wife do not know that she enjoys her wedding night with a handsome man and thus they cannot sleep a wink, "full of fear and anxiety for their daughter. They did not believe their eyes when they saw her leaving the room, safe and sound, in fact, joyous and happy. They began to shower her with questions, but their daughter, who had always respected them, refused to answer." Eventually, they wear her down. [67] Similarly, in a Moroccan story, a girl wed to a golden horse is drugged each night—a common way to account for her ignorance concerning the nocturnal visitor [68]—and her parents convince her to discover who her husband is. She succeeds, loses him, and then embarks on a successful quest to win him back. He forgives the transgression but imposes the harsh condition that she sever all relations with her parents. [69]

At other times the theme is rendered in less extreme terms, but nonetheless, the bride's separation from the parental home is seen as a precondition for the married couple's future. In an Italian tale, the animal groom almost dies as his wife prolongs her visit with her parents, and when she returns, he exacts the promise that she always "remain and never go away any more." [70] The thematic significance of such motifs has already been discussed in terms of exogamous marriages, in which the seeming expulsion from the parental home is a traumatic event that may well inspire the bride to consider her husband a beast. It is not strange that she will come to see him as human only as the psychological if not literally physical distance between her former and present home widens. Both parents, not only the family patriarch, may represent her earlier allegiance. Thus the need to transfer loyalty from father to husband is only one factor in the transition she must experience,[71] and psychological studies of the animal groom tales must account for the bride's relationship to each parent as well as both parents, especially since her parents as a couple provide the model for her own life. This is as true in Cupid and Psyche tales as in life itself.

It is possible to challenge not only the idea that animal groom tales— as a group—concern the transfer of the bride from father to husband but also the idea that such a transfer is about love. For what some stories depict is a mere assignment of authority over the woman *by father to husband*. What sometimes results is the woman's conflict between father and husband. In a West Highlands tale, a farmer helped by a dog to find lost cattle allows the animal to wed his youngest daughter. During each of three pregnancies she returns to her parental home, where she apparently is cared for during her confinement. Although warned by her husband not to reveal the secret of his human form and not to stay until the child is born, each time she does so, and the child is stolen by its father to the accompaniment of fairy music. After the third time, the father demands to know whom she is married to, and unable to resist his authority, she defies her husband's prohibition about discussing the marriage.[72] This "Griselda," however, has little reason to trust her spouse, and it may be that she is appealing to her father's protectiveness as much as responding to his authority. A story from the United States depicts a Psyche who is able to resist her sisters' pressure to disclose her husband's identity, but "thought surely she ought to tell her own father what her man's name was."[73]

Similarly, a Middle Eastern bride supposedly married to a beast makes apparent in public her admiration for a handsome warrior. Her angry father suspects her of infidelity and thus feels himself publicly disgraced by her behavior, and to placate him, she disobeys her husband and confesses that the admired stranger is her lawful spouse in his human form.[74] The protective and the authoritarian father are often difficult to distinguish, and such stories supply a harsher context for the father-daughter relationship than tales in which a young woman weds a beast to protect her father from the animal's wrath, her obedience certifying her worthiness to experience ultimate happiness in marriage. Perhaps these stories of Beauty and the beast provide but a veneer other versions had no need for or were willing to dispense with.

The question again arises, who tells these stories? Tales of a search for the lost wife (Type 400) have been found to be favored by men, tales concerning a search for a lost husband (Type 425) favored by women,[75] in both cases the searcher's gender correlated with that of the most likely teller of the tale.[76] But again, a female narrator in no way guarantees a feminist point of view, whereas a male narrator may for many reasons prove insightful concerning woman's lot; the apportioning of tale types to male and female narrators consequently raises as many questions as it answers. Why would men favor a tale in which the supposed quest on which they are engaged typically ends in failure? This will be a central concern in chapter 7, on Orpheus. For now consideration will focus on what there is in Cupid and Psyche tales that expresses peculiarly female interests.

One argument has been that the amorous longings expressed in the Cupid and Psyche tales constitute a subject that appeals to a female audience (of course, by now it should be clear that the stories are more likely to depict harsh reality than romantic feelings). Interesting in this regard is Calvino's analysis of the superior female storyteller who was the source for Giuseppe Pitré's famous collection of Italian folktales. Pitré heard them from a nursemaid, an illiterate old woman named Agatuzza Messia, who was, according to Calvino, always "ready to bring to life feminine characters who are active, enterprising, and courageous, in contrast to the traditional concept of the Sicilian woman as a passive and withdrawn creature." With approval, Calvino notes that she scorned the Cupid and Psyche story so popular in Italy precisely because of its sentimental treatment of love, refusing to romanticize a love that does not in the end benefit woman.[77]

That romantic love benefits neither woman nor man is obvious in an animal groom story from Afghanistan, related by a male narrator to an all-male audience. A serpent's wife is egged on to discover what she has been forbidden to know, how her husband's snake skin may be burned so that he will retain only his human form. When her stepsisters succeed in getting her to ask the tabooed question, her animal husband slapped her on the mouth so hard that blood flowed from her lips. . . . Then he felt bad, put her head on his lap, and told her, "Foolish human being, why do you ask me such things? What if you and I have enemies?"

He nonetheless provides the forbidden information, she burns the snake skin, and he disappears.[78]

Discernible in his reaction to his wife are three stages that might well appeal to his male audience: first, he demonstrates an aggressive male forcefulness in response to her readiness to transgress limits set for her; second, his tender feelings suggest that at heart a man is not such a bad fellow after all; and, third, he will prove what such a man would believe to begin with, that his wife's stepping out of place is but a sign of essential female weakness, and that his natural tenderness probably should be overcome in order for him to control that member of the species who is the source of all trouble. Even if other versions did not convey the same message, and many do, it is clear that in this one, the search for the lost husband and the couple's reunion mark not so much female energy but penance: the woman must learn her place once and for all. Is this the kind of tale that women could enjoy or tell? Perhaps Agatuzza Messia neglected the popular Cupid and Psyche tale less because of its theme of amorous longing than because of the ultimate female capitulation. In sum, it is hard to demonstrate the existence of romantically erotic themes (in contrast to motifs concerning destructive lust) except perhaps in the so-called classic fairy tales. To argue that sentiment in the Cupid and Psyche tales makes them particularly appealing to women is only to perpetuate the stereotypes on which the stories draw. If the narrative group is favored by women, something other than romantic love underlies it.

It is not only important at least to contemplate (if not necessarily to know) who tells the Cupid and Psyche tale but also to decide whose story is being told, Cupid's or Psyche's. It has been argued that animal groom tales are "heroine tales, not hero tales, for the interest in them is centered on the disenchantment brought about by the maiden who comes to love the prince in his beast form."[79] But the matter is not so simply resolved. There can be distinguished, for example, two different versions of the same story: one of them ends when the animal is disenchanted, and one virtually commences at this point. In the first instance, the husband in need of disenchantment is the chief folklore character, and the tale concludes when he becomes human. But because the woman's means are frequently violent (such as throwing the frog against a wall or burning his animal skin, sometimes against his will), these are stories in which the energy and resourcefulness that she evidences must be modified, and her initiative constitutes the very offense for which she loses her spouse. From this point her search commences, and the story becomes that of a Psyche who undertakes trials to win back her husband.

Therefore, establishing the focus of interest in Cupid and Psyche tales may depend less on determining which character, male or female, is the more active one than on deciding upon the narratives' central themes. If Psyche's passive submission at the beginning and, arguably, at the end of the narrative is the point of the story, Calvino's professed agreement with Agatuzza Messia view that Psyche is *not* an example of an active, courageous, and enterprising woman holds. But if Swahn's emphasis on the successful quest for the lost husband holds, then the feminist interpretation of Cupid and Psyche gains support: a determined heroine undertakes and endures an arduous journey and painful travails to achieve her goal. Whether the paradoxical relationship between her courage and her goal—to win back her husband and assume woman's traditional role—is perceived will depend upon individual narrators, discerning members of the audience, and scholarly commentators whose exposure to the vast tradition defined by Tale Type 425 may vary widely in degree.

Again, some versions of the swan maiden story are considered "male" Cupid and Psyche tales,[80] and narrative motifs attached to mortal men in some stories can be found correspondingly attached to mortal women in others. For example, both men and women frequently prove unable to resist boasting of or showing off the supernatural mate even though doing so has been forbidden. Both men and women seek to identify their mysterious lovers, again, even though they are denied such knowledge. In such cases the taboos are identical, as both men and women are told not to light the revealing lamp or ask the unknowable name. As a result, many critics treat shifts in gender as but one of many common inversions of motifs; in the preface the view was presented that the change in the sex of the supernatural suitor is common in folktales[81]—as if to say just this is to say very much. A similarly casual approach to gender is found in the argument that the "widely distributed myths in which a husband or a wife transgresses some 'custom'—sees the other's face or body, or utters the forbidden name—might well have arisen as tales illustrating the punishment for breaking the rule."[82] But unless equality between the sexes is presumed to have existed among the early peoples who told the tale, there must have been even in earlier times some significant difference between forbidding men knowledge of their wives and forbidding women knowledge of their husbands.

There are obvious and subtle differences that distinguish story groups in which the husband is the supernatural partner from those in which the wife is. Often a woman thinks she has wed a monster to discover that he is in reality a handsome youth, whereas a frequent theme is that a man who thinks he has wed a woman learns that she is a monster—or at least comes to perceive her as such (see chapter 6). These differences do not, of course, always hold, and most narrative motifs have their literal thematic obverse with regard to gender. But to study animal groom and animal bride tales is to discover that reversals in the motifs usually bring with them thematic changes that speak to the conflicts between man and woman. And where the erotic motif in the story is strong, such conflicts appear only that much more emphasized.

Students of Western medieval literature have long recognized the connections among erotic fantasies, power, and supernatural mates. Marie de France's bird man tale, the *Lay of Yonec,* has been distinguished from its Celtic folklore sources precisely on the matter of the heroine's assertive personality. In both folklore and literary version, the supernatural lover visits frequently, but only in *Yonec* does the lover come "at the wishes of the lady,"[83] visiting his married mistress "whenever she expressed an ardent desire to see him,"[84] her desires communicating themselves to him and thus acting as a summons. She exercises in the love affair autonomy denied by her husband, her liaison with her shapeshifting lover claimed to reflect a time in Irish history when a woman, "married to a man of equal rank and fortune with herself," was "comparatively independent, and had the power of divorce. She took part in affairs, and even went out to war."[85] This possibly submerged presence in a Cupid and Psyche type tale of the autonomous Celtic fairy who has been contrasted with the submissive swan maiden[86] makes it particularly difficult to sustain as a feminist heroine the woman who wins back her husband, because her very search for him is a sign of submission. The narrative tradition itself—moving through folklore to literature—suggests that in some instances, a strong female character has been replaced by a weak one, the restoring of her autonomy being merely a literary fantasy. And if a Psyche desperate to win back her husband can only be a dubious model for women seeking to achieve some independence within marriage, what can be said about Psyches who defy the taboo imposed on them and cannot rectify their error—the Semeles and Elsas whose mistakes prove irremediable? In the literature based on swan knight legend, whose folklore roots have already been noted, such gender-related themes are more significant than has been acknowledged by commentators.[87]

The core of the swan knight legend involves a woman sorely in need of a champion who can defend her in combat. When one mysteriously appears, he warns her never to attempt to discover his origins, a taboo she eventually breaks, to his sorrow and her fruitless remorse, for their separation is irrevocable. In Wolfram von Eschenbach's *Parzival,* the heroine, by now familiar in this book, spurns ordinary suitors and acquires a supernatural mate:

> Now there ruled in Brabant a duchess of surpassing beauty, noble of birth and irreproachable in conduct. So pure and holy were her thoughts that she remained indifferent to the many suitors whom her land and her beauty attracted, though among them were princes and kings. Finally the lords of her realm became impatient and displeased because she would accept none of her wooers. She called together the lords and made known to them that she would give her hand to none except one whom God should send.

When her champion rescues her from the danger her resistance has placed her in, nothing would seem to account for her fatal error in asking about his origins—unless the very idea of "lords of her realm" suggests that the space she lives in is never her own. Eschenbach merely poses a rhetorical question: "Happy were the years that followed, and lovely children were born to the duke and duchess. But one day, alas! the duchess asked the forbidden question—why did she so despite the warning?" An audience accustomed to viewing all mortal women as the daughters of Eve might take the answer to be self-evident.

The duchess in Konrad von Wurzburg's *Swan Knight* is less an idealist than a woman determined to remain free of male control. A widow with a daughter, she must fight to retain her dead husband's wealth after her brother-in-law invokes a German law forbidding women to inherit property. When the swan knight defeats the pretender, he wins the duchess's daughter in marriage. Lineage and inheritance having already been established as important, it is consistent that when the swan knight's wife "looked at her beautiful children she longed to know of their father's parentage. At last she could restrain herself no longer."[88] In an Indian analogue, it is a desire to be assured of her husband's high caste, a concern for her own status, that provokes the heroine to force from her serpent husband the secret that irrevocably separates them.[89] But in the *Swan Knight,* there is the additional theme of woman's autonomy: it is plausible that a duchess who asserts her right to property will raise a daughter who not only endeavors to be convinced that she is wed to an appropriately aristocratic husband but also strives to exercise a control over her own life that requires she have his trust. That once he is lost the swan knight husband cannot be recovered inverts one of the most important elements of Cupid and Psyche type tales.

In the "Lohengrin" section of the *Wartburgkrieg,* a medieval source of Wagner's famous opera, Elsa's fight for her inheritance is also attached to her right to choose a husband rather than have one chosen for her. Lacking the might to enforce this right, Elsa must find the champion who will settle the matter for her in combat. When she later asks the forbidden question concerning his origins, it is in the setting of a combat, and what happens parallels the Middle Eastern folktale discussed above in which the heroine who is openly favorable to a strong and handsome warrior is forced to disclose to her father the forbidden secret of her animal husband, that he is capable of taking human form. Similarly, Elsa and the Duchess of Cleve watch Lohengrin fighting in a tournament. Elsa is goaded by jealous, taunting women, and cries in vexation in her husband's arms until he publicly proclaims his identity and is lost to her forever.[90] This is the version of the swan knight legend that comes closest to the myth of Zeus and Semele.

The arbitrary demands made on such women have not rested easily on those who treat their story. In Pindar's odes, Semele is granted a place in Olympus among the gods: her desire to behold divinity is recognized as being something greater than female curiosity or a crass desire for status.[91] And a defense of Wagner's Elsa—that she was a "loving woman who must have the full confidence of her husband so that she may withhold from him nothing in her heart, that she may give herself to him in the fullest sense"[92]—reveals how uncomfortable a modern world might be concerning any taboo that denies woman knowledge of her own spouse. Elsa will be perceived as frustrated in her efforts to retain independence as part of a relationship that rests on more equality than the taboo admits. Her story hence provides a suitable point for focusing attention on the taboo motif itself and its gender-related significance in animal groom tales.

While the taboo motif in animal groom and animal bride type tales has drawn commentary, taboos are generally dismissed as mere narrative devices, "one of the numerous related tricks of which the epical technique of the folk-tale makes use in order to carry the plot further—the appearance of a prohibition in the chain of motifs in a tale implies that someone will violate" it.[93] In contrast, MacCulloch's explanation of a taboo he finds particularly "baffling" is that early storytellers were likely to view "women at all times, and especially at various critical epochs, as highly dangerous,"[94] and his account has the virtue of linking the taboo to gender. The argument to be made here and later, in chapter 6, is that taboos can frequently be distinguished according to who it is, a male or female character, who must endure the prohibition. Even when the prohibition is identical, subtle differences in meaning may exist. For example, both human men and human women are enjoined not to speak of the supernatural spouse to others. When the men break the taboo, it is usually to enhance their position among other men, hardly a praiseworthy act but one associated with the male prerogative to assert status in groups, and certainly less blameworthy than the act by which women utter that which they are forbidden to speak about. For woman is stereotypically perceived to be a troublemaker who cannot keep her mouth shut, who indulges in the mischievous gossip that, because it affects outcomes, is associated with power and is thus "potentially a challenge to [man's] control of the hierarchy."[95]

In general, taboos imposed on the wife in Cupid and Psyche tales are often intended to keep her in her place, to prevent her from achieving some autonomy by knowing who her husband is, seeing him, or being able to disclose his identity to others.[96] Those imposed on the husband in animal bride tales frequently concern some kind of abuse (for example, the prohibition against physically hurting the animal wife or insultingly referring to her animal origins).[97] This is not to say that taboos are never arbitrary plot devices, nor to deny that the same taboos may be found in both story groups, but only that the taboo motif possesses more thematic significance and is more gender oriented than is ordinarily granted.

The necessity of controlling women appears to supply the reason for the taboo in a story in which a Moroccan Psyche disobeys her husband twice, the second time after he has forgiven her for her first transgression. But other narrative motifs appear to illuminate the meaning of the prohibitions. First the woman insists on seeing her husband although forbidden to do so; then, apparently encouraged by his leniency to continue asserting herself, she permits her sisters to incite her to find out his name. Eventually she must sever all relations with her family as her husband finally gains full control over her.[98] Significant in this tale is the repeated disobedience, the violation of two of the three most popular taboos in Cupid and Psyche tales at issue, both prohibitions concerning knowledge without which a woman remains at a distinct disadvantage in the marriage. Again, disobeying her husband appears from one perspective to be her attempt to balance the power in the relationship, and from another perspective reinforces his belief that because woman is inclined to destructiveness, she should be denied power.

Other versions of Psyche's tale reinforce the idea that the wife's reason for defying the taboo is sufficient reason for imposing it. Such a position necessitates a blatantly antifeminist narrator, as is the one who tells an Italian tale about a bride warned not to disclose the name or nature of her supernatural mate. "The maiden promised," relates the story, "but she was a woman" and so gives in to her sister's cunning mischief making.[99] In the same collection, another Psyche breaks two taboos: she wants not only to know her husband's name but also the contents of a box that must not be opened. The perils of such typically destructive female inquisitiveness appear in an Indian tale when the heroine reproaches herself for the irrevocable loss of her husband: "Loud and piercing was the cry which she gave forth when she realized the extent of her misfortune, and wept and cursed for the remainder of her life the folly of her impertinent curiosity."[100]

But curiosity had not been her only motive. The narrative depicts a serpent groom with two wives, one of whom would rather lose than share her husband. It is she who incites the other to ask the tabooed question. The story thus reflects tensions that might be expected to exist in polygamous marriages. In addition, the forbidden question has not to do with her husband's name, but rather his caste, and her concern may reflect a legitimate social reality.[101] In Lang's version, the serpent prince's dismay is as pronounced as Lohengrin's and Zeus's as they provide Elsa and Semele with the forbidden but sought-for knowledge: "he said sadly: 'Do you still insist that I should tell you my secret?' And the princess answered 'Yes.' 'If I do,' answered the prince, 'remember that you will regret it all your life.' But the princess only replied 'Tell me!' "[102]

That women are mischievously curious and defeat their own interests is not, however, the worst charge that has been leveled at them. In the *Pentamerone,* a woman's disobedience not only deprives her of a prized lover but also deprives him of his hoped-for salvation: like Eve she has led a man to his fall.[103] However the story is told, Psyche cannot win. Even the passivity demanded of women in these stories gain them as much scorn (sometimes disguised as pity) as their prying and supposedly destructive curiosity. A young Greek woman drugged at night is not even aware that she is being visited by a demon lover. Thus she goes off to sleep, and when the Lord of the World Below comes to bed, she is not aware of him. "So the time passed by."[104] Deprived even of the pleasure to be enjoyed with demon lovers, this Psyche appears to symbolize the stupor in which women seem required to live as a permanent condition.

Such an inert woman may even lack a substantive reason for breaking the taboo. In the story from Afghanistan discussed above, the arbitrary conditions of the wife's life are highlighted. No reason is given in this version for the father's marrying his daughter to a snake. No reason exists for her asking the parent how to burn her husband's animal skin, because, on her own, she is entirely content. Responding to her sister's goading, she complies as automatically as she receives her husband's blow when she asks the offending question. His ensuing tender-heartedness, which he comes to regret, at least demonstrates his ambivalence, which thereby confers some identity upon him, whereas she is so unresisting as to suggest that the very definition of woman involves a kind of blankness.

It is not only a domineering or abusive husband who victimizes Psyche. In the Indian tale mentioned earlier, about a stepmother who arranges her stepdaughter's marriage to a serpent, the older woman becomes jealous of the bride's happiness and incites her to the catastrophic act: she knows that if her animal son-in-law were to reveal his name, "he would be obliged to return again to his former home underground," and so she encourages her stepdaughter not to "rest day or night until he had" revealed his secret. After the young wife embarks on a search for her husband, her mother-in-law (like Apuleius's Venus) acts out her own hostility by setting difficult tasks the repentant bride must perform.[105] Whatever anthropological or psychological explanations the story may elicit, it also suggests that young women are made passive when other, older women whose roles make them angry and punitive cooperate with patriarchal systems by exploiting the very elements in it that have led to their own misery.

This is not to deny the relationship of the taboo motif to the power struggle in the marriage. The swan maiden, for example, frequently supplies the excuse a husband needs to attempt to control his wife by whatever means are necessary. When, to cite an instance, the Bulgarian Samodiva exploits her husband's desire to show off the dancing of his beautiful and talented wife by tricking her magic clothes out of his possession and thus escaping him, she may be said to be meeting exploitation with exploitation. She is, after all, a captured bride forced to bear the son that confers more status on her husband than on herself. Yet her scheming substantiates the view that women are untrustworthy, that their wiliness will defeat even the most vigilant husbands. The inherently blameworthy wife has surrendered the right to be treated fairly, and therefore no opprobrium attaches itself to the man who has abused her. Psyche's breaking of the taboo only confirms such premises.

In Cupid and Psyche tales, women prove themselves virtuous by abiding by the conditions of their marriage, by seeking to recover husbands lost when the taboo was broken, and by accepting animals as husband. Conversely, repulsion would mark their deficiencies as women and wives. When, for example, a Spanish Psyche holds up the forbidden light, her husband reverts to his frog shape, which now becomes a permanent factor in his wife's life. She is embarrassed and pretends to her friends that her husband is away on a trip.[106] Similarly, a Magyar bride on the way to her dreaded wedding with a beast covers her loathsome groom "with a shawl, as she did not wish to let the whole town know of her misfortune."[107] She hardly seems to deserve her good fortune when he becomes a handsome man, in contrast to a Basque bride who willingly allows the whole town to see that she has wed a serpent.[108] Perhaps the most worthy of all is the Russian wife mated with a snotty goat, for as repulsive fluids oozed from parts of his body, "the unfortunate girl never stopped wiping him with a handkerchief, for she was not a bit squeamish. The goat was pleased—he combed his beard in his pleasure."[109] The sexual symbolism indicates a pleasure experienced only by the male beast, the woman being merely acquiescent.

Woman's worth is frequently on trial in these stories. When a Greek bridegroom gives finer gifts to his sisters-in-law than to his bride, the latter betrays the secret of her strange marriage, failing her test.[110] And when a Roman bride of "The Dark King" pays the traditional visit home, she not only brings lavish gifts but also boasts, " 'That's nothing. You should see the beautiful things that are scattered about in my new home, just like nothing at all.' " She accepts her family's plan to kill her husband, who they convince her must be a monster to whom she need feel no commitment.[111] An unpleasant character, she is not a typical Psyche, and in her portrayal an antifeminist tradition partially submerged in other versions of the animal groom stories nastily comes to the foreground.

Frequently witchlike older women foreshadow what young Psyches will develop into. It is the prurience of some French crones that results in the broken taboo:

Once there was a girl who lived all alone in a castle. A young man came to see her every day with the idea of marrying her later on. Every evening the old women came to spend the evening with the girl. They said to her, "Oh, Mademoiselle, when you are married we'll come and see you in bed."[112]

When the women spy on the wedded pair, the offended supernatural husband disappears. The literary descendents of these old women who live vicariously through younger women have been met with in the previous chapter and have their well-known literary descendents: Juliet's nurse is only one, but perhaps the best-known, example. Often they are or should be in charge of young girls but instead instigate or aid in the young women's rebellion. Their counterparts are, of course, the helpful older women Psyche frequently meets and receives help from on the journey to find her lost husband. The coexistence of these antithetical female characters within a story so fraught at the outset with ambiguities concerning gender relations indicates another thematic layering in the tales' structures, one that reinforces the more obvious themes.

The extent to which the Psyche character measures up to her culture's ideal is central to these stories. Many Psyches are not only assertive but also defiantly rebellious. One tale begins with a young Greek woman imprisoned by her father in a tower. One day, while she is playing ball, she shatters the glass of her chamber and an eagle flies in and kisses her. After this the "princess ran away and went to seek her lover."[113] But not all who defy their father's authority retain their independence. In a Basque story a widower's three daughters set out on their own to explore the country, an uncommonly adventurous undertaking for young women. The third becomes the prisoner of her animal mate, and, significantly, must learn to curb the courage and independence that had led to the pair's union in the first place. In her wanderings,

She went very much farther into the wood, and she was caught, and kept prisoner by a serpent. She remained there crying, and not able to eat anything; and she remained like that eight days, very sad; then she began to grow resigned, and she remained there three years.[114]

As woman's imprisonment and woman's rebelliousness are played off against each other, the outcome is usually the subduing of the deviant impulse.

Some Cupid and Psyche tales present a veritable "taming of the shrew" motif. In one story, a dog's wife musters all her energy to escape her beast husband, whom she calls a " 'great, foul, small-toothed dog,' " until she realizes that if she wishes to visit her parents' home, she must learn to be compliant. She henceforth refers to him as "Sweeter-than-a-honeycomb," at which point he is transformed into a handsome youth.[115] In the fairy tale of the "Frog Prince," it would appear that the releasing rather than the repressing of rage leads to the disenchantment, the frog being transformed when his human wife throws him violently against the wall (Bettelheim thinks she is finally asserting herself). But acquiescence to an animal husband and violence against him are not always contradictory. When the serpent's wife in a German story asks to attend a party at her parents' home, her animal groom insists that he will accompany her despite her protest that his horrible form would terrify the guests. Faced with his adamance, she gives in: "If you wish it, so must it be."[116] During the dance, she appears in public with her loathsome groom, and when she steps on his tail and crushes it, he is transformed into a handsome youth. Such versions of the Cupid and Psyche tale suggest that the wife's acquiescence to her husband's will is a precondition for the transformation of what would otherwise remain a

wild man, her violent act being the counterpart to his beastly form, and
both partners being humanized and, one way or another, subdued.

There may be no great satisfaction in differentiating Psyches who
have no spirit, who are, that is, passively obedient to male authority,
from those whose spirit must be broken to make them obedient. Paradoxically, however, the Psyche character may be equated with Eve,
mother of all female disobedience, in those very stories in which she
evidences the least initiative, almost as if the storyteller were unable to
portray a fully realized female character and could only project onto a
blank narrative canvas negative female stereotypes. Sometimes, however,
Psyche's active energy draws the storyteller's admiration. Calvino tells
the story of one who must remain loyal to her husband while he travels
around the world in the form of a tortoise in order to be released from
an evil spell. He leaves his wife a ring with magic properties, but either
its presence in the story is gratuitous, perhaps a remnant of another
version, or it is intended to emphasize that entirely on her own she meets
the challenges posed while he is away, for she never invokes its power.[117]
And frequently a beast's humanization is dependent on a woman's strength,
not her weakness. But even then, woman's strength constitutes a means,
not an end, her courage redounding to her husband's benefit and only
indirectly to her own, her happiness being experienced *through* him.
Most Cupid and Psyche tales, even those that portray Psyche in her most
favorable light, seem to make that assumption. This subject will be
returned to.

Distinctions can be drawn between wives who have full knowledge
concerning their mysterious husbands but may not disclose their secrets
to others, and those who must live in ignorance of their spouses' identities. The Scottish wife who bears three children to a mysterious husband
is finally wearied with her "way of living," and "at length ventured to
ask an old woman who frequented the castle, why her husband assumed
the appearance of a Brown Bull through the day, but came home a
handsome young man at night." The key words "why" and "ventured"
are consistent with the argument that Psyche takes a more active role in
her own story than other fairy tale heroines.[118] This woman is not
merely being curiously inquisitive, and her willingness to take risks in
order to have some control over her existence is highlighted by the
Grimm's story of "The Singing, Soaring Lark," in which her counterpart
marries a lion that turns into a handsome man. The two "lived happily

together, remained awake at night, and slept in the daytime."[119] To sleep in the daytime is effectively to isolate the sexual part of the relationship from all else, to shut out the world beyond the bedroom because it is the troubled realm in which the relationship will be tested. The woman married to the brown bull ventures outside the room she shares with a handsome young man, willing to confront reality by asking "why" her life is as it is. She similarly displays her strength of purpose when, on her search for her lost husband, she successfully obeys the prohibition against looking behind her at the crucial moment when her husband might be lost to her forever. This female Orpheus, so to speak, succeeds where her renowned male counterpart fails. But even here it may be difficult to find an outcome to Psyche's tale that leaves her with the independence she once evidences. Her ability *not* to look negates the question concerning her husband's secret, reverses her need to *know* what it has been denied to her to understand. More than most variants, this one highlights the paradox of the Cupid and Psyche type tale.

Psyche tales suggest that women should not expect happiness as their lot, a theme made explicit in an Egyptian version. A desolate princess who had broken a taboo and lost her husband cannot even muster enough spirit to embark on the journey to find him. Instead she tries to find out if there is another woman in the world as unhappy as she. The complaints she subsequently hears are paradigmatic. One woman's husband beat her, while another preferred another woman and, to make matters worse, her rival was old and ugly. A third woman's husband divorced her and the lover she took married another. Finally, an old poor woman tells her a tale so pitiful that the princess resolves to search for her own lost mate. When she finds him, he must be rescued from a spell, and the strength she displays in her determination to save him may be derived from her having unflinchingly confronted the common plight of her sex.[120] It is the unpleasantness in one wife's life, however, that suggests an essential deadlock in the Cupid and Psyche narrative pattern. In one serpent groom tale, the loathly groom cannot divest himself of his "venomed breath" whatever his wife does, and she is forbidden to inquire into his problem.[121] This husband is, of course, pathetic, but the inability to disenchant the animal may be closer to reality than some of the supposedly happier endings.

That women may suffer at the hands of the men on whom they are nonetheless dependent emerges as a theme from the Countess d'Aulnoy's working out of the Cupid and Psyche type tale in her story of "Gracieuse and Percinet." Abandoned by her father and victimized by her step-mother, Gracieuse distrusts Percinet and refuses shelter in his magic world, until one terrible mishap after another drives her to him, her final acceptance of her supernatural lover constituting as much a despairing admission of failure and dependency as it is an apology: " 'You are revenged for my hesitation, Percinet; but I feared you were of the same inconstant nature as other men, who change as soon as they are sure they are beloved.' " This didactic tale delivers a double message to any young woman inclined to forget that whatever her view of men, it is a man's world. Psyche's rebellion is specifically cited in another d'Aulnoy fairy tale, "The Green-Serpent" (discussed below), as a paradigm for the heroine's error, and Gracieuse is chided, asked what her fate would have been "if thy fond and faithful guard, / Thy Percinet, had not been ever there!" [122]

But in no group of Cupid and Psyche stories is the condition that the heroine lives under as starkly set out as in those that contain the already mentioned Patient Griselda motif. Even in this relatively benign Irish version, the wife's lot is a terrible one. Married to a dog, she is told by him that after their third child is born, he will be disenchanted and able permanently to retain his human form.

"But there is one condition; and it is a hard condition. If, during the years of enchantment, you shed a single tear, or make a single complaint, what you have done [by remaining strong up to that point] will be fruitless, and I shall be in my enemy's power more completely than ever." [123]

At least she is not *merely* being tested, as is Griselda in Chaucer's "The Clerk's Tale," where obedience is demanded for obedience's sake and the wife's relationship to her husband is symbolic of the human relation-ship to God. The Irish folktale reveals, nonetheless, that the man's self-actualization may be predicated on his wife's pain and deprivation. In contrast to Psyches who may not cry is one who cannot win her husband back until she fills a barrel with tears: [124] but the antithetical motifs are only two sides of the same coin.

The gains and the losses involved in Psyche's compliance with wom-an's role involve some of the most important themes in her story. Not only does Psyche fail to retain the independence symbolized by the broken taboo, since the reunion with her lost husband is ultimately dependent on her submission to his authority, but also coercion defines virtually all of her relationships, even those with the women whose support she should be able to count on. But in a male-dominated society, female bonding itself spells trouble: the women who support a wife in her rebellion are going to be the source of her trouble—or her husband's. In the *Rig Veda* Purūravas finds his vanished Urvaśī surrounded by her sister Apsaras. Her rejection of him is couched in language that perhaps significantly moves from the first person singular—"I am hard to catch and hold, like the wind"—to the third personal plural: there "are no friendships with women; they have the hearts of jackals." [125] In Apuleius, Psyche's sisters, driven by envy, convince her that she must be married to a monster, for why else would she be forbidden to see her husband; and thus they goad her to the forbidden act. In another version, concern for the bride provokes the same outcome: "her friends told her there must be something wrong with her husband, some great deformity that made him not want to be seen." [126] In one version, it is her sister, not Psyche, who performs the forbidden act and turns on the light. [127]

What Psyche's "sisters" do is attempt to raise her consciousness. Frivolous as the comparison may seem, Psyche being told that she is wed to a monster is not so different from modern women being encouraged to believe that their basic discontent results from marriage to male chauvinist pigs. [128] From the feminist point of view, women reaching out to other women to make them aware of their condition would be an example of female bonding; from another perspective (often but by no means exclusively male), such sisterly support is but coercive peer pressure. Even on this point, some Cupid and Psyche tales prove ambiguous: without some kind of group influence, Psyche might have remained submissive if not content; and without her latent discontent, group pressure probably would not have worked.

Contemporary women's groups have been open to the same objections leveled at other forms of group therapy: groups are often geared to collective aims rather than the personal goals of the person seeking guidance. The individual who resists the group may be subject to criticism and even abuse concerning a resistance or even silence maintained in the face of group pressure. [129] Similarly, some versions of the Cupid and Psyche tales focus on the pressure on the wife to reveal her secret. One from the Basque country tells how sarcasm is used to push a woman into disobeying her husband's prohibition that she not speak of him, the repetition in the story of "epousée" and "poussée" emphasizing her helplessness to live without either her husband's or her peers' coercion.[130] In a Tagalog story, a wife reveals her husband's name and rank only when mercilessly beaten by jealous older sisters,[131] and a Scottish wife discloses her secret when her sisters threaten to burn her.[132] The Algonquin wife of Katahdin, spirit of the mountain, makes the conventional visit home bound by the usual promise of secrecy concerning the identity of her husband. Her people (in this instance, not just women), however, are unable to "restrain themselves from talking to her on what they well knew she would fain be silent," forcing her to leave them.[133] The determination of the Algonquin woman not to reveal her husband's secret sets her apart from the others described above as capitulating to group pressure. But no less than they does she experience a push-pull situation, conflicted as she is by her desire for independence from as well as attachment to her culture. Perhaps the cosmic significance of her marriage to a nature deity suggests that she has already detached herself sufficiently from the mundane world to resist its coercion.

Equally afraid of the group that pushes her toward or pulls her away from her mate, Psyche frequently finds her entrance into marriage terrifying. A Romanian gypsy princess agrees to marry a snake because she is "afraid to say no,"[134] and in a similar story from modern Hungary, it is not clear whether the bride's shrieks when left alone with her serpent husband express terror or loathing. Only gradually does her outrage give way to her acceptance of the snake into her bed.[135] In an Armenian-American story, the serpent groom who could allay his wife's distaste as she passively submits to his embrace declines to do so: "The snake insisted on sleeping with his wife. He would lick her face until she was unconscious and fell asleep. When he was certain she was asleep, he would get out of bed, take off his snake skin and put it under the pillow."[136] In contrast, a Polynesian woman is allowed to get used to the unpleasant touch of an eel: "This occurred again and again," until she became accustomed to the eel, after which its form changed to that of a handsome youth.[137] A male narrator from Kentucky deems a bride on the whole fortunate because her frog husband performs the household tasks, but nonetheless sympathizes with her having in her bed "his warty old skin and his toad-frog eyes. Living with a man-sized toad-frog would give a girl the creeps, it seems to me."[138] The bride of the Cossack

"Serpent-Tsarevich" agrees to wed a serpent only if her dowry consists of twenty outfits of clothing that she puts on all at once. When her groom insists she remove these layers of clothes, she agrees to do so if he will do the same: he "cast off one of his skins, and she cast off one of her twenty suits of clothes."[139]

Such stories, of course, support Bettelheim's argument that the new bride must learn to undo the repression of sex, and the Cossack tale is perhaps more optimistic than some other versions about eventual compatibility. More frequently the stories indicate that all that is required of the wife, and all she can look forward to, is resignation and compliance in the marriage bed.[140] As earlier noted, a drugged bride is common in Cupid and Psyche tales. In a story from Mykonos, a sedated wife who is astonished to become pregnant empties her nightly draught into a hiding place and experiences an "awakening" into what might be viewed as both higher consciousness and sexual maturity. That she loses her husband after this audacity, however, suggests that some cultures do not encourage undoing the repression of sex—if that is what a wife's accustoming herself to the reptile's touch is about. The submissive wife is to be kept passive in all areas of life, and the merely acquiescent acceptance of the husband's embrace in a stupor is in some stories a desirable state of things.

The cruelty that many women associate with the initiation into their sexual lives is exemplified in the Danish ballad of "The Serpent Knight," in which the lady refuses an animal groom, hoping to escape him by merely agreeing to a kiss:

> The linen so white betwixt she placed,
> And the laidly worm she kissed in haste.
>
> With his tail of serpent up strook he,
> From beneath her dress the blood ran free.[141]

Having overcome her by force, he is transformed into a human and she marries him. How she really feels may be reflected in the vaginal serpent legends still popular among Mexican-American women in Texas. These are held to reflect a specifically female viewpoint that extends among those who hold it to their entire role in marriage and childbearing. The "animals enter the female reproductive system, where they may hatch a whole litter and mutilate or kill the woman, or (in one text) they may merely wiggle around in her vagina and drive her crazy."[142]

A tale that seems more explicitly than most to depict the cultural necessity (in contrast to some erotic necessity) for undoing the repression of sex comes from the Zuñi. A beautiful young woman possesses a "peculiarity of character," a "passion for neatness and cleanliness of person and clothing," and an inability to "endure the slightest speck or particle of dust or dirt." To maintain this physical purity, she defiles a sacred spring by obsessively washing herself. The serpent of the spring disguises himself as a child whom she takes into her room. That she accepts the child into her life at all seems to expand the themes of the story, since, in effect, she becomes a mother without her fastidiousness being subverted by sex or childbirth. But when the serpent reappears, she is forced to wed and move to the abode of the fearsome creature. During the journey he is transformed into a handsome man determined to control his bride. Whenever "she staggered with fear and weariness and was like to wander from the way, the Serpent gently pushed her onward and straightened her course." But then he asks gently if she is tired, and the voice, so changed, "thrilled her wonderfully with its kindness." [143]

Another form of defilement, of breaking religious, moral, and social codes, occurs when the woman in the animal groom tale is not fastidious enough—when, in effect, Psyche favors her serpent over the human groom into which it is transformed. That these two themes create a kind of counterpoint may be illustrated by the fact that just as the Danish ballad quoted above portrays the brutal defloration of the woman by the serpent, so another, "The Fight with the Worm," depicts the conflict that develops between a young woman and her people because she is too attached to hers. When the daughter of Sir Helsing receives a snake from a shepherd boy, she "cherish'd" it until it grew so foul and fierce that neither parent any longer had access to their daughter. [144] Again, the Eskimos tell of the girl who nurtures a growing snail in her bed, [145] and there are other examples of this motif—which was touched on in the previous chapter. According to Max Lüthi's analysis of animal groom tales, such stories might reflect an earlier, erotic form of the narrative that was transformed over time, weakened because "at the crucial moment, every time, the animal bridegroom turns into a young man," the folktale no longer understanding its own symbols. [146] His is a different view from that of Joseph Warren Beach, whose study of the animal bride and groom tales distinguishes between bestiality and true eroticism.

There are, in any event, Psyches who have no difficulty obeying fathers who have promised them to beasts, whose only fear is that they will be separated from their pets, even when disenchantment results in handsome human husbands. An Italian daughter tells her father "at once that snakes had always pleased her," and in a piece of explicit imagery, the serpent "shook his tail in token of great joy, and making his bride mount it, carried her away."[147] An Italian princess similarly asks her father to buy her a crab as a pet.[148] Ordinarily, however, the woman's pleasure in her animal is something to be distrusted and curbed. When a young African woman finds great joy with a strong lion, her kin destroy the beast.[149] Animals of various kinds represent for young women a call of the wild against which society often appears powerless. In an Arikara tale, a young woman must be tied down while her family contrives to kill the elk she wishes to mate with, after which she is confined until she recovers from her crazed desire.[150] The elk has much in common with the horse lover popular throughout the world. In stories from India and from Turkey, a man owns a horse that has a special affinity for one of his daughters. In the Indian story, the girl is not aware that it is in reality a horse that has sexual intercourse with her in human form,[151] but in the Turkish narrative, the bride's delights are linked to a rich fantasy life: in the daytime, she had a "horse for a husband and a stable for a dwelling. By night the stable was transformed into a rose-garden and the horse into a handsome youth."[152]

Where the story explicitly approves of the young woman's learning to repress her sexual desires, her mother—again—appears as herself and not in disguise (a witch). An African woman discovers that when she is away from home, her daughter visits a serpent. In order to put an end to the relationship with the beast, she deliberately frightens the girl by asking, "why do you amuse yourself with a serpent? It will kill you, my child." Convinced by her mother, the serpent's young mistress helps kill the beast. Similarly, the young woman in another African tale defies her mother's prohibition against marrying a leopard and claims that however much her parent protests, she will follow her own desires.[153] Like young women who defiantly invoke the presence of demon lovers, this one must learn to heed her female parent. The leopard proves a demon that the daughter barely escapes. But folktales also depict the dangers of too much repression. In a Caddo story, an "adolescent girl was lying alone. A rattlesnake came and lay with her." He warns her not to tell her family or friends about him, but she does, warning them, futilely, "If you kill the rattlesnake, I shall die. I am dying now."[154] From India comes the story of a girl who has a tree for a lover, her parents killing her when they destroy her mate.[155]

This struggle between nature and culture is dramatized in the bear husband stories widely told among North American tribes. In Bella Bella versions, a woman becomes the animal's mate after stepping on bear dung,[156] eventually escaping the animal in some versions, whereas in another, she merely pays the conventional visit home, reaffirming a commitment to her people and their values, but eventually returning to her animal spouse. In an Armenian-American version of the "Bear Husband," the reversion to nature, although an unwilling one, proves irreversible. A young woman is kidnapped and is forced to live with her beast (there is no romantic transformation to a handsome young man) until she escapes and he is killed. But the signs of her deviance are no less symbolic than Hester Prynne's scarlet letter: "Marian lost all her beauty and became black in color. Her clothing was reduced to rags, and heavy dark hair covered her entire body."[157] In a Mexican-American dog lover story, the family of the woman who gives birth to a litter of puppies "had to take the girl out and kill her because she was more animal than human by then."[158]

Animal groom stories may reflect human perversity and deviance rather than the beautiful process through which sexual repression is overcome so that love may flourish. Despite the argument that in early times shapeshifting was not "considered to be the essentially evil and unnatural thing that it afterwards became,"[159] it is perhaps *because* man and beast once lived in such close proximity, *because* the line between wildness and civilization can be so fragile, that the boundary between them had to be defended so vehemently, even if to do so meant allowing people occasionally to cross the line (see discussion of Duerr in previous chapter). In contrast, Jameson straightforwardly interprets both animal bride and animal groom tales in terms of human erotic fantasies; when the partner is a "shapeshifting male," the narrative reflects female fantasies "as widely distributed" as erotic male fantasies.[160] Animal groom stories frequently reveal how threatening it is to her people that Psyche prefers her beast lover to a human husband.

Not surprisingly, such tales introduce a female character familiar from demon lover tales: the woman whose amorous liaison with the devil follows from her rejection of ordinary suitors. In animal groom tales, a particularly angry family may abandon the rebel and leave her to fend for herself. What was previously noted about the necessity of Eskimo women to marry and add a provider to the family, extending its kinship ties,[161] is probably true of many peoples. From Angola comes the story of a maiden who mates with a strong and fierce lion, and who "would not permit men to court her," despite the number of suitors attracted by her beauty. "There came a time when the inhabitants of the region moved away to a far country. Her father and mother went with the other people, but they would not permit their daughter to go with them, saying to her, 'Since you will not agree to marry, we are leaving you here all by yourself.' "[162] Similarly, the Senecan tell of a woman who must be rescued from a great serpent. Beautiful but proud, she has spurned many young warriors and also turns a deaf ear to her imploring mother.[163] Comparably rescued is a young African girl who marries a monkey later killed by a human hunter. But like the young woman who cannot erase the visible signs of living with a bear, this one is tainted by her animal and disdained by the hunter (and implicitly other appropriate men): "She has been raped by a monkey and I want nothing to do with her."[164]

Young women who take animal mates are often believed to have resisted a proper upbringing. A story from Africa about a young woman who marries an owl depicts a petulant, spoiled "little girl who cried to have her way in everything" and too often got it. When another young woman in the same story leaves home after her family exhausts its patience with her, she must do penance by marrying a leper whose skin must be burned as the animal groom's skin must be in so many other versions.[165] That rebelliousness may be intrinsic to maturity but nonetheless needs to be suppressed is the theme of a Tahltan tale in which a young woman had just "finished the training that girls undergo at puberty." When a toad is transformed into a young man and proposes marriage, she does not realize he is an animal and accepts; in this story the animal groom is a demon to be overcome rather than disenchanted.[166] That disobedient girls are vulnerable to such deceptions is a theme in an African American story in which a young woman consistently rejects her parents' choice and gets a bearhog for a husband, a demonic animal "who had changed himself into a human being to go courting."[167] A generalized moral for these tales comes from an African monkey groom tale: when young women select husbands on their own, they "are the ones who initiate the matter—and trouble along with it." The narrator exhorts, "Friends, let no one spoil his child through over-indulgence."[168]

Often female rebelliousness is linked to sexual lasciviousness—although, as has already been noted, anthropologists report that when women are allowed more autonomy by their societies, their folklore depicts them as less lascivious and more likely to resist the advances of demon lovers than they are in narratives of people who restrict female independence.[169] Again, the correlation may not be exact: women might conceivably be granted independence by those whose stories nonetheless express male anxiety about gender roles. In any event, in a Jicarilla Apache tale, a rejected suitor becomes curious about a woman's attachment to her pet dogs, follows her, and kills her as well as the "dog while it was still on her in the position of sexual intercourse," later summoning her relatives, who weep for shame.[170] Less explicit bestiality is found in a Salishan version in which a young woman stays away from home with a handsome man for several days. When she returns, she takes him back as her pet dog. When her parents hear them laughing together in bed, their suspicions are aroused and they kill the dog.[171] An Eskimo parent threatens to wed his daughter to a dog if she continues to turn away suitors, and she "warned him that if he said this often she might take him at his word."[172] Similarly, another unmarried girl responds to her father's taunt that perhaps she would prefer to marry a dog by replying that she would. When she finally accepts a man who does attract her, she discovers that he is, indeed, a dog, much as women who heedlessly say they will marry the devil find themselves his bride.[173]

The Coast Salish are among those who depict the dog as a trickster who pits his cunning against a woman whose very resourcefulness sets her apart from other women, and, as was seen in the previous chapter, marks her as a likely target for demons: she is "always out digging material for baskets that she could sell, or picking berries."[174] Such women do indeed appear superior to the human suitors they spurn, although the stories make clear that whatever their special qualities, they must defer to the customs of patriarchal tribes. Sometimes, however, the admixture of the dog husband with the Cupid and Psyche type tale softens the portrait of the rebellious woman. The Quinault tell of a young girl who was very fond of her dog and allowed it to sleep at the foot of her bed.

Every night he would change into human form and lie with the girl, and in the morning, before it was light, would turn back again into his dog shape: so no one knew anything about it. After a time she became pregnant; and when her parents found it out and knew that the dog was the cause they were greatly ashamed, and calling the people together they tore down the house, put out all the fires, and moved away from the place, leaving the girl to die.[175]

Such folklore characters often seem less rebellious than emotionally troubled, ignorance of their lover's real identity being a projection of inner confusion. The Thompson are one of the native tribes that tells how a woman marks her lover with paint or creates some other notable sign when he lies in her embrace (much as Japanese Psyches attach a thread to their serpent bridegrooms), and when she discovers that he is a dog, is "overcome with shame," in one instance going home and refusing to "talk or eat."[176] In a Blackfoot version, a "very nice girl" inadvertently makes an unwise wish, declaring aloud to a dog she fancies, " 'I wish you were a young man, then I would marry you.' " When her ill-fated wish comes true, he reminds her, " 'Well, it was your fault, you wished it,' "[177] a dialogue that suggests some insight into unconscious desires. In general, the dog lover tales are studies in forbidden impulses (or warnings *against* exogamous relationships), and this one shows how dangerous it can be to undo the repression of sex. Frequently the family whose daughter mates with a dog leaves her;[178] in one instance, a mother deprives her daughter of food and snatches back the marriage robe she passed on to the young woman, withdrawing not only sustenance but also the emotional support of a secure heritage.[179]

Lasciviousness is usually the reason for taking a serpent lover, the woman's sexuality constituting an expression of unrestrained nature. In one Eskimo version, the symbolism is bypassed altogether when a woman summons not a serpent or water monster but a disembodied phallus from a lake.[180] When an Algonquin woman lies down to sleep, she sees upon awakening a "great serpent, with glittering eyes, crawl from the water, and stealthily approach her. She had no power to resist his embrace." Later the evil power that has possessed her is exorcised as, one after another, the serpent children to whom she gives birth are murdered. The need to purge such evil is the point of another Algonquin story about a woman who has caused the death of five husbands in a single year. The sixth husband discovers she has a serpent lover who injects her with poisons she then transfers to her unwitting spouses. But her final spouse refrains from sharing her bed the night he witnesses her coupling with the snake, and, unable to rid herself of the deadly venom, she dies.[181]

A clergyman who had collected tales of serpent lovers from the Canadian Carrier, and who focuses on the phallic significance of the snake as animal lover, notes that this folktale group reenacts the "fall of the first woman," Eve. Few myths, he writes, "have been more generally diffused than that of the woman and the serpent. It is well nigh impossible that such a notion be not founded on fact, nay, on a fact with momentous consequences, since it has left its impress on peoples so utterly devoid of all kinds of literature as the American aborigines. Woman, serpent, and guilt—always of a lascivious character—are the three points which seem inseparably connected."[182] It is difficult to decide whether it is his attitude toward women or toward the natives he collected from that is more condescending, but it cannot be denied that he has caught what is frequently the import of the serpent lover tales.

Sometimes these stories have less to do with morality than the more straightforward concern that the aberrant woman will fail to perform household tasks. The Salish, who substitute a stallion lover for a serpent, relate how a woman "grew careless of her household duties" because she "always wanted to look after the horses."[183] An Eskimo husband similarly notices that his wife gathers very little heather and follows her to her bizarre rendezvous with a beast.[184] And the husband in a Tahltan story notices that his "wife was always sick and could do little work, and that she only brings him little firewood for the family's use."[185] In Ojibwa and Blackfoot versions, the tardiness in bringing home the wood rather than the meager quantity of it arouses the man's suspicions.[186] In these instances the husband is portrayed as fulfilling his role by hunting, whereas the fires on which the game is to be roasted are neglected by his spouse, a female malingerer.

Blatant self-interest rather than neglect leads a Menomini wife to subvert her husband's ability to provide for his family:

A couple lived together in the forest with their two children, a boy and a girl. The man lived by hunting, and, like all hunters he never touched the dandruff scales from a woman's head. One day, however, his wife was careless, and she scattered her dandruff so that it fell upon him and broke his luck as a hunter.

... The woman had done this purposely, in order to kill her husband and so be free to marry a he-bear with whom she was enamoured.[187]

That a dutiful husband can be victimized by an oversexed wife is also the point of a Carrier tale in which, again, the man tries to observe societal taboos—"He always slept away from [his woman] when he was preparing his traps, and he observed faithfully all the ancient prescriptions"—but the woman undermines his efforts in order to consort with an animal. His abstinence contrasts with her lack of control: "Each time that he returned home from a visit to his traps he found his wife with her face painted and her hair carefully combed."[188]

Just how dangerous to their families such wives are is emphasized when the woman's failures at home are focused on her children: indeed, in an Algonquin tale, a woman's very childlessness despite the "passionate" nature that leads her to a serpent lover indicates her deficiency in woman's most basic function.[189] But where children do exist, they may be the victims of their mother's aberrant nature. The children in a Saulteaux story cry all day while their mother enjoys her paramour.[190] Among the Senecan, the woman's mating with a bear is deemed the cause of her son's being puny and sickly.[191] In another Saulteaux version, a man who kills a good many deer comes home to "find his children had been crying all day." His wife lies, ironically—perhaps deliberately so—linking their offspring's unhappiness to her traditional role: " 'When I leave them in the tend while I go to get firewood, they always start to cry.' " But he does not believe her and eventually discovers her animal lover.[192] The children's gender may extend the narrators' distinction between victimized males and female victimizer. The son may objectify the betrayal of the father. The Senecan husband who discovers his wife with her lover, says, "now I know why you abuse our boy."[193] In an Ojibwa tale, a son actually brings about his mother's downfall. He is curious about why, each day, she dons fine clothing as his father leaves the house, only to remove them again just before the latter returns. The boy alerts his father to this odd behavior and the tale takes its usual course.[194]

The female perspective is noticeably absent in stories about how a wife and mother betrays her family for an animal mate; her actions are apparently presumed to speak for themselves. Sometimes when she is given her lover's flesh to eat by her angry husband, she assumes the animal form that symbolizes what she has been all along. In a Caddo version, the husband recognizes his wife when he comes across a serpent but passes on and does not acknowledge her.[195] In other animal groom stories, defiant women who spurn ordinary lovers are at least given their say about what it is they reject in their ordinary lives. But these tales focus on how the woman's animal nature (symbolized by her lust for a beast) devastates her family and people. This theme is further emphasized when the Indian serpent lover tale is prologue to another widely distributed story pattern: the angry husband decapitates his wife, whose disembodied, rolling head pursues their children, who must flee the vengeful mother.[196] Whatever the moral intent of the storytellers, there are few stories that depict so emphatically the female rage accompanying a woman's need to undergo more and more repression of her own needs in order to fulfill her function in the family and the tribe. Thus few stories reveal so pointedly her rejection of her role as a bastion of culture, civilizer of the male animal.

The benefits and losses experienced by the man, the woman, and the couple itself when the animal husband is disenchanted and becomes a human being form muted but significant themes in Cupid and Psyche tales. The beast husband freed from his nonhuman form assumes with pride the status that men enjoy in patriarchal societies. Often he inherits a kingdom he can now rule unimpeded by the deficiencies implied by his animal form. True, he relinquishes his exclusive tie to nature, that is, freedom to satisfy basic drives unconstrained by society's requirements, but the stories say he has won more than he has lost. (In enchanted animal bride tales, as will be seen in chapter 6, women appear to lose status when they are humanized.) Similarly, for the Psyche character to play her role as the one who civilizes the beast, she must accept that which in one way or another and to one degree or another she had earlier rejected. She must finally acquiesce to a role that she has had little say in defining. Yet, ironically, passivity is not necessarily a virtue in her, and a too-easy submission to the influence of others, as was seen, often endangers her husband as effectively as her own rebellion might. In short, many Cupid and Psyche tales indicate that a woman must experience not mere acquiescence to her place in society, but rather a full and conscious acceptance of that place and a full realization of what is required of her (as well as what is offered her).

From the conflict between wildness and civilization thematically rendered in animal mate stories emerge complex and often paradoxical themes. People who live close to nature and thus more closely associate animal lives with their own may be less inclined to distinguish reality from fantasy. Bestiality, as Ernest Jones has argued, may reflect "a maiden's dream of being pursued or attacked by rough animals," the unconscious releasing during sleep of impulses she has been taught to repress. Since animals "therefore lead themselves to the indirect representation of crude and unbridled wishes," the disenchantment of the beast husband also speaks to the disenchanter's subduing of her own basic drives.[197] But the rationalization of the animal-human mating, the transformation of the beast into the prince, for example, is a sign of how distanced societies have become from basic human instincts—to cite Lüthi again, the story has forgotten its own symbols. The suppression of Psyche thus becomes a cultural precondition for the eventual socialization of man—which has been made her duty. It is interesting to consider the argument that "human males, not the females themselves, are the ones who imagine that females are frequently involved in sexual contacts with animals of other species."[198] Man would thus impute to woman his own fantasies, and then would expect woman to relinquish them so that he might also.

In his study of the wild man figure (Beauty's beast looking somewhat more human than animal) in medieval literature, Richard Bernheimer takes up a ritual game in which "instead of being hunted and buffeted about by men, the wild man was found by little schoolgirls got up in their prettiest dresses, who tied a red ribbon upon him and brought him captive to the village."[199] In the image of these young maidens can be found the ambiguities and ironies that result from charging women with the task of disenchanting the beast to whom they may feel powerfully drawn. On the one hand, imputations to women of bestial impulses perpetuates male notions of inherent feminine evil; but on the other, denying women their physical drives and resultant fantasies effectively denies them as well some essential participation in a nature-culture conflict and reduces them to innocent schoolgirls—with potentially disastrous results. For then they must play the part into which they have been cast. Equally problematic is Neumann's Archetypal Feminine, a goddess who takes "human form" to rule "among and over the animal powers." According to Neumann, it is precisely because "man is a creature of instinct living in the image of the beast or half-beast," dominated by "the drives of the unconscious," that he requires a female figure who "is an embodiment of all those psychic structures that are superior to instinct," that is, in short, "culture bearing."[200] Animal groom stories frequently reveal a storyteller's full awareness of the paradoxes involved in charging the same being responsible for the fall of man with his redemption. Women are being asked to do what it is either impossible or too costly for them to do, and then, because they have difficulties fulfilling their roles, they are frequently accused of being the source of human problems.

In his *Facetious Nights,* Straparola begins an animal groom tale by praising God for creating man as more than a mere animal, and by addressing the female audience to whom the story "of one who was born as a pig, but afterwards became a comely youth" appears to be addressed. The tale depicts a devoted and nurturing mother who nonetheless indulges and spoils her pig son. Still, she remains a model for the woman who will eventually civilize (disenchant) him. When the pigling grows up and begins to talk like a human being and explore his environment, he remains attracted to mud and dirt, which "he would always wallow in" after the "manner of pigs," returning to his parents covered with filth. That his eventual wife is to emulate his mother is indicated when he murders his first two brides because they do not respond tenderly to him, driving his sharp hooves into their breasts. A third wife turns to her mother-in-law for advice, and the alliance between the two assures the further emotional nourishment of the man for whom a woman's breast is so crucial an emblem. Most stories, of course, are not so obvious in theme and symbol; Straparola's, however, supplies a gloss on the folklore that stands behind his literary rendering of the animal groom story.[201]

To tame a man is, of course, to domesticate him. A Turkish dragon prince devours bride after bride until one who can appease him appears.[202] A Tortoise Prince in the *Dravidian Nights* takes human form at night to visit his divine mistress, but assumes his beast shape as he returns in the morning to his wife. The destruction of his animal shell is necessary to cement the domestic relationship that reflects his role in the larger culture.[203] In a French beauty and the beast story, the animal form is the explicitly external sign of a flawed character. As the reformed beast admits, "All I could think of was revelry and battles; nothing did I know of pity and charity. Beggars disgusted me, with their rags and their sores. One day, when I mocked at a poor man who asked for bread at the door, I beheld myself changed into a Beast."[204] Belle-Rose, as her name implies, will change her husband from an insensitive, aggressive man to one whose transformation will supposedly redound to her benefit, bearing out the motto appended to a Chinese animal groom tale: "wise and dutiful devotion may change a beast into a man."[205] But a Turkish version suggests that the symbolic metamorphosis never is and perhaps never should be complete, that some kind of original sin can never be overcome even by the most devoted woman—or that in a complex symbiotic fashion, the couple's relationship demands the perpetuation of their roles as fallen man and redeeming woman. When the Psyche character follows a black cat to the otherworld, she witnesses his transfiguration into a handsome youth. But the "girl saw that on one of his cheeks was a beauty spot as black as coal. There and then love entered her heart for this strange and handsome youth."[206]

Historically, women's status was supposed to be enhanced when her civilizing influence was recognized. Her personal happiness, then, was won not through the gratification of her own drives, but through the sacrifice of immediate pleasure for her own and her culture's long-range goals. If she plays her part as nurturer, or so many animal groom stories make clear, she will win at the end a devoted and passionate lover-husband instead of a beast. Psyche's story seems to illustrate the process that all of womankind is to undergo, and the human who emerges from the animal skin of her beast reveals the triumph of civilization.

At the end of the nineteenth century, Ralston ironically—and seemingly inadvertently—pointed out the price woman would have to pay to humanize her mate. When the animal skin is destroyed, writes Ralston, the beast does not merely disappear, but he "loses his transforming character and settles down into an *ordinary* husband."[207] That the woman may end up with less than had attracted her to begin with is implied in a Bantu story of a "Girl Who Loved Danger." The heroine insists, contrary to good sense and contrary to any idea of romantic love, that she will mate with Snake-Man. She courts danger and the excitement that accompanies it; nonetheless she remains the usual instrument through which the beast is released from an evil spell—"now that a maiden is willing to wed with me, I can break the witchcraft and reveal myself to my father."[208] Moreover, the serpent's transformation restores to his mother-in-law the honor lost when her daughter proved so headstrong. Gender roles are defined emphatically in this version. But whether the daring wife is content with what Ralston would call her ordinary husband, when it was a dangerous animal she had sought, is a question raised but not answered by this African animal groom tale.

For to civilize a man is not only to domesticate him but sometimes to dominate and manipulate him as well. And thus the struggle for the man's redemption becomes another element in the power struggle between man and wife. A comparison of two tales with a common motif can illustrate the point. In a Kalmouk tale, a wife burns a bird cage whose importance she does not understand until after her mistake. Because the cage had housed her husband's soul and protected him from demons, he is placed by her in great jeopardy. Once again has Eve eaten the apple and Pandora opened the box. In penance the wife "went back home, and built a cage like to the one that was burned, and wooed the soul of her husband back into it; and thus was her husband delivered from the power of the gods and daemons, and came back to her to live with her always."[209] And yet the rebuilt cage seems to imprison him while keeping her out, some features of the story paralleling Ibsen's treatment of Nora's doll house.

In an Armenian-American tale, a wife similarly attempts to control her own life when she asks her mother-in-law for help in destroying her husband's animal skin. Unlike the pair in Straparola's story, the two generations of women seem allied with each other *against* the animal man. And so it is consistent that the husband's rebuke be directed against his mother, the older and seemingly more powerful of the two women: " 'Mother, you waited this long, couldn't you have waited three more months? When my child was born, I would have burned my snake skin voluntarily.' But how were they to know what his plans had been?"[210] The narrator of this story is a woman, and her concluding question appears to highlight woman's helplessness, although it also sounds like a whining excuse. She justifies her sex's attempt to manipulate events whenever the opportunity arises, but the story points to the usual debacle caused by female meddling. In this version, however, the husband appears in a very poor light. His protest is reduced from the ominous threat issued by animal grooms found in other variants to the whimper of the still-dependent child, one whose domestication has been, if anything, too complete, Ralston's ordinary husband reduced to his most wimpish form, or James Harris, the demon lover, rendered not only average but almost contemptible.

As an instrument of grace, Psyche supposedly enjoys the secondary gains that result from her beast husband's liberation: his improved ethical behavior and a tenderness that she otherwise would not receive from him. But again, the Cupid and Psyche tales ordinarily focus on how the heroine must subordinate herself to her husband in order to achieve his immediate and her ultimate good. And so if there is one theme that reverberates through these tales, it is that of *acceptance,* as the heroine proves to be either appropriately obedient or reverses the act of disobedience that separates her from her husband. Romantic love, then, as was suggested earlier, seems but an invention to encourage woman to play her traditional role. A South African bride is urged by another woman not to fear her serpent bridegroom, for she will come to experience his affection if she will submit. As the snake embraces her, "he put his head just at her heart, the woman being perfectly quiet all the while." [211] Without fantasies of love, often represented by supernatural lovers, it might be difficult to make women into wives and mothers. A Zuñi frog lover story tells how a young woman enters into an alliance with a Kachina man, who eventually leaves her, instructing her to marry and treat her husband well: "I cannot stay with you for life because I belong to other people"; only after death can they be reunited in Kachina Village (the otherworld). Thus when a Zuñi woman dies and goes to the Kachinas, "she always lives with her first husband."

The Zuñi, explains Ruth Benedict, believe that it is the function of the supernaturals "to keep people from making mistakes, and one of the most likely of these mistakes is that of reluctance in regard to cohabitation." [212] The tale of the woman who marries a Kachina suggests that if romantic love is more important to woman than man, it is not because women belong to the more sentimental sex but because in an unequal relationship, woman gives up more than man in her adaptation to society (especially if she has left her own people to live with her husband's). She requires the kind of inducement that the supernatural folk offer—a love that ordinary husbands rarely offer or abandon too soon after courtship. The Cupid and Psyche type tale also belongs to those in which a former love retains its hold on the woman, the return of, or to, a demon lover bringing into sharp contrast wish fulfillment and the cultural necessity represented by a human husband. As has been said of Madame de Beaumont's "Beauty and the Beast," when Beauty "accepts at the end of the story, the marriage she rejected for so long, she still looks for her dear Beast, which she does not recognize in the handsome Prince that took its place." But the happy outcome reflects reality: "one senses here a tendency to give up childish wishes on the part of the young woman, a ready acceptance of a reality considerably more satisfying than her dreams. In short, the girl had matured in a triumphant acceptance of reality and [of] the Beast as sex and part of adult existence."[213]

This restatement of the psychological interpretation of animal groom tales begs the question of what the story heroine has *given up* for this acceptance of reality when she learns to prefer the prince to the beast. The generally human development of the individual bypasses any gender-specific meaning. It is possible to distinguish between those Psyches who wed the beast in obedience to a parents'—usually a father's—command, and those who precipitate the crisis themselves by asking for something the father can get only at the price of handing his daughter over to a beast. A further differentiation can be made. There are those young women who request a modest gift, often a flower, the humble request like docile obedience indicating that in asking for so little, they have already reconciled themselves to a humble life and will ask for as little from their husbands as they have from their fathers. Such women are unlikely to prefer the beast to the handsome youth. But there are also those daughters, such as the one in an Iraqi tale, who asks for "Clusters-of-pearls," not jewels but the name of her fantasy lover.[214] That she does not require costly material possessions is in her favor; nonetheless, the juxtaposition in the imagery of wealth, fantasy, and demon lover invokes the ambiguous motives of the runaway wife in the Child ballad.

What the young woman asks for, the way the storyteller interprets her request, and the way that cultures view the fantasy element in Psyche's desires help illuminate the degrees of loss and gain she is perceived to experience when she and her husband unite to live their mundane existence. In a French tale, the request for a rose is made in such an imperious fashion—"Oui, mon père, c'est cette rose que je veux; ne reviens pas sans l'avoir"—that it is hardly a surprise that the beast dies, leaving the woman unhappy the rest of her life.[215] One who treats her father with such disrespect, who is so self-absorbed, is hardly the kind necessary to transform and preserve the beast. A similar theme can be found in a story that infuses a Pygmalion motif into the Cupid and Psyche narrative: a young woman fashions a dream lover out of jewels, sugar, almonds, and other delicacies, because no suitor her exasperated father finds will suit her.[216] In such an instance, it is the rebellious woman who is the beast: "like some feminine ape [she] hated the idea of a tail; like enclosed land reserved for shooting, she resented the approach of any man." Her father's misery is expressed in metaphors of the space that ordinarily defines his world, but that she has appropriated for her own.[217]

As seen earlier, blame for such behavior is often laid at the feet of permissive parents who are stuck with what they themselves have created. The "proud and presumptuous" Maliane of a Basotho tale is indulged by a father who allows her to spurn her people: "She never ate with the other people out of the communal dish, but always received her food separately. She never did any work, other people had to wait on her, and, when she was rude and impertinent, her father only laughed." Not only does Beauty not tame the beast, but her serpent husband takes over what should have been the father's role: it "beat her with the tail as a real man beats his wife with his stick. She ran and he followed her. She ran and he beat her with his tail."[218] The tale's imagery links female submission to male sexuality with a concomitant capitulation to male authority.

The earlier-mentioned Bantu story of "The Girl Who Loved Danger" combines swan maiden and animal groom narrative patterns to portray a woman's conflict with male authority and her failure to be appropriately womanly. When some bathing girls find their clothing stolen by a monster, most of them retrieve their garments through supplication, but the willful heroine, "different from all the other girls of the tribe," will not resort to such subservience. She "was bold as a boy, and ever off on some new jaunt. And the more peril she met, the better she was pleased. Her father saw that the spirit of some warrior ancestor had, by a strange mistake, taken his abode in this girl." Later, and still defiant, she marries Snake-Man, whose transformation to a human man coincides with her final acceptance of woman's place.[219] In a similar African story, a monster borrows snakeskins to appear more attractive to a woman whose preference for a beast husband is a corollary to her insistence on choosing a husband for herself. Interestingly, this story is narrated by a male member of Limba society, described as one in which women enjoy considerable autonomy.[220] If so, the story's narrator, who depicts the final capitulation of the independent woman to her husband, advocates limitations to such freedom. The breaking down of woman's resistance to male-dominated culture becomes in another African tale part of a ritual not unlike the deflowering of the new wife. A serpent is told by a girl's tribe that "she is your wife. If you can catch her, she will go with you." Thus begins the chase that the heroine must lose if she is to win: "It is according to the customs of our ancestors for the girl to run away and for the man to bring her back."[221]

Beauty's obedience to her father, then, has far-reaching implications in animal groom stories, and it is difficult to find that at the end of the tale Psyche is enjoying some rightfully earned autonomy, that, as Kolbenschlag has claimed, she is one of the few heroines of fairy tales who has reached maturity before the tale begins, that both the princess and the frog are destined to be changed. At first, "the princess obeys her father, but her anger and outrage intensify, finally liberating her personality from the father-image (superego) in an act of self-assertion." Noting that every language and culture has its version of "Beauty and the Beast," Kolbenschlag manages to evade the paradoxes of its variations and problematic endings by a leap (like Neumann's) into gender-free and pure abstraction: more than any other tale, this one "celebrates self-knowledge and self-transcendence."[222] Attractive as this view may be, an analysis of the heroine's self-transcendence through a sampling of animal groom tales reveals that the higher good served is society's, that the heroine of animal groom tales plays her part by elevating man above the level of beast, and that this is a feat usually achieved when she accepts her place as subservient to him, properly "womanly" as her people define that attribute.

The point may best be made by recalling those stories in which Psyche is irrevocably separated from her mate or in which the customary disenchantment of the beast does not take place. Sometimes an animal skin is prematurely or impetuously burned; at other times a secret whose disclosure is unwisely demanded leaves the heroine eternally bereft and her animal mate forever trapped in his beast form. A Chinese story describes what may happen when the heroine asserts herself too much, her husband retreating further the more she proclaims her selfhood. In it, a woman gives birth to a conch:

When he grew older, he would come out of his shell, as does a snail, but would withdraw into it again quickly when tired or frightened. After he attained the size of a man, he would frequently emerge from and sit upon his shell, but would never wholly depart from it.

When he marries, his bride follows the advice of his grandmother and hides the shell. "As the bridegroom could neither find his shell or account for its absence, he lived without it, and appeared like other people." But when he regains his protective covering, he crawls away to sea, "from which he never returned." This tale appears to be a swan maiden story in reverse, the timid bridegroom taking over the role of captured bride, escaping from his spouse as soon as his magic "garment" is recovered.[223] This animal groom is perhaps not animal enough, and his final transformation may have demanded more of the forcefulness associated with the animal lover than he was capable of. But the basic point of the story seems to be the same one found in other animal groom tales. To be more of a man, to be a man at all, is a goal thwarted, not aided, by the women in his life. It is not always the case—perhaps it is rarely the case—that when Beauty is more her*self*, the beast becomes a man. His humanization too often demands that her selfhood be modified on his behalf.

Do animal groom stories indicate that Psyche must always *lose* in order to win? Certainly enough of them do to require some amendment on the part of feminist critics who find in Tale Type 425 the active heroine lacking in most classic Western fairy tales. But there are also animal groom tales in which some mutual need unites the married pair, some accommodation by both woman and man allowing the marriage to exist. There are, for example, stories in which the animal's skin is destroyed and the human bridegroom, instead of being angry and disappearing, requiring that his penitent wife undertake an arduous journey to win him back, expresses gratitude for his deliverance. In a Philippine monkey groom story, a "princess of unspeakable beauty" is shut away in a castle "so that no one might discover her existence." She effects the transformation of her animal groom and he rescues her.[224] Similar reciprocity is to be found in the *Dravidian Nights*. A prince learns the art of shapeshifting from a master who becomes his enemy. In the form of a parrot, the prince hides in a princess's room, where he becomes her pet and her nightly lover. She remains awake one night and discovers that pet and lover are one. Together they outwit the evil master and marry.[225] Similarly, a version of the popular Japanese Tom Thumb stories (which resemble animal groom tales) depicts how the diminutive hero rescues a princess from "*Oni*, one of the evil spirits that appears in the form of animals and toads." To repay him, she uses a magic wish that she has been granted to make him as tall as ordinary men.[226] The Irish tell similar tales. In one can be found a mutual disenchantment: a king's daughter suffers from a spell whereby she may not be seen by any man except her father unless she is wearing a veil (curiously, the story says she may not gaze on any man's face without her face being covered). To be free, she must marry a prince. She has a vision of her redeemer, a speckled bull who with alacrity agrees to marry the enchanted maiden: " 'I will, and welcome!' said he. 'But the way I am, I won't be of much use to her or to any other woman.' "[227] In helping him shed his beast form, the princess serves her interests as well as his. Even the disobedience of another Irish Psyche appears in a positive light, for only when the young woman defies her father's injunction that she not open a locked room can she disenchant a hound she, too, had seen in a vision.[228]

A Spanish animal lover strikes a bargain with his bride. He believes men are deceived before marriage by the fair exterior of women, only to find themselves married to a figurative if not literal beast. Accepting the toad's premise that exterior appearances mean little, a young woman is persuaded to marry him. He is transformed into a handsome youth, and she retains her earlier identity (that is, remains fair). The story is optimistic insofar as the bride is promised by her animal husband that if she does her part and subdues woman's basically deceitful and shrewish nature, he will prove less a beast than a bride may expect her husband to be.[229] Marriage is in this way rendered a bargain, in which the marriage ceremony is an implicit pledge that both partners will attempt to obliterate their least pleasant qualities for the sake of the other.

In the eighteenth century, the Countess D'Aulnoy incorporated the Cupid and Psyche story into her own fairy tale of "The Green-Serpent." Her heroine, Laidronette, is cursed with excessive ugliness. Nevertheless she is beloved by a serpent from whom she cannot help but shrink. In his palace she is treated with love and luxury, so that she begins to fancy she is less disagreeable to look at. She consents to marry an invisible lover who visits her only at night, and promises not to try to see him until the final two years of a seven-year spell have ended. He gives her the story of Psyche to read as a warning against trying to hasten the period during which he must remain unknown.

The weakness 'tis of womankind
  Witness the first created;
From whom Pandora was design'd,
  And Psyche imitated.

Each, spite of warning, on the same
  Forbidden quest intent,
Of her own misery became
  The fatal instrument.

Psyche's example fail'd to save
  Poor Laidronette from erring;
Like warning she was led to brave,
  Like punishment incurring.[230]

Laidronette's mother and sisters believe that the happy ending of the Cupid and Psyche tale misleads her, and they precipitate the ensuing crisis. The Countess d'Aulnoy's story infers that Laidronette cannot learn from Psyche's lesson, that she must *experience* Psyche's disobedience and Psyche's final enlightenment, although it would have been better if Psyche's tale had done its didactic work. At one stroke in this story, then, d'Aulnoy confirms that woman's best interest rests on submission to male authority, but, ironically, has negated the rhetorical value of the story group on which her own tale rests.

Yet the treatment of the Cupid and Psyche tale in "The Green-Serpent" points up the tensions inherent in the tale, tensions that help explain the interaction of fairy bride and fairy groom tales. The swan maiden who returns to her demon lover in the otherworld, and the mortal woman who humanizes hers so that they may live in society, illuminate woman's problematic role in society, one tale portraying fantasies of escape, the other accommodation to woman's traditionally defined role. Whatever optimism exists in the story, however, is canceled when the folklore behind Cupid and Psyche stories is transformed into demonology, as in the incubus type tales to be explored in the next chapter.

# CHAPTER 5

# Swan Maiden and Incubus

The Gandharvas who reclaim Urvaśī for the divine world are depicted as variable beings. They are musicians to the court of Indra; they are associated with love matches in which brides choose their husbands. But they are also the mythical wild men of Hindu mythology,[1] a race that haunts the "air, the mountains, the forests," with the power to cause illusions and even madness. The carefree existence reflected in their "free sexuality and their love of wine, women and song"[2] appears more ominous when their powers as voluptuaries are associated with the kinds of erotic dreams not easily distinguished from nightmares. They are, that is, the Hindu incubi.[3]

The incubus appears in two folklore patterns that sometimes remain separate and at other times are combined.[4] "Incubus" may refer to a loathsome hag or animal that emanates a suffocating influence on a dreamer, who awakens to experience difficulty in breathing.[5] "Incubus" may also denote the nightmare itself. And "incubus" is also a term for the lascivious demon imagined to visit young women in their sleep in order to have sexual relations with them (the demon can also appear to men as a succubus). The intermingling and even seeming confusion of these beliefs informs and transforms many swan maiden and demon lover tales.[6]

The ease with which popular folklore may be transformed into demonology is illustrated by a Renaissance account of how a pregnant woman confesses to her parents that her lover is "a handsome youth who would mysteriously appear in her room, go to bed with her, and then vanish." The parents spy on the pair and break down the door to find "her in the embrace of a hideous monster." When the Gospel of Saint John is read, the demon disappears. The girl had apparently been under a spell and has seen not a demon but a handsome lover who "would most appeal to her sense of beauty and most arouse her desire."[7] Hungarian folklore depicts similarly suspicious parents who wonder why their daughter is getting progressively thinner, going about with a "sort of dizzy look." She is visited by a "vampire-like creature" that, like the incubus, can appear as either sex. The demon can also appear as a revenant, overcoming its "victims by taking on the guise of an absent or dead lover."[8]

From the demonologist's perspective, supernatural lovers demonstrate a human readiness to enter into relationships with devils, and in the demonologist's hands, familiar themes shift decisively toward pathology. As G. L. Kittredge has noted, incubus lore involves the Cupid and Psyche tale fallen upon evil days.[9] Thus a narrative ordinarily favored by women commands the obsessive interest of men, often clerics, gripped by a fear of feminine evil, sometimes forcing women under torture and threat of death to reveal their secret fantasies as if they were acts really performed in the service of the devil. Animal grooms are no longer enchanted princes but are instead were-animals or the familiars of witches, those lesser demons attached to women who have entered into unholy pacts. Incubi themselves, according to some beliefs, are fallen angels, and the ambivalence bound to result from such a conception is reflected in a deadly war between flesh and spirit. Finally, the swan maiden appears not as the timid fairy who flees her captor, but as a nightmare demon who torments as well as escapes her human lover. Woman herself is perceived as inherently demonic, eager to enter into unholy alliances.

The swan maiden's readiness to desert her family thus has less to do with a flight from mundane reality than a morbid antipathy toward woman's most sacred role. She is sister to the succubus Lilith, who not only entices men to their doom but also devours other women's children or substitutes changelings for human babies spirited away by the other-world. In some parts of Scandinavia, female nightmare spirits and were-animals are specifically associated with the pains of childbirth, confirming the biblical premise that as a result of the fall, motherhood was doomed to begin with woman's agony—a seemingly fitting punishment for the being who initially tempted man to evil. Demon children, in turn, play a role in tales that speaks to a hatred of parenting that has reached virulence. The stories recounted in this chapter will be familiar from previous chapters, but the atmosphere that surrounds them will reveal that the fears arising from conflicts discussed earlier have escalated into terror.

According to some folklore, the swan maiden is herself the nightmare, a human being, frequently one whose love has been slighted, and who as nightmare demon is enabled to approach the beloved object.[10] The "mara" slips through the keyhole, or any other aperture in a building, and sometimes presses its victim to death.[11] But it can be caught by closing up the opening through which it has entered. One "mar-wife" story tells how a young man tries to catch the demon who is tormenting him, enlisting the aid of a friend, who witnesses how the victim is afflicted and "promptly plugged the hole."

The mar-ridden man fell in love with the girl, married her and had several children. On one occasion, however, he was about to show his wife how she had come to him. He pulled out the plug, and the wife disappeared through the hole, never to return.[12]

Why should the victim be so attracted to his victimizer? Unlike psychologists, who have little difficulty understanding this contradiction (however much their explanations vary), storytellers have to manipulate narrative details to transform the female character into a more benign creature. In one version, the encounter is shifted from night, with its often fearful visions, to early morning, when demons traditionally vanish: the son of a clergyman sees "sun-beams coming in through a knothole in the floor," their splendor matched by a "woman of marvellous beauty."[13] A Scandinavian tale recounts how a young man is "ridden" each night by the persecuting "mara," who, it turns out, is no one more fearful than the girl next door awaiting the man who can release her from an evil spell.[14]

But not all nightmares are beautiful maidens to be rescued; the "mara" is not only akin to the swan maiden but also appears as an "old, ugly woman," a witch.[15] Both meek swan maiden and frightful sorceress have been traced to the image of the mare goddess in Hindu and Indo-European mythology. The swan maiden and demon lover tales can, according to Doniger, be seen as antagonistically posed against each other. After the mare goddess was split into the images of the good and the evil mother, the "auspicious (albeit dangerous) white mare" was "given a malevolent evil black alter ego," so that the "model of mortal woman and immortal man rose above the model of immortal woman and mortal man" (that is, the Cupid and Psyche tale prevails over that of the swan maiden). The goddess is thus "demoted to ignominious mortality and passivity."[16] To extend this argument, the swan maiden, debased already by her captivity by a male-dominated world, is debased still further when her captivity is justified because she represents an inherently feminine evil.

A tale from the Caucasus (Georgia) exemplifies the turn a swan maiden tale can take. After a man is changed by his unfaithful wife into a dog, he becomes a shepherd's helper whose fame in killing and driving away wolves spreads. He is taken to the palace where it is hoped that he may rid a princess of her nightly torments by brownies, that is, malevolent nightmare beings. On his first watch, the dog man sees twelve "swans enter the bedchamber through the closed doors, [after which] they choked and trampled upon the sleeping princess." His wicked wife proves one of the demonic swan maidens, and the avenging husband not only releases the princess from her nocturnal oppression but also transforms his wife and her diabolical lover into an ass and a she-ass. Here are joined the images of the swan maiden and the horse, in its denigrated form of an ass. Moreover, the story plays out the theme of the male and female struggle for dominance: the evil wife takes the form of the male ass and her lover becomes the female animal, acting out in their enchantment the roles they assumed when the domineering, dangerous woman had her way.[17]

Urvaśī's appearance as both water bird and female horse links the timid swan maiden, on one side, to the incubus-nightmare on the other.[18] The etymological confusion in English between "mare" as incubus and "mare" as female horse can be related to a general duality between the nightmare astride its victim, and the nightmare depicted as a horse— that is, one who is ridden.[19] Whether the nightmare is equine or equestrian[20] is a distinction that seems linked to the ambiguity surrounding the nightmare dream itself: both voluptuous pleasure and agonizing pain and terror are reported as sensations.[21] Doniger describes how the prototype of "the nightmare who presses down on the sleeper or has intercourse with him while lying on top of him" is "the mare who rides perversely astride her son/husband instead of being ridden."[22] This ambiguous "mare" can be found in a large body of folklore.

The Salishan relate how a chief's rebellious wife frequently rides one of his stallions, eventually cohabiting with it while growing "careless of her household duties." The people notice the affinity between the woman and the horse, and when her husband discovers her unnatural affair, he shoots the stallion. After crying and refusing to go to bed (cohabit with her husband), she disappears for a year: "it was discovered that she had gone off with some wild horses," among whom she is discovered, grown hairy and resembling them. As the herd is attacked, the wild horses run away, but the woman

could not run as fast as they, and was run down and lassoed. She was brought to her husband's lodge; and the people watched her for some time trying to tame her, but she continued to act and whinny like a horse. At last they let her free.

The story ironically restores the unregenerate wife to a parody of her traditional role: transformed into a mare, she ends by bearing colts.[23]

An Icelandic tale similarly depicts a rebellion against woman's domestic role in terms of the aggressive woman and the ridden man. The fairy Hild is cursed by her mother-in-law to work on earth as a housemaid, a position she fills well, although she and the farmer never fall in love (perhaps he recognizes she is no ordinary woman). Once each year Hild returns to the fairy world by riding a mortal whose dead body is found the next day. The desperate farmer employs a worker who outwits Hild before he becomes her next victim.

He pretended to be fast asleep, and felt that she was busy fixing something in his mouth; he realized that it was a magic bridle, but he let her put it on him. As soon as she had bridled him she led him out by the easiest way, got on his back, and rode as hard as she could till she reached a place which looked to him like some sort of deep pit or cleft in the earth.

This is a reverse disenchantment, because Hild is returned to the otherworld, not integrated into the human realm. Her good fortune nonetheless depends on a masculine strength that restrains her, overpowering the murderous rider of men.[24]

"Hild" belongs to those folktales in which a woman is followed on secret visits to the otherworld, detection of her sojourn putting a stop to them. Stories of mares and galloping demons often combine with comparable stories in which the woman sneaks off to attend a witches' sabbath. A Czech farmhand, for example, subdues his employer's wife when he pursues her to unholy festivals "where the witches were having their feast."

Now, when he came there, the farmer's wife knew him, and, to hide herself from him, she turned herself into a white horse. But he did not lose sight of the horse. He mounted it and went to the smith with it, and told him to shoe it. Next day the woman had four horseshoes on, two on her hands and two on her feet. And she had to stay like that always![25]

Similarly, a Scottish blacksmith is victimized by a female demon he does not at first realize is his wife, who "puts a magic bridle" on him and rides *him* to the wild moors where such "vile creatures hold their hideous feasts." The blacksmith's brother, a hunter, conceals himself until he is able to capture the witch by flinging a bridle over her head. When she is transformed into a gray mare with a lost shoe, he arranges to have it replaced by her blacksmith husband. She becomes sick, a doctor finds the horseshoes nailed to her hands, and she is condemned to death as a witch.[26] Both hunter and blacksmith have pursued their symbolically male occupations, both intent on subjugating the witch/horse/woman.

A similar tale from New Mexico depicts how a suspicious husband follows his wife and mother-in-law to a cemetery where he watches them eating human flesh and burying the bones. They turn him into a dog, but he manages to regain his human form, after which his "wife becomes a horse and her mother a mule. He rides them to death."[27] Not only humans but also animals are victims of the perverse female rider, and charms are invented to protect the stabled horses at night. A queen is a great lover of horses:

In particular she had one horse which was dearest of all to her, and filled her thoughts both sleeping and waking. The stable-man had noticed several times that there was something wrong with the horse, and came to the conclusion that it was being ridden by a night-mare, so one time he seized a bucket of water and threw it over it, and lo and behold, the queen herself was sitting on its back.[28]

Doniger has described how "aggressive woman thus rides astride, like the castrating mare," the image playing "upon the more usual notion (of which it is a self-conscious inversion) that every actual sexual act is, by implication, a fatal battle." Such role reversals "occur in several forms in the myths and icons. The inverse position in sexual intercourse, with the woman on top, is a reversal of hierarchical patterns of authority."[29]

Several folklore motifs may be thus explained: for example, that the risk of a man's being mar-ridden is especially great if he lies on his back;[30] and, concomitantly, the Hebrew account of Adam's first wife,

Lilith, who rejected Adam's authority over her, symbolized by his forcing her to accept the prone position during sexual intercourse (see further discussion of Lilith below). The swan maiden tale itself speaks to male anxieties: man's fear of female sexuality, his anxiety that his wife will not be satisfied by him, and the resulting dread that his manhood will be destroyed in the power struggle waged between them. This traditional fear of women makes coherent the transformation of the timid swan maiden into the nightmare demon, the transformation, that is, of the victim into the victimizer. As a woman's story, the tale of the swan maiden can, as has been argued, speak to fantasies of escape from the dreariness of earthly life. As a man's tale it can speak to fears of victimization and abandonment. The wife becomes an extension of the bad mother and hence the oppressor. Man's very dependence on woman can lead to his sense of being mistreated, to a belief in feminine evil, and to a power struggle that often takes on elements of pathological dread and hatred. And when this fear of women exploded into mania during the witch trials, the world began to resemble, as Gregory Zilboorg has described the period, "a veritable insane asylum without a proper mental hospital."[31]

The belief in relations between humans and otherworldly creatures had existed for centuries, such relations having been called one of the "most interesting bits of folklore in the Middle Ages."[32] How a piece of folklore became a theological matter concerning heresy, and how the definition of a witch became reduced to "a woman who has had sexual intercourse with the devil,"[33] are problematic issues confronting scholars of witchcraft—as already noted in chapter 3. Among the most extreme of the inquisitors, male anxiety had indeed passed into mania. According to the nineteenth-century work of John Fiske, it was Christianity that made a nightmare demon of the mara (swan maiden) and that adopted the theory that Satan employed these seductive creatures as agents for ruining human souls: the "Mara belongs to an ancient family, and in passing from the regions of monkish superstition to those of pure mythology we find that, like her kinsman the werewolf, she had once seen better days."[34]

To enmesh the swan maiden in a web of heresy, it was necessary to make sexual relations between human and supernatural being the means to an end rather than an end in itself. Bernheimer has described the situation:

As the incubus changed from a wood demon into a devil the story of women's relationship with him was decisively modified. For now a moral choice seemed to be involved in the proceedings. The intercourse between woman and devil was now conceived as a conscious act of apostasy by which the witch, who had sought such contact, sealed her compact with the evil one.[35]

A similar progression has been traced from the lascivious but "essentially healthy" supernatural lovers, the Greek gods, to Hebrew demons who, in general, indulged natural sexual desire, to the demons believed by Christians to seduce humans in order to "corrupt and degrade men and women and lead them into eternal damnation by way of irremediable sin."[36]

A Basque tale bowdlerizes the usual demonological treatment of a folklore theme but nonetheless illustrates the connection that developed between satanism and human sexuality. One Bidabe must make one of two women his bride, one seductively beautiful, the other not only skilled in domestic work but also a diligent churchgoer. Bidabe follows his sensual appetites only to learn his error when he finds his ill-chosen fiancée at an unholy convocation where witches worshipped "an ugly fat man" who "seemed to be the king of these creatures. As they marched slowly before him each one made a low bow and planted a kiss upon his great toe."[37] Ordinarily, planting a kiss upon the devil's posterior is one of the perverse acts believed to take place in witches' rites,[38] but rendering the Basque story more acceptable also renders the demon more ugly than frightening, and the whole scene more ridiculous than threatening.

In fact the fathers of the early Catholic church rejected the incubus belief; until about 1100 a.d. they were skeptical when faced with popular superstitions, regarding "night monsters as illusions—the projections of sex dreams or unhealthy imaginations." But later the incubus "captivated the imaginations of theologians and clerical story tellers alike." It has been explained that folklore was no longer waved aside, if for no other reason than that the schooled intellectuals had to deal with popular "beliefs if only to reclassify or dispel them. In turn, the theologians maintained and perpetuated the popular superstitions by recording and commenting on them."[39] Thus the church, which may have begun with a keen insight into psychological processes, may have eventually come to understand the implications of its own position (or, to follow Ginzburg and Duerr, may have started to reconsider the meaning of the witches' confessions), finally burning an extraordinarily high although still controversial number of people, mainly women, often saving their souls by extracting from them lurid descriptions of their unions with demons and then destroying the bodies whose concupiscent desires had led to sin. Zilboorg has ironically noted that the whole field of clinical psychiatry was covered by theologians whose text was Leviticus: "A man also, or woman, that hath a familiar spirit, or that is a wizard, shall surely be put to death: they shall stone them with stones; their blood shall be upon them."[40]

It has been argued that the dreamer who submitted to the incubus experienced weak reality testing to begin with and that the church came to confirm the actuality of the fantasy. Thus a "kind of mutual validation persisted through the centuries between certain dreams, which have such vivid reality for the individual, and the reinforcing influence of the myths and attitudes of the society that supported the belief in this reality."[41] But such historical analyses tend to deemphasize the specific pathology of the inquisitors whose pornographic fantasies, according to Masters, combined an impossible asceticism and hatred of the flesh "with a practical libertinism seldom rivaled in all of history."[42] Psychological factors are probably to be counted among the others that caused theorists of demonology to range from the "very credulous to hard-headed," from the honorable Johann Wier and Reginald Scott to the bloodthirsty Nicholas Remy, Jean Bodin, and the authors of the infamous *Malleus Maleficarum*.[43]

A corollary to the question of why so many more women than men were executed for witchcraft is the question of why the devil, who could take on either a male or female form to tempt mortals to sin, assumed the incubus's shape so much more often than the succubus's. On this matter conflicting views are found. According to the misogynistic demonologists, women, being the more lascivious and less rational member of the human species, were the devil's easier prey, more likely to attract him and less likely to resist.[44] One fourteenth-century bishop reports that the nuns of a particular convent were so familiar with their incubi that they were not afraid of them; therefore he was unable to dispel the demons' influence with "penances and advice and preaching."[45] A nineteenth-century medical treatise contradicts such a view: admitting that virgins (and pregnant women) were liable to attacks by the incubus, its author maintains that in general "women were less liable to nightmare attacks than men."[46] The changing role of women in society may well account for shifts not only in theory but also in people's actual experiences. Studies performed in recent times, when equality between the sexes has been greater, indicate that men and women seem equally subject to the same anxieties and thus the same kinds of nightmares.[47] And significantly, as noted in previous chapters, anthropologists have reported that where women in a society enjoy relatively higher status than women elsewhere, their folklore reflects this difference: they are less likely to be the prey of demon lovers, or they manage to outwit the unwelcome suitors. In short, the incubus visitation may be a measure of women's position in society. Holbek has pointed out that nuns were the witches' obverse just as the sabbath was an inverted mass. Ironically, both witches and nuns are closely associated with incubi.

Anthropologists are particularly interested in incubus lore, and although they characteristically study it in culture-specific contexts, their findings usually transverse geographical boundaries. A particularly useful study for understanding the importance of gender where it comes to beliefs concerning demon lovers concerns the Iban people of New Guinea, whose popular assumption is that a miscarriage indicates that the father of the unborn child was not its mother's husband but an incubus. Hence the woman's grief over her loss becomes mixed with guilt about her own sexual behavior, about why she should have attracted the attentions of the demon. At the same time, "mingled with the feelings of fear and hatred" that the incubus evokes among the Ibans, is a measure of fascination with the demon as a "consummate lover and an arch philanderer."[48] It is noteworthy that Western demonology elevates such fascination into sadomasochistic fantasies, for copulation with the devil was according to his consorts by no means always pleasurable. The oversized or icy or scaly (or all of these) phallus of the incubus was described more as an instrument of torture than of pleasure[49]—which perhaps serves as another link between demon lover and inquisitor. But commentators have been more inclined to emphasize the guilt and remorse felt by the frightened woman who confessed to witchcraft than they have been to analyze the dynamics of the dialogue between her and her prosecutor.

Insofar as accounts of these confessions were written by men in their treatises on witchcraft, they constitute a man's story. Perhaps many accused witches intuited the extent to which they were feeding the inquisitor's own sexual imagination and thought they might save their lives if they revealed what their questioners wanted to hear. If so, such

women were in a sense dummies through whom inquisitorial ventrilo-
quists spoke, giving voice to male fantasies. For it may be speculated
that the incubus visited more often than the succubus because, like the
Iban men, the inquisitors experienced vicarious pleasure in identifying
with this potent lover. In contrast, the succubus is indeed like the castrating mare, threatening to man's self-image. For example, the *Malleus
Maleficarum* relates the ridiculous but for that no less dangerous story
of how in "front of his wife and friends, a man was forced to have
intercourse with a succubus. He kept at it three times; but when the
succubus wanted to recommence, the man fell to the floor worn out."[50]

The so-called witch's account of her demon lover's cruelties might
render old folk material in a form particularly satisfying to those who
were fascinated by the incubus and might even have identified with it.
Kittredge may have understated the case that links the incubus belief
with the Cupid and Psyche tale. The demon lover who consorted with
accused witches was not only very different from the supernatural lover
who visited Psyche, but was even more malign in being more perverse
than the spirit who carries off the carpenter's wife in the "Demon Lover"
ballad. Thus the so-called witch inverted woman's role as the civilizer
who transformed the beast, for if she unleashed the fantasies of her
interlocutor, she actually aroused the animal in him. Destroying her
despite her confession (or perhaps because of it) and contrition might
then have been the inquisitor's unconsciously desperate gesture toward
restoring his own internal equilibrium as well as readjusting cultural
order.

The necessity of subjugating inner demons by eliminating the threatening female influence is reflected in the power struggle between the
nightmare–swan maiden and her victim. It is not enough to reduce the
fairy/witch to human status and bend her to male will; she must, again,
be destroyed or, as many stories have it, mutilated. Short of that, she
must be rejected by the man who has come to associate her with his
animal or fallen nature. But the fairy as nightmare demon will not
always be so readily controlled, and sometimes the ensuing struggle will
destroy the man instead of or as well as the female devil. The legendary
story of Vanlandi tells how he leaves his wife for ten years although he
had promised to be gone only three. No Penelope, this wife consults a
sorceress, bargaining "with her either to bring Vanlandi back to Finland

by means of her witch-craft or else to kill him." At first the spell is successful and Vanlandi becomes eager to return to his wife, "but his friends and advisers prevented him." He then becomes sleepy, but "he had not slept long before he called out and said that Mara was treading him." Although his men tried to help him, "when they took hold of his head, she trod his legs, so that they nearly broke; then they turned to his feet, and she depressed his head, so that he died."[51]

Vanlandi's fate is highlighted by his powerful status as a chief at war in conflict with not only his enemies but also those companions whose advice undermines his own inclinations. His conflict is reflected in his struggle with his wife and her alter ego, the sorceress who sends the nightmare demon. The wish to keep his promise to his wife, however belatedly, is interpreted by male companions as weakness. The fury of his wife and his failure to reconcile this tug of war between masculine and feminine interests is raised to a level of national conflict and even takes on cosmic significance in light of the names given to the wife and her father (Drift, daughter of King Snow). Questions of male and female mastery make the proper relationship of husband to wife a central issue in the very stability of the universe.

Incubus lore transforms the animal groom tales just as it does the swan maiden tale. Not every suitor who appears to a woman in animal form is waiting to be released from an evil spell unwillingly suffered; these creatures are also emissaries from some infernal region. The Ibos are not the only ones to hold that "incubi are really animals" that "may assume human shape at will."[52] Were-animals of various sorts bear the same relation to frog princes as the incubus does to Psyche's Cupid. Christina Hole, in the tradition of the evolutionists' emphasis on a cultural development that is reflected in folklore, traces the belief once prevalent among peoples that humans could change into animals. Totemism frequently made of the affinity of man and beast a tight system of belief, and "shapeshifting was not in the early periods of thought considered to be the essentially evil and unnatural thing that it afterwards became."[53] In any event, Western demonological input into well-known folk narratives is reflected in three variations of the animal groom tale: animals are often the forms assumed by demons such as the nightmare; witches, Circelike, can turn men into beasts (according to the *Malleus Maleficarum* it is one of the ways that witches infected the venereal act); and witches who enter into pacts with the devil acquire assistants in the form of animal familiars that often become the witches' lovers.

In the realm of demonology, the lustful incubus found kin among "vampires, werewolves, witches, the devil, and other supernatural blackguards."[54] The abnormal sexual relations assumed to exist between a witch and her incubus are reflected in the account of the "eminent scholastic Guillaume d'Auvergne, bishop of Paris," who credulously writes of Lucifer that God permits him "to appear to his worshippers and adorers in the form of a black cat or a toad and to demand kisses from them; whether as a cat, abominably under the tail; or as a toad, horribly, on the mouth." Fiske describes similar associations with the devil attached to were-animals: "Lycanthropy became regarded as a species of witchcraft; the werewolf was supposed to have obtained his peculiar powers through the favor or connivance of the Devil; and hundreds of persons were burned alive or broken on the wheel for having availed themselves of the privilege of beast-metamorphosis."[55] The folklore associated with the were-animals has been the subject of many studies, ranging from the sensational to the sanely considered inquiry into the subject.

As were-animal, the swan maiden is frequently claimed to assume the shape of an animal to torment her victim. In the following story, the husband asserts control over his prospective bride with a brutality besides which the traditional theft of clothing or other customary forms of capture are rendered benign. Instead of merely plugging up the hole through which the nightmare (in the form of a cat) enters his room, he catches the animal and nails it by one paw to the floor. The next morning he found "a handsome naked woman" with a "nail driven through her hand." Long after, when the couple had had three children, he uncovered the hole: "she escaped through it instantly in the shape of a cat, and never returned."[56] A similarly "terrible case" recounted by Fiske reveals the extent to which the maiming of the animal, like the shoeing of the witch/horse, is a device for controlling the supposedly wayward woman. A gentleman described as a "helpless hunter" is attacked by a savage wolf and manages to cut off one of the forepaws of what will prove in the story to be an "unfortunate lady." Later he meets a friend to whom he shows what had become a "woman's hand, upon which was a wedding-ring." The friend recognizes his own wife's ring, and, his suspicions aroused, he finds her "sitting by the fire in the kitchen, her arm hidden beneath her apron," a bleeding stump.[57] She is burned as a witch, paying with her life for the unresolved conflict between the "unfortunate lady" and the "helpless huntsman," he, in the end, proving, with the aid of his culture, less helpless than she.

A less sadistic but more provocative variant tells how a girl in East Prussia was, unknown to herself, "every night transformed into a black cat."

In the morning she used to feel exhausted as after a heavy dream; but the fact was that in her transformed state she used to go to her betrothed lover and scratch and torment him. One night he caught the cat and tied it up in a sack, in which he found next morning no cat, but his naked sweetheart. The parson of the parish cured her.[58]

Here it is the demon animal, not her victim, that suffers the nightmare. Religion cures her of her demons, a more humane healing than the mutilation often used to control the animal. (One might recall, here, the practice of female circumcision by which some people control female sexuality.)

Folklore from the United States offers a somewhat pragmatic rendering of the stories described above. In "The Devil's Pretty Daughter," a blacksmith is ridden by a witch whom he catches and shoes. She proves to be a rich merchant's missing daughter, found naked in a barn with horseshoes, and so "they just hushed the whole thing up and sent the girl off to a big hospital somewheres."[59] The connection between medical healing and exorcism is of anthropological interest, for some believe the "confession" of the supposed wrongdoer may have pragmatic advantages. The rebellious female may find herself trapped by her revolt, alienated from her people, and exorcism at least offers her a way back to culture. "The 'bush of the were-animals' appears in many respects to be like the subconscious mind"; it is an "area of submerged, private identities." Confession "rectifies the 'deceit' of such a double existence, harmonizes the submerged with the public identity."[60]

This discrepancy between private fantasy and public existence was developed by Michelet in his portrait of the housewife whose maladaptation to domestic life makes her prey to demonic animal lovers who reflect her fantasies and her guilt. The anxieties of her day are described as "trifling" compared to the "torments of the night" in which she cannot sleep, racked by her devil, who takes "a hundred hideous forms" and "persecutes her without mercy," stealing "horrid kisses from her shuddering mouth" even when she tries to repel him with Christian signs. " 'No! not that; you must *not* do that.' "[61] That a man might in ignorance sleep while his wife received her incubus constituted a prevalent belief during the witchcraft era, controversy arising about whether women actually left surrogate images of themselves in bed while attending the devil's orgies, or whether confessions of such visits merely reflected the delusions resulting from the devil's power.[62]

Such scholastic disputation led to considerations about the kind of women most likely to attract demons, the consensus being in accord with Ernest Jones's contention that of "the sexual activities of the Devil no more need be said; it is sufficiently illustrated by the Abyssinian proverb: 'When a woman sleeps alone, the Devil sleeps with her.' "[63] But the witch who leaves her sleeping husband in bed as she attends orgiastic sabbaths or who entertains her incubus while her spouse sleeps unknowing beside her may be far more dangerous to society than the nun who entertains her incubus in her cell. For the marital relationship and the family unit is held by most societies to be essential to group survival.

A Maori folktale describes the double life of Whanawhana, kidnapped by the fairies against her will, her existence involving an oscillation between the home she shares with her husband and the otherworld. "In the morning, while she lay in a deep sleep made heavy by the incantations of the fairy, she was borne away again through the clouds. She awoke, and there she was, lying upon the fairy mound in the bush —and before her stood her [supernatural] husband." If Whanawhana's erotic experiences lack that admixture of fascination and loathing that characterizes the sleepless nights of Michelet's bourgeois housewife, it may be because her dreams are described without the taint of demonology that is reflected in Michelet: Whanawhana is not vilified for a predisposition to sin; she is not tormented by guilt. Nonetheless, she too must undergo an exorcism to rid her of her demon lover, to unite her daytime and nighttime existences so that her lawful husband will assume his place in the center of her life.[64] European tales, in contrast, often reveal confusion on this point: although successful "cures" banish the evil demons, the woman must somehow pay a physical or psychological price for their visitation.

The early European demonologists believed that female depravity, manifested in women's sexual fantasies and unbridled sensuality, was linked to women's unfeminine ambitions and desire for power. The *Malleus Maleficarum* is unequivocal on the subject:

Three general vices appear to have special dominion over wicked women, namely, infidelity, ambition, and lust. Therefore they are more than others inclined towards witchcraft, who more than others are given to these vices. Again, since of these three vices the last chiefly predominates, women being insatiable, etc., it follows that . . . among ambitious women

those who are more hot to satisfy their filthy lusts are more deeply infected.[65] It is difficult to imagine any seemingly logical statement that could more fully express a fear and loathing of women. And much folklore and literature is based on what happens when such beliefs enter the marital relationship. The interaction of misogyny with witchcraft beliefs informs, for example, Nathaniel Hawthorne's intriguing and powerful story, "Young Goodman Brown," where even the suspicion of his wife's communion with evil turns a husband against his wife for their entire lives.[66]

What is being argued here is that the controversy over a woman's presence at a sabbath where she consorts with demons and animals while her unsuspecting husband sleeps unawares cannot rest too heavily on the insane beliefs of rabid inquisitors, although these exploited age-old beliefs in what was at least in part a transformation of folklore into demonology. To put aside for the moment the arguments of Duerr and Ginsburg, it can be noted that moderate thinkers believed that fantasy lay behind many confessions, but that although they helped put an end to the atrocities visited on women, they did little to alter the essential misogyny concerning a natural feminine inclination to the perverse. For if the dreaming self is the other self—literally, according to some society's belief that during a dream, the dreamer's soul actually exits the body to sojourn abroad,[67] or figuratively, according to modern psychology—then what such fantasies imply is that those who insisted that women actually attended witches' sabbaths may have rendered literal a still-significant metaphor. Not ignorance but rather an all-too-keen appreciation of female fantasy and how it subverted attempts to keep woman in her place may have helped to drive the most extreme antifeminists to their positions.

What was happening in distant centuries may be illuminated by a contemporary perspective in which equality for woman is reflected in woman's right to sexual satisfaction, and in which sexual fantasy is viewed as an essential route to that satisfaction. The incubus is in effect invited to join the married pair. Modern woman is urged to rid herself of guilt experienced if she actively and deliberately imagines that her husband is someone else, and her hopefully enlightened husband is encouraged not only to tolerate but to appreciate the value of this ménage à trois.[68] A contemporary short story depicts a young married woman's discontent in the double sphere traditionally deemed her place, kitchen and bed. Twice she ironed her husband's "shirts without washing them. He wore them, never knowing. Hemming his trousers, she inadvertently cut one leg an inch shorter than the other. He wore them never knowing. She faked orgasm one night," and on the next pretended he was a popular actor.[69] His oblivion is comical but also can evoke the folklore of women who fly away to orgies, leaving effigies of themselves in their beds, their husbands failing to recognize the substitution. Today, Chaucer's Wife of Bath could take satisfaction in the incubus's return: he has not only regained his power but is no longer deemed subversive.

That a woman only dreams of rather than commits literal adultery with her incubus would, again, not necessarily console the distrustful husband who intuited (or consciously recognized) that her erotic dreams portended trouble for him. Again, it was perhaps not ignorance but astute psychological insight that made the early Catholic church modify what Ernest Jones called its practical but unpopular early views concerning the incubus as a projection of human fantasy. Fortunately, the practical view would eventually triumph and the controversy shift from religious heresy to a folkloristic debate over the relation of popular narratives to real dream experience. The swan maiden has herself been explained as a dream creature, her sudden disappearance likened to awakening from a dream,[70] just as the "origin of the whole conception [of the incubus] may be traced to the nightmare."[71] Jones takes it as given that dreams have played an important part in many popular beliefs: the soul's capability of existing independent of the body; the revenant's power to revisit the living; the transformation of human beings into animals or other beings; and the existence of night flights to distant places. In contrast, the main criticism Swahn directs against an earlier scholarly work on Cupid and Psyche is that its author's prodigious effort is expended to prove a questionable thesis, that these stories have their origin in dream experience.[72]

The question of dreams in swan maiden and demon lover narratives raises an apparent contradiction. Those who write on the nightmare emphasize the isolated and isolating terror of the victim; despite "its universality," the nightmare "remains a strictly individual experience."[73] But the lore of the incubus involves collective images mustered by the dreamer to explain or deal with the dream experience. Not only dream lore, then, but the folktales that invoke it require consideration of both the individual and collective nature of the incubus.

To the present time, the debate of Chaucer's cock and hen on the subject of dreams and their meaning has not abated. A distinction remains between the naturalistic explanations of a dream (for example, the food eaten before sleep, or the random workings of the brain) and the insistence that dreams have meaning in the life of the dreamer.[74] Rather than try to decide whether dreams give rise to traditions, or traditions to dreams, it may be more profitable—at least for the study of folklore and literature—to consider how the human experience of conflict between fantasy and reality creates a myriad of relationships among real life, dreams (of many sorts), aspects of religious beliefs, and the narratives people invent, adopt, and retain to deal with these. Jones cites Hobbes's *Leviathan* to illustrate the premise on which he has based his study of nightmares and demonology: Hobbes had written that from ignorance of "how to distinguish Dreams and other strong fancies from Vision and Sense did arise the greater part of the religion of the Gentiles in times past that worshipped Satyres, Faunes, Nymphs, and the like; and nowadays the opinion that rude people have of Fayries, Ghosts, and Goblins, and of the power of Witches."[75] It has similarly been observed that in "all fairy tales and all mythology, a remarkable conformity to the deranged ideas of sleep occurs, and the stories of the lower races; as, for instance, those of Schoolcraft's 'Algic Researches,' read far more like the recollection of bad dreams than like the worn ideas of a once pure religion, or of a poetical interpretation of nature."[76] Perhaps it is because at least sometimes dreams might be transformed *into* swan maiden and demon lover narratives that dreams themselves in these tales are not usually literal narrative motifs (perhaps the dream element is often taken for granted). Thus when a story specifically cites a dream to explain a character, it provides an opportunity to see how the storyteller perceives the relationship between private and public self.

A Siberian folktale relates simply that there "was a girl who refused all men, but the Sun came during a dream, made her his wife and took her aloft upon [a] white deer."[77] In another Siberian story, dutiful and rebellious daughters are distinguished according to what they dream. The elder of two daughters obediently reports to her father that she had dreamed of marrying a merchant's son. The younger, having dreamed of marrying a goat, is forbidden even to cross the threshold of her home. "However, she was disobedient, and when she went out a goat lifted her on his horns and carried her beyond a steep bank." Interestingly, it is not the obedient daughter who triumphs in this tale, but the one whose deviant impulses are expressed through dreams and who proceeds to a happy life, successfully disenchanting her beast husband.[78]

That dreams may lead to adaptive rather than maladaptive behavior is also suggested when a kind-hearted young Burmese lady is solicitous of a snake, which she allows to sleep in a basket beside her. She "had a strange dream that night; she dreamt that a handsome young prince came and shared her bed. The dream was repeated the next night, and so in the morning the dreamer told her mother about it."[79] That a loathly toad is really a handsome prince is knowledge also acquired in a dream by a Lusitanian girl: "in her dream, she was advised to take the prince for her husband, and all would turn out happily."[80]

Frequently, the dream motif in folktales highlights the contrast between actual life and an only longed-for existence. A Wichita tale makes explicit what is usually a submerged motif in star husband tales, linking the journey to star land directly to wish fulfillment ordinarily realized only in dreams. On the same night that a young woman thinks that a brightly twinkling star would be the better spouse than normal choices would afford her, it seems "that in her dream she was with this man whom she had pointed out and desired for her husband."[81] The Caddo relate how the girl who married Wild-Cat had refused all previous suitors, becoming enamored of a handsome youth who visits her home, eating with her family but paying no attention to her. Thinking about him in bed, "she fell asleep and dreamed of him," dreamed that she "saw him coming to her." Awakening, she "closed her eyes and prayed that her dream would come true. When she opened her eyes the young man was bending over her, begging her to go with him. She arose and followed him out into the darkness." Her brothers and father wander a long time in search of the woman, the parent's death in the wilderness being paradigmatic of the subversive influence of her unrealistic yearnings.[82]

Insofar as dreams lead to deviant rather than adaptive behavior, the influence of the woman's dream lover must be, if possible, exorcised. A Maidu serpent lover story relates how "every night, when it was nearly dark," a girl

went bathing, and did not miss a single night. Then she slept, and dreamed to herself, kept dreaming, dreamed every night, dreaming of the same person. And once she went to bathe, and, having gone bathing, she did not return until morning.

Finally her longings are materialized in a great snake that crawls into her house, looking steadily at her, which she takes as a signal to go with him. Her father helps her get rid of this loathsome suitor.[83] This tale contrasts with the Caddo story to the extent that culture effectively counters the forces represented in the dream.

Whether the woman's dream increases or decreases her share of responsibility for her and her people's fate is not a simple matter. That she dreams of her demon lover suggests that she is particularly disposed to welcome him. The dream might point up incomplete or improper socialization, the dreamer's propensity for subversive behavior reflected by *and* in the dream. But dreams are often held to be external visitations and the dreamer is thus relieved of responsibility both for the dream itself and what may ensue. Folktales indicate that many cultures understood (if variously interpreted) the interaction of internal and external factors in demonic visitations. Societies may pragmatically attempt to reintegrate the individual into the group. The Ibans of New Guinea supply an instance of how a community perceives of and deals with what Western cultures would now deem emotional illness.

Not only miscarriage but also infant mortality is attributed by the Iban to demonic parentage, the bereaved mother—again—needing to deal with both grief and guilt. One such woman confesses that she had dreamed of having sexual intercourse with her husband, but that when she awakened,

she heard the noise of a door being opened and glancing up she saw, in the pale light of dawn, that the door of her sleeping apartment was ajar. At the same time she noticed [her husband] still fast asleep beside her. With a pang of anxiety she realized that she had just been visited by an incubus who, to deceive her had assumed the appearance of her own husband.[84]

A great deal of folklore is echoed in this account, including the famous Greek myth of Amphytrion. In any event, both the individualistic and collective aspects of the woman's dream are invoked in exorcising her internal and external demons. It is *she* who has been visited and who must undergo the ritual, but her people recognize her plight and are familiar with the demonic invader.

As cultural symbol, the incubus supplies the dreamer with a method of coping with a stressful situation, since the dreamer can argue that the visitation came without summons. Nightmares about demons, then, are not necessarily "the most personal expression of the unconscious," not, that is, to be uncritically used to explain fairy tales, which are communal in nature.[85] As Vincent Crapanzano has argued, dreams about demons recognized by a culture allow the "drama of individual experience" to be "played out on a collective stage," averting the "horror of private fantasies and visions—hallucinations—and individual compulsions and obsessions that haunt the Westerner entrapped within an ideology, an idiom, of extreme individualism."[86] Furthermore, the person who attributes affliction to demons avoids another source of guilt; instead of placing responsibility for misfortune on others who as members of the same society are bound to the sufferer and may be blamed for the affliction, the dreamer can place blame on mysterious forces from the outside. Feeling less threatened, the victim's people are less likely to punish and more likely to muster resources to seek a cure for the malady.[87] To extend this argument, although women are traditionally seen to be especially likely conduits for demonic influence, there may be, again, a particular impetus to "cure" them of their illness rather than blame them for it. To depopulate a people by executing its witches is not only a sign of communal madness but also a self-defeating course of action, depriving the community of the sex that bears babies, that is associated (for better or worse) with civilization, and that is held to mediate between nature and culture.

To return to the dream as a narrative motif in demon lover stories, the tales sometimes indicate that if a woman dreams of a demon lover and is subsequently visited by him, she will appear to have summoned him. When the dream forms part of the narrative, it tends as a literal motif to break down the value of the incubus as a collective symbol, directing the significance of the dreamer's experience back to herself. Her predisposition to reject her culture, the appearance of her incubus, and the aftermath of their union are depicted as resulting in permanent harm to herself, to some members of her family, or to her entire people. Often her "cure" depends on how effective her people are in invoking her cooperation as they exorcise the evil spirit. The dream of the Caddo girl who mates with a wildcat foreshadows the debacle to come, but the private fantasies of the young Maidu woman who takes a serpent for a lover are erased by her male relatives, fathers and brothers who are the implacable foe of her demon. Because the Maidu story concludes with the successful reintegration of the Maidu woman in her society, her dream may be seen as safety valve that has the additional value of alerting those around her to her danger.

In the Lusitanian story, it is, again, the vision of a handsome youth in her dreams that helps the woman to disenchant the man/beast she must actually live with—perhaps a corollary to the Zuñi belief that if human beings did not in their youth consort with supernatural lovers, they would remain unwilling to enter into human marriages.[88] In short, the world's folklore, like the world's theories, offers a wide range of dream interpretation.[89] Frequently the folk indicate some insight into the unconscious in their awareness that there not only exists a conflict but also a relationship between dreams and reality, the private and the public life. It may be true that they would not be likely to articulate this conflict in terms totally consistent with modern psychology,[90] but their narratives suggest that the folk are astute in their understanding that some are more prone than others to demonic visitations.

These folklore themes have been wittily rendered in Jorge Amado's novel *Dona Flor and Her Two Husbands*. Married for the second time to a staid bourgeois pharmacist, Teodoro, Flor misses the exciting sexual relationship she had had with her deceased first husband, Vadinho, who was in other respects a ne'er-do-well. When Vadinho appears as her revenant, making love to her while her husband sleeps, he correctly insists that he had materialized in response to Flor's summons. And because he *is* a projection of her inner self, he is also capable of articulating her dilemma, warning her that he cannot "be Vadinho and Teodoro at one and the same time." Teodoro can give her comfort, security, respectability, conjugal fidelity, "these noble (and tiresome) things that she needs to be happy"; and he, Vadinho, can offer his "fiery" love that makes her suffer but that she cannot do without. Her living husband is her "outward" face, her revenant her "inner," the lover she "does not know how and can't bear to evade." By the end of the book, Flor exorcises her guilt rather than her incubus, happily settling down to her split existence.[91]

That Amado's novel is essentially antifeminist, inspired by the cliché "that women respond to sexy and charming scoundrels, and that stable 'nice' men are supposedly almost asexual" is a charge that has been leveled against it. For the book's theme appears to be that granting woman her sexual freedom ultimately guarantees that she will submit to male domination in other, more fundamental areas of the domestic relationship.[92] Like other wives who are encouraged to utilize their sexual fantasies rather than understand why they need them in order to enjoy the pleasures of the marriage bed, Dona Flor need not question why her differing needs must be met as they are, nor what there is in ordinary domestic life as she and Teodoro understand it that makes it necessary for her to summon an incubus. Widespread folklore, however, conveys a potentially more subversive message than Flor's practical accommodation to what she perceives as her reality. For the popular themes that Amado has both utilized and illuminated suggest a more fundamental problem in the marital relationship, one that cannot be dispelled simply by arguing for the usefulness *to* husbands of the cuck-olding incubus.

Ancient myths, folktales, and dream theories reflect the essential tension between wildness and civilization. The nightmare, which has been associated with the goat god, Pan, has been described as approximating "lost, dead nature," repressed until it returns in dreams that inspire "demonic emotion." The dreamer returns "by instinct to instinct."[93] Because the demon whips up both desire and anxiety, "every possible gradation is to be observed between the pleasurable excitement of voluptuousness on the one hand and extreme terror and repulsion on the other." The incubus in one aspect is the nightmare, in the other the gallant lover.[94] It became necessary for Western society at least to counter the way the Middle Ages merged once separate beliefs in "a demon under orders from hell" and in "a creature from the woods subject to no higher rule than that of his own overbearing passion."[95] The incubus, that is, was to be returned to his ancient association with healthy nature, eradicating his connection to the terrifying nightmare, to sin, and to guilt. The romantics made his redemption one of their explicit goals, although not without a naggingly persistent ambivalence about their task and his essence: it might be possible to envy at least the simplicity of older theological beliefs.

But ambiguities surrounding the incubus in Western cultures predate Christianity, and demon lovers have been traced to Genesis 6:1–4: "When men began to multiply on the face of the ground, and daughters were born to them, the sons of God saw that the daughters of men were fair; and they took to wife such of them as they chose." These lines have provoked puzzlement and controversy. The story appears again in the Book of Enoch and is associated with Satan's rebellion and the idea of the fallen angels. Were women the cause of the angel's fall because they awakened male lust, or were earthly women merely the instruments by which Satan enticed followers already prone to succumb? And, in terms of misogyny, does it matter? For it has been said that the "belief that angels could be seduced by women shows how ravening the sexual desires of males (including angels) were thought to be; and how irresistibly tempting in a carnal way women were considered to be."[96] Such ideas were discussed in the previous chapter: to disenchant the beast, woman must quell her own natural instincts. Somehow, and conversely, just by being female, she is held responsible for the male lust that caused even the angels to abandon heaven.

Whatever the exegesis on Genesis 6, commentators are generally in accord in attributing to the mating between mortal women and supernatural men a profound cosmic disorder and the introduction of sin into the world. The argument has been made that those who wrote the Book of Enoch "were not playing with a folktale," but dealing with a central problem of religion.[97] The story of the fallen angels has been treated as an account of the first fall, to be succeeded by the second fall story that occurred when Eve ate the apple.[98] The angels lusting after women "introduce the principle of evil into humanity" and "disturb the moral order of the earth by deeds of lawlessness." From the very beginning of the concept of original sin, "the flaw or weakness inherent in the structure of human personality" is caused by or at least closely connected with what is known in the "language of technical theology as 'concupiscence.' "[99]

The influence of Genesis 6 can be discovered in folklore. In some cultures, the fairy folk are thought to be descendants of the fallen angels

or the fallen angels themselves. Supposedly, the Danish Bergman originated in this way, for when our "Lord cast down the wicked angels from
Heaven they could not all get to hell together, and some of them settled
in the mounds and banks." They are "just little devils, the whole lot of
them."[100] Conversely, Genesis 6 has itself been traced to a folk tradition: "the J author has picked up a story that is fairly routine in the
mythologies of ancient peoples throughout the world, a somewhat *dise-
difying* tale of divine and human miscegnation that led to the birth of a
monstrous growth of supermen" who represented "a world strangely
out of joint."[101] Once the folktale had been placed in such a moral
context, and once the original or first fall was associated with lust, the
emphasis would inevitably fall on the perversity of natural instincts. To
rescue nature and to rescue the fallen angels from their subsequent
reputation as demons would often become a joint venture.

In the seventeenth century such a rescue was attempted by Ludovico
Sinistrari, who divided incubi from devils by attributing natural substance to the former and condemning the latter as purely immaterial
beings who assume illusory shapes or who inhabit dead bodies (reven-
ants) in order to copulate with witches who have sworn themselves to
the devil.[102] When, at the beginning of the twentieth century, the Rosi-
crucian Reuben Swinburne Clymer translated Sinistrari, he emphasized
the distinction between demon and incubus by omitting the pejorative
word and designating the incubi as "elementals." In so doing, he was
part of the process by which not only the incubus but also nature itself
was to be redeemed. According to Clymer's interpretation, the fallen
beings of Genesis 6 are the nature spirits, gnomes, salamanders, undines,
and sylphs. He goes so far as to explain the birth of Jesus by arguing
that Mary was impregnated by a salamander.[103] He also seems to have
built on some lore derived from Paracelsus and popularized in the nineteenth century, that female elemental spirits seek union with mortal men
in order to gain salvation. He produces his edition of Sinistrari so that
some of God's daughters may be saved.[104]

Combining his interest in folklore (as interpreted in the Romantic
age) with dreams, the nineteenth-century French author Charles Nodier
created his sprite Trilby, who gave his name to a later literary work in
which his diabolical counterpart, Svengali, was a far more ominous
demon. The direct source for Nodier's fiction was Sir Walter Scott, and
Nodier might have been familiar with the Scottish writer's theories

concerning the way folklore was transformed into demonology after the Reformation,[105] for Nodier's treatment of his material is consistent with Scott's ideas. Nodier announces that his theme is based on a popular folk motif: "Like all popular traditions, this one has journeyed round the world, and is found everywhere. It is 'the Devil in Love' of all mythologies." But Nodier's Trilby hardly seems to be a devil; this "goblin" is "more mischievous than wicked, and more frolicsome than mischievous."[106] How and why he becomes a demon lover supplies the theme for Nodier's novella.

Trilby is in love with Jeannie, wife of a fisherman, and his habit of "disturbing the sleep" of young girls with "incomprehensible but pleasant dreams" invades the tranquility of Jeannie's life as Vadinho disturbs that of Dona Flor. However, the "innocently-voluptuous dreams" that Trilby brings to Jeannie in her sleep-induced "illusions" hardly seem comparable—even after allowance is made for the literary restrictions of Nodier's time—to the frenzies experienced by Flor in the embraces of her revenant. It is only after a guilt-ridden Jeannie reveals the existence of Trilby and her church arranges to exorcise her supposed demon that Trilby begins to resemble an adult sexual being: "The capricious child was succeeded by a youth with fair hair, whose slender form, so full of elegance, vied in suppleness with the rushes growing on the shore; he had the delicate pleasing feature of the elf, but developed into the imposing outlines of the chief of the MacFarlane clan." Jeannie, looking at his new form, mourns the disappearance of her former, seemingly more innocent, love. It would appear that once Jeannie's innocent longings are subjected to the moral scrutiny and rituals of her culture, the mischievous sprite begins to assume the appearance of a demon lover, and her troubling but mildly erotic dreams take on the qualities of nightmares (insofar as her daytime sufferings increase as the result of her guilt-inspiring dreams). Thus in Trilby is reproduced the process that some commentators on incubus lore find in the transformation of elementary spirits to devils. To cite Bernheimer once again, this change decisively modified the woman's relationship with her wildman lover, for she is held by her people to have entered into a conscious pact with evil. Jeannie's death conveys romanticism's critique of the harm done to individuals when their instincts are rendered in terms of an evil to be exorcised, and illustrates as well the damage caused when women internalized this negative concept.[107]

The mythologies of many peoples depict the incubus's double face, the demon resisting any simplistic designation of "good" and "evil." For example, the Gandharvas are both "radiant beings who sing sweetly on the mountains" and dangerous creatures, "especially at twilight," when together with the Hindu nightmare demons, "they roam about and haunt forest pools."[108] Similarly, the Roman Faunus is both a kindly spirit "who caused crop and herd to flourish," and the mischievous "spirit who sent the Nightmare."[109] The Teutonic Schrat is a comparably ambiguous nature being,[110] and the "house man" of Finno-Ugric myth is generally a "kindly and useful spirit," who, however, "when he is given cause for anger, annoys sleepers in the form of the nightmare, tangles hair and beards in the night, and hinders the successful conclusion of tasks."[111] The double aspects of these supernaturals point to essential human conflicts, and to banish the demonic to nonexistence and thus eliminate this ambiguity is only apparently a satisfactory solution to the guilt invoked when people are exhorted to control their appetites. So long as the incubus remains at least a valid symbol for woman's conflicts, nature cannot be simply redeemed without trivializing her dilemma. For even assuming that nature can be completely freed from its conflict with culture, the question remains, what constitutes the "natural" woman? This is a particularly perplexing question when the role of children is introduced into swan maiden and demon lover stories.

The association of incubus lore with Lilith, the female demon who not only seduces men but also murders children, focuses attention on an aspect of the incubus–swan maiden story that is particularly troubling: the desertion of her offspring by the runaway fairy, an act traditionally condemned by society as not only criminal but "unnatural." Even modern psychological attempts to detach female development from an ideal of masculine development tend to extend the paradigm of a woman whose moral basis for behavior emerges from a self-definition essentially predicated on caring relationships with others (rather than on the abstract ideas that man's idea of morality rests on).[112] These are the very premises contradicted by the swan maiden's desertion of her family, who thus appears to escape not only mundane domestic reality but also the concomitant definition of woman herself, be it based on nature itself or some natural psychological development less amenable than some would have it to cultural alteration. In any event, the swan maiden as mother supplies her story with one of its most complex aspects.

The Patient Griselda motif frequently found in Cupid and Psyche tales depicts the mother-child bond as so strong that the husband can exploit it to ensure his wife's submission and obedience. In contrast, it will be remembered that the Bulgarian Samodiva tells her husband that her kind are not meant to be wives and mothers, and her ritual recovery of her virginity after she deserts husband and son is a symbolic rejection of such roles. That in some stories the swan maiden takes her children with her or continues to tend to their needs even from a distance points to narrators who cannot imagine or will not perpetuate the dangerous idea that woman's rebellion against her domestic role could include child abandonment, that she could sacrifice her child to her own search for self-satisfaction.[113]

But if "natural" is defined as an obedience to basic instincts and drives that are psychologically as well as physically self-preservative, transcending what has been called the cultural and "human yoke of purposes," "natural" in this sense meaning "impersonal, objective, ruthless,"[114] the swan maiden's flight *from* her children is also *natural*. For when the swan maiden gets back her animal covering, she not only flees her family but also appears driven by some instinct to do so. That motherhood is not necessarily tied to some maternal female essence is reflected in the story of a woman who is pursued by a satyr or wild man who represents nature incarnate. Like the captured swan maiden, this mortal woman is carried to his abode and forced to marry him and bear his children. When he is sufficiently confident in her to leave her alone, she escapes him. He cannot entreat her to return although he plunges a knife into one child and then into the other. He finally kills himself. She, impervious, "could not go back to that life with him."[115] It cannot be rationalized that she has given birth to a demon's and not a human's child: the folklore concerning otherworldly lovers has a multifarious relationship to definitions of what is and what is not "natural" behavior.

Sometimes the children in swan maiden and demon lover tales become the mythological parents of extraordinary, often heroic human beings. Such is the star boy whose mother had preferred a star husband to an ordinary mortal. Melusine, about whom more will be learned in the next chapter, was the legendary founder of the noble French house of Lusignan (according to legend, an entire nation, Luxemburg, owes its origins to her), and her inability to become fully human is reflected in the strange children to whom she gives birth. And Lessa writes of

Madagascar that it is "rich in swan maiden stories, which are principally concerned there with establishing the origin of royal families or tribes."[116] A folktale from Assam depicts both the antipathy felt by the swan maiden toward her children and their eventual high status in their society. When children were born to Nongriji Kongor, "the girl did not like her home or the children. One day she left her husband and children and returned to her lonely cave. The youngsters were very fond of their mother whom they could not induce to return." But the "people loved them for their good qualities and took them to be the children of the gods and respected them." One of this swan maiden's children became the "god-king" of his people.[117] In Welsh folklore the swan maiden known as the Lady of the Lake, who leaves her family when the taboo that has bound her to her human home is broken, "appeared suddenly, and accosted her eldest son" to announce that he would be a physician, assisting the human world by relieving people of pain and misery "through healing all manner of their diseases."[118]

The incubus is similarly cited as the father of extraordinary men: Alexander, Seleucus, Plato, the elder Scipio, Augustus, Hercules, Merlin,[119] and various local aristocrats and heroes, such as the Baron of Drummelzier, who, according to Sir Walter Scott, was born of the baron's lady and the spirit of the river Tweed.[120] Even if the child is demonic, he is extraordinary, as in the medieval stories of Sir Gowther and Robert the Devil. Moreover, the pseudomedical practice of incubation that was often used to cure infertility is described in such a way that the healing god sometimes resembles a demon or serpent lover as he appears to the female patient and impregnates her.[121] Such examples may satisfy a fantasy in which, according to Ernest Jones, erotic wishes and ego are "fully brought into harmony," since the nightly visitor is "not an evil spirit but actually a divine being."[122]

The attempt to achieve such harmony motivates the heroine of Kleist's *The Marquise von O*, a widow ignorant of her child's father's identity, her pregnancy no longer permitting the marquise to ignore a secret life she had hidden not only from others but also from herself. The morally upright marquise avoids self-reproach by transforming a completely human, flesh-and-blood man into an incubus, at first relegating him to the angelic rather than demonic realm to avoid self-reproach as well as the moral opprobrium attached to her illicit act. But as the reality of her situation is forced upon her, the father of her child is transformed into a demon, the thoughts and emotions of this woman traveling the same path supposedly traveled by the incubus in Western civilization.[123]

The marquise and her society equate moral purity with woman's sexlessness; but since motherhood is associated with female sexuality, it is also potentially sinful. Not surprisingly, then, lascivious female demons influence the mother-child relationship. Again, among these demons, Lilith remains archetypal, two noteworthy themes being featured in the lore that surrounds her: female submissiveness and motherhood. Where the former is deficient, the latter is conceived of as perverted. Lilith, who flees Eden because she cannot live there the equal of Adam, becomes a "demon of vengeance against the children of men":[124]

When God perceived that it was not good for man to be alone, He first created a mate for Adam out of the dust of the earth. But the two did not get on at all; for Lilith had no feminine submissiveness about her, since her origin was identical with Adam's. She soon left him and, by pronouncing the Ineffable Name, flew far away. Adam complained to God, Who despatched three angels to force her to return. They found her among the billows of the Red Sea and threatened to drown her, especially when she declared her intention of molesting infants during the early days of their lives. But finally they let her go on this condition: if children were protected by an amulet bearing the names or pictures of the three angels, she would do them no harm. She had further to accept the penalty, imposed by God when she refused to return to Adam, that a hundred of her own children should die every day.[125]

The point of contention between Adam and Lilith is that "when he wished to be with her, she took offence at the recumbent posture he demanded. 'Why must I lie beneath you?' she asked. 'I also was made from dust, and am therefore your equal.' "[126] It has been said that Lilith represents a human desire to satisfy sexual desires outside the obligation to perpetuate the human species, to be mistress and even wife, but not mother.[127] Demonology thus assigns to Lilith two roles, the seducer of men and the murderer of children.[128] Still, modern feminists take her as a model and symbol for the reason that "Lilith was the first woman to challenge masculine supremacy," reaching a "decision similar to that of the end-of-the-nineteenth-century Nora in Ibsen's *Doll's House*."[129]

As a demon who is believed to mother devils who help her prey on humans, Lilith is the female counterpart of the Indian nightmare demons: "they lie in wait for sleeping women, at the wedding procession, at the first nuptials, and just after childbirth; they haunt the women as licentious, permanently excited sex spirits with large testicles, and they enjoy killing newly born children . . . they are capable of driving women into a frenzy."[130] Lilith is similarly associated with male frenzy and perverse sexuality, a combination that made Dante Gabriel Rossetti's poem, "Eden Bower," one of the most suggestively pornographic poems of the nineteenth century. In addition, Lilith's connection to parturition makes her "the chief figure on the 'childbirth tablets' still hung on the walls of the lying-in room in the East and in eastern Europe." The lore in this matter is diverse, complex, and ambiguous. Lilith is permitted to "kill all children which have been sinfully begotten," and this permission extends even to lawfully wedded couples whose relationship transgresses Jewish law. And in her bloodthirstiness, Lilith turns on her own children (born of demon fathers) when no others are available to her.[131] No negative concept of motherhood is lacking in her portrait.

Ironically, one of Lilith's punishments for her feminist inclinations is a kind of fertility problem—if one reads as symbolic that a hundred of the children begotten by devils should die each day. And thus the curse of her childlessness surrounds Lilith with pathetic qualities, and she has been described as a Lady of Sorrows, her grieving voice heard in the night, "like that of Rachel weeping over her children."[132] In this aspect, Lilith has thus been linked to the legendary La Llorona of Hispanic folklore,[133] whose story is varied, its themes in most instances, however, focusing attention on the relationship between gender and demonology.

In one story, La Llorona is a beautiful woman who does not want her first child when it is born and so "threw it into a stream and did so successively with her other three children as they were born." When she dies she is made a penitent who must haunt "streams at the edge of towns and in wooded places," attempting to gather up her murdered children. Because many have heard her wailing "O, my children!" she is known as the weeping woman.[134] As a folklore character, La Llorona has been argued to be an import from Europe, her ancestry traced to one Kunigunde Orlamunde, a widow whose ruling obsession is the wish to remarry. When word reaches her that Albrecht the Fair has said that if "four eyes" were not in the way, he would make her his wife, she misinterprets his words. "The possibility of remarriage intoxicated Kunigunde," who decides her children are the obstacle to her remarriage, and she kills them by thrusting a needle through their heads. But she is in error: Albrecht had been referring to her parents, and her act of infanticide so horrifies him that he rejects her. In remorse, Kunigunde crawls on her knees between two cities and finally enters a convent. Many legends grew up about Kunigunde, most revealing the troubled relationship between man and woman in which the latter, dependent on marriage for sustenance and respectability, comes to view her children not as beloved people but as the signs and manifestations of her social inferiority. One story tells how a man makes a woman pregnant, later mocking her: "He carried his scorn to the point of jeering at her and her child as she stood at the window of her home. At length the young mother became so enraged that when she met the knight in the street she threw the child under his horse's feet, tore the sword from his scabbard, and stabbed him." When he dies, she is executed for her crimes, and since that time a "White Lady appears at the spot of the double murder and attempts to lure young men with her pale beauty. All who speak with her die within the next few days."[135]

Like Medea, women who react violently against their subordination to male power frequently act out their fury through infanticide. Others give birth to unclean spirits—demon children. But in Hispanic folklore, male culpability is depicted indirectly, one group of La Llorona stories making clear that the ghost does not choose her victims at random but rather attacks men who in one way or another have already denigrated women. La Llorona "appears to men who have been drinking, have visited houses of prostitution, or are tempted to take advantage of defenseless women." Hence her victim is portrayed as woman's victimizer, and if the man does not die, he "suffers extreme fright or becomes insane."[136] The revenge motif, it has been hypothesized, probably preceded the infanticide theme, the guilt for the murderous act being shifted to the man, the woman becoming a "blameless, pitiable creature, who, after death, still seeks to avenge her lover's deceit."[137] The story, so interpreted, becomes a woman's story, representing the female point of view with regard to what has been designated "an implicit folk model of the antagonistic aspects of male-female relations."[138] But the legend of La Llorona reflects a wide variety in the attitudes and feelings of narrators, who, taken together, are no more than Euripides likely to reduce to simple dimensions the story of a woman who is revealed in three aspects: siren, murderer of children, and betrayed, grieving woman.

Echoes of the legend can be found throughout the world. The Singhalese have a Lilithlike demon they call Bodrima, "the ghost of a woman who died in childbirth and in great agony," and who harbors vindictive feelings against men, whom she chokes to death whenever the opportunity presents itself. Women respond ambivalently to this demon and their own identification with her, and she fears them, especially when they carry brooms (their symbolic tie to their role) and verbally abuse her. But they also feel compassion for her (having perhaps disliked that role), and "often leave a lamp and some betel leaves where she may get some warmth and comfort from them." [139] How much sympathy is offered or withheld from these folklore characters is frequently dependent on how the storyteller interprets the infanticide theme.

In a story from Mexico, no motive is offered for La Llorona's seemingly arbitrary killing of her child, but in another version, a mother's "baby was always crying and she didn't like it. And then one time it rained and rained and she threw it in the river and drowned it." [140] As reported, the account appears almost neutral, no apparently overt judgment being made concerning her response to the irritability women experience in meeting the demands of their infants. In contrast, a variant from California depicts the phantom as a "woman who killed her three sons in order to be free to pursue her own wicked life," her choice of words conveying the informant's attitude. But here is a case where translation and paraphrase combine to miss an important ambiguity found in the original language. "De la llorona solamente sé que era una señora que tuvo tres hijos. Y que . . . los mató para seguir ella su vida *libre*" (emphasis added). It is not the woman but the *life* that is specifically described as free. [141] This version of the La Llorona legend echoes the "Demon Lover" ballad in which the carpenter's wife is promised a trip to the land of sweet liberty.

That a mother may also reject a child for no other reason than that she does not like it is a theme to be found in the swan maiden tale. Lessa recounts an Oceanic Polynesian tale in which Hina "becomes weary of the filth and disobedience of her children, whereupon she escapes into the heavens, leaving her husband and two boys behind." [142] Today, some women are reported as taking the line "that they will never be free until they get [their] children off their backs," a complaint that has been described as "unique and apocalyptic." [143] To the contrary, stories emanating from the legend of Lilith suggest that it is a cry beginning with creation itself.

Infanticide, historians and other social scientists point out, reflects social and economic reality as much as, perhaps more than, psychological states of mind. A majority of the world's population faces difficulty in supporting children, and emotional nurturance will be effectively thwarted when survival itself is paramount. Jonathan Swift's "A Modest Proposal" may refer to the Ireland of his time, but reflects as well a universal problem. But a study of attitudes toward children in early times—that is, before the nineteenth century—is very difficult, and in a recent account of how the medieval period coped with the economics of child raising through two systems of abandonment—*expositio* (the exposing of children in hopes of rescue by one able to care for them) and *oblatio* (placing children in a monastery or convent to pursue a religious life)—the point is made that children, "seldom seen and rarely heard in the documents, remain for historians the most elusive, the most obscure." For these little children are absent from the written records, and there is "something mysterious about the silence of all these multitudes of babes in arms, toddlers, and adolescents in the statements men made at the time about their own existence."[144] But as is true of the subject of witchcraft, for those who will let the record speak through folklore, there is an abundance of material about the parent-child relationship, linking economic and psychological factors—although it is the latter that will be emphasized in the following discussion.

Nightmare and werewolf infants in folklore reflect the demonological strain in the swan maiden tradition. These aberrant offspring are, of course, variations of the demonic child found throughout folklore. What should be considered is the extent to which the demon baby is an extension of the child abandonment and infanticide motifs to be found in swan maiden and demon lover narratives. If it is such an extension, the demon child story could be expected to echo familiar themes: the struggle between husband and wife, and the rebellion of the female partner against her role in domestic life. Some widespread Scandinavian lore focuses on the connections among swan maiden and demon animals, the pain of childbirth (with which—again—woman is specifically cursed after the fall), the problems of mothering, and the demon child:

When a woman is about to become a mother for the first time, and is afraid of the pains of childbirth, she can escape from these if she choose. She must go before daybreak to some place where there is a horse's skeleton, or the membrane that encloses a foal before its birth. If she sets up this, and creeps naked through it three times, in the Devil's name, she will never feel any pains, but to her first born there clings the curse, that it becomes half a brute; if the child is a boy, he will be a were-wolf, if a girl, she will be a nightmare [that is, swan maiden/mara].[145]

Some folkloristic and literary treatments of the demon child will be familiar from earlier chapters. Among these are tales that recount strange births, the parents wanting a child so badly that even an animal seems preferable to childlessness. The popular medieval story of *Robert the Devil* begins with the mother's desperation.[146] Similarly *Sir Gowther* tells how a woman wishes for a child wherever it may come from. The devil fathers her child, later tormenting her with the promise of a son of bad character.[147] In an Irish tale, a man would willingly "make a communion with the Devil" if this would result in a son or daughter who could be his successor.[148] A story from the West Highlands similarly explains the birth of a bad son, this time combined with swan maiden/animal groom/incubus motifs: "There was once a great gentleman in Ireland, who had three daughters, and they went to bathe. One of them went to sleep, and when she awoke, she felt the most amazing sensation. She saw a seal making off a little way from her. She became heavy."[149]

Demon child tales form a counterpoint to stories in which swan maiden or incubus is parent to a hero. When the child is aberrant, however, narratives tend to pay more attention to the tension between the human and supernatural parent, their conflict mirroring the relationship between real husbands and wives. Sometimes the impersonal mating symbolized by the animal (seal) who impregnates a woman and then moves indifferently away from her is rendered as blatant abuse. In *Sir Gowther,* the stranger who comes "disguised as the husband" behaves toward the wife with "brutal violence." In the story of *Tydorel,* the queen's demon lover is instead "a model of courtesy," but threatens that "if she reject him, she will never more know joy."[150] That their sexual relations and childbirth become the focal points for the struggle between man and woman is spelled out in the story of "L'enfant voué au diable": the parents have vowed for religious purposes to have no further sexual intercourse and when the husband breaks the vow, his wife retaliates toward their child as well as him: "forced to submit, she commits to the devil in a moment of spite the child she would bear."[151]

The demonic child in folklore and literature (and, today, film) reflects complex attitudes toward parenting in general and mothering in particular. The strange child born to a mother who will settle for any form of child depicts a strong drive toward childbirth and nurturing. But when the offspring is portrayed as a demon baby, one finds in such stories the mother's anger about her husband, child, or both; disappointment concerning her expectations for the child; and the psychological and behavioral problems she faces in childrearing. She experiences, in short, difficulty in coping with her role. The folktale group that presents these themes in a particularly concentrated form involves the *changeling* belief, in which, as Hartland explains, an "apparently human babe is an imposter" that, belonging to a different race, "has no claim on the mother's care and tenderness."[152]

According to Hartland, who studied the changeling as thoroughly as the swan maiden, the changeling involves "a belief that fairies and other imaginary beings are on the watch for young children, that they may, if they can find them unguarded, seize and carry them off, leaving in their place one of themselves, or a block of wood animated by their enchantments and made to resemble the stolen person."[153] Changelings are sometimes linked directly to incubus lore, for the incubus, as was seen, appears in some cultures as a creature who preys on children, sometimes the very offspring he has fathered. In Finno-Ugric myth, an

evil household spirit of Tartar origin is the Suksendal, which is believed to disturb the peace of the people of the house. It creates disturbances in the night, troubles people in the guise of nightmares, and has sexual intercourse with people in their sleep, appearing in the form of a man to women, and in the form of a woman to the men. Further, it deposits changelings in the place of children left alone in the house.[154]

In many cultures, vulnerable newborn babies, lacking the benefits of modern pediatrics, were viewed as innocent victims of demonic agents, and various charms and amulets existed to protect the infant from the likes of the incubus, Lilith, and other malevolent fairies. Among Christians, baptism was the crucial event, and the baby needed special protection until this sacred rite could be performed.

A look at changeling stories reveals two themes that might explain the mother's rejection of her baby and her seizing on the idea that she owes it no special tenderness. In general, the changeling is deformed and ugly, but it is also depicted as an extremely fretful child who drives its mother to her strongly antipathetic feelings. The "yelling every night" of one changeling "deprived the whole family of rest; it bit and tore its mother's breasts, and would be still neither in the cradle nor the arms."[155] The mother of Robert the Devil not only gives birth after a torment-

filled labor that lasts eight days, but also perceives from the very beginning that her child manifests bad instincts, never ceasing to cry and
kicking at its nurses.

From Cornwall comes the report of a woman who believed the "fairies had changed her baby, because it was very small and cross-tem-
pered."[156] Such a mother might be instructed by popular superstition on
how to test for a changeling or on how to recover her own child, but the
procedures she would have to follow, such as burning the child with
fiery turf held in tongs, do little more than suggest that child abuse itself
has been absorbed into folk motifs.[157] Evans-Wentz, a credulous re-
porter on fairy faith among Celtic peoples, is nonetheless repelled by
such practices, which reflected the paradoxical belief that the demon
folk were sufficiently attached to their own children that exposing the
changeling or subjecting it to punishment would summon the true mother.
Weak and sickly children thus became in reality the "objects of systematic cruelty at the hands of even their own parents." Evans-Wentz also
makes an interesting connection between the changeling and the demonic child. He reports a case from Brittany in which the black color
and deformity of the child is seen as but the outward form of mental
pathology: the changeling has "all the possible vices; and he has tried
many times to kill his mother. He is a veritable demon; he often predicts
the future, and has a habit of running abroad during the night."

The changeling belief might be a response to the birth of a deformed
or otherwise abnormal child. But folktales describe the interchange between the deviant child and the repelled parents or mother. Because
mothers provide child care, it is to be expected that stories would
emphasize the female parent's response to the strange offspring. That a
generalized antifeminism will attribute neglect to her when her baby is
"changed" suggests that the changeling may be suffering as much from
psychological as from physical problems, and that the mother's own
difficulties in adjusting to her role may be as important in explaining the
child as the child is in explaining the mother. Difficulties with the baby
have also been explained by the demon possession theory,[158] but this is
not a useful distinction unless one takes the theory seriously—or, at
least, understands it as a significant metaphor for the disturbed relations
between parents and child.

The demonic or possessed child has become a familiar figure in popular culture. In the 1970s the United States experienced the coming

together of two phenomena. On the one side women were proclaiming their freedom from childbearing in a loudly announced decision to refrain from motherhood or in defiant acts of child desertion. Among middle-class families, as was noted in chapter 2, women were now significantly outnumbering men who abandoned their families. The temper of the times is reflected when one author expresses with satisfaction that among the runaway mothers he had interviewed, only a few expressed any guilt over what they had done. And one of his interviews involves a mother who would appear to be describing a changeling rather than a real child when she admits openly, "One of my kids I don't like."[159] Coincident with this rejection of the maternal role was a spate of American novels and films based on a theme described as the " 'demonic invasion of the womb.' Children, in various stages of development, and mothers in various stages of vulnerability or violation, have been the principal figures in these parables of possession. One thinks of *Rosemary's Baby, Demon Seed, The Exorcist, Audrey Rose,* and *The Omen.*"[160] The last is the most ominous; the changeling as anti-Christ must be murdered before it succeeds in killing its unwittingly adoptive father as it already has its adoptive mother (here is the family romance from the parent's perspective). The mutual race to destroy is won by the demon child.[161] Interestingly, the movie was reviewed in an American magazine that had one month earlier featured an issue that posed the question of whether America was beginning to hate its children.[162]

Naturalized versions of the demonic child appear in Joyce Carol Oates's collection of short stories entitled *Marriages and Infidelities,* for it would be difficult to find a more unpleasant group of youngsters. Indeed, their parents find them so. An adulterous mother notes that she is not expected to love strangers' children, so "why must she love the one" who is "said to be her son." In another story, a young son displays a touch of the demonic: "I have never seen this child before and he does not know me. His face is a stranger's face. He is the child of strangers, people I would never meet. And yet there is something familiar about him—his face—a boy of about five, knowing, condemning, sly." Still another mother, a psychiatric patient eager to leave her husband, comments on the unattractiveness of her children, with their "thin chests, narrow shoulders." A pretty child in another story hates and physically abuses her brother, while a beautiful girl's autism widens the chasm between her parents. The only good child in this volume is a dead child, and his mother, married to an insensitive hard-hat, is able to idealize her deceased son: "I think of Jackie and of how he would not have grown up to be a man like these men." She has substituted a dream for a real child because only in a dream would that disaster have been averted. Jackie's father is one of the decidedly distasteful men who appear in these stories.[163] And so Oates's female characters can be related to such folklore characters as Lilith, La Llorona, and other White Ladies, for both children and mothers inspire horror, revulsion, and sympathy.

It is woman herself who will be most aware of the difficulty of reconciling her varying roles within the framework of day-to-day living. The mother whose "changeling" child vexes her waking hours and deprives her of sleep will find it difficult to fulfill her husband's fantasies of the ideal erotic partner, mother, and domestic servant. But even assuming a husband's full cooperation in his wife's quest for selfhood, or her being relieved of most of—at least the most onerous—domestic chores, the union between wife and mother is not going to be easy to achieve.[164] But where that cooperation is lacking, a woman may people her fantasy life with a variety of demons, a supernatural lover whose symbolism is a projection of her guilt, and a demon child toward whom she directs her rage. But these demons are also reflections of man's belief in essential female perfidy. It may be the kind of husband portrayed by Oates who believes his wife is not only capable of abandoning him but also capable of leaving him with a "changeling," destroying their legitimate offspring and substituting for it a demon child.

That the demon child defines a woman's lot and thus plays a significant part in her story (her autobiography and her fantasy) is the theme of Jane Addams, the renowned American social worker whose essay on the "Devil Baby at Hull House" explores the meanings of a rumor that had circulated in Chicago, that a demon infant was being cared for at the settlement house. The story, writes Addams, developed as it might have centuries earlier as a response to the imperative needs of anxious wives and mothers. Addams recalls the theory that woman "first fashioned the fairy-story, that combination of wisdom and romance, in an effort to tame her mate and to make him a better father to her children." Chicago's poor women made up the majority of the public eager to see the so-called devil baby, often dragging with them their reluctant spouses. Among these beleaguered wives and mothers, the folklore of the demon child helped to explain the "hundreds of women who had been humbled and disgraced by their children; mothers of the feeble-minded, of the vicious, of the criminal, of the prostitute." In the legendary devil infant was the embodiment of their lives.[165]

Addams's sympathy for these women in her eloquent essay lends the piece its strength, but her analysis of the fairy tale tradition behind the demon baby belief has its disturbing implications. The women who clamored to see him responded to the infant devil as if to some lost memory that had flickered only to die again. Addams must speak for the poor women of Chicago, who had lost touch with most of their own inherited folk traditions and therefore had few sustained outlets through which to articulate their pains. They illustrate not only the loss of potential insight but also the loss of solace provided by a living folklore.

# CHAPTER 6

# The Animal Bride

Icelandic sagas tell of Helgi the Bold, victorious in battle because his swan maiden beloved, Lara, brings him good fortune. But one day Helgi raises his sword so high that he accidentally cuts off the swan's leg, after which his luck deserts him.[1] A similarly hapless accident is the subject of a modern song in which one Polly Von wraps about herself the symbol of her domesticity, her apron, is mistaken for a swan, and is shot by her fiancé.[2] Bahamian folklore supplies a comparable story. Whenever a young wife takes off her human clothing and sings a particular song, she becomes a bird. Discovering her secret, her husband terrifies his wife by vocalizing the song; she "knew if he kept going, she would turn into a bird right in front of him," but he continues until the transformation takes place. Then he shoots her.[3] These hunters and warriors are prototypes of men who kidnap rather than woo their wives, their aggressiveness destroying the fragile connection between the vulnerable bird maiden and her forceful mate. It is their masculine self-image that Urvaśī appears to exploit when she goads Purūravas into recovering her stolen sheep, turning man's vaunted strength against him.

Often the traditional might of warrior and hunter is needed to rescue a swan maiden held captive by an evil being; at other times, the male folklore character is required to summon a very different kind of courage, that which he frequently cannot muster (for example, kissing the female frog). His failures appear to derive from his own negative beliefs concerning woman, his conviction, for example, that what is natural in her makes her particularly sinister or repulsive. Doniger notes that according to such views, "women and demons are dangerous, demonic women are *very* dangerous."[4] Demonic women often appear, however, to be themselves the invention of the men who fear them. Such a premise can be romanticized, as happens when the Chinese fox wife is held to reflect "the eternal mystery of woman, her power and her elusiveness."[5] In one well-known story group, a loathly hag can be transformed into a beautiful woman if a would-be hero discovers what it is that women most want. It is a woman who supplies the ironic answer: sovereignty over the man upon whom she is otherwise dependent, who is more likely to hurt or disappoint than support her.[6] Yet, woman's desire for some power is traditionally held against her, is translated into a pernicious feminine trait that justifies man's endeavor to keep her in her place.

These masculine attitudes are revealed when a single tale relates how three Scottish men marry seal maidens, one conducting a significantly different courtship from the others:

Two elder brothers began to tell the girls how much they loved them and what a good life they would have once they were married. A dress of silk, a bed of softest feathers, they promised, butter, too, and cream. In the midst of this the youngest remained silent. "What will you give your bride?" demanded his brothers, "speak, man, offer her something." But the youngest brother said nothing, for his heart was stirred with great love and he knew the gift that he must offer.

Without condition, he returns her stolen sealskin, and she subsequently pays him voluntary visits at infrequent but regular intervals. Meanwhile, his brothers and their reluctant brides settle down to unpleasant domesticity; the men grow "fat and lazy, their docile wives doing all the work." One, regaining her animal skin, escapes to the sea. Learning the wrong lesson from her flight, the third brother "decided that the only way to hide the skin completely and for ever was to burn it."[7] In other folktales, the destruction of the animal hide forever ties the animal mate to the human world, but in this instance, the house is destroyed and the seal wife burned to death.

The periodic visits of the seal maiden to the husband who would not hold her by force are reminiscent of Urvaśī's meeting with Purūravas after she declines a permanent reconciliation. But neither Scottish nor Hindu tale clears a path toward a relationship viable in the human world. This essential pessimism in swan maiden tales supplies a context for considering those versions that do conclude with a so-called happy ending. For in contrast to the captive fairy wife who yearns for the rarified atmosphere of the supernatural realm is the swan maiden who is instead an enchanted human being held captive by an evil persecutor, awaiting the hero who will release her from her spell. Reidar Christiansen has commented on these "two radically different redactions" of the swan maiden tale, "based on a different conception of the nature of the mysterious lady," noting that in the "European oral tradition both stories have lived together for a very long time," and that it is "strange to observe how the essential difference can be seen in most variants."[8] It may not, however, be so strange; in the very juxtaposition of these two redactions can be seen woman's ambiguous role.

Typical of the motif of the enchanted swan is a Danish story about three sisters carried off by a wicked fairy, allowed to revisit their old home only on Midsummer Eve.[9] The story evokes versions of the swan maiden tale found throughout Scandinavia (as well as in other lands) in which a young man secretly on the lookout for mysterious intruders that damage his or his father's property discovers maidens dancing in the meadow and takes the dress of one of them. When, in one story, the princess agrees to marry him, he returns the garment, but his trial is not over. She is a troll's captive and her deliverer must find the troll's palace, kill her captor, and restore to life those he has imprisoned.[10]

That the swan maiden story can be found in antithetical redactions sometimes renders the tale paradoxical. A Spanish father orders his daughter killed when she refuses to wed the wicked knight chosen for her. She escapes her fate by assuming a swan's form. Victim of a tyrannical patriarch, she is also a prototype of the deviant woman—a disobedient daughter. In her transformation she is analogously split, becoming a pitifully enchanted bird maiden and at the same time a siren who combs her long hair and lures the story's hero to danger. On one side the father's alter ego is personified by the evil suitor. On the other side the woman must be controlled, rescued from her own waywardness by a man virtuous enough to deserve her but also strong enough to master her.[11] Thus are combined two themes: disenchantment as a means of uniting husband and wife; and disenchantment as a means of taming the shapeshifting woman.

Some swan maidens first escape their mortal husbands and then invite them to embark on an adventure to win them back. In an Armenian folktale, the fairy virtually leaves a forwarding address: she can be found in "The Country of the Beautiful Gardens."[12] A Tibetan swan maiden similarly begins by proclaiming her freedom—"After being seized and bound, after having laughed and played, like a cow freed from its bonds, will I fly away"—but nonetheless bestows on her husband specific instructions about where she may be located. And when, in his final trial to reclaim her, her husband must pick her out of a crowd of identical fairy women, she responds obediently to his command that she step forward and identify herself.[13] Similarly, a Siamese fairy about to be ceremonially sacrificed escapes her husband (the swan maiden's fate is literalized in this version), issuing a warning that her spouse not undertake the journey to find her but nonetheless leaving anchorite talismans for his protection should he make the attempt: "the holy man gave him all that his wife deposited there, not forgetting her paradoxical wish that he would give up the pursuit."[14] Such versions yield a further paradox: the swan maiden's husband rarely appears as weak as he does when the couple is reunited because it has always been the fairy wife's intention that he recover her.

Instructions about how and where to find the lost spouse are also a feature of Cupid and Psyche tales. But from that point commences the trial that is also the wife's penance, and however courageous her actions, what ensues is acquiescence to her husband's will (which is not ordinarily the case even when the mortal husband wins back the wife lost through some blunder on his part). The order that has been disrupted in the marriage has been restored, and following her husband's instructions is what the erring wife must learn to do. In contrast, the swan maiden has escaped subjugation to her husband, and her willingness to map out her escape route is an inconsistency that can be turned by storytellers into a negative feminine trait: women are fickle, unpredictable, and unstable, the very reasons why they must be restrained. But such explanations do not sufficiently account for her inconsistency, and other rationalizations can be found in the stories.

Love is often invoked as an explanation, but conflict-free sentiment is often trivialized. The speech to her sisters by a Polish swan maiden who escapes her groom on their wedding day and unaccountably regrets her flight is worth quoting because it hovers on the edge of parodying romantic love: "I am thinking of the prince, my husband. I love to think of him, and I am so sorry for him, poor fellow! To think I left him for no fault at all; and when we loved one another so dearly! Oh! sisters! I shall have to leave you, and go back to him; only I fear he will never forgive me, however I entreat him, for having behaved so unkindly to him."[15] He had naively counted on her affection for him when he had returned her stolen clothing immediately after the marriage ceremony (or else he thought human rituals more binding than they proved to be), and his determination to find the runaway and win her back appears to indicate some maturing on his part. But since she already regrets her flight and is ready to come back, it hardly seems to matter whether her husband is strong or weak.

Princesses requiring disenchantment and fairies who coyly invite their mortal husbands to follow them do render the swan maiden story a fairy tale as that genre is commonly understood. The stories would seem to illustrate the adage expressed in one of them, that "true love overcomes everything."[16] But the coexistence of the two swan maiden patterns suggests that more problematic issues—not so easily resolved—are embodied in the confrontation between the everyday world and the supernatural realm. Happy endings are rare even in the West, and it is an error to think they are characteristic of European treatments of the swan maiden tale.[17] But wherever the stories are told, the significance of the disenchantment motif, the returning of animal groom or animal bride to a world of social interaction, of obligations to others, and of the pains and tensions of a mortal existence, cannot be encompassed by the explicit or implicit formulaic conclusion that husband and wife live happily ever after.

The reason why mortals follow supernatural mates to fairyland hardly strains understanding. As Yeats writes in "The Stolen Child," humans thus escape a world more full of weeping than they could hope to understand. It is Yeats's fairies who themselves supply the images that help resolve the more perplexing question: why should the supernatural folk, released from human necessity, seek in human mates the imperfections of mortal life? The oatmeal bins in which little mice disport themselves, and the warm hillside on which cows contentedly low speak to a comfort that offsets the sorrows of the world. That those who live with the fairies are seized with an unbearable longing for home is a common theme in folklore. In Scandinavia, seals are sometimes depicted as mortals who "have intentionally drowned themselves in the sea," indulging in the ultimate escape from earthly reality and finding their earthly paradise with the sea folk, only to yearn at times for the old life: "Once in the year, on Eastern's Eve, they can take off their skins, and enjoy themselves as human beings, with dancing and other amusements, in caves and on the flat rocks beside the sea."[18]

From the perspective of the dead or of those imprisoned in a world forever sundered from humanity, it is the mortal world that is the earthly paradise, an idea that forms the basis for a Scottish tale that relates how an evil woman had enchanted her stepchildren, who must live most of the year as seals: "in order to make her cruel act yet more cruel, she added one further touch. Three times each year, at the fulling of the moon, the unfortunate children would automatically acquire human form and walk among men. By doing this they would be better able to realize what a wonderful life had been denied them."[19] A significant number of animal brides find themselves drawn to the mortal realm, seeking out rather than being captured by their human husbands. If they are suffering a spell, they of course need disenchantment. In an Irish tale, "three swans came every day to be in the water and swim in the lake." When they see a prince accustomed to fishing there, they approach him to explain that they were transformed by a jealous stepmother and need his aid. But as seen in chapter 1, the Oceanic swan maidens studied by Lessa similarly take the initiative in finding human mates. They not only willingly enter the human world but also readily assume the domestic tasks that ordinarily repel fairy wives: in many Malaysian tales the "tidying of houses and the eating of [human] food" is characteristic.[20]

Sometimes her willing acceptance of woman's domestic role leads to the animal bride's disenchantment. A tale from Brittany relates how a man weds a swine who bears nine children, then is subsequently freed from her animal state. The original problem had been her own mother's distaste for her role; she had found all babies ugly. God had punished her with a bestial infant. The swine wife is saved by love of a man but even more by her own readiness to be a mother.[21] Similarly, an alpine swan maiden is a princess, and both she and her companions are turned into birds because, as one of them explains, "the princess did not want to be married."[22] In these stories disenchantment is a symbolic rendering of woman's completed domestication. But for the swan maiden to acquiesce to woman's traditional place necessitates a human husband. Thus a Korean swan maiden explains that the fairy wife of a mortal is a princess for whom no suitable matches could be found in heaven.[23] But to find a human is sometimes to act in ways conventionally deemed unfeminine, to initiate the union. Jameson claims that the aggressive animal bride is the projection of a male erotic fantasy. A Chinese man who desires union with a fox wife need only go to the places they haunt hoping to find him.[24] More practical is Hatt's commentary on a variety of fox wife, the "mysterious housekeeper" who secretly cleans the house of a bachelor or widower while he is out working: she is held to reflect "a typical wish-idea, natural for lonesome men." For the story of the solitary man's "home being kept in order and provided with food in a miraculous way is told everywhere with almost the same features."[25] The mysterious housekeeper will be further discussed below, but it can be noted here that once again it is the husband's, not the wife's, needs that are invoked to define the narrative pattern.

The man who imagines a perfect female partner (whether his emphasis is on the erotic or the domestic) typically also fears her and is likely to turn her away. The aggressively forward woman is seen as a kind of "wild woman," depicted by Richard Bernheimer as so "obsessed with a craving for the love of mortal men" that she goes out of her way to obtain it.[26] Bernheimer's description thus confirms what Jameson's informants report, that Chinese fox women "are near us at all times. The pretty woman who smiles at you in the street, the wife of your bosom, your daughter, your female slaves, your maidservants, may be foxes and one cannot be too careful in one's behavior towards them." Not surprisingly, men respond with ambivalence to the fox women's attention: "Their purpose may be to steal your vital essence or they may give you valuable instruction in sexual hygiene."[27]

If fear of woman, often rooted in a fear of nature itself, is commingled with erotic fantasies in which the man symbolically throws off civilization to enter into an unnatural relationship, then the husband of an animal bride may find himself in conflict with the motives that led her to initiate the relationship in the first place. It is perhaps because man cannot untangle his own response to woman that stories frequently raise the question of whether or not he is obligated, willing, and/or able to disenchant the animal bride. The motifs of domestic life that pervade the mysterious housekeeper stories, for example, indicate that fantasy and reality must somehow be reconciled, that the unreality of erotic fantasies cannot adequately explain the disappearance of the animal wife. But even granted that the ultimate male wish is for the wife who will perfectly minister to both domestic and sexual needs, there still remain questions concerning why it is that instead of depicting how the ephemeral dream relationship dissolves in the light of common day, the stories more frequently emphasize how the man subverts his own good fortune.

As noted earlier, Lilith fled Eden after refusing sexual subordination, but her rebellion can be extended to other aspects of the marital relationship. An ancient Persian legend attributes a human "fall" to a division of labor in which woman is assigned to domestic work. So long as Meschia and Meschiane hunted together, discovered fire, made an ax, and built a house, "they for a long time lived happily together." But after they set up housekeeping, "they fought terribly, and, after wounding each other, parted."[28] Many animal bride stories depict man's *need* for female ministration, and the tales address the requirement that woman devote her life to supplying it. That man would not, however, envy woman's lot is reflected in an unusual Irish "swan maiden" tale—almost a parody of the tradition. An enchanted ass comes to a great house every night and he "washes the dishes and scours the tins, so that the servants lead an easy life of it." When, inspired by exuberant gratitude, they offer him a present, he asks for only "an ould coat, to keep the chill off him these could nights." But "as soon as he gets into the coat he resumes his human form and bids them good bye, and thenceforth they may wash their own dishes and scour their own tins, for all of him."[29]

Welsh swan maidens are, again, prized as good housekeepers,[30] but an Eskimo animal bride rejects her husband's world not only because she cannot eat human food (perhaps a reversal of the folklore motif in which humans who eat the fairies' food must remain with them) but also because she "will not help" by taking on woman's tasks.[31] So bound are women to their domestic chores that, according to a story from Assam, swan maidens are not exempt from them in the otherworld. Although a mortal husband who has lost his fairy wife is chided that "she belongs to the sky [so] how can she set her mind on this earth?," the benefits to her escaping are limited. She and her sisters are depicted as having "to cook" and "to put the cocks and pits in their cage and sty," but the fairy is so deficient in these areas that her father, the sun god, complains about it, noting that she does not "weave" or "do any other work."[32] In a Bengal story, a woman discovers her son's wife has been replaced by an evil spirit precisely because the imposter cleans so well, whereas her daughter-in-law is "weak and languid, and took a long time to do the work of the house."[33] Conversely, animal brides frequently prove worthy of disenchantment by demonstrating domestic skills. In the Caucasus, a childless couple possesses an unusual pig that "took the pitcher, went to the well, filled the pitcher and brought it home," also knowing "everything there was to know about housekeeping."[34] In a Georgian variant of the frog wife tale, three brothers and their brides live in a communal household in which the frog proves as adept as her sisters-in-law at carrying out domestic chores.[35]

Frog wives are at least as ubiquitous in folklore as frog husbands; but whereas the animal groom need not display any particular skills to warrant the devotion of his human bride (although, admittedly, his often luxurious abode indicates his ability to provide well for a wife), frog wife narratives often rest heavily on the animal bride's domestic accomplishments. When, in a story pattern whose variants are widespread, brothers acquire spouses, one of the men seemingly cursed with an animal wife, she often proves the most skilled at the tasks assigned by her father-in-law, the king, and wins her husband the kingdom. Thus she must be superior in needlework, cooking, or baking. Sometimes the mysterious housekeeper motif enters the frog maiden story. While a Greek prince and his father occupy themselves with traditional male occupations (hunting), "the frog was putting [the prince's] house in order": she "stepped out of her skin, and lo! she was a beautiful princess." Nonetheless, "she rolled up her sleeves, lit the fire, and cooked the game," after which she set the table, served, "and then stepped back inside her skin and sat down in her corner."[36]

Man's psychological dependence on woman is sometimes expressed through the imagery of household work. A Senecan hunter separates from his mother to live alone in the forest. Mysteriously, his cabin is cleaned regularly and his food prepared. When he discovers the lovely moose woman who is the source of his good fortune, he thanks her for being "very kind" to him, and she responds that she knows he was "starving for lack of a woman's aid" and thus came to him to be his wife.[37] A Pygmalion motif is sometimes added to the mysterious housekeeper tales told by North American native tribes. In one version, a lonely man treats a piece of wood as if it were his wife, until a real woman appears to assume the care of his house, remaining hidden until the time when she burns the stick of wood and reveals herself.[38] The Kwakiutl tell a compelling story of how a chief owns two slave girls, one of whom dies in a fire warming herself, the other of whom tries suicide, ultimately escaping. She comes upon a house into which she peers and glimpses "two images of women [that is, two unreal surrogates]. There were piles of mountain-goat wool and spindles." She hears the man greet his images by pleading, "Please speak to me," expressing his loneliness.

When the escaped slave woman becomes his mysterious housekeeper, he believes his images are materializing and thanks them for "becoming real persons." When she spins wool, he also thanks the images for "beginning to work." The story proves a creation myth in which a people's origins are conceived of in terms of man's longing for both a companion and a housekeeper.[39] But since the emergent society is structured along conventional lines, the woman who had escaped slavery seems almost to be returned to it. The difference in her lot would depend upon her husband's continued tenderness, but animal bride tales frequently describe how the affection that should bind the couple breaks down. As a myth, the Kwakiutl narrative ironically confirms contemporary arguments that man more than woman benefits from marriage as it is traditionally constituted.

The reason why a man might long for a real woman who will ease his loneliness and keep his house, even to the point of forcing a reluctant fairy wife to assume the role she usually resists mightily, is easy to comprehend. What, again, remains puzzling is why the man blessed with a mysterious housekeeper, often an animal woman who takes human form to meet his requirements, typically destroys his good fortune. The stories provide various explanations; for example, the Iroquois widower who fashions a wooden doll that miraculously comes to life disobeys the taboo that he refrain from sexual relations for a specified period: but "the desire of the man to once more clasp his wife in his arms was too great," and when he surrenders to his desire, he finds himself "holding the wooden doll!"[40] Perhaps an etiological element in this story concerns female sexual frigidity, resulting from the man's unwillingness to allow his wife time to become accustomed to him. But as a narrative group such stories suggest a more fundamental breach in the relationship between man and wife.

A common feature of the story is that something in the wife repels the husband. For example, a fox wife accepts her "duty" to keep house and expresses the hope that "she had performed her labor in a manner satisfactory" to her husband, but he had "detected a musky odor about the house and inquired of her what it was." She confesses that she emits the odor and says that if he is going to find fault with her, she will leave —which she does.[41] It is, in short, the specifically animal nature of his wife that disgusts the man, a theme that will be explored shortly. The point now is that the man blessed with a seemingly ideal mate instigates her flight from him. What differs in the tales' focus is whether blame lies squarely with the husband or whether some attribute in the wife is invoked as a mitigating circumstance.

Two Kodiak hunters, one old and lame, the other young and handsome, live alone. The younger consistently drives away a grouse and eventually wounds it, while the other makes it a pet and builds it a nest. When the grouse proves to be a mysterious housekeeper and the smoke coming out of the chimney a sign of the clean house and warm supper awaiting the men, the younger kills his companion to take the beautiful woman as wife. But the grouse, a swan maiden, finds her stolen skin and escapes, reminding the man that she had originally sought him out: "three times you chased me away. The last time you hurt me. I will not be your wife now."[42] As a portrayal of male insensitivity, however, the Kodiak story cannot begin to compete with the Irish tale of the "Nine Days' Sickness of Ulsterman." Here the fairy not only displays exemplary domestic skills but also initiates lovemaking, laying "herself down beside" her husband and placing "her hand on his side." But she makes a demand characteristic of Celtic fairy lover tales, that the man not speak or boast of his unusual spouse. When he subsequently enters a race, he cannot resist bragging that with his wife's help he could easily win. By now she is advanced in pregnancy, but, challenged to produce his wonder woman, he forces her to run the race. She "succeeds in winning, but at the end of the course she is taken with birth pangs and brings forth twins. Her dying cry causes all who hear her to suffer the weakness of a woman in childbed for four days and five nights—a form of debility which returns upon the Ulstermen periodically for nine generations."[43]

"The Nine Days' Sickness of Ulsterman" brings together many themes. The husband's pursuits outside the home as competitive hunter, sportsman, or warrior necessitate a fierceness incompatible with his wife's requirement for tenderness and consideration. By meeting traditional standards of masculinity, he undermines his position within the very household his masculine strength is supposed to uphold. His emotional failure sharply contrasts with his wife's willingness to serve him, even if to do so means relinquishing the advantages of the fairy life. Her sacrifice effectively highlights his deficiencies—or perhaps the deficiencies of the masculine model for his behavior.

Nowhere, perhaps, is this difficulty in finding an adequate masculine image by which to live revealed as starkly as in a group of stories in which it is the mortal man rather than the woman (Psyche) who must perform superhuman feats in order to win back the lost spouse. Holmström says the man's ability to complete the tasks makes him worthy of his swan maiden wife,[44] but his argument not only bypasses the differences between animal bride and animal groom tales, but, more to the point, also overlooks a significant story group in which the fairy, not the hero, performs the impossible feats. For when the supernatural male character carries out the superhuman tasks, the traditional male-female relationship has been sustained; but when the supernatural female performs them, the traditional relationship has been inverted, with significant implications for the stories. That the male character is in effect *not* being a stereotypical man, that rather than rescuing the woman, he needs to be rescued by her, is consistent with another, almost unique feature of animal bride tales, that the animal woman is often unable to shed her beast form. When the longed-for disenchantment does take place, it is frequently because she has effectively succeeded in disenchanting herself.

When the animal bride effects her own transformation, her husband consequently acquires benefits he hardly seems entitled to, such as rule of a kingdom. If he is, for example, in competition with his brothers to produce the most beautiful fabric, his supernatural wife obligingly weaves it for him. And if a beauty contest must be won, the animal obligingly transforms herself into a ravishing princess. The husbands in such tales often appear in very poor light. A French prince keeps a frog wife whom he fantasizes to be a "beautiful woman who will not make me envious and whom no one will search to take from me."[45] He is not anxious to change his circumstances. And the prince who marries a frog in one of Calvino's tales does so out of pure self-interest, needing to win the competition with his brothers. When he calls the frog and she asks who summons her, he arrogantly responds, "Your love who loves you not." To which she responds, "If you love me not, never mind. Later you shall, when a fine figure I cut."[46] True, some husbands may show as much devotion to frog wives as do maidens to their frog princes, but their good characters do not significantly alter the composite portrait of ineffectual human husbands, some of whom actually leave it to their wives to decide how they are to be disenchanted. Such is the case when a French animal bride asks her future husband to put his fate in her hands—"Trust in me, Bedoce, trust in me. Your wife I'll be"—and he acquiesces as passively as women in corresponding animal groom tales.[47]

The sequence according to which a taboo is broken and tasks are assigned in animal groom tales is significantly reversed in animal bride stories. Psyche disobeys her husband, loses him, and in her ensuing search, she must (with his help) complete the work assigned to her. But characteristically, in animal bride stories a successful completion of tasks is a precondition of the marriage, the animal bride or her kin needing to insure their deliverance and therefore helping the man with the superhuman chores. It is only then that some taboo is imposed upon the human partner. Such a pattern characterizes the famous relationship between Jason and Medea,[48] a variant of a widely distributed folktale group in which the supernatural woman first helps the man perform the labors necessary for her or their deliverance, and is then betrayed by him, often when he abandons her for a bride from his own people. Although the substitute bride is usually rejected after the fairy wife ingeniously establishes her identity, the story motifs are the same ones that take their tragic turn in Euripides' play.

When Jason is sent by Pelias to capture the Golden Fleece, he must recover it from King Aeetes, whose sorceress daughter Medea uses her magic powers to help him yoke the bronze-hoofed oxen, sow the dragon's teeth, slay the soldiers who spring from the strange planting, and drug the monster that guards the tree on which the fleece is hung. When Medea learns that her father plans to slay the Argonauts, she escapes with Jason, thus saving his life. Euripides' dramatic focus is on how, when Jason subsequently discards Medea, she kills not only his new fiancée but also her and Jason's sons. But the ambiguity of this classical masterpiece is already rooted in folklore sources, with their rendering of the power play between the two main characters. And because Jason can take his place among the indifferent or brutal hunters and warriors who slay their swan maiden wives, it will come as no surprise that in the folktales the Medea character often is just that, a swan maiden.

Thus it is an unheroic Jason who supplies the prototype for his counterparts in these widely told stories. Sometimes the male folklore character is a gambler who owes money to an ogre or magician, and, like the hero of Sir Gawain and the Green Knight, has a year to locate his supernatural debtor and make good on his pledge. Often the ogre's daughter is a swan maiden who takes a fancy to him or, in some instances, finds her own freedom contingent on his, and after extracting from him a pledge to marry her, agrees to help him defeat her father. Desiring entry into the mortal world, the Medealike swan maiden is placed in the ambivalent position of relying upon a man less powerful than she, a man whose position in culture is, however, secure. The story develops in various ways, all of them illuminating the essential conflict.

In an Armenian story, a young man under threat of death must capture a prize bird for a king, and to succeed he must perform the tasks set by a bird maiden who has her own reason for killing the monarch. Thus she joins with the young man, directing their mutual endeavor; but "as soon as she learned that the King was dead, [she] threw off her feathers and became a beautiful maiden. 'I did everything for your sake,' she said to the Prince. 'Now you are the King, and I shall be your Queen.' "[49] Similarly, a Basque swan maiden can achieve religious salvation (one way of looking at the disenchantment theme) if she can find some hero to rescue her from her devil father.[50] But a Tyrolian version takes its place among that group of swan maiden tales in which the bird maiden is suffering an evil spell. St. Anthony directs the errant gambler to an enchanted princess who is not the magician's daughter but is rather "a child of our people, whom he stole from us."[51] In such variants, feminine weakness and dependency are equated with woman's salvation.

Not all supernatural women are willing to trade their autonomy for the subordinate role of wife. In a French tale, a cat woman helps a prince win his father's kingdom by performing the requisite tasks for him, but declines to be his queen and instead finds him another bride.[52] The Brunswick Malecites tell a similar tale of a young man who shares a meal with moose woman.

When he asked her, "Where is your husband?" she told him that she had none. "I live alone," said she. After he had finished the meal, he said, "I am going home now, but I will come and see you again. Is there anything that you want?" She replied, "No, I have everything that I want."[53]

That the supernaturals miraculously supply human needs is a common theme in folklore, and no more would have to be read into this story were it not the case that in so many animal bride tales, the animal shape embodies self-sufficiency whereas dependency comes with the female human form.

In sparring for control, the mortal man and fairy woman often strike a bargain. In one story he is "Evil Christian," and she is the devil's daughter, who performs his tasks in exchange for a pledge of marriage: presumably, their union will lead to mutual salvation.[54] But sometimes the Medea character strives to preserve her independence, agreeing to perform tasks only if her stolen clothing is returned, a narrative pattern to be found among the "Blanca Flor" stories popular in Hispanic countries.[55] The pact struck in such tales usually highlights the man's desperate need of help, as in a Polish story that tells how a father pledges his son to a monster and a swan maiden rescues the prince from his fate.[56] In an Irish variant, a prince must forfeit his head to a giant one year after his first encounter with the monstrous being, and he returns the swan maiden's garment for the same reason Gawain retains Lady Bercilak's, a desire to save his life.[57]

When the husband in the Scottish tale cited at the beginning of this chapter returns his wife's sealskin, she rewards him with freely paid visits (implicitly sexual), each partner yielding something *to* the other. In Jason and Medea tales, however, each partner extracts what he or she wants *from* the other. Because their blatant bargaining derives from the woman's power, some storytellers appear to try to diminish its importance. In a Skidi Pawnee tale, a husband will die if he cannot pick out his animal wife from the "many buffalo of her size and age" chosen to confuse him. Because his son and not the wife herself helps him make the proper identification, strength and initiative remain in the male realm.[58] Similarly to downplay female power, another variant romanticizes the bargain struck between the mortal in trouble and the bird maiden whose stolen covering he will return only if she agrees to help him:

Eligio came forward, and said, respectfully, "Fair lady, I know what it is you seek, and I will help you to find it; but first promise to do me a great favour." [Then] their eyes met, and both owned, in the depth of their own hearts, that the other bore the very image which for a year past their fancy had conjured up.[59]

In a West Indian variant, a trickster's very ability to fool the swan maiden adjusts the balance of power between them:

"Ho-day! what is become of my clothes? Ho-day! who has stolen my clothes? Ho-day! if any one will bring me back my clothes, I promise that no harm shall happen to him this day. O!" This was the cue for which the youth had been instructed to wait. "Here are your clothes, missy!" said he, stepping from his concealment; "a rogue had stolen them while you were bathing, but I took them from him and have brought them back."[60]

As parodic versions of romantic courtship, such stories suggest that sentiment is but a veneer to conceal the devices by which men win power over their women.

Other storytellers, often female, portray the man as weak and passive —sometimes implying sexual impotence. From Serbia comes the story of how a man sleeps as a swan (peahen) maiden tries to arouse him with caresses: " 'Awake, my darling! Awake, my heart! Awake, my soul!' But for all that he knew nothing, just as if he were dead."[61] Dormant "heroes" abound in such tales. In a Mexican story, the fairy woman lulls her beloved to sleep in order to defeat a rival; when she joins the prince in bed, he seems unaware that she is there.[62] A Basque swan maiden tears up trees by the roots as a display of strength, insisting that as she performs this task for her lover, he must keep his eyes closed.[63] Similarly, in the Grimm's tale "The Drummer" the superhuman feats are achieved while the man sleeps in the fairy's lap,[64] while in still another version, the fairy emphasizes how "While thou didst sleep I did the work."[65]

In a story from South Africa, the man is only symbolically asleep, suffering from a weakness of will that thwarts the bird maiden, who in frustration threatens to turn him into an "enormous hairy spider" from whom everyone will flee. If he does not do his part to assure their union, he will, she tells him, "live a life of loneliness and misery."[66] Male passivity is carried to unusual lengths in a French frog princess story, for in this version the hero does not even want to compete with his brothers for their father's kingdom. He is described as unambitious, unwilling to look for the precious cloth that supplies the object of the princes' quest: "Let my brothers have the crown. It makes no difference to me."[67] A similar character is bookish, lacking the energy expended by his brothers on physical activities, so convinced that he cannot master his brothers that he is defeated before he makes the attempt. Concepts of manliness thematically pervade these stories. The wastrel gambler of many Jason and Medea tales is said in one variant to be squandering "all the time he ought to have devoted to more manly pursuits,"[68] and one swan maiden in need of a hero's strength to rescue her from captivity asks him if he is "man enough" for the endeavor, to which he replies that he is "man enough for that and more too."[69]

Sometimes the female characters are amused by what they perceive as the disparity between masculine self-esteem and their sleeping or otherwise passive lovers. When one of these is unable to perform the tasks set him, the princess "laughed to see him helpless; and said she would do the work for him."[70] This theme is more fully developed in the Norwegian tale of "Mastermaid," where each unperformed task drives home the hero's dependence on a troll's female servant to rescue him from the dire consequences of leaving the work undone. Twice he begins by affirming his ability to do what is set him, finally to admit helplessness. The third time he does not even pretend to resources he can draw on, and when Mastermaid asks him how he will "go to hell and fetch the fire tax," he responds, "Well, that's for you to tell me!"[71] The idea of a woman who is both master and maid is derived from the story type itself. The performance of the difficult tasks by the female partner— even if she is a supernatural being possessed of magic powers—disrupts the conventional pattern in which the man rather than the young woman is master in the relationship.

Some storytellers seem compelled to reconstitute the usual balance of power. In the American story of "The Devil's Pretty Daughter," the Medea character is subdued by marriage itself: "a preacher come along, so her and Alf got married without no more foolishness. She took up piecing quilts and making soap and having babies, and never mixed in no devilment."[72] But a Celtic fairy bride is denigrated to the position of servant, a domestic apprenticeship she must serve as a precondition for her eventual marriage to a prince.[73] Two frog bride tales make a similar point. In a French version, the wife must submit to a test period determined by her future father-in-law, for despite her ability to perform extraordinary feats, it is essential to "see her in her house to know what she's good for."[74] A Mexican father-in-law similarly visits his son's home to find the fairy woman in the kitchen preparing the evening meal.[75] In all three variants, the patriarch establishes the pattern whereby the wife takes her subordinate place in the marriage. But probably no other supernatural wife is as compliant as Indra's daughter in the *Dravidian Nights*. Not only does she perform the requisite tasks that save her husband's life, but she also provides him with additional wives and becomes but one partner in a polygamous union.[76]

Forcibly domesticating the swan maiden is not the only avenue by which power is restored to the male folklore character. Sometimes the supernatural woman paradoxically uses her strength to undermine her own position. In a French story, the Medea character provides counsel instead of physical strength as she helps her future husband defeat her father, coaching him on what to say and do as the two men confront each other. As she stands behind the scenes, she seems to be already preparing herself for human society.[77] Not all stories portray such compliance, however. For example, when the Norwegian Mastermaid first successfully rids herself of unwanted suitors and then receives an invitation to the marriage at which her lover is about to wed another, she sends a response whose import is that she will not surrender her position so readily: "Give my regards to the king and say that if I'm not good enough for him to come to me, then he's not good enough for me to come to him."[78] When they are reconciled and wed, however, there seems no way for her to preserve this independence: the folktales that unite the lovers in the human world seem unable to find a way out of this impasse, perhaps because in real life it is an impasse difficult to surmount.

The substitute spouse motif supplies important plot elements and themes to these stories: in Euripides' dramatization of Medea's story, Jason's intended marriage to another instigates the final tragedy. The folktales, in contrast, usually supply a happier ending, although even here gender differences are significant. Women show great ingenuity in proving their identity and establishing their rightful place in their husband's lives, but their very endeavor is directed to a future that will deprive them of, rather than enhance, their will. When, in contrast, the story involves a substitute groom, the rightful spouse may retain his dominance by confronting his wife with her perfidy, sometimes dealing with her harshly. A Turkish husband cloaked in invisibility disrupts his wife's wedding, the "princess [being] overcome with fear" because she suspects that some malevolent supernatural power has been invoked against her. Her husband's reproach concerning how she has deceived him with another man is merely verbal—"Have I deserved such cruel treatment?"[79] This wife is more fortunate than the one in a Grimm tale; her husband first interrupts the marriage and then follows the weeping bride to her chamber:

She said, "Has the devil power over me, or did my deliverer never come?" Then he struck her in the face, and said: "Did your deliverer never come? It is he who has you in his power, you traitor. Have I deserved this from you?"[80]

The story implies that his abusiveness toward his wife confirms his fitness to rule the kingdom.

Physical punishment can be found in both animal bride and animal groom tales, one of the best known of the latter depicting how a young woman forced to live with a frog flings him in anger and disgust against a wall and in this way disenchants him. But when the animal is a woman, the themes are worked out quite differently. In animal groom tales the successfully disenchanted beast takes up his position as master over his bride, subduing in her that very strength that made it possible for her to bring the male brute within the boundaries of culture. In animal bride stories, however, the male character need only act as the forceful man he must remain after the disenchantment takes place. The theme is exemplified in a story in which a young man has to be coached by a cat woman to perform an act of which he would earlier have been incapable.

"Now, remember, you have undertaken it solemnly. This is what you must do. When you come in, you will find me sitting on the kitchen stove; you must then seize me by my two hind-paws, and dash me upon the hearthstone till there is nothing left of me in your hands, but the fur!"[81]

At first, he had demurred, for he had thought that his wife would require nobility and courage from him rather than harsh strength. But to be a man involves submerging rather than displaying tenderness. Also noteworthy is the place where he will perform his brutal act, the hearth and stove that symbolize woman's domestic role.

Mexico provides a less subtly refined version of this tale, "La Perra," in which a prince's ready willingness to abuse a little dog guarantees that she can count on him for the cruel act that will disenchant her. As she tries to persuade him to take her to a ball, he responds by kicking her violently.[82] This theme was met with in chapter 4, a German snake groom similarly forcing his reluctant bride to dance with him until her treading on his body transforms him into an appropriate husband. But the harm she inflicts is part of her essential obedience to her husband, upon which woman's civilizing role paradoxically rests, whereas the dog woman is merely abused. To juxtapose animal groom and animal bride tales in this context is to recognize that the completely socialized woman is an asset to her family and society, whereas the completely socialized man is not. The husband who does not remain at least in part an animal is not really a man—or so many of these tales strongly suggest.

A folktale group that reveals woman's precarious dependence upon man as rescuer tells of a youth who for various reasons sets out to find a beautiful woman confined within an orange (or some other fruit or vegetable); it is the story upon which Sergei Prokofiev based his opera *The Love for the Three Oranges*. Typically, when a young man cuts open the fruit, a beautiful woman emerges and asks for a drink of water. Having none at hand, he watches her perish. This happens a second time, but the third attempt finds him wiser (or cannier) as he supplies the life-saving beverage. The pair then set out for his country; but when he decides his bride ought to be received by his people with pomp and ceremony, he leaves her behind, usually hidden in a tree beside a body of water. While he is gone, a loathly servant comes to fetch water and sees in it the reflection of a beautiful woman she mistakenly takes to be herself. When she discovers the truth, she turns the orange maiden into a bird, takes her place, and by stratagem convinces the returning prince she is his bride, suffering, however, some temporary changes in appearance. They are wed, and the story proceeds with how the orange maiden must overthrow the false bride.

Narrative elements from the three oranges tale frequently combine with motifs from swan maiden stories, orange maidens often proving to be swan maidens or coexisting in tales with them. In an Indian story, an ugly woman pushes the beautiful Rání into a well when the latter asks for water. Two dove maidens dwell in the house and Rání's husband can recover his wife only if he steals their dresses. One proves to be his reincarnated wife, who implores, "Oh, give me back my dress. If you keep it I shall die," going on to echo the orange maidens who plead for water: "Three times has God brought me to life, but he will bring me to life no more."[83] And when a Greek man throws the lemon girl into water (rather than offer her water to drink), she becomes a swan maiden who swims about looking for her sisters.[84]

The orange maiden story deals blatantly, if symbolically, with the dependency relations between man and woman. As is often the case when a large narrative pattern is studied, it is the absence of a motif in one variant that highlights its very significance in another. For example, the young man in one version opens each of three oranges and leisurely chooses for himself the most beautiful of the three women who emerge from the fruit, the other two subsequently disappearing. His needs, such as they are, are the story's only concern.[85] In contrast, his counterparts in other variants experience sharp anxiety as they lose first one and then another of the orange fairies because they do not immediately grasp what is required of them. In a Portuguese version, the maiden who emerges from the cut fruit asks in vain for the drink without which she will perish.[86] But a perhaps cynical Polish storyteller has embroidered on this theme, extending the request for the symbolically life-bestowing substance to a demand for pretty dresses, so that a genuine need has been rendered as female manipulation, which the man interprets as permission to master the woman: " 'Aha! now I know what sort of lemons these are,' said the prince; 'stay, I won't cut them up so lightly.' From the cut one he ate and drank to his satisfaction, and thus refreshed, proceeded onwards."[87] He is not the only character engaged in a competition with a fairy wife to determine whose requirements in the relationship will prevail. In an Italian version of the three oranges tale, the two characters address each other as "Love" while their desires are simultaneously announced and denied, the term of endearment perhaps being ironic, since it obscures drives for survival and self-gratification that have little to do with sentiment.[88]

If the story of a princess who emerges from the fruit cut open by a man suggests his sexual exploitation of her, it also seems to teach a lesson, that it is not in man's long-range interest to gratify himself at woman's expense, that he would do well to accept temporary deprivation in order to satisfy an ultimate thirst. Thus although there is something pathetic about the orange girl who emerges from the fruit, begs for water, and dies because the man is unable to supply it, the narrative makes possible an exploration of the mutual demands husband and wife make *of each other*. In an Indian variant, it is the man who must be saved by the life-giving water. In one tale, the man cuts open the fruit from which emerges a woman so beautiful that he faints from astonishment. "The princess fanned him, and poured water on his face, and presently he recovered and said to her, 'Princess, I should like to sleep for a little while, for I have travelled for six months, and am very tired.' " But despite his dependence on her, patriarchy prevails: " 'After I have slept we will go together to my father's palace.' "[89]

The three oranges and Jason and Medea story groups share the motif of the substitute bride that turns *Swan Lake* into a tragedy: the man confuses the evil bride with the woman to whom he has pledged himself. The tale of the three oranges is also linked to animal bride stories as the imposter's blackness (or some other perceived negative trait) serves a function similar to that of the animal skin, allying woman with gross nature, the converse of which is the ideal of the pure and submissive wife. Ballet fans know that the challenge to the female dancer in *Swan Lake* is that she usually dances both roles, Odette and Odile, and that she must dance them differently, demonstrating that the evil and pure swans are at the same time different and essentially similar.[90] They also reflect two folkloristic aspects of the animal mate: the beast as enchanted human and the beast/human shapeshifter as demon. The substitute bride motif often portrays man's difficulty in working his way out of a confusion originating from an internalized nature-culture dichotomy.

The blackness[91] of the substitute bride in three oranges tales is clearly symbolic. Where she is not specifically black, she is often ugly and swarthy, such as the Arab girl in a Turkish variant[92] and the imposter in a Norwegian version, where one would not expect to find a dark-skinned woman.[93] In a German tale, the pretender is a gypsy, essentially "other" in most cultures;[94] comparably, the false bride in an Indian story is a woman from a lower caste.[95] A Moorish woman can be found in a Spanish variant,[96] and in many Hispanic examples, the stories omit the early motifs of the cut fruit and focus instead on the conflict between a wife and a wicked Negress who tries to impersonate her.[97] Sometimes it is sufficient that the imposter fail to meet some feminine ideal. In one French tale, she has "reddish-brown hair, and her skin is sprinkled with freckles."[98] She may be likened to a witch[99] or an ugly hag, that is, to the loathly lady of folklore and literature. A significant gloss on the theme may be provided by an Indian folktale, in which the beautiful daughter of a king wanders so long in search of her love, Majnún, that she "was no longer beautiful and had lost her teeth" by the time she meets him. Only if he cuts open a piece of fruit will she be restored to her original beauty.[100] This variation of the three oranges motif draws attention to the psychological "splitting" that informs these stories, fair and foul women existing as alter egos.

The tendency of the male folklore character to split the female object may be related to a theme found in many of the three oranges tales: the young man is compelled to seek the orange girl as punishment for arbitrarily offending an old woman, for example by throwing rocks at her. That his action is a crime against woman herself (similar to the rape at the beginning of Chaucer's "Wife of Bath's Tale") is suggested by a version of the story in which the offended hag is transformed into the prototype of the maiden he must now seek: her hair becomes as blonde as straw, her wrinkles disappear, and she is changed into a splendidly dressed, beautiful woman, for he had insulted a fairy.[101]

That fair and foul may be projections of psychological qualities is particularly suggestive in a Mexican story in which a "blonde, blue-eyed, and very good" folklore heroine is portrayed as a kind of prelapsarian Eve, who, living in comfort, "woke up with a whim" one day and demanded her husband "take her to live in a very leafy tree that grew by the edge of the river." Asking her "anxiously" how she could "abandon her palace where she has everything she needs" (that is, the advantages of civilization), her husband gives way to her persistence. Her ugly black maidservant enters the story as a projection of her mistress's subversive longing for nature, the maid representing both the serpent intruding on paradise and, as substitute bride, postlapsarian woman. "And this Negress had come to hope she would marry the prince. An impossible thing. How could the prince take notice of such a horrible-looking woman?"[102]

When, in a story from Athens, the black imposter promises to turn white, whiteness is an attribute not merely of beauty but also of the virtue lacking in the impersonator.[103] A similar promise in a German story that the substitute will be clean again implies the eventual triumph of society over her waywardness. She explains to her bridegroom that she had "come out of [an] egg," and because the sun was shining on her, she was "all black." She assures him, "If I can clean myself in my room, I shall be fair again."[104] The egg, more than any of the fruits popular in the story type, symbolizes the rebirth of the woman, her blackness thus being rendered some original sin that must be wiped away. The room in which she may be cleaned depicts the cultural space in which she must establish herself. And she does become fair again insofar as the story ends with the restoration of the true, virtuous bride.

In the mythologies of many people, the "dark woman and the dark man are most frequently on the side of evil, sex, and destruction."[105] In Sri Lanka the incubus is known as the Black Prince,[106] and in both animal groom and animal bride tales, blackness itself constitutes a blight from which the enchanted being must be freed. In many animal groom tales, a young woman is imprisoned by a black man instead of the traditional beast,[107] the blackness being intended to symbolize that which the beast represents. And women who take black paramours, such as those in the Greek story and in the frame for the *Arabian Nights,* reveal their own depravity.[108] In these themes can be found a clue not only to three oranges stories but also to animal bride tales in general. If black = animal = nature = evil, then it seems to follow that the female animal is, according to traditional associations between woman and nature, an even more dangerous creature than the male beast, and thereby will be even more difficult to disenchant. The Mexican folklore character who leaves her castle to live in the woods has in effect reverted to type, and, again, it is possible to understand her moral connection to the loathly woman who serves her and tries to substitute for her. But the narrator's question—how could the prince take notice of such a horrible-looking woman—can be more than rhetorical, focusing attention not on the distinction between the fair and foul woman but instead on the man's perception of these distinctions—perhaps on man's perception of the women.

That the blackness or animal form of her mate may be a symbolization of woman's essentially base character is suggested in a French tale, where a woman's secret rendezvous with her lover has been discovered by the Virgin Mary, who turns her into a frog: "You shall become as ugly as you are pretty now."[109] Thus these stories reveal that the loathsome form, blackness, or animal shape of the folklore character is reflective of a sin of a specifically sexual nature, and the fair-foul antithesis thus speaks to a distinction between innocence and experience. In a story from the Dodakanese, a beautiful girl emerges every night from a bay tree to enjoy the rest of a garden, while a prince keeps watch and spies among what seem to be golden oranges a sleeping (that is, sexually innocent) girl, whom he "stoops down and kisses" very lightly, strewing roses over her before departing. But when the young woman, a combination of sleeping beauty and orange princess, awakens, she knows something is different, and, uneasy and grief-stricken, she is refused admittance to her former abode: "A girl who's kissed and cuddled so, into the bay-tree may not go."[110] In this rejection is implied a taint of foulness associated with the man's erotic attention. No Eve, she is nonetheless portrayed as fallen and is expelled from Eden.

Virtue and evil may be distributed between true and false brides in order to protect the purity of the former, the innocent one who must serve as a model for her sex. Her alter ego is not only wickedly lascivious, but in many versions she also refuses to perform the domestic tasks assigned to woman. The imposter is frequently a slave or servant (despite her power to enchant the true bride), and it is when she comes to fetch water that she finds reflected in the water the beautiful image that she mistakes for herself. Typical is the reaction of the Arab woman in a Turkish story: "If I am as beautiful as that . . . my lady shall not send me to fetch water again!" And "so saying she smashed her jug, and went straight back to the house."[111] Here, however, the narrative faces a potential problem in its establishing of such dichotomies as fair and foul, wicked and innocent, rebellious and docile. The class distinctions embedded in the story make it difficult for the true bride to demonstrate her domestic virtues to the detriment of the imposter. It is perhaps for this reason that many of the stories in the three oranges group incorporate the motif of the mysterious housekeeper. In the Turkish tale just cited, the bride, transformed by her rival into a dove, establishes her worthiness to win back her groom by happily performing the tasks her loathly rival rejects: "She set to work to sweep and clean, until the house was as fresh as a rose, and then she set about cooking some food." In Calvino's version of "The Love of the Three Pomegranates," the imposter pierces her rival, whose blood turns into the fruit tree. An old woman picks up one of the fruits: "Every morning the old woman went to Mass. And while she was at Mass, the girl would come out of the pomegranate, light the fire, sweep the house, do the cooking, and set the table. Then she would go back inside the pomegranate." Reports to the husband about these domestic miracles set in motion the ultimate reunion with his beloved.[112]

On one side of these tales, then, is a woman fair in looks, sexually innocent, and proficient in domestic tasks. On the other side is a loathly hag whose blackness may very well symbolize depraved sexuality as well as generalized evil, and whose rebellion against domestic work is but one, if a crucial, aspect of her deviant character. Not every version works out these oppositions. The Mexican woman who prefers a natural environment to her luxurious home is certainly not bound to domestic chores. And yet the pattern holds. She effectively rejects her society in favor of the natural life, her retreat to the woods being depicted as a regressive act for which she must be punished. Her reversion to a state of nature is reflected in the character of her wicked maidservant, who as substitute bride is virtually living out the logic of her mistress's rebellion.

By absorbing narrative motifs from swan maiden and mysterious house-keeper tales, the stories of the orange girl depict an extreme splitting of the female image, creating an ideal of femininity that depends almost completely on its antithesis.

That antithesis involves a variety of folklore characters who can be subsumed under the category of the wild woman, creatures neither purely human nor purely animal who are, however, projections of the unrepressed human "able to call up forces which [her] civilized [sister] has repressed in [her] effort at self-control." [113] The wild woman appears in many shapes, ranging from loathly lady to beautiful temptress, and virtually all supernatural female folklore characters are imbued with features of the wild woman, that is, the animal side of the human being. A recent description of a wild woman in contemporary American folk-lore points to her struggle with patriarchal culture: "there is scarcely a community in Texas without its resident wild woman or loathly lady, usually said to be trying to avenge some wrong associated with a man." [114] Whether or not such a character can be perceived as a female Caliban, daughter rather than son of the wild woman Sycorax, cursing man's attempts to civilize her, what animal bride tales indicate is that this is what man has traditionally thought her to be.

It thus becomes possible to understand better one of the themes surrounding the fair-foul woman as she emerges from folklore to take her place in literature. The loathly lady is able to create the illusion of beauty to captivate a man, and "may also terminate the deception by revealing her identity through some vicious act." [115] If she is but a volatile figure out of a man's dream, essentially his invention, however, she has less control over these transformations than would appear. She can create her illusion of beauty only so long as her male partner submits to his own erotic fantasy and becomes in effect her wild man partner, abandoning reason and self-restraint. This was Chaucer's theme: once the knight in "The Wife of Bath's Tale" allows his loathly bride to make decisions for both of them, whether in the future she is to remain loathly but faithful to him, or be lovely but untrue, he has inverted the values of a hierarchical culture so that what is foul now appears fair to him.

A woman could make the same error, and demon lovers attest to this mistake. Nonetheless, animal groom and animal bride stories differ in that the animal groom's disenchantment seems to be based on an assumption that the human form is the true form, the bestial shape some aberration (except in stories where a demon's human form constitutes a deception), whereas a basic assumption about woman is that her beast form defines her essential being. Moreover, natural woman frustrates man's attempt to control the wild man within, and thus woman poses a danger in his ever-constant struggle to rise above the beast. As was seen in the chapter on animal groom tales, the woman may prefer the beast to the prince, may prefer, that is, debased nature to the confines of civilization: it is then *she* who is the animal, her beast paramour virtually an extension of herself.

Many explanations exist to account for the particularly negative portrayal of animal brides. One is a generalized antifeminism often reflected in folklore, but a more specific argument is that woman's menstrual cycle and ability to bear children emphasize her link to the natural world. The bleeding woman gives special significance to the shapeshifting motif that defines both animal groom and animal bride tales, and has supplied an explanation for Melusine's demand for weekly privacy during which time she assumes the form of a serpent. As was seen in the discussion of the star husband tales in chapter 4, female fantasy is sometimes linked to woman's periods, and in a Shuswap tale, it is when a woman menstruates that she becomes the wife of a grizzly bear, whom she mistakes for a handsome man. Later she becomes a bear herself.[116] In many cultures the menstruating woman is considered unclean and must be secluded to avoid contaminating her people. That animal brides are sources of pollution is indicated in Japanese stories of clam or fish wives: when men marry their mysterious housekeepers, their soup begins to taste better. But later they discover that their wives urinate in the food and express their disgust so openly that the women leave.[117]

Blood supplies an explanation for the man's repugnance concerning his supernatural mate in the Celtic tale of the "Daughter of King Under-Wave," which begins when Diarmid accepts the advances of a loathly lady already rejected by his more squeamish companions. She is transformed into a beautiful woman and together they live in her magnificent palace until his growing aversion and her disappearance end the relationship. The source of his repugnance is not clear: perhaps the domesticated couple has become subject to the squabbles that characterize human marriages; or Diarmid may be a Tannhäuser sated with Venus. Be that as it may, when she is gone, he searches for her, finds her ill, and must supply a life-preserving elixir: "He put a gulp of blood into the water in the cup, and she drank it. She drank the second one, and when she had drunk the third one there was not a jot ailing her. She was whole and healthy. When she was thus well, he took a dislike for her; scarcely could he bear to see her."[118] There is, of course, something vampirish about her drinking blood, female vampires being one variety of the wild woman. But the periodicity of her transformations from loathly hag to beautiful woman suggests the link between female monsters and menstruation.

Wherever asceticism prevails as an ideal, female sexuality will be enough to make a woman appear loathly. In a medieval religious tale, a clerk is plagued by the tempting figure of a beautiful woman, until he fasts for enough days to subdue his flesh. Then she reveals herself in her "true" form, a hideous hag.[119] And Jewish folklore contains the story of a man who marries a rabbi's daughter renowned for her erudition in religious matters, only to be repelled when he removes her veil and discovers her animal face. Although he is moved by pity to consummate the marriage, he leaves the next day, and the son born grows up and seeks his father, eventually effecting the reconciliation of his parents and transformation of his mother.[120] This story has been assigned to the tale type involving the recognition scene between an estranged father and son, and the animal nature of the woman has been relegated to at best minor importance in the story.[121] But this may be another example of how the analysis of a tale that overlooks the significance of gender reiterates the original offense to the female character: the extreme polarization of the intellectual and the physical is embodied in the animal woman, and it is she who suffers the effects of this man-made dualism.

The male werewolf reflects similar beliefs concerning man's periodic reversion to his brute nature, and of course men are not exempt from the opprobrium attached to the animal side of human nature (although no biological explanation comparable to female menstruation is offered by stories or commentators). Nonetheless, the *animal* in the animal bride appears to be a more significant feature of animal mate tales than of the corresponding animal groom stories. For even if it is true, as Holbek contends, that a female audience might imbue the animal groom with as many bestial attributes as are given to animal brides, merely confronting the mate with his animal nature is not typically the reason for his disappearance. In contrast, it is frequently enough to discover the woman's animal origins, to remind her of them, or to allow her contact with her natural element for her to disappear. One story tells how a hunter forms an alliance with a beaver woman who requests that he build her a bridge to prevent her feet from touching water. He neglects one spot and she reproaches him for his carelessness: "I only asked thee to help me dry-footed over the waters. Thou didst cruelly neglect this. Now I must remain for ever with my people" (that is, imprisoned in her animal form).[122]

Native American folktales provide many instances of the woman's difficulty in concealing her beast form. The Menomini tell how when a man had first met a bear woman, she had looked just like a human being and had not revealed her dual nature. But in her husband's home "it now and then became apparent who she was."[123] A Modoc bear woman tale concerns a character who is a woman by day and a bear by night. Her human mate has never discovered her animal form but is nonetheless repelled, for despite her beauty, he is aware of her strangeness, and of a strength that particularly disturbs him. He "was afraid to be in a strange house with such a powerful woman." She, in turn, knows that he is suspicious and is afraid to go to sleep before he does, for "he would see her when she was a bear."[124]

He is not the only folklore character put off by his wife's animal nature. In a Pawnee tale an unfaithful wife is killed by her husband, less for her adultery than for bestiality. Although he mourns for his lost wife, he uses his bow and arrows, a symbol of his power over nature, to kill her, "for he did not like to see her with the horse's tail."[125] In Norwegian lore it is the *hulder's* cow tail that reveals not only her supernatural but also her animal origins, and in one story, she admits in an impulsive moment that she is sometimes tempted to kill and roast her children, after which her husband never feels the same way about her.[126] A contemporary and satiric rendering of the Slavic *Russalka* reiterates such themes. The fairy wife is nauseated by cooked food, finds human clothing intolerable, and is horribly bored by female tasks such as embroidery. The prince, her husband, believes Russalka is under a spell. He is right, claims this witty feminist writer, "although he'd got it all backwards: Russalka's paleness, her sluggishness in the cold, her slippery skin, her odd smell, and her strange eating habits—these were not the work of enchantment (as the Prince thought) but the only things left about her that were natural. The enchantment was all the other way."[127]

Such an author would find in swan maiden stories (of which *Russalka* is a version) an apt paradigm for the idea that civilization is antiwoman, and would hear from the folklore of the past voices that echo her own themes. But one story element unites traditional and modern renderings of the animal wife theme: the man's revulsion against his spouse not only derives from presumptions of innate feminine corruption but also ironically thwarts his wife's attempts to conform to his world.

According to stories told by the tribes of North America, if women are not properly socialized when young, it will be virtually impossibly to subdue their disruptive animal instincts. A young girl has no inkling of what she provokes when she urges her older sister, who has no lover, to imitate a bear. " 'No, younger sister, if I did it, I should turn into a bear.' 'Well, do it, that will be more fun.' "[128] Playing animal is tantamount to becoming one in other tales. Widespread is the story of the woman who takes a bear lover and herself turns into a grizzly to revenge herself on the family or tribe that kills her animal mate. The Jicarilla Apache have been described as believing that women are mentally and morally weaker than men, that they are more likely to succumb to erotic passion, and also that they are more inclined to quarrel. They tell stories in which sexual perversions usually involve women, and in which the theme can be found that too few societal restraints release the animal in woman, whereas too many awaken the beast in man. Thus when a sister and brother are left without parents to supervise them, it is she, not he, who becomes a deer;[129] whereas, in another story, an overprotective mother confines her son too much and when he finally escapes from her to join other boys in play, he becomes a buffalo.[130] The boy's mother is herself a buffalo woman, her childrearing practices as inappropriate to his role in society as is her animal nature. When he becomes an animal, it seems to be because she, not the men among his people, was his model.

In a recent and significant change of emphasis, the deer woman tale told by storytellers on a Ponca reservation has shifted from a story about a temptress preying on men to one about a female seducer who leads girls away from their families to the cities, where they live evil lives. The deer woman continues to exist in native lore, "but now as the head of a prostitution ring, and until she is destroyed, Indian women will remain in danger."[131] Clearly, however, the narrative's central point remains unchanged despite the shift from young man to young woman as victim:

deer woman is a negative prototype of female animalism, continuing to victimize men but also encouraging other women to exploit their essentially animal nature.

So long as the woman retains her tie to nature, so does she retain some power. According to Tom Peete Cross, the Celtic fairy, "at first an animal *sans phrase,* becomes a supernatural woman in animal form, and finally a fairy maiden whose power resides in her clothing"—that is, a swan maiden.[132] But since the loathly lady lurks beneath the fair exterior, the animal form assumed by the woman will be as fearful and repellent as that taken by the animal groom. It would thus be wrong to believe, as does Max Lüthi, that the folktale hero who marries an otherworld bride "notices nothing disturbing about her,"[133] fails to perceive, that is, the wild woman in the fairy. Animal bride stories show that a husband is likely to feel threatened not only by the fairy's purely instinctual self, which arouses his, but also by her potential for what Kapferer describes as the disordering of both nature and culture.[134] This threat and its consequences is exemplified in the Maori tale of "The Fairy Woman of Takitimu": "Truly she was desirable, but there was danger in her beauty. No mortal could safely wed a fairy woman, as she clearly was, for her enchantment might bind him to the mountain for all time." Like the animal skin that can be burned, the fairy's spell can similarly be destroyed through a fiery exorcism that strips the woman of her power. Thus a physical struggle ensues in this story, and in a moment when the husband's attention wanders, the fairy makes a successful dash for freedom. The image of her escape echoes the swan maiden tales: "Like a bird flying from the snare of the fowler, she raced for the safety of the friendly forest. In an instant she had gone."[135]

The theme of the burned animal skin highlights another difference between animal groom and animal bride tales. Usually the animal is a human suffering an afflicting enchantment, and frequently when he or she is asleep, the human partner destroys the animal skin to prevent the reversion to the beast. Sometimes the animal mate is grateful for the act and the disenchantment has been successfully achieved. But at other times, the destruction of the beast covering is an assault and precipitates the catastrophe by which the spouse is lost and must be won back, the struggle between the social and the natural being not so easily resolved.

Where the woman too early destroys the hide of her animal mate, she has seized an initiative ordinarily denied her, and her subsequent trials are—as the chapter on Cupid and Psyche contended—a kind of penance. But where her destruction of the animal skin is timely and the hero is disenchanted, he is also—again—socialized, elevated above raw nature, exchanging the negative ideal of the wild man for the higher ideals of civilization. And ordinarily the animal groom wins more than he loses in this adjustment, enjoying the unique gains given only to men in society, such as the rule of his kingdom. Only occasionally will a tale imply that civilization brings with it discontents, and in some instances the animal groom will resist mightily his transformation to humanity. In a Turkish story, for example, the folklore hero not only provides instructions about how to burn his skin but also admits to the woman who will carry them out that he will not readily relinquish his tie to the wild:

Tell my parents to build a bath one hundred meters from the palace and place a large pile of firewood near it. Then, tomorrow night, when I shall come and spend the time with you, have the feathers burned while I am asleep. But make sure that the bath is a hundred meters away, for if I sense that the feathers are being burned, I shall rush madly to them and perhaps be burned to death in the fire.[136]

And, indeed, he makes a last desperate attempt to retrieve his animal covering, restrained by his father and soldiers, prototypes for what he is to become. Similarly, in the Grimm's fairy tale "The Donkey," a king arranges to have his son-in-law's skin burned, and the animal wonders how he is to evade the yoke of culture: "Now I shall have to contrive to escape."[137]

In animal bride tales these themes are related to the basic swan maiden tale. Typically, the captured brides plead urgently for the return of their stolen animal skin or clothing, and this urgency reflects their resistance not so much to society as to male domination. Occasionally, however, the supernatural realm does appear to issue a veritable call of the wild summoning the woman from civilization. In one story she responds to her rescue from demons much as the Turkish bird lover reacts to the burning of his bird feathers. A cotter happily marries a young woman whom the fairies have been as yet unable to seduce from "this world of love and wedlock," and overhears their plot to steal her from him and substitute in her place a wooden effigy. Because he has been privy to their scheme, he can contrive to save his wife. But while he holds her fast in his arms, she reacts against the restraint: "She speaks, cries, entreats, and struggles," but he "will not move, speak, nor quit her."[138] A seal maiden story from Scotland works a variation on this motif. Even the return of her sealskin will not allow the wife to return to her people: the seals, she says, would not touch her and could not help her because of the "blessed water on [her] face and forehead." One night she is allowed to join the sea folk, but she is correct—none of the seals will come near her because of the holy water that more effectively than burning had destroyed her animal essence.[139] From the fairies' point of view, it is the human and not the animal world that is tainted, human clothing, not the animal skin that is odious. When, in a star girl tale told in Panama, the swan maiden is seized by a mortal boy, she tells him bitterly that he can let her go: "I'm already stained with the smell of your skin, so where could I flee to get away from you?"[140] This merging of themes—the swan maiden's flight from domestic life and the animal bride's reversion to pure nature—defines an essential difference between the disenchantment motif in animal groom and animal bride tales. The burning of the animal wife's skin, like the burning of the animal husband's, represents the triumph of culture over nature. But whereas the man whose beast hide is destroyed rises, again, to the full status conferred on him by society, the animal bride's conversion almost always implies a loss of status, a transition from freedom to control, not only the internal control that society demands of all its members but also the specific control of her husband.

Several stories can be invoked to illustrate the loss suffered by the fairy wife forced to endure domestic bonds. A modern Greek tale relates how a man traps his mysterious housekeeper by destroying her outer covering. She threatens that if he burns it, he will "suffer much trouble," but he does not heed her, and although she "went on serving him and was as his wife," the story ends with a premonition of future domestic discord as their relationship goes the way of most marriages.[141] Another mysterious housekeeper who seems willing to perform domestic tasks only so long as she retains her animal skin is a character in an Arawak tale, whose language makes very clear what the burning of her dog skin means: "With the pelt destroyed, the white spirit could not retrieve its own identity and *had no choice* but to remain a woman."[142] Similarly, a Greek story tells how a jackdaw discards her feather covering to become a "lovely damsel" at night, putting it back on in the morning, "when she resumed her bird shape." When, after begging her in vain to discard her feather dress, the prince burns it, the smell of burning causes her to rush too late to the oven to rescue it. "But before she arrived it was utterly destroyed, so she *had to remain a woman* for the rest of her life." [143]

To remain a woman is to be deprived of whatever choices are implied in the shapeshifting motif, an idea to be found in an Albanian swan maiden tale in which the wife who flees her husband's home leaves word where he may find her. No fool, he burns after their reunion the magic garments whose retrieval had made her escape possible, and no options remain to her but to be his wife. Ironically, she herself lights the fire in which her garment is burned, and she lights it in order to perform the housewifely task of washing clothes. But this is a swan maiden who has consistently sent out mixed signals, having internalized man's world at the same time that she rebels against it. [144] In three of these four examples, the fairy wives will freely assume woman's domestic role provided some autonomy associated with the animal covering can be retained. Conversely, domestic tasks become onerous when choice is denied. Thus while both animal groom and animal bride stories reveal that burning the animal skin means that the transformed person will become fully human, only for the animal bride does the social contract spell not only the loss of freedom but also the diminishment of status.

Thus the burning of the animal skin or some analogous act in which the animal woman is harmed or maimed may come to symbolize virtual wife abuse. Horrific mistreatment frequently results from the clash between a woman's striving for autonomy and the man's need to dominate. In a French tale concerning a cat woman, a man awakens one night to find that his wife is gone; when she returns, she will not account for her absence. He bolts their door, but she manages nonetheless to get in, and after awhile he decides to stay awake to see how. When he sees a white paw come through a cat hole to unlock the door, he hacks it off. "Nanon did not come near the house for three days. On the fourth day she came home. One of her hands was missing. After this she never went out at night." [145] Similar mutilations were discussed in the chapter on the incubus; it is rare in animal groom stories but frequent in animal bride tales that the real and symbolic wounds inflicted on the beast must persist in the continued life of the human. For apparently only animal brides must be forced into such extreme submission to societal rules.

The female animal skin represents instinctive patterns of behavior to which woman may cling as a guarantee of freedom, also sustaining, however, the antifeminist view of woman's easy regression to a state of nature. To assign her the role of civilizer is a way to control her, but when that role redounds to her disadvantage, her autonomous self may be aroused and her "animal" nature may erupt in a quest for freedom. Such themes appear to inform a curious novella by David Garnett, *Lady into Fox,* based on widespread folklore. A man watches his wife's metamorphosis into a vixen and then her progressive reversion to type, until, beyond any help he can offer, she is the victim of hunters and is torn to pieces by the human-trained dogs that pursue her. The heroine, Silvia, had been a conventionally, perhaps too properly raised young woman, whose socialization, however, may have remained incomplete because of the early death of her mother and invalidism of her father. "That she did not grow up a country hoyden is to be explained by the strictness of her governess and the influence of her uncle."

Instinct and upbringing compete to explain Silvia, who was "always a little wild at heart," although "living in so wild a place" might also have contributed to what happened. But in her youth, she was well behaved, the animal being revealed—perhaps—only to her husband in their intimate moments. Even after her transformation, Silvia ludicrously tries to remain a lady, but her reversion to nature becomes more and more pronounced, and for a time her husband follows her by implied acts of bestiality against which his socialized self finally reacts in self-revulsion. Soon, however, Silvia abandons all traces of the human, there no longer remaining even the chance that she can remain a house pet. In the wild she finds a fox whose young she bears. But before that, the narrator—perhaps fearful that his point will have been missed—spells out what must be taken as a gloss on Garnett's theme. While a fox, Silvia meets her old nurse, Mrs. Cork (the nomenclature is too obvious), and fears interference in the struggle between her and her human husband. For he "was always trying to bring her back to be a woman, or at any rate to get her to act like one," whereas she appears to have "been hoping to get him to be like a beast himself or act like one."[146]

Garnett's novella explores the ambiguities of repression, of both too much and too little, but its treatment of gender also illustrates essential themes in the folklore behind it. The strictly brought up girl's reversion to nature might help advance more enlightened principles of child raising. But such enlightenment would still appear to serve the ends of her husband, whose own ties to male-dominated culture are strong. The pathos of the novella's ending, the fox wife's death at the hands of hunters, echoes the stories of swan maidens slain by insensitive or brutal human lovers.

The split between Silvia the woman and the fox is reflected in a mother-daughter pair in Giovanni Verga's short story, "La Lupa." The she-wolf is a widow so lustful that she is shunned by her community, and the story's narrator associates her with a variety of folkloristic wild women, not only the female werewolf but also the vampire and succubus. Her ravening desire for a young man inspires her with the idea to make him her son-in-law and thus keep him available to her. The daughter's growing love for her husband is paralleled by her increasing accommodation to a patriarchy she appeals to against her mother. And the son-in-law, who had eventually submitted to the older woman, evidences by his determination to kill her his subduing of his own instinctual self. And so the story ends with the she-wolf moving toward him, at the same time aggressive and imploring, while he raises a murderous weapon against her:

The She-wolf saw him come, pale and wild-eyed, with the ax glistening in the sun, but she did not fall back a single step, did not lower her eyes; she continued toward him, her hands laden with red poppies, her black eyes devouring him. "Ah! damn your soul!" stammered Nanni ["Ah! malanno all-anima vostra!"— balbetto Nanni].[147]

The folklore of the animal bride provides a special context for understanding this ending, and it is not necessary to argue for Verga's conscious use of folk motifs to recognize the irony of his conclusion. The hunters and warriors who slay their animal mates do so with a special brutality derived from their traditional notions of masculinity. By depicting Nanni as stammering as he raises his weapon against the she-wolf and as he utters the curse that is tantamount to his self-exorcism, Verga has succeeded at one and the same time in upholding the patriarchy Nanni represents and subverting the masculine image that bolsters it.

The destruction of the animal spouse's skin represents a kind of exorcism, and such ceremonies have long been the object of studies concerning the cultural significance of exorcism rites performed over women.[148] For understanding the folklore of the devil's or animal bride, certain distinctions should be recognized. On one side, exorcism banishes the evil spirit that has invaded the woman, and the devil's bride is returned to her proper role in society. On the other side, animal brides portray the externalization of some essential female nature that must be altered or at least controlled in order to extract woman's compliance with patriarchal culture. The view of the female animal mate is thus as harsh as that of the devil's bride, and as a result equally harsh treatment of her is depicted as justified.

It does indeed sound "like a poor joke" to argue that "in certain cultural settings, demon possession and exorcism provide a road to woman's liberation." Not only is there prestige in being possessed by a devil or a god, but the person being possessed will also become the center of attention. "The meek wife becomes, for a few hours, a vehicle of the unknown; the old maid can be invitingly sexually passive or active; the virginal nun can escape her anonymity, become a center of attention for male priests, while being manhandled by 'the devil.' " Moreover, women undergoing exorcism rites could with impunity make ordinarily forbidden demands, and their husbands could "at times be persuaded to be more considerate toward [them]." [149]

To ask why in most cultures more women than men require exorcism is essentially to ask why more women than men were tried for witchcraft. An answer to the former query may be implied in a study that covers both men and women in Ethiopia, each of whom must undergo exorcism to "carry on his normal role in the community." [150] That intended gender-neutral phrase is both deceptive and illuminating. If woman does experience liberation in exorcism rites, it is at best a temporary one. *Her* normal place in society is subordinate to *his* normal place—as the folktales make very clear. There are, of course, feminist polemical implications in this distinction. But that is not the point being stressed. Both men and women in folklore mate with beings from the otherworld, sometimes animals whose duality suggests a nature-culture conflict, at other times fairies who reflect the human imagination's capacity to conceive of a world better than the one to which people must realistically adapt. What folktales suggest is that for woman the conflicts between nature and culture on one hand, and fantasy and reality on the other, are more problematical than for man, because woman's usual position in society makes the lure of raw nature and the appeal of the otherworld potentially even more enticing than they are for man. Perhaps only the male artist can identify with woman in this respect, which is why the nineteenth-century European writers were drawn to a female persona and the essential otherness that marked her, frequently portraying the fairy woman as a muse.

Folktales express the perhaps unconscious understanding that so long as man battles the otherworld's attraction for woman instead of assessing more astutely woman's relationship to it, he will fail in his repeated attempts to bring woman fully under his control (short of destroying or losing her altogether). He will be unable to disenchant the animal bride even when she longs to be freed of her animal form and even though her transformation will effectively domesticate her. It would seem that the animal bride cannot become fully human until her would-be deliverer frees himself of his perceptions of her *as* animal. His fear of her as beast appears to symbolize a more generalized fear of female human sexuality that paralyzes his will: women will almost invariably kiss frog princes, whereas a noteworthy number of men cannot kiss the frog princess.

A Portuguese story, "The Little Tick," suggests that men, at the very least, have as much difficulty as women undoing the effects of sexual repression. When the male folklore character spends the night in a palace where he is served a sumptuous if lonely supper, and where "a good bed appeared for him to take his rest," he is awakened and frightened by coming into contact with something "very cold and clammy." He "soon became accustomed to the sensation," however, and begins to hold long conversations with the tick, which, when he agrees to marry her, is transformed into a beautiful woman.[151] But in a story from German medieval literature, an enormous pressure must be exerted on Wolfdietrich before he comes to the same point. He "gains his wife by overcoming his natural revulsion against a hairy monster which treads upon his heels," a "creature" who has the "impudence to demand his love." When he refuses, she takes her revenge by making him mad, and he wanders the forest as her counterpart, a wild man. Only when he agrees to marry her is he disenchanted—as is she.[152] A similar tale from South Africa contains undertones of the swan maiden tale. When a prince sees a green water monster, he "held his breath with horror," but soon "this hideous creature touched the water [and] the green skin fell away," there standing in its place the "loveliest maiden he had ever beheld."[153]

Female werewolves represent the fearfulness of such creatures, but stories about them frequently deny the possibility of disenchantment. In a Persian tale, a man learns that his son is fated to be torn to pieces by a wolf. As a result, the child is hidden away and tutored privately so that he can be protected from the outside world. But when the time comes for him to marry and he finds himself alone with his bride, no sooner does he put his arm around her waist, "than she suddenly turned into a wolf and tore him in pieces. When she had done this, she turned again into the same girl as she was before," one so out of touch with her own nature that she cannot explain what happened: " 'I don't know,' said she, 'but I know this much, that I turned into a wolf and tore him, and then again I turned back into myself.' "[154] Again, in "La Lupa" Verga works out these themes by splitting the female image between the dangerous mother and her docile, socialized daughter.

The vagina dentata motif found in many animal bride tales focuses not only on the dangers of female sexuality but also on the specific threat it poses to male sexuality. Typical in its basic outline is a story from the Kiwai Islands, which is untypical, however, in its suggestion that the attribution to woman of sexual evil may be an essential projection of male fear and suspicions, in this case revealed in a dream. A man is approached by a woman but declines to have sexual relations with her, "for her vulva was provided with sharp teeth and opened and closed continuously like a mouth. Again and again he tried to muster up courage but shrank back every time." In anger, the woman attacks him and he flees into water after which he finds, "to add to his horror," that he is threatened by a crocodile. Just as the animal is about to catch and to devour him, "he opened his eyes."[155] The complexities of the dream motif were discussed in chapter 5. However this story is read, it takes its place among those in which a man proves unable to summon the courage necessary to disenchant his animal mate.

That an unwary man will be literally or symbolically castrated by the animal woman is a theme in many stories, an example being the Thompson tale of a woman "of very handsome appearance and enticing manners," who is accustomed to wander through the mountains where she offers herself to men who pass by, "every one [falling] victim to her wiles." But her "privates were the mouth of a rattlesnake," and thus "many hunters never returned home," their "bones" becoming plentiful in the area where the wild woman roams.[156] Similarly, in a Zuñi narrative, a young man is horrified by a snake that speaks gently enough to him, but will, he fears, bite him and devour his flesh while he sleeps.[157] An Algonquin story tells how two girls are changed to water snakes after they fall into the habit of absenting themselves from their people every Sunday to run around naked and swim in the lake, "wanton, witch-like girls, liking eccentric and forbidden ways."[158] The phallic shape of the female serpent, of course, only highlights the antagonistic confrontation between male and female sexuality in animal bride stories.

It is the castrating power of the deer woman that the Poncas especially fear when they describe how her chosen victim "could not go to any other woman, no matter how much he loved and wanted her. The Deer Woman held him with her magic eyes," but killed him when she "trampled his genitals with her knife-edge hooves. Even if he had lived, he would never have been a man again."[159] As noted above, in this contemporary retelling of the traditional Ponca tale, young women become prostitutes under deer woman's influence, but the essential themes remain unchanged: the prototypically evil woman spawns other female deviants, whose unbridled sexuality attacks the basic fiber of society, which is often linked to male sexual prowess.

About this theme, animal mate stories are frequently ambiguous. Sometimes male sexuality is equated with nature *and* culture, whereas despite the critical role woman plays within culture, female sexuality (outside the context of childbearing) tends to be associated only with nature. But at other times, animal mates of either sex represent the dangerous lure of gross matter. Bear spouse stories of North America are often particularly explicit on this point. Frequently a woman must step on bear feces to qualify as the animal's wife;[160] correspondingly, men who take bear wives are drawn to the beasts' completely unsocialized behavior, and at the same time are repulsed by it. That woman is victimized by such ambivalence appears to be the point of an Ojibwa story that tells how "Bird-Hawk lived with a woman; very much he hated her, for attempt was made by her to be intimate with him; and so throughout the whole of every night he was kept awake by her. Truly no desire did he have to be intimate with the woman."[161] It is *because* he recoils from her that she becomes a bear. The Chippewa convey a similar theme by playing an interesting variation on the burned animal skin motif. The "Bear Girl" of the story's title marries a man who finds himself repelled by his bride. "She would sit by her husband, and he'd start moving away. When they went to bed, her husband bundled himself up in a blanket and turned the other way. She told her husband that she was very sad that he did that. She said, 'Since you don't like me

anyway, just make a big fire and throw me in,'" adding that when
" 'I'm all burnt up, smooth out the ashes.'"[162] In another version of this
story, a beautiful woman emerges from the fire, refusing, however, to
share her husband's bed.[163] Woman's uncontrolled lust as well as her
frigidity seem to reflect not so much on her as on her husband's perception of her.

Scholars who have looked for the folklore sources of such narratives
as Chaucer's "Wife of Bath's Tale" have traced them to what is called
the *fier baiser* (fearful kiss) motif, which can involve either a male or
female folklore character who must be freed from a loathsome shape in
order to become human. In animal bride versions, a woman is for one
reason or another forced to assume the ugly and horrifying form until
she receives one or more kisses from a man, or until her rescuer can hold
on to her long enough for the spell to be broken. According to commentary on the *fier baiser*, "not every man or woman will have the kindly
courtesy or the physical courage to undertake the adventure,"[164] although the examples supplied indicate that men are particularly noteworthy for being unable to summon sufficient valor for the endeavor.
The annals of German lore, for example, are said to be "strewn with the
failures of men who could abide the first and second trial, but not the
last" (either the kiss is itself the last trial, or a final kiss cannot be
bestowed).[165] Such men could be compared to the husbands and fathers
met with in earlier chapters, who are unable to rescue women taken by
the otherworld because the stolen are tainted by it in ways their own
culture rejects.[166] This theme shows up in a Hollywood movie that
remains a favorite among film enthusiasts, *The Searchers*, in which a
young girl kidnapped by Indians becomes the object of her brothers'
extensive search, only to be rejected by them when they discover she has
been an Indian's wife.

It is possible to distinguish in folklore and the literature influenced by
it three different forms of a tale that involves the female beast who must
receive a hero's kiss to be disenchanted. Sometimes the loathly lady is
the aggressor and bestows the kiss on the unsuspecting hero who has no
chance to resist. At other times, the male protagonist musters the necessary daring to bestow the kiss, displaying his courage and proving his
worth as a man as well as disenchanting the woman. In such stories,
ladies who must be rescued from dragons seem to merge with those who
must be rescued from their own dragonlike forms. And, finally, there is

the version popularized in "Hippocrates' Daughter" from Mandeville's *Travels,* a tale in which a character known elsewhere as the Lady of the Land (in Morris's *Earthly Paradise,* for example) is deprived of a chance to be human because her would-be deliverer is too repelled to touch her.[167]

With literary embellishments and graphic detail one version describes the ordeal such a man faces when although "sick with horror," he is resolved to "dare everything" for the sake of the woman he had first encountered as a ravishingly beautiful woman. Then he sees a huge and hideous toad. "Its moist skin glistened under the cold light of a silver moon, while its great eyes burned with a green and baleful light," and its mouth was "wet and slavering." A "toad he had expected, but not this loathsome bloated creature. It might be some evil spirit, sent to destroy him with its embraces." As it approached him he "leaped back, thrusting out his hands to ward it off, and covered his face. 'I cannot touch you,' he moaned; 'you are too horrible.' "[168] By comparing this story with the Portuguese tale of the little tick, it is possible to achieve a better understanding of the fearful kiss motif. The wet and slimy toad's mouth provides as repulsive an image of female genitals as the vagina dentata motif provides a fearful one.

Some stories illustrate that a man might face a multitude of dangers less fearfully than he confronts a woman's sexual demands. A humorous variation on the theme can be found in a Spanish story where jousters competing for the hand of an ugly bride try "to get run through themselves" rather than defeat their opponents. When one of the reluctant suitors wins the repulsive maiden, he thinks of armed combat as easy, but he "could not bring himself to kiss the Princess as he was expected to do," much less marry her.[169] Not so funny is the story of "The King of the Golden Mountain," told in Turkey and in the Grimm's tales, as well as in America as "The Snake Princess."[170] The hero who wishes to disenchant a serpent woman undergoes many tortures successfully, including being beheaded. But again, his ordeal seems nothing compared to physical contact with the female snake. Revulsion toward the animal bride, especially if, as one French critic has argued, her phallic-serpentine shape suggests her usurpation of male power and dominance, is the central theme in the widespread "Melusine" legend.[171] As punishment for a transgression against her mother, Melusine must one day each week assume the partial shape of a serpent. But if a mortal husband will allow her sufficient privacy to guard her secret, she will win a human soul. Unfortunately, Count Raymond of Lusignan is so appalled by the strange children Melusine bears him that he intrudes on her in seclusion and discovers her secret, whereat she is transformed fully into a serpent, and, deprived of her salvation, she flees her family.[172] This French legend has been linked to the frequently told Japanese story concerning a female snake lover.[173] And sharing these motifs are the equally popular Japanese crane wife tales, which tell how a bird woman lives with a man, periodically asking to be put in a cabinet and left alone for three days, a time she uses to secretly produce a fine cloth he can sell for much money. Not content to leave things alone, he peeks into the cabinet, and as a result loses his bird wife and also the prosperity her skill had made possible.[174]

Common features link Melusine and swan maiden tales, and one version of the fox wife story not only combines these two narratives but also illustrates their connection to a larger animal bride pattern. A man who is cared for by a mysterious housekeeper finds and hides her fox skin so that she remains his wife and bears his child. For a time he is content, but one day he becomes "annoyed at something and accused her of having been a fox." Asked to prove this, he takes out her fox skin, which she seizes, vanishing.[175] What distinguishes the Melusine type tale from the swan maiden story is that revealing the wife's animal nature or taunting her with it triggers the catastrophic end to the relationship. A Japanese legend tells of how a fox woman elects to live in the human world, and at first her husband is happy with her and their son. The disaster occurs when he discovers rice planted upside down (comparable to Melusine's strange children). Unexpectedly returning home, he discovers his wife's fox tail. She has no choice but to leave him, although the story continues as such legends often do, telling how the animal mate bestows good fortune on the people it had lived among.[176] This husband is blessed with a plentiful rice crop and larger-than-ordinary profits. The animal spouse is an emissary from nature, bringing with its visitation to earth nature's dual capacity to nurture and destroy. Thus a story with a disastrous ending can also be transformed into one that explains good fortune and cautions about behavior that will subvert it. But when the tale is thus rendered ambiguous, the wife's animal form being linked to her higher, not her lower essence,[177] her husband's culpability is paradoxically even more emphasized than when the story ends with a debacle.

Whatever reason is given for the husband's error, it remains the case that he cannot leave well enough alone, that he sabotages his own good fortune. Often, again, some unusual feature of his wife or their lives together piques his curiosity or arouses his alarm, and he thereby discovers her fox's or serpent's tail, or some other sign of her animal being. These phallic shapes, again, suggest that a struggle for power ensues as the woman takes on the attributes ordinarily given only to men and thus asserts herself in a relationship in which woman traditionally plays the submissive role. In Japan, however, the serpent also represents powerful emotions, not only sexual passion but also jealousy and hatred. A popular story tells how when a woman is rejected by a Buddhist priest (his asceticism perhaps analogous to male revulsion in other animal bride tales), she becomes an enormous serpent and pursues him until he hides under the large bell of a temple. "But it was in vain, for the furious monster flew over the gate, wound itself around the bell and whipped it with its tail so vehemently, that it became red-hot and burned the priest to death." [178]

Because animal wives ordinarily anticipate the effect of their true nature on their mortal husbands, they usually try to hide its signs (that is, emulate society's ideal woman). The Norwegian *huldre* woman provides a significant example, and many tales center on what happens when her characteristic cow's tail is spied beneath her properly long skirts. In one story, a young man tactfully points out that she is "losing [her] garter," and is rewarded with good fortune. Another scornfully tells her that she carries "a rare train" about with her, and falls ill and dies. [179] The pathos attached to the Melusine group of swan maiden tales emerges from the prodigious effort made by the animal bride to live with man on his own terms, while he thwarts her—even when to do so is not to his advantage.

The husband who undermines his own good fortune in forcing his animal wife to leave him despite her willingness to minister to his needs makes him one of the most puzzling characters in folklore. For despite her relatively low status vis-à-vis man, woman is the member of the human species on which the home, an essential element in culture, rests, and her disappearance from it thus extends her husband's loss to his people in a profoundly material as well as psychological way. Ancient fears of women or myths of feminine evil seem to rest at least in part on the anxiety that woman will exercise an ever-present potential for widespread destruction of the social order. And animal bride tales reflect these fears and myths in more forceful ways than animal groom stories.

The fear of woman is, again, linked to a fear of nature, and the Melusine type folklore heroine may reflect

the universal desire for solitude during the performance of certain physical functions, shared by man with the higher animals, ... an extension of the organic instinct for safety and self-preservation. These functions, especially the nutritive, sexual, and excretory, are not only of supreme importance in organic life, but their performance exposes the individual to danger, by rendering him defenseless for the time being.[180]

The seclusion of women by some peoples during such times as childbirth and menstruation might in this context, then, not be unwelcome. Melusine, in fact, is punished with her serpentine form after spying on her mother when the latter had been about to give birth. In what may be only an apparent reversal in such motifs, Urvaśī's refusal to see her husband naked may be connected to her requirement that she retain the right to withhold herself sexually. The Melusine type character may mask her true essence in order to protect herself from man himself, who may emphasize the animal in her in order to diminish it in his own self-image. The struggle for dominance in the marriage thus becomes a struggle over self-definition as well.

That a woman may achieve autonomy over her life as well as equality in the marital relationship may in folklore be her ultimate fantasy (or her husband's, born of his most essential fear). Animal bride stories suggest that a husband will accept his wife for what she is—if he indeed does so at all—only when compelled. A Norwegian tale concerns how a man gets a *huldre* woman for his wife by force (laying the barrel of his rifle over her), sees her baptized, and lives well with her and their child until one night the fairy wife reveals something of her "savage" nature, and the "peace of the home was destroyed." He resorts to taunting her with this savagery and beating her, which she endures for some time, until, driven beyond endurance, she demonstrates her own superior strength by twisting an iron rod "like steel wire round her husband, who had then to give in and promise to keep the peace."[181] Doniger points out the phallic significance of the iron rod, in which case its vulviform shape once it is twisted around the man highlights the gender basis for the married pair's struggle. The triumph of the woman is noteworthy, but the story's characters and themes are familiar: the fairy forced to submit to a domestic relationship even though it is antithetical to her nature; the aggressively domineering husband whose rifle allies him to the hunter who slays his swan maiden; the control over nature (baptising and thus converting the animal); the revelation of the wife's character to the disgust of her husband; the degenerating situation within the home; and the power struggle that, in this version, subdues the husband rather than his wife.

Celtic folklore provides a wider context for this domestic struggle. The loathly lady is held to have originally been a symbol of Ireland herself, in a linguistically significant phrase its "sovereignty," and the hero's successful disenchantment of her allows him to rule over the land. When "sovereignty" "developed into the more domestic meaning of predominance of the woman's will in marriage," a group of narratives developed, the most renowned version of which is Chaucer's "Wife of Bath's Tale." [182] The knight who had raped a woman, equivalent perhaps to the placing of a rifle across the *huldre* woman, can only escape capital punishment by discovering the answer to the question of what it is that women most want, the correct response being, again, dominance over their husbands in marriage. When the loathly hag who supplies the answer is apparently transformed into a beautiful woman, it is not only because the knight has married her but also because he has allowed her that very control woman is supposed to require. Chaucer's tale has been held to be a rationalization of the animal bride type story. [183] That woman most wants to be dominant in marriage—that is, to be symbolically the man—is therefore tantamount to nature taking back control it had ceded, however reluctantly, to culture.

The threat to human civilization supposedly posed by woman's nature would therefore seem to justify the aggressive character of the hunter with which this chapter began. In a tale from the Alps, the disenchanted animal woman expresses her gratitude to the man who had pursued her into more and more dangerous terrain. She had been a rebellious child, unable to "resist the call of the mountains," wishing to be a "fleet animal and race about as they do among the steep rocks by day and night," *significantly* "giving the hunters a good run." Her punishment had been to achieve her heart's desire, to become in fact a beast, and only yielding to the hunter returns her to human status.[184]

The sovereignty of the fairy woman is frequently reflected in the way in which she, like Urvaśī, imposes the taboo that her human husband must heed if their union is to last. And just as taboo motifs in animal groom tales prove thematically significant and not always mere narrative devices to keep the story going, so are they important motifs in interpreting animal bride tales. What the husband is prohibited from doing covers the whole gamut of the problems with which wives have traditionally been able to identify. For example, in some native North American tales, an erring husband leaves his wife and tribe to follow a female animal and to live with the herd, only to return to his own people and take up his former life.[185] His return is complicated: on one side, he is expressing his rootedness in human society; on the other, his infidelity speaks to the precarious foundation for any social contract. Sexual unfaithfulness reflects not only a moral issue or even the potential to hurt a wife, but also man's sometimes weak commitment to the values by which the human world strives to achieve a balance between contrary forces. In a story told by the Skidi Pawnee, for example, sexual infidelity is the cause of the rupture between a man and his buffalo wife, is in effect the broken taboo.[186]

Another prohibition underscores woman's domestic role. The Lillooet tell of a widower who discovers that his dead wife returns to nurse their child. With the help of a shaman, she is recalled to life, but he is warned "to take very great care of his wife, and to give her tasks by degree, as it would take a very long time yet for her to become just as she had been before her death." Over the years the woman improved "so that she was now able to do most of the work she used to do, much to the joy of her husband." He, however, increases the demands he makes on her, insisting she take on increasingly more domestic chores, and she dies again.[187] In a story from India with a more specific swan maiden frame, the sisters of the supernatural bride warn her husband to "be careful not to grieve or trouble her. Do not make her cook or serve up; moreover, touch not her hand or her foot."[188]

These sisters have actually imposed three taboos. The first is a generalized injunction to treat their sister well since she has no choice but to remain with her husband while he possesses her stolen garment. The second is not to subject her to onerous tasks she would presumably be free of in the otherworld, not to turn her into a mere drudge. The third prohibition, not to touch her hand or foot, echoes Urvaśī's demand that she not be forced to submit her body to Purūravas against her will. Folktales, that is, reflect woman's desire that in her most intimate relations, she *not* be treated as an animal. Thus a need to respect a bride's timidity until time and experience have allowed her to overcome it constitutes the basis for the taboo imposed on a husband in a Shoshonean tale. He is ordered not to touch his wife "before the end of ten days. On the eleventh night you may sleep with her. If you touch her before that, she will run away and return to [her father]." On three separate occasions the husband breaks the taboo, each time remaining abstinent for four to eight days, but eventually forcing himself on the woman before the requisite time has elapsed.[189]

Similar themes pervade the Orpheus tales widely told by North American tribes, in which the taboo imposed often seems intended to protect the wife recovered from the otherworld against physical or emotional abuse. Wives who die are thus equated with swan maidens who flee their domestic homes, and in one tale a man who "scolded and beat" his wife all the time caused her to get sick and lose the will to live. Dying in childbirth, she nonetheless comes back because both husband and baby "were suffering without her." But he breaks his promise not to mistreat her, and she turns into a dove and flies away.[190] Some stories indicate that psychological abuse is even worse than physical harm. In a story told by the Crows, a buffalo wife tells her husband, "I don't care whether you beat me, but do not call me names"[191]—that is, he is not to reproach her for being an animal. From the Lipan Apaches comes a variant on this motif that is both curious and enormously significant. A man captures a white pigeon who warns him, "You stole me and took me away but don't you dare call me your wife."[192]

This swan maiden understands that "wife" means not only domestic drudgery but also a loss of autonomy for which there appears no adequate recompense. Calling her "wife" is thus tantamount to stealing her feather garment, or worse, burning it. It binds her to a world in which the taboos wives impose, demands to be treated with dignity and to be given some freedom in their roles, are more likely than not to be broken, even though it appears contrary to man's self-interest to defy the prohibitions. In the struggle for power between the sexes, man asserts himself with brutal aggressiveness; but he also proves in animal bride tales to be passive, weak, dependent, more frightened of his animal wife than women are of animal grooms. The tales of female disenchantment discussed in this chapter invoke conventional paradigms of male power and analyze models of behavior employed by men to sustain masculine self-esteem. The stories of animal brides therefore lead almost inevitably to the Orpheus narratives to be discussed next, to the ironically failed *quest* to win back the lost wife.

# CHAPTER 7

# Orpheus's Quest

Most swan maiden stories begin with the capture of the fairy wife, her enforced stay in the mortal world, her eventual escape from her domestic life, and her husband's setting out to bring her back—the latter motif being used by folklorists to characterize the story, making the husband's rather than the wife's experience the narrative focus of interest. Hartland explains that the "one idea" that runs through the swan maiden tale is that a man unable to retain his supernatural wife "must pursue her" to her own land and "conquer his right to her by undergoing superhuman penance or performing superhuman tasks—neither of which it is given to ordinary men to do."[1] And, as already noted, according to the tale type *Index*, wives *search* for their lost spouses, whereas husbands who have lost fairy wives embark on *quests*[2]—a particular irony given that the searching women characteristically win back their spouses and the questing men characteristically do not. Their failures are exemplified in the *Rig Veda*, in Purūravas's attempt to find Urvaśī and, despite his reproach that it is she who first enticed and later rejected him, her refusal to be reconciled: "I have left you, like the first of the dawns. Go home again."[3]

This book has focused not on the husband's search but on those motifs in the swan maiden story attached to the fairy wife and to woman's role in human society. It has also tried to redress the scholarly emphasis on animal groom tales by paying at least equal attention to animal brides, additionally arguing that both story groups belong to a larger narrative pattern in which swan maidens play important roles. This chapter, however, will shift the earlier emphasis to consider whether the ineffectual husband is typified in the myth of Orpheus and Eurydice. Is Orpheus's story as it appears throughout the world's folklore to be interpreted as a narrative about a husband's grief over his dead wife and about his futile attempt to return her to the world of the living, or as a powerful story about failed marital relationships? Whether Orpheus can be linked to the typical husband of the swan maiden hinges on three controversial issues: whether the world of the dead must be sharply differentiated from other supernatural otherworlds; whether Eurydice resembles the swan maiden; and whether Orpheus's failure establishes a special brotherhood between him and other husbands or lovers whose claim to be the superior sex is in these widely distributed folktales rendered dubious.

The tangling and untangling of features associated with the realm of the dead and with fairyland are intrinsic to studies of the medieval poem *Sir Orfeo*, a compound of Celtic and classical mythology in which a king must recover not his dead but his kidnapped wife. According to one commentator, the Orpheus myth is thus transformed to join tales of the "abducted, of those wrongly imagined to have died," death itself losing "its bitterness and finality," being "swallowed up in enchantment."[4] The general view, however, is that even if they "spin the same theme,"[5] stories about the dead involve different worlds than those about the abducted. But even Katharine Briggs admits that although at "first sight the commonly received idea of Fairyland seems as far as possible from the shadowy and bloodless Realms of the Dead," yet, "in studying fairy-lore and ghost-lore we are haunted and teased by resemblances between them."[6]

In *Sir Orfeo* scenes of carnage appear out of place in the Celtic fairyland; conversely, a virtual wonderland instead of an inferno is portrayed in the widespread Orpheus tales related by North American tribes. Ake Hultkrantz, who has studied these stories, notes that one would expect the dead to be "described in terms of horror [that] would provide a more effective dramatic frame for Orpheus's expedition to rescue his love."[7] That motifs of death and of capture easily combine is illustrated by a seventh-century Chinese tale in which a man's wife is stolen by a spirit, and he follows them to a place where he finds women at play, singing and laughing. Although told that his wife is ill—a reminder of human mutability and mortality—he finds her dining on "all kinds of delicacies."[8] If abductions to fairyland are read as "similes of death,"[9] then the merging of apparently disparate realms can be explained: popular beliefs can supply consolation to bereaved persons who may imagine their loved ones experiencing another, better life, rather than dying.[10] In fantasy, if not in fact, the lost one could even be won back.

Rather than differentiating fairyland from the world of the dead, or attempting to reconcile them,[11] it might be more useful to focus on their common denominator, which is their *contrast to the actual world*. Both the dead and humans captured by the fairies are imagined to exist beyond the pains of human life. Those half in love with easeful death may find themselves drawn to the pleasures of an imagined world beyond this one, at the same time guiltily reacting to worldly commitments by expressing this guilt with images of an inferno.[12] To restrict the Orpheus narratives to stories involving the death of a spouse, or to tales in which the hero is actually named Orpheus or Orfeo—as some have restricted them[13]—is to overlook this psychological tension, one intrinsic to stories of marriages between beings from disparate realms.

But no differentiation between the realm of the dead and fairyland would appear as striking as the apparent dissimilarity between the sorrowfully yearning Eurydice of Roman mythology and the defiant swan maiden who will not return to the human world. In native North American lore, the dead wife must often be "conducted to the world of the living although she is reluctant and unwilling": about a Comanche wife it is said, for example, she "was happy where she was."[14] And in a story from California, the husband who has buried his wife witnesses her rising from the grave to begin the journey to the otherworld. He tries to seize her, but he "could not hold her," subsequently following her and overhearing her conversation with the ruler of the dead:

"Do you think you will go back to him?" She said: "I do not think so. What do you wish?" The chief said: "I think not. You must stay here. You cannot go back. You are worthless now."[15]

Insofar as a wife is dead, she is indeed worthless to a husband who must meet his practical and emotional needs among the living. This confrontation between longing and reality is underscored when the husband in this story is allowed a single night's visit with his dead wife, following which she vanishes and he awakens to find himself alone. "Worthless," however, acquires further associations from other disappearing wife tales. If the woman has tasted the pleasures of the otherworld, she may be unable or unwilling to readapt to her old way of life, which is perhaps why men who recognize the mark of the supernatural people on their wives, daughters, or sisters often reject them. The chief of the dead may also realize that the wife's reluctance to return to her husband speaks to essential conflicts between the pair, or her essential unwillingness to conform to a society that cannot claim her obedience beyond the grave. Perhaps "worthless" connotes what her people perceive to be the subversive implications of her reluctance to go back to the world.

Native American Orpheus tales frequently echo swan maiden narratives. Often the dead wife must literally be seized by her husband, sometimes during a dance from whose circle he forcibly pulls her, this seizure paralleling the manner in which swan maidens are captured to begin with.[16] And the taboos imposed on the husband concerning the trip back to the world or life together after the return are the same prohibitions that are imposed on the husband who takes a fairy for his bride.[17] In short, if, as has been claimed, American Indians relate *real* Orpheus stories, theoretically differentiable from the folklore of kidnapped (rather than deceased) wives, it is noteworthy that the Eurydices of these tales more closely resemble the swan maiden or offended fairy wives than they do the mythological Eurydice.

But Eurydice may be a more ambiguous figure than appears from a simple reading of her story in Vergil or Ovid. She is a dryad, a nature divinity, and thus she is implicated in the complex dichotomies with which humans imbue nature itself. Robert Graves argues that Eurydice was originally a "goddess of the underworld," an embodiment of the moon goddess, "the serpent-grasping ruler of the Underworld," to whom male human sacrifices were offered, "their death being apparently caused by viper's venom." According to this interpretation, Eurydice's death by snake bite is but a distortion of an original myth that has been rationalized. Although his interpretation has been challenged, Graves is not alone in attaching to Eurydice associations with dangerous or malevolent female deities.[18] She has been associated with Melusine,[19] her connection to the legendary serpent-woman reinforcing the possibility of reading the Orpheus and Eurydice myth as another narrative about a failed marital relationship rather than a tragic story in which lovers are separated by death.

Marriage and family are paradigmatic structures of a society undermined when one of the wedded pair subverts the relationship; but conflicts within the marital relationship reflect internal strife as well. Orpheus tales are permeated with these layered themes. *The Mahabharata* tells a story strikingly similar to the Roman myth. In the Hindu story, a young woman of semidivine origins is beloved by a mortal man. Shortly before their marriage, she steps upon a serpent that bites her, causing her death. Her betrothed, maddened like the Celtic Orfeo, wanders grief-stricken in a forest, where he is approached by a mysterious male figure who tells him that if he will agree to give up half his life to his wife, she will return to life and the two will live happily together. He agrees and the bargain is fulfilled.[20] To give up half of his life is perhaps symbolically to grant the wife that which would make it possible for her to adapt to an earthly marriage without a total alteration of her semidivine status. But however the Orpheus story is told and however it is understood, to make Eurydice a passive character, merely the object of her husband's search, is to deprive her of an important role in a very complex story.

In the European Middle Ages, Eurydice was a prototype of feminine evil, an allegorized embodiment of irrational human sensuality and passion,[21] and the associations of Eve with the serpent only served to reinforce the idea that Orpheus's descent to the underworld symbolized man's descent to his lower nature. Eurydice has, again, also been connected to "the earth goddess,"[22] sometimes associated with the female ruler of the dead. Eurydice's death, then, has been understood to parallel the kidnapping of Proserpina, who, "by the very nature of her myth," is not only the "maiden torn out of her innocent activities by Pluto's violence, but also the terrible and threatening goddess of the underworld."[23] Consistent with these associations is the name given to Orfeo's wife in the medieval poem, Heurodys or Heurodas, which echoes Herodias, called "one of the darkest and most sinister figures in the medieval vocabulary," which may be why King Orfeo's wife has been marked as worthy of the devil's attention, the demon appearing in the medieval narrative in his guise of fairy king.[24] To invoke here motifs from other narratives, the serpent woman has found her natural counterpart in the serpent man.

In the story of "The Snake-Hawks" told by the Skidi Pawnee, for example, an ordinarily faithful wife is attracted to a young man while her husband is away with a war party. Her lover proves to be a snake, and in order to follow him to his domain, she too assumes a serpent's shape. Her son, missing his mother, embarks on a search for her, and when he finds her, she keeps him by her side. The husband must therefore find both wife and son. When he is reunited with the latter, he learns that his wife is "living with Yellow-Headed-Snake. So the man went into the tepee and took some strings, caught the snake and tied it up." He spares the woman, however, for she had taken her son in. "But if it had not been for the boy he would have killed her."[25] The serpent world is the place from which the woman must be literally and symbolically retrieved, but the phallic woman is also dangerous. Only because the Pawnee wife displays a maternal inclination can she still be saved.

The Pawnee wife reflects a paradox that has already been raised in an earlier chapter, one concerning the question of nature and motherhood. Is the so-called maternal instinct natural and the flight from motherhood therefore inherently unnatural; or is the desire for personal gratification the most essential of natural drives? To counter the argument that Eurydice is an avatar of the serpent goddess by insisting that she is merely a dryad, that is, a nature spirit, is not necessarily to purge her of potentially negative associations. Dryads will be perceived of as being as pure or as tainted as nature itself. It will be recalled that in Greek lore, the swan maiden is sometimes a naiad enjoying a carefree life until married: when she escapes her human husband, she is obeying the irresistible and antisocial pull of her natural habitat.[26]

Similarly ambiguous attitudes toward nature can be found in other cultures that produce the Orpheus type tale. In versions from both New Zealand and Japan, the lost wife is transformed into a vengeful female who not only refuses to return to the upper world but also continues to wreak havoc from the otherworld: "in the Maori [creation] myth as well as in the old Japanese myth [of Izanagi and his quest for Izanami], the great mother-goddess changes into the goddess of death, parting from her husband, who tries in vain to win her back from the underworld."[27] This is a myth of feminine evil submerged in the figures of Eurydice and Heurodys, the portrayal of the latter in *Sir Orfeo* reflecting the eventual triumph of civilization, the fate of the former in the Roman myth suggesting the difficulty attendant upon the struggle.

In short, Eurydice is a character who acquires more complexity the deeper one goes to unearth her origins in folklore and myth. In contrast, Orpheus appears relatively unambiguous despite the three separate traditions with which he is associated: Orpheus the musician, Orpheus the religious teacher, and Orpheus the lover[28]—which is not to deny that the relationship of these roles to each other is enormously complex, but only to contend that Orpheus's position in the swan maiden narrative is less problematical than Eurydice's. Still, it is Orpheus's renown as well as the fact that Tale Type 400 is defined by the husband's search for his wife rather than the motives for her disappearance that combine to raise the provocative question of why in the widespread folktales about him Orpheus is characterized by failure. This question is especially provocative because in earlier versions of the myth, Orpheus triumphantly returns with his wife to the world. There is in commentaries both on the Orpheus myth and on the swan maiden tale an intriguing parallel: as time went on and the narratives altered, the wedded pair was less likely to be reconciled. In this light, Ovid's ending to his version of the Orpheus myth picks up added and ironic significance, for it has been noted that Ovid's Orpheus dies "not for his love of his wife but from his hatred of women," being torn to pieces by enraged maenads.[29] Each age has fashioned Orpheus in its own image, "giving him new attributes, emphasizing certain of his deeds at the expense of others, and even changing the course of the narrative to make the Orpheus myth conform to the values of the day."[30] It is, of course, doubtful that one could simply identify *the* values of any age. But as will be shortly argued, Orpheus may typify a kind of husband presently receiving considerable attention.

In India, easily recognizable motifs from the Orpheus myth are frequently found in combination with the theme of the swan maiden's stolen garment. These motifs include the music played in the otherworld to induce its ruler to relinquish the captured wife; and the "look" taboo, the injunction that as he leads his wife back to the world, the husband may not look at her. In some Indian tales the prohibition is specifically linked to the swan maiden pattern: after gaining possession of the fairy's garment, the man must not gaze at the captive for a specified period of time. The typical outcome is illustrated in the *Dravidian Nights* when Indra's daughter tempts a man with visions of her beauty to forfeit his long-range goals for the immediate satisfaction of beholding her beauty.[31] And in a comparable story from New Goa, the swan maiden pattern is central; when the man glances behind him, "the dresses went back to [the sorceresses] and they flew away."[32] Both stolen garments and taboo depict a power struggle in which to retrieve the fairy wife is, in effect, to learn to subdue and control her, to overcome her seductive power—to learn, that is, how to be a husband.

Another and obvious link between the Orpheus and swan maiden tales clusters about the need to retrieve the lost wife not merely from the otherworld but also from its monarch—that is, her demon lover. Other folktale types come in here, such as those in which a husband envied for his beautiful wife must strive to keep her; or narratives concerning the nocturnal journey of a woman to the otherworld, until she is eventually followed and prevented by "proof of her escapade" from returning there.[33] Common to these stories is the idea that a powerful rival must be persuaded or forced by the husband to relinquish his wife. But so long as the supernatural rival embodies the longings and dissatisfactions of the wife, her husband's struggle ultimately comes back to the essential problems in his marital life. Such narratives once again depict the dual theme of Orpheus's strength and his weakness. If, in some way, the lost wife helps him in his battle with his rival, then his own ingenuity and forcefulness are diminished. What is often perceived as Orpheus's special strength, his skill in music, is ironically the very point in which, for Plato, his essential weakness lies: he is an artist rather than a man of action. Actually, this differentiation collapses in many stories. The Orpheus character may prove himself a man of action by following his runaway wife to the otherworld, where his music becomes the means he employs to get her back.

The importance of music in the Orpheus story is reflected in what is held to be an analogue to the British Orfeo narrative, a widely distributed Scandinavian ballad, "The Power of the Harp." A bride informs her groom that she is doomed to be taken by the supernatural folk on her wedding day, and despite the husband's best efforts to surround her with armed protectors, her prophesy is fulfilled. But the bereaved bridegroom plays his harp so movingly that the demon releases not only his bride but other women stolen before her as well.[34] These themes point to an interesting feature in the Gandharvas, Purūravas's rivals for Urvaśī. In Hindu mythology these demigods are also the musicians at the court of Indra.[35] Similarly, in Scandinavian folklore, the Nekk who steals the bride as well as the husband who wins her back are musicians—if not necessarily in the same narratives. In chapter 3 a comparable link between the demon lover and the human husband of Child 243 was discussed. In their simultaneous unity and duality, they represent the runaway wife's conflict. From the Orpheus stories, however, emerges another possible meaning usually submerged in the story pattern. The common features that link the antagonists who compete for the woman who, through flight or through death, dwells in the otherworld may symbolize an essential split in the image of masculinity, one that parallels a significant duality in the husband's *self*-image. The failure in the Orpheus story suggests a concomitant failure on the part of man to find a model upon which to pattern his behavior, to win, to hold, and, if necessary, to regain his lost wife. In that sense, these stories also reveal the weaknesses of patriarchal culture.

One way to make a story serve society is to depict culture's advantages over nature. A New Zealand tale tells how Mataora falls in love with Nuvarahu, a Turehu woman whose people dwell in the underworld and eat raw food. For a time, all is well, but a quarrel between the husband and his jealous brother leads to the beating of the woman, as if she were to blame for this rupture of male bonds. "Angry at this treatment, she fled back to the underworld, but her husband grieved for his lost wife and resolved to seek her." Widely distributed variants relate that this strange folk not only preferred raw food but also cut open a woman when she was about to give birth, so that she died. The husband who brings her back to his world shows her the way of normal childbirth, and in so doing, demonstrates the superiority of the mortal realm.[36]

Although Mataora may teach his wife and her people a safer kind of childbearing (as if man could claim credit for "natural" childbirth), and although woman's natural function is used to anchor her in a social world man controls, a husband may be particularly insecure when his wife becomes a mother, because he essentially remains powerless before both her physical condition and her emotional responses to her role. As Holbek points out, in folklore it is at important transitional points in human life that people become susceptible to the influence of the supernatural folk. Eurydice is childless, but, again, the swan maiden has no qualms about leaving her children behind in her escape from mortal ties. If she does return on their behalf, that return characteristically excludes concern for her husband or is reversed when her husband evidences those traits she fled in the first place by breaking the taboo imposed as a condition for their reconciliation. But Orpheus tales frequently reveal a significant theme that places the husband's plight at the center of these stories: any woman's husband was once another woman's son, and the way the former son treats his wife may reflect the outcomes of that earlier tie. When his wife herself becomes a mother, the symbolic struggle with the otherworld to which she may at any moment return is intensified.

Irish folklore is replete with wives taken by the fairies shortly after they have given birth, and undoubtedly the stories tell of the physical dangers in which a woman is placed merely by fulfilling this natural function. But as well as depicting a woman's death in childbirth, these stories also appear to portray what today would be called postpartum depression. In such instances, the failure of a husband to retrieve his wife from the otherworld speaks to his essential impotence in dealing with his wife's reaction to childbearing and motherhood.

A particularly suggestive example of a wife especially vulnerable to the otherworld when she is, effectively, most "natural"—about to give birth—tells how other women are hired to attend her. But when her labor starts, a "great tumult" arises in the room, which suddenly darkens. The nurses, "much flustered," take a long time to relight the candles and when "they could see again they [find] to their horror that [she is] lying dead." But the town's minister decides that it is "no Christian that is lying there, but some senseless substance that has been shaped to look like her." To get his wife back, her husband must wait until her spirit returns to her home and he must hold her fast until dawn, which suggests not only the capture motif in swan maiden tales but also the general resistance some women put up against returning to home and family after they are free of them. In this instance, other women are blamed for what had originally happened, in this case because *as women* (nurses) they had not prevented the catastrophe: "she would never have been stolen if the women hired to nurse her had not been drinking too much as they sat up watching her."[37] Their deficiency in the birthing room seems symbolically extended to some essential failure in helping the new mother accept her maternal role.

That although women must be relied upon, they cannot be fully trusted to sustain the social relations on which culture rests is also suggested in an analogous story, in which, again, a woman is neglected by the nurse hired to help her through, in this case, some unspecified illness. She is thus vulnerable to a "multitude of elves [who] came in at the window," after which she remembers nothing more until she sees her husband standing over her. When he finds his wife among a troop of fairies, he forces them to release her, going home to burn the effigy they had left when they took her, an act reminiscent of burning the animal wife's skin or performing some other rite to silence in her the call of the wild.[38] In his stalwartness, this husband is not alone in folklore, but he does provide a contrast to similar characters, who, as Scott notes in his *Minstrelsy*, usually lose courage at the critical moment.

Scott associates the husbands' abortive attempts to save their wives with Orpheus's failure, and among his examples tells the story of a farmer from Lothian whose wife is taken by the fairies. She appears to her husband and instructs him in what to do, begging him "for her temporal and eternal salvation, to use all his courage to rescue her." But when the husband sees the fairy host, he stands "frozen with terror." That this is no failure of love, as Katharine Briggs claims, but rather only a "failure of nerve" is debatable.[39] Such a husband resembles the father who chooses to leave his daughter in the otherworld: the mark of the trolls, like the sign of the animal-woman, designates an improperly socialized woman.[40] The radical view that what Orpheus must not see when he looks at Eurydice is the remnants of the powerful snake (phallic) woman can be sustained by a widespread folklore tradition. Psychologically, man first creates his model of woman much as Indian and Eskimo husbands create wooden dolls to serve as wives; then, when nature or some weakness in culture subverts the unrealistic ideal, man experiences anger and revulsion, his own misconceptions rebounding on him as his marriage collapses.

In a story from Alsace-Lorraine, a man must choose between his wife and the town that deems her a witch whom, in its hatred, the community is determined to burn. When her husband agrees instead to her captivity in a single room, a paradigm for woman's confined space and limited range of experience, the "look she turned on her husband, when he falteringly informed her of his promise, [could cow] the boldest bystander."[41] As Doniger says of the myth to which the swan maiden story can be said to belong, there are two patterns, the one in which the woman flees the man "because he is superior and the one in which she flees him because he is inferior," both of which versions are "based on contrasting perceptions of the power balance between the two main participants."[42] Orpheus narratives illustrate this paradox very well. If the man proves superior, that is, overly domineering, the woman can only be returned from the otherworld in an act of seizure that reenacts the original winning-by-capture. On the other side, passive husbands equally fail their wives because they impute their own weaknesses to women instead of questioning cultural models for masculine behavior, models, the Orpheus story suggests, men cannot readily live up to.

A husband in a complex Australian aboriginal story, who is both strong and weak at different points in the tale, unable to sort out the conflicting demands of wilderness and civilization, proves incapable of rescuing his "water-girl" (that is, animal bride) from a pathological family situation that may well symbolize her entire society. She had been the object of her father's incestuous desire, and when as punishment he is transformed into a crocodile, she continues to flee him, the disturbed relationship with this male parent foreshadowing the ultimate debacle in her marriage. Meanwhile, the mother who should ideally have protected her daughter had failed to do so, perceiving the younger woman as rival rather than victimized fellow woman. Thus the water girl remains helpless in a male-dominated world, and her eventual marriage by capture is consistent with the conditions of her life: her husband to be "grabbed at her long tresses that floated on the water about her and winding these around his left arm he gathered the helpless girl in his arms and fled from the accursed pool." On the one side he has rescued her from the crocodile, but on the other, he takes over the patriarchal role. Now the "accursed pool" becomes nature itself, and as he performs a kind of exorcism and holds her over a fire so that her slimy covering is burned away, vast swarms of leeches flow from her pores.

The—significantly—male narrator warns that with her adaptation to her husband's society, the story has not ended. At first the formerly "useless" water girl lives as a proper young woman who talks her husband's language and thus understands his customs. Her husband has a "very happy time" of it in "dry time," but when it rains, "everywhere was danger for she was still half water-girl." "Wet" and "dry" become signifiers of nature and culture, and after the husband dreams of soft voices calling to his wife and understands that because she responds, she is lost to him, he begins his search for her. Tortured by sun and heat, he eventually watches the lagoon in which his wife has joined her water girl sisters dry up. But just as he advances toward his wife, he feels raindrops: he has found her "too late" and now he has lost her forever.[43]

It would be difficult to find another story in which the paradox of man's strength and weakness comes together in such a clearly defined psychological pattern. The father who betrays his daughter is succeeded by the husband who in one sense rescues her, but in another retains her through force. The story points to themes found in analogous tales. Man deludes himself when he thinks that in controlling nature by erecting social structures he must now sustain, he has taken the final step toward resolving the essential conflicts in his domestic life. The husband who saves his wife by burning the effigy left as a substitute by the fairies, for example, is matched by the one who lays his sword across the supernatural folk who took his wife. Often mined and subsequently forged raw metals symbolize the triumph of patriarchal civilization. (It will be remembered that the Norwegian *huldre* wife driven beyond endurance by her husband's abuse is able to bend an iron rod, undermining the man's power over her.) [44] To defeat the fairies with forged metals is comparable to the exorcism that banishes demon lovers, to the maiming of the animal or the burning of her skin, and the distinction between rescuing and controlling the woman collapses. What is extraordinary in the aboriginal tale is the extent to which the narrator sees the vicious cycle perpetuated, and the extent to which he recognizes that it creates a situation before which the ineffectual husband is helpless—"Manbuk come too late now"—doomed by his ambivalent relationship to his wife.

Jack Zipes has argued that central to most folktales is the "concept of power. Where does it reside? Who wields it? Why? How can it be better wielded?" From a contemporary perspective, folktales "are filled with incidents of explicable abuse, maltreatment of women, negative images of minority groups, questionable sacrifices, and the exaltation of power." [45] Zipes's argument appears to require a political content folk narratives do not always disclose; nevertheless, on the psychological level, power also operates as a significant factor in the way people orient themselves in their societies. In three variants of the same tale from India, a husband's attempt to win his fairy wife from the demon ruler of the otherworld sets in motion a struggle between the wedded pair in which retaining his wife clearly necessitates the husband's destroying in her what the demon lover represents. A comparison of the three versions reveals that although the stories conclude with the same outcome, the reconciliation of the separated pair, significantly varying degrees of power wielded by the Orpheus character over the swan maiden underscore the significance of power itself as a central theme in the narratives.

The consequences of a prince falling in love with a fairy rather than an ordinary woman is depicted in the first of these tales, "The Perfumer's Daughter," when an anxious father dreads offending his wife and daughter, whom he therefore allows to set the terms of the daughter's marriage. The bride will be allowed each night to return to her father's home. That she actually spends this time at the court of Indra is, ironically, less of a lie than might appear. An imagined world in which women have such power of choice is as different from the ordinary domestic realm as is the otherworld of constant revels. Indra is thus a projection of the father's indulgence, and since the fairy bride splits her existence between two worlds, the prince's task is less to rescue her from Indra than to undermine the influence of the divine realm by establishing his own dominance over her. To do so, he needs to find, and succeeds in finding, a male role model quite different from the indulgent or hedonistic "fathers" who have allowed his wife her way. Much of the story involves how difficult it is for him to follow the instructions supplied by his mentor, a "grand master," the fairy almost succeeding in sabotaging her husband's resolve to subdue her by exercising her seductive power over him.

One way for this husband to master his fairy wife is to force her to consummate the marriage. When at his insistence, she successively relinquishes the seven veils behind which she hides, she expresses the rage that inspires his fear that "perhaps on the morrow she might not return." His concern is well founded, for she is a swan maiden, and what her mortal husband must learn from his mentor is how to take possession of his wife's garments, not looking at her until she is fully under his control. He succeeds at the first task, but as the fairy follows him, a Eurydice led by her Orpheus to the earthly realm, she uses feminine wiles against him: "My lord! my love! oh, stop and turn but once, and I will follow you and be your slave for ever." Unable to resist this chance to conquer her, he first seeks further reassurance that she will go with him and then looks back, at which point she without remorse seizes her clothing and escapes the necessity to make good on her unwilling promise. Her duplicity constitutes part of the prince's education, and when he is given another chance to recapture her, he is ready to follow to the letter the advice of the grand master. When he does so, proving himself at last a man, Indra surrenders the swan maiden.[46]

The story's focus on the husband's need to control his wayward wife is even more pronounced in the other two variants. In "Prince Amul

Manik" the husband achieves control over his wife not by stealing her clothes but by an act that can be compared to holding the water girl over the fire to burn away her leeches, or cutting off the cat woman's paw, or shoeing the mare who in her human form is thus maimed, or burning the animal bride's skin to prevent her return to nature. For from the outset Prince Amul follows closely the instructions he receives from his grand master, and tears from the swan maiden's body her fairy wings, a more overtly brutal act than stealing her clothing: "You have found your match at last young lady; this time I shall not let you go in a hurry," to which she replies that she is at his mercy: "I yield, prince; you have beaten me fairly."[47] In "The Kotwal's Daughter," the prince with a fairy wife who will not yield herself to him asks in anger, "What's the use of this marriage to me?" From the beginning he decides that surely it will not "beat [him] to master one weak woman." Of the three husbands, he needs the least help from a grand master to dominate his wife, his masculinity as defined by patriarchal culture being already quite developed at the beginning of the story.[48]

Thus, in a noteworthy progression, "The Perfumer's Daughter" describes how a prince's maturity, as defined by his people, derives from his developing obedience to an older male model; "Prince Amul Manik" depicts a prince lacking initiative of his own but sufficiently respectful of patriarchal values to steel himself against feminine allure and to follow the lessons of his mentor; and "The Kotwal's Daughter" supplies an almost ideal portrait of a prince portrayed as already so manly as to require from his teacher only the merest outline for a plan to subdue his fairy wife. He can supply the specific strategies for himself.

The Pawnee similarly tell a tale in which to win a wife from the otherworld is visible proof of masculine power. When the uncles of a dead woman visit her grave and her spirit emerges from it, her husband must hold her fast: as the young man holds the girl, she "jumped up and down" and he was "thrown upon the ground and she got away." When she sees him again, she taunts him with, "Why, young man, you have no strength at all." She warns him that a fourth escape will mean the final end to their union: "Young man, if you care for me and want me to stay with you, you must use more strength than you have shown." Significantly, he must hold her until her uncles come and touch her. In a brutal and perhaps sexually symbolic gesture, he "puts his legs around her," at the same time twisting her hair with his hands, shouting for help from his companions.[49]

Marriage, manhood defined by exclusively male models, dominance over the woman—in all these stories, the three are so obviously connected with each other as to suggest that the "Quest for the Lost Wife" is a euphemistic designation for the tale type. But the Pawnee story also harkens back to themes treated in the previous chapter. The fairy or animal bride often appears willing enough to live under patriarchal rule if her husband is both strong enough to disenchant her and considerate enough to retain her. What constitutes such strength and how it must be employed to support the relationship involve, of course, the critical questions raised by the stories. The answers will vary from society to society, storyteller to storyteller. What seems apparent, however, is that the required strength usually operates against rather than in favor of sustaining the relationship, while at the same time, weakness and passivity on the husband's part are equally destructive. It is difficult to define traditional masculine strength in positive terms, and man's bafflement pervades the Orpheus story. And if it is a tale generally told by men,[50] then another problematic issue has been added to the matter of male self-image: what accounts for man's pessimism as he contemplates his ability to maintain a relationship with woman? There are, however, other themes to be explored before some speculation on this subject is offered.

This book has consistently argued that taboos are *not* mere narrative devices to initiate the separation of the married couple; that despite some overlap, different taboos exist in animal groom and in animal bride tales; and that even where the taboos are the same, in a significant number of instances gender affects the way the taboo motifs are treated. It is not surprising that prohibitions surrounding how a wife is treated supply important themes in Orpheus narratives. In a Pawnee version, for example, a husband is granted the return of his dead wife with a series of seemingly unconnected statements by the rulers of the otherworld: "All of us agreed that we would send the girl back. You can see her now, but she is not real. You must be careful and not make her angry, or you will lose her."[51] The otherworld has relinquished the wife, but in returning to life, she does not yet belong exclusively to the world of men —in this sense she is not yet real. Thus the husband must be wary of how he exercises male prerogatives.

In a Wichita Orpheus tale, a father extracts from his son-in-law the promise that if his daughter is restored to the world, her husband will be faithful and refrain from hurting her. The man is "anxious to live with her again, and would not for anything mistreat her if he could live with her again."[52] That such promises are rarely kept suggests how even the most fantastic themes in folklore mirror reality. And it is perhaps a sign of how meaningful taboos are in these tales that a husband is frequently bound by more than one prohibition. Many times he succeeds in heeding one, but fails in another. A Sioux version of the widely distributed "Ghost Wife" story relates how a woman dies after very arduous childbirth. To get her back, her husband neither looks at nor touches her for four days. But years later he betrays a more fundamental bond and compounds his betrayal by rationalizing it as an advantage to her. The "man fell in love with another woman. He told his wife: 'I shall marry a second woman, and she will share the work with you. You'll have someone to talk to when I'm away hunting. Things will be more pleasant.' "[53]

Even allowing for differences between the Sioux's view of marriage and monogamous relationships ideally based on romantic love, and admitting the possibility that a moralistic element has been added to the story by a disapproving collector, the tale reveals that polygamy as a system places woman in a vulnerable situation, its supposed advantages perhaps being essentially a male myth.[54] In this story the value of polygamous relationships serves to rationalize the husband's self-gratification. The rationalization is especially exposed within the context of the broken taboo motif, the other woman exemplifying the husband's betrayal of the marriage. It is hardly surprising that the Sioux wife disappears again, this time for good. As will be seen shortly, however, polyandry is equally dangerous for a woman, for she can be blamed for the tensions and resultant aggressions among the men with whom she lives. The point now is that these tales derive their significance not so much from *how* the wife is mistreated, but from the fact *that* she is. And mistreatment itself can be defined both positively (an act performed against the wife) and negatively (a failure with regard to meeting her needs). The wide variety of ways in which the relationship between the man and woman can break down because of some misadjustment of power is thematically evident in the "Mudjikiwis" story group widely narrated in North America; it is a narrative recognized to be thematically allied to the Orpheus tale.[55]

"Mudjikiwis" usually involves a swan maiden or mysterious housekeeper (or both) who enters the household of many brothers, one of whom she marries. Mudjikiwis envies his brother this beautiful and useful wife, and when she resists his attentions, he injures her, whereat she disappears and her husband can only get her back if he meets certain conditions, such as the instructions to "cling" to his wife as they stand poised at the edge of a mountain, and to hold her "tighter than ever" until they are back in his tent.[56] The instruction may be analogous to the requirement that a husband whose wife is to be taken by the fairies hold her fast until the danger has passed, or to the injunction that the animal mate whose beast covering is about to be destroyed be prevented from interfering in that process. Although the husband in the "Mudjikiwis" stories thus appears to be a more sympathetic character than his aggressive and destructive folklore fellows, he and characters from other tales come to resemble each other as the matter of *how* brute strength is manifested evolves into one of *when* it is. "Mudjikiwis" expresses the central ambiguity present in Orpheus tales: the strong husband holds the wife to prevent her escaping him; the weak one "clings" to her because he thinks that only in this way can he retain her.

In a version of "Mudjikiwis" narrated by the Plains Cree, the very existence of a woman in the house carries with it implied if symbolic taboos or comparable injunctions: the men are now constrained to "hunt hard and not let [their] sister-in-law hunger or be in need." She is not to be allowed to chop wood, and she cannot be expected (euphemistically) to "attend" to all of them, her tasks being restricted to cooking and mending their clothing.[57] But her role in this household, which is itself a paradigm for male-dominated culture, is a contradictory one. Unlike cooking and mending, chopping wood is a marginal activity performed both by men and by women. In this variant it appears to be a masculine task, and when the woman performs it, she seems to have intruded into masculine space, thus releasing man from his role as protector and unleasing his aggressive and competitive behavior. Thus it is while this fairy housekeeper is at the woodpile that Mudjikiwisis tries to rape her; when he fails, he shoots her in the leg.

He is not the only character in whom lust is associated with masculinity, and for whom lust provides an incentive to dominate a woman, to disregard, that is, the taboos that would ordinarily protect her.[58] In a Zuñi Orpheus type tale, a husband who loves his wife so much that he will follow her to the land of the dead is warned by an old owl—his grand master—not to allow the impatience of youth to overcome his judgment: "Let not your desire to touch and embrace her get the better of you, for if you touch her before bringing her safely home to the village of your birth, she will be lost to you forever." In this story unbridled sexual desire is blamed for the human fall into mortality: if the young lover had "practiced patience and self-denial for only a short time, then death would have been overcome." This loss, as well as the lust are, however, rationalized, death having the practical advantage of population control. Thus the betrayal of the woman is, ironically, conceived of as a myth of human necessity.[59] On another level, however, the story suggests that the man has failed precisely *because* he has been unable to distinguish between sexual drives and human affection. For it is because woman is *not* to be facilely equated with nature that she is, in this story, lost.

For often the husband's failure to meet not some material but rather some emotional need leads to his wife's departure—either in the first place or after she is recovered from the otherworld. Often ruptured affectional bonds raise issues concerning why man's image of his own masculinity need come into conflict with woman's need for tenderness. In a Maori tale, Hutu's failure to return Paré's love is the reason for her death. She is a chieftainess, that is, a woman who, like fairies, enjoys the special status of having men accountable to her. But where she can extract obedience, she cannot command affection. When her people want to kill Hutu for his hard-heartedness, he requests three days to bring her back from the world of the dead, where he employs trickery to rescue Paré, making up with cunning and strength for his earlier lack of sensitivity. The essential conflict between the pair has been sidestepped, for although Hutu, unlike Orpheus, succeeds in recovering Paré, it would be necessary to invoke a conventional male logic to argue that his efforts demonstrate love.[60] In a Pueblo tale, a lack of sufficient caring on the part of her husband is offered as the reason a serpent demon gets power over a wife. When the husband fails to heed an injunction that she not be left alone, her demon lover tells her, "Your husband does not love you. . . . He did not do as he was told." Her people echo this sentiment (a rare instance in which the demon has the support of the community), justifying the wife's desertion of her lawful spouse.[61] And in a Bantu bird maiden tale, a groom similarly fails to heed a warning not to leave his bride during their wedding procession. Distracted by his male companions who take off to hunt an animal (that is, who typically behave like men), he loses his wife. When he finds her, she is a green bird and laughs as she reproaches him: "Was it not you that took me from my father's kraal, and left me on the highlands, while you went off with a land lizard?"[62] Her laughter is difficult to interpret: she seems to express both anger and a teasing invitation that he win her back.

These examples of emotional failure are significant because they suggest that even were it true that romantic love is an invention of modern Western literature, its elements not to be read into narratives where they do not apply, the importance of emotional bonds in the marital relationship has probably always been recognized. The breakdown in the attachment of husband and wife is a significant feature of some of the world's most widely told stories. So long as the family supplies society with a basic structural unit, the affective tensions within the family will be crucial aspects of daily life and the narratives that grow out of it. "Mudjikiwis" provides a good example of the conflict between group interests (symbolized by family) and individual needs, a conflict that will often rebound against woman, because despite her supposed role as keeper of the hearth, she may nonetheless exercise the least direct control over the tensions within the group.

The pragmatic rather than emotional advantage of tenderness toward a wife is suggested by a Blackfoot Orpheus tale. A husband successfully resists the temptation to look back at his dead wife as he returns with her to the living world. But then his efforts to control his wife sabotage his self-control. Not long after their reunion, "this man told his wife to do something; and when she did not begin at once, he picked up a brand from the fire, not that he intended to strike her with it, but he made as if he would hit her, when all at once she vanished, and was never seen again."[63] In another tale, a husband inadvertently beats his wife to death because he has underestimated her strength and thus overestimates his need to protect her. When his wife and the "bad sister" who impersonates her begin to fight, he assumes that his beloved will get the worst of the battle, and so the "poor young man started forward to part them, but he knew not one from the other" (his error is comparable to the prince's failure to distinguish Odette from Odile). So, "thinking that the bad one must know how to fight better than his beautiful maiden wife, he suddenly caught up his stone-weighed hoe, and furiously struck the one that was uppermost on the head, again and again, until she let go her hold, and fell back." [64]

The Yuchi tell of a more calculated, mass murder, the obscurity of the story seeming to be related to the theme of death as inexplicable and mysterious. For no stated reason, four Yuchi men decide to kill their wives. Almost as inexplicable is their decision to get them back: "There is no such thing as death. So let us go and hunt them." [65] If the translation is faithful to the original, the conception of the quest for the lost wife as a "hunt" exposes the reality at the core of the relations between women and men whose abuse of their wives is a virtual acting out of masculine stereotypes. Such a basic conflict explodes when an Eskimo swan maiden attempts to win her freedom by feigning death, and her husband goes through the motions of mourning her. "Meanwhile the wife arose again, and began walking about the tent in which her husband was. Then he took his spear and killed her." [66] In the end, the husbands who kill their wives in error and those who do so deliberately reflect the same destructive pattern: neither male brute strength nor passivity, forceful domination nor overprotectiveness, is conducive to success in marriage.

As a group, Orpheus tales reveal many motivational layers where it comes to the searcher's contrary patterns of behavior. Aggression and anxiety are only two aspects of what causes the husband to act. Other reasons emerge from man-made myths of feminine evil. Flight and quest may be contrary responses to a similar underlying problem. It has been argued that because of the association between Orfeo and Orpheus, commentators on the medieval work have often failed to notice that Orfeo does *not* undertake a "long search for Heurodis"; indeed, he passively suffers the blow of fate that deprives him of his wife. Moreover, during his deranged wanderings in the wood, his kingdom is left without rule [67]—a clear disordering of culture by nature. In a similar tale, the *Rose of Bakwali*, the husband who has lost his wife to Indra "rolled on the ground through excess of grief," and the "fairies, pitying his condition, took him up and cast him in a forest on earth." For three days he lies senseless; on the fourth, he opens his eyes to confront reality —his wife is gone. [68]

As Bakwali's husband wanders through the forest, asking the very trees to direct him to his lost wife, his disorientated behavior resembles the bewilderment experienced by men faced with what they perceive to be some eternally mystifying quality in woman and in their relationship to her. What it is that woman really wants is a question that would appear to "appeal to and be posed by a woman" [69] (Freud perhaps being a notable exception), but when it is, it is usually posed in a story told about men. Parallels can be drawn between the knight in Chaucer's "Wife of Bath's Tale," who must return with the correct answer to this query in order to expiate a crime against woman (a rape), and the folklore Orpheus character, who must retrieve his wife, frequently after having offended and thus lost her. For Ovid's Orpheus can be portrayed as a misogynist who more out of self-interest than love goes in search of his wife.[70] And more misogyny than he might wish to admit may exist under the bewildered lament of what can be deemed a modern Orpheus, the man who today has lost his wife not to death but to her quest for a liberation he fears and thus despises. Two such "Orpheuses" have described their loss in terms that highlight the extent to which they are both aggrieved and confounded: their accounts provide a significant gloss on the ancient myth of Orpheus and its folklore analogues, whose themes and motifs they seem unwittingly to have employed.[71]

From the pseudonymous Albert Martin's point of view, his marital life had been idyllic, and he cannot fathom why his wife had wanted to leave him and their home. After asking himself the question for two years, he says, he still had only the "reality that she did." As to how she *could,* "the fact she *did* and I never could *understand* it says a lot about what happened to both of us." Something had made her change profoundly, but no therapy they received or books he "hungrily read" supplied the insight he sought in order to win his wife back.[72] Joined to Martin's pained and reproachful account of his broken marriage is another, more cynical voice that not only expresses bewilderment concerning how his marriage disintegrated but also admits to powerlessness in stopping the inexorable movement toward its permanent dissolution. He writes in an ironically conceived *Letter to My Wife* (that she is not interested in hearing from him is part of his pain) telling her that he is staggered by the "alacrity" with which she had given him up, as if he were "no loss at all." He too had sought help in therapy but is struck by his ludicrous situation: "To go to a psychiatrist not because the defects in our marriage bothered [her] but because they didn't."[73]

Perhaps these contemporary Orpheuses are representative of what has been incorrectly described as a peculiarly modern phenomenon, that "of the passive, submissive wife who suddenly and inexplicably turns around and leaves her shocked husband." Like Orpheus, abandoned husbands have been described as going "to extremes to win back a woman who had rejected them," many "seemingly strong, self-contained, 'independent' men [having] been brought to their knees." Like the princes of the Indian tales, they will consult the grand masters of the counseling profession to learn how to restore traditional order to their homes and lives.[74] As Holbek suggests, they illuminate one of the important themes symbolized by Orpheus's quest: in winning back their lost wives, they can also restore their self-esteem. But psychologists may be less effective in helping them achieve their goals than in explaining their predicament. Because a woman has been a man's lifeline since his infancy, her leaving him in a state of unrelieved dependency is "often life-shattering."[75] Contemporary Orpheuses often resemble the mythical husbands who become wild men of the woods in their frantic and random wanderings. And folk narratives prove especially illuminating when it comes to explaining Orpheus's plight.

A man's dependency on women goes back to his infancy and his first relationship to a woman, his mother. This dependency pattern may affect for good or ill ensuing relationships with other women. Realistically, however, requirements for masculine behavior perpetuate this dependency because a man cannot fulfill his traditional role outside the home unless someone else cares for his children in it. Scott relates the story of a widower who first mourns his dead wife and then commences with the pragmatic plan of forming a new marriage, which, for a "poor artisan with so young a family, and without the assistance of a housewife, was almost a matter of necessity."[76] But folklore also depicts the emotional helplessness experienced by the man deprived of his child's mother, the dependency of the infant being real enough but also a symbolic projection of the adult man's needs. In a Malaysian story, the baby deprived of the absent mother's breast "did nothing but cry," its misery profoundly affecting the "father's heart." Faced with his own inadequacy in the situation, "he thought of ways to get into heaven too" —that is, die or retrieve his wife.[77] The Pawnee depict a similar predicament. One night a widower "took [his] child in his arms, and went out from the village to the place where his wife was buried, and stood over the grave and mourned for his wife. The child was very helpless, and

cried all the time. The man's heart was sick with grief and loneliness."[78]
Such a merging of his own and his child's unhappiness causes the husband in a Visayan swan maiden tale to "weep bitterly, especially as he
did not know how to take care of the child. So leaving it in the care of a
relative, he set out to find the way to heaven."[79] The emotional component in these stories is only highlighted by way of contrast when the
motivation to retrieve the lost wife lacks the pathos supplied by the
helpless child and rests instead on practical domesticity: a widowed
hunter "had to do his cooking, mending, and making fire, for now there
was no one to help him."[80]

That if woman had not been created, man would have had to invent
her is an idea found in folklore when a Pygmalion theme is attached to
Orpheus and mysterious housekeeper tales. Such stories often become
creation myths, such as a tale from New Britain in which two men plant
a sugar cane. While they are away, "the stalk burst and from it came out
a woman who cooked food for the men and then returned to her hiding
place." When they discover the mysterious housekeeper who is the
source of their help, they seize the woman and "[hold] her fast," all
humans descending from these original matings.[81] Such a myth legitim-
izes woman's domestic role, making it both part of the original order of
things as well as a role that woman herself has chosen. But the sugar
cane also symbolizes the advantages that accrue to the husband as he
finds in his female partner not only subsistence but sweetness as well.
The husband-wife relationship in this way replicates the mother-son
bond. And in mastering his wife, a man essentially reverses what had
happened early in his life when he could not prevent his separation from
his mother. Evidence from the folktales for such a reading will be
provided shortly.

To reestablish this early tie and to assure that his wife serves him, a
man must enforce the social assumption that to do so is indeed her
mission in life. The subduing of the swan maiden wife in the Indian story
of "The Kotwal's Daughter" (discussed above) is followed by an event
Purūravas might have fantasized about in the face of Urvaśī's refusal to
return to him. After being mastered by her husband, the prince who has
used his cunning to immunize himself against her allure and trickery, the
fairy rushes across the room,

fell at his feet and cried, "Forgive me. I have committed many faults against you.
All this time I have not even spoken to you." "Oh," replied the Prince, "you are

a celestial nymph, and I'm just an ordinary man. Why should you deign to have anything to do with the like of me, and how should I presume even to look at you, much less touch you?" At this, the girl began to weep bitterly and entreat him piteously to be merciful to her.[82]

Despite his pretense at self-effacement, the prince's very recapturing of his runaway swan maiden speaks its own message, and she has not failed to receive it. Again, not only his domestic well-being but also his very masculinity is at stake in his effort to control her.

That the equation between masculinity and a man's ability to control his female partner may only mask a dependency on woman is implied in an Esthonian Melusine type tale. The man is a dreamer, unable to succeed in the family business and thus spurned by his family. When he takes a mermaid wife, his need to cling to her prevents him from fulfilling the requirement that he allow her her weekly seclusion. He intrudes on her privacy—not because, like Raymond of Lusignan, he is suspicious of her, but because he cannot bear the anxiety of her absence.[83] He takes his place among similarly weak and gullible folklore characters who cannot distinguish the false effigies in their beds from the real wives who sport with incubi or fly off to witches' revels.[84] Fictional and nonfictional Orpheuses remain obtuse where it comes to their wives' motivation for leaving them. Albert Martin, who describes in idyllic terms the plot of land on which stood the home he shared with his wife, resembles the husband of a Korean swan maiden who mistakenly believes that "not even the beauties of heaven could tempt her to leave our home and children."[85]

The idea of a childish Orpheus returns this discussion to the significance of the inquiry concerning when and why the Roman myth of Orpheus's failure replaced an earlier version of the classical myth in which he succeeds in rescuing Eurydice. His renowned failure has been explained in two diverse ways. Either Orpheus did not comply with the condition that was imposed and looked back at his wife, or "the gods scornfully rejected his plea and mocked him with a phantom." The latter version is Plato's, and, again, the philosopher believed the gods scorned Orpheus on the very grounds that in most folk versions of the story win their favor. That is, "being a lyre player," he was conceived as lacking in manly courage, singing not acting,[86] deciding on what Yeats would call perfection of the work over perfection of the life ("The Choice"). According to such a view, the story of "Kusa Jataka," a variation on the

Cupid and Psyche tale, would supply a more adequate model of the husband whose manliness is to be emulated. For in this tale, the warrior's acts are sufficient for "Beauty" to perceive the prince beneath the "beast." Earlier his wife had ignited a lamp to identify her mysterious husband, and she had been horrified by his ugliness. When she leaves him, he follows her to her father's home, and when there "came an opportunity for him to display his matchless strength and courage," his wife admires him so much that "she resolved to overcome her dislike, and once more to accept him as her husband."[87]

But perhaps more striking is the argument that contributing to his reputation for weakness is Orpheus's ignominious end: he is torn to pieces by angry women. From classical versions, then, emerge two Orpheuses, one the sorrowing figure whose unwitting betrayal of his wife rebounds upon himself; the other the insensitive misogynist engaged in a psychological battle of the sexes, whose death at the hands of the maenads is therefore just. That possessed women might have destroyed Orpheus over fury at his weakness challenges, however, the argument that demon possession is a stratagem for women to correct, if only temporarily, a power imbalance, a means for expressing without retribution their rage at a male-dominated society. Many storytellers appear to understand that men may try to dominate women at least in part as a reaction to *depending upon them.*

Again, Orpheus tales thus impugn the assumption that the anxious husband of contemporary times is a peculiarly modern phenomenon, shrinking in emasculating fear from today's swan maiden as she reaches for autonomy. The argument has been made that only in recent years has it "become increasingly apparent that the gender orientation known as masculinity has serious and troubling limitations and, consequently has put the male in crisis." Among other things, modern man is "fearful of abandonment by his increasingly autonomous and powerful woman."[88] Men are frequently advised that they should benefit from rather than fight the changes by redefining masculinity—not necessarily because to do so would be to recognize the legitimate requirements of woman, but because if man gives woman what she says she wants, he will be relieved of many of the social, economic, and even sexual burdens attendant upon being the so-called stronger sex.[89] Insofar as the argument implies more rather than less dependence on woman, it is an ironic one.

It is men, not women, assert some, who are constantly in search of self-definition. Biology, it is claimed, early lets a woman know about herself and the roles she is to play, whereas a man defines himself in terms of his relationship to her.[90] She knows what she can do that he cannot, bear children, whereas it is hard for him to find areas exclusively his own according to which he is a "man." Thus any role change by the woman throws her husband into potential chaos, posing a threat not only to his domestic security but also to his pursuit of self-definition. Modern studies describe the masculine dilemma—Orpheus's quest—in psychological and sociological rather than narrative modes of discourse, but widespread themes from folklore can be recognized in their arguments.

That the forcible seizure of the swan maiden, her escape, the need to pursue her to the unknown place to which she has fled, and the often futile attempt to win her back are closely bound up with images of masculinity is obvious in a Tyrolian story. When a cowherd sees three white robes floating in the wind and cannot identify their source, he is "seized with an unutterable terror." In a comforting rather than seductive fashion, the fairy overcomes his fear, looking "smilingly behind" as she enters the mountain into which he is to follow her.[91] He is not the only terrified man who resists even his traditional role as the swan maiden's captor. In a Spanish tale, a man is frightened to find himself suddenly transformed from poor fisherman to lavishly attired gentleman. The story pointedly depicts how he imputes evil to his fairy benefactor because he is himself anxious about whether he can live up to his new role.

"I am enchanted. That princess is indeed a mermaid, and has cast a spell over me. I am undone, my eyes deceive me, and what I take for so much grandeur is but a deception." Saying which, he started to his feet, and hurried towards his village as fast as his legs would carry him.[92]

If it is true that the Orpheus tale is as favored by men as the Cupid and Psyche tale is preferred by women, then male storytellers appear to be expressing through these narratives their difficulties in achieving self-definition consistent with stereotyped ideals of manhood. The typical success experienced by Psyche and the equally typical failure encountered by Orpheus can be profitably analyzed in the context of a recent study of the difference between the ways in which men and women respond to their own fantasies: "women would see deprivation followed by enhancement, whereas men would see enhancement followed by deprivation." In contrast to women,

men showed a preference for extreme endings, which revealed itself most clearly in the tendency of men to see any decline or fall as abrupt, total and final. The possibility of a resurgence or second chance, which is implicit in the female pattern, does not seem very real for men. Perhaps an important difference is that woman is socialized to lose (or give up) control without panic, and that she picks up as a positive concomitant to her submission confidence of recovery in the face of failure or suffering.

Men, on the other hand, may be more prone to see any "loss of conscious ego control as total and absolute—'once you slip, it's all over.' "[93] Masculinity, that is, demands that men never slip—once the fairy wife is lost, she is not likely to be won back. Thus she must be initially won and held with whatever force is necessary.

To *learn* to be a man, according to many who write on the subject, means successfully to separate from the mother and to turn to the father, who is at one and the same time a helpful and wise role model and the threatening authority figure often portrayed in folktales as an ogre-tyrant. If the swan maiden–Orpheus stories, then, can be understood at least in part as depicting a conventional maturation process on the part of a hero on an archetypal journey toward self-realization, it is not surprising that in the tales, father-son and mother-son relationships frequently provide significant themes, and that success and failure with regard to the fairy wife are related to the male folklore character's ability to work through these difficult relationships with his parents.

In the analysis above of the three Indian stories in which men wed to fairy wives find themselves unhappy because the fairies' power interferes with the satisfaction of their own desires, the importance of male role models was noted even if the character of the "grand master" was not discussed in any detail. Male authority, however, is divided between, on one side, the mentor who provides instruction about how to capture the fairy wife, and, on the other, the demon lover from whom she must be taken. These powerful men can be seen as split-off aspects of the whole father. In all three tales, the hero confronts a fairy wife he cannot control; that is, he is not yet a man. To become one, he must use one aspect of the father figure as a model in order to defeat the other, in order to supplant his rival. Similar patterns are found in North American Orpheus tales, in which the presumed ruler of the otherworld has his counterpart in tribal chiefs who instruct bereaved men about how to retrieve their wives from the rulers of the dead.

The demon lover as authority figure, and the Orpheus character's rivalry with him, suggest an oedipal struggle in which the hero's emerging identity is in question. In chapter 5, the relationship of a father figure to an incubus, "an inaccessible being with supernatural powers who is besetting [the rightful husband] by stealing the favors of his libidinal object choice," was invoked as an explanation for the New Guinea concept of the incubus as father of a miscarried or stillborn child.[94] A similar oedipal conflict can be located in a Chinese story in which a man entranced by a woman in a painting is suddenly transported into her world, where he marries the image. But before the marriage can be consummated, a figure "clad in golden armour, with a face as black as jet, carrying in his hand chains and whips" comes to see if *all* his women are accounted for. The new bridegroom hides in terror under the bed, soon to emerge into the real world. The picture on the wall changes to that of a married woman (that is, a mother figure), and the man forgets his adventure.[95]

The father's direct role in his son's maturation can be illustrated by two Slavic variants of the swan maiden story. The Yugoslavian tale of "The Tsar's Son and the Swan-girl" places the young man between his father and another older man in such a way that each plays a conflicting role in the prince's growing to manhood:

Once upon a time there was a tsar, and he had a son. When the boy grew up, he went hunting one day and lost his way. He went hither and thither through the woods until he came into another kingdom. There he lighted upon a hut in which he found an old man, whose white hair reached the ground and whose beard fell down to his waist.

That the young man has "lost his way" implies a separation from the male model whose importance the son may not yet appreciate. He must agree to serve the old man for three years to win as a reward a wife and home of his own—the goal according to which a young man symbolically replaces his father in a normal sequence of events.[96]

In earlier chapters, it was seen that sometimes the swan maiden's son prevents the reunion of his parents. The male child may warn of his father's imminent arrival in the otherworld, thus preserving his exclusive tie to his mother. The opposite has also been met with, for example, in North American native folktales in which the boy allies himself with his father against the "bad mother"[97] (the one who has betrayed them both with her demon lover). Neither story pattern reflects a child whose parenting has provided him with a satisfactory model for a male-female relationship. Reappearing in swan maiden tales as the fairy's husband and faced with an elusive wife who replicates the bad mother image, he can only hold on to her if his rival, her demon lover, proves magnanimous, which does not necessarily improve his self-esteem, or if some authoritative male figure teaches him how to subdue her, which may only convince him of how tenuous is his hold on her.

Today, in novel and film, a female therapist may represent the feminist cause and unabashedly ally herself with the rebellious wife against the husband. In folklore, her counterpart is also a powerful woman, often a witch who is the female counterpart of the ogre father figure. The Orpheus character thus must struggle not only against the male rival but also against the mother-wife he strives to overcome. Sometimes his success against the witch presages his symbolic overcoming of the father-rival by demonstrating, finally, a successful if paradoxical use of the masculine model. To return to "The Tsar's Son and the Swan-girl," the young man begins as a very passive figure: he has lost his way. He continues to display this passivity when he allows his mentor to pick his bride from a group of swan maidens. Then he turns the magic garment over to his mother for safekeeping, and she, of course, eventually returns these to *her* rival so that the swan bride may escape. The older woman, that is, effectively impedes her son's achieving his own identity as a man, becoming a duplicate, that is, of the husband with whom she has already been engaged in a power struggle. The family pathology in these stories is continuously rebounding on the family's members through its literal and symbolic representatives of an essential gender conflict.

Thus the tsar's son, who has so far had no active role in the sequence of events that so profoundly affects his life, must begin his trial by defeating the witch who sets him a series of impossible tasks. As he successfully meets each challenge, he achieves an increasing pride in his own manliness, expressed in a growing aggressive anger toward the old witch, who capitulates in fear: "Oh, woe to me—he is stronger and more furious than I. I had better let him go before he kills me." Thus, where the youth earlier endangered himself by entrusting his mother with his swan bride's clothing, he now vindicates himself by overcoming the witch. Nonetheless, he remains dependent on his fairy wife, for—as typical in Jason and Medea tales—he could not have performed the tasks without her aid.[98] Why, then, does the fairy help her husband conquer the witch, who remains a projection of her own potential to dominate the relationship? For the witch's demise or defeat foreshadows her own submission to her husband. As compensation—or so the story suggests—her husband's conquest of the female ogre may assure her that she no longer has a powerful rival in her mother-in-law, that her husband has successfully overcome his dependence on his mother and has shifted his primary allegiance to his wife.

Such a reading of the Yugoslavian tale is sustained by looking at a Czechoslovakian version of the same story, where it is made even more explicit that to be a man, the swan maiden's husband must separate from his mother. In this case his father has died, and his mother only allows her son to seek his fortune in the world and "[fits] him out for the journey" because she perceives some benefit to herself from his maturity: the strong son will take care of her. But a male sorcerer he encounters advises him to create a separate life instead: "When you get home, if you haven't got a household of your own, have one built, and then pluck those three feathers out of the dove and hide them away so carefully that no human eye can see them." But, typically, the young man relies on his mother, who returns the stolen feathers to the captured wife, her son's immature reaction being to "weep and wail." On his search for his lost wife, he must perform tasks for the devil's grandmother, this time without help from his fairy wife. And the crone is to be feared, for if he does not defeat her, he confronts a dire fate: "the Devil's grandmother always cuts off the servant's head and hangs it on a hook."[99] Again, the symbolically castrating mother must be overcome for manhood to be achieved.

The Hawaiians supply another twist to such themes, the possessive mother being merely supplanted by the possessive wife, herself a kind of witch. When Hiku, a demigod who lives alone with his mother and is never "permitted to descend to the plains below," gains his mother's reluctant acquiescence that he be allowed to "see the abodes of men and to learn of their ways," he becomes the object of Princess Kawelu's passion. "With her wily arts she detained him for several days at her home," and when he is about to return to his mother's house, "shut him up" and "thus detained him by force." It is his mother's earlier words warning him not to remain away too long that inspire his determination to "break away from his prison." Kawelu dies of grief but Hiku descends to the otherworld and brings her back.[100] His success speaks to his emergent manhood, and presumably he not only can distinguish wife from mother but can also prevail over both.

If it is at least in part true that Eurydice herself can be traced to the "bad mother" represented by the powerful and destructive goddesses of the otherworld—deities who project images of man's fear of woman—the characteristic failure of Orpheus raises doubts concerning the basis for happy endings in some swan maiden tales, such as those told in Yugoslavia and Czechoslovakia. The folklore hero whose quest for his lost wife is successful defeats a witch by adopting the model of the patriarchal male figure whose negative counterpart he must frequently conquer as well, both because he must supplant the rival father figure and because the demon lover represents his wife's subversive protest against the role her husband will insist she adopt. Fortuitous conclusions (so-called happy endings) to Orpheus type tales seem to indicate that in one way or another, and for one reason or another, a husband's masculine identity rests on the eventual subjugation of his wife. But Orpheus remains a renowned failure, and his usually aborted attempt to retain his wife indicates not only that men have little confidence that they can live up to traditional definitions of masculinity but also that men must seek other models to preserve even the most traditionally conceived of marriages. The woman who prefers her human husband to her demon lover, like the swan maiden who willingly returns to the mortal world, both of whom will be discussed in the next, concluding chapter of this book, seems to make her choice *despite* rather than *because of* the stories' logic.

# CHAPTER 8

# Etain's Two Husbands: The Swan Maiden's Choice

Previous chapters have argued that to "rescue" the lost fairy spouse from the otherworld is frequently to parallel her original capture, and that these magic tales convey the realistic idea that to win and hold a wife by force involves a perilous marriage at best. The conflict between husband and wife is, moreover, subversive of the well-being of most societies, whose structures mirror and thus rest on the stability of family relations. Fairy visitants to the mortal world do indeed prove a "tester of human relations,"[1] and the swan maiden tale is not an encouraging one. Even fairy wives who coyly invite their husbands to follow and win them back perpetuate in the very games they play the symbolism of capture. There are, however, swan maidens who choose the human world, as Lessa has argued, as well as mortal women who spurn the advances of demon lovers, preferring reality to the imagined pleasures of the otherworld. Even Ibsen's Nora, who slams her famous door on an unsatisfactory marriage, does so with few illusions about what she faces outside her doll house. As will shortly be seen, Nora appears to have been modeled on the swan maiden, but Nora's final decision involves Ibsen's characteristic inversion of his folklore material. In both her resemblance to and her difference from the swan maiden, Nora helps define her folklore ancestress.

And thus the concluding chapter of this book picks up the one theme that is omitted from the story of Purūravas and Urvaśī as it appears in the *Rig Veda* and the *Satapatha Brahmana*, where the promise that Purūravas will dwell among the Gandharvas and thus be reunited with Urvaśī in the divine realm is the only reconciliation these lovers can enjoy. Their fate is a persistent one in the swan maiden tale. It is reenacted on stage each time a penitent Prince Siegfried and his sorrow-ful Odette fling themselves into the swan's lake, having thwarted the evil Von Rothbart but having done so too late to live in the real, that is social, world. A similar, parodic version of the ballet's ending is the closing scene of the Hollywood film *Splash* in which a young man in love with a mermaid stands poised with her at the edge of a dock as his people close in on them, intent on capturing the water creature. Together man and mermaid plunge into the water, the aftermath of their story being left for the audience to imagine.

In a late dramatization of the Sanskrit tale, the *Vikramorvasiyam,* Urvaśī proves her claim to have loved Purūravas by returning to earth, and according to one commentary, the play omits the conflict expressed by the "vigorous conversation" that characterizes the hymn.[2] It is diffi-cult to know how to read this alteration in the story. On one side, it represents a sentimentalization of the story consistent with some kind of idea of romantic love. But on the other, it may be truer to day-to-day actuality. If dwelling with the Gandharvas is a symbolic stage in wom-an's life as she moves toward, not away from, her human husband,[3] the play's ending may paradoxically be more, not less, realistic as its female character adapts to the world. As Holbek has described the heroes and heroines of traditional magic tales, "they are measured according to the qualities they need in order to function as adult, responsible members of their communities."[4]

And some folklore does suggest that strength, both physical and moral, rather than conformity may characterize the woman who spurns or resists the otherworld. In such cases the demon lover may be recog-nized by his victim as a diabolical seducer and the woman may triumph over the threat he poses by outwitting him. Such narratives are fre-quently related to the Bluebeard pattern, appearing, for example in the widespread ballad known in its English version as "Lady Isabel and the Elf Knight" (Child 4). The ballad tells how a demon preys on women for their wealth, killing them after they have eloped with him. He eventually meets his match in the courageous woman who cunningly gains control over him, until he begs her—usually in vain—to spare his life.[5] Like "Lady Isabel" and the heroines of the prose "Robber Bridegroom"[6] tales, many female folklore characters neither submit passively to patriarchy, symbolized by male dominance in its most malig-nant form (for example, Bluebeard), nor spurn reality. They choose an existence on earth because they are not so easily deceived by the allure of the otherworld.

But the woman who can, who *has to,* decide between two husbands and hence two ways of life becomes a character who, from any feminist perspective, remains ambiguous and hence problematic. The choice of reality over fantasy suggests strength and emotional health, but the "reality" a wife elects is so affected by social and cultural determinants that it may be difficult to view her decision to live in her husband's world as other than capitulation. Previous chapters have looked at folktales in which a reconciliation between the mortal and the forfeited supernatural spouse results in the loss of some freedom and the compensatory gain of status for the human man, and both loss of freedom and loss of status for the fairy woman. The cultural, ethical, and psychological issues raised by the swan maiden story show no immediate promise of resolution. Is it really true, as Wordsworth would have it, that the prison to which we doom ourselves no prison is? One perspective for consideration of this matter proves to be an important theme in the folklore: *choice* itself. And some well-known folklore heroines draw attention to questions of woman's choices: Alcmena, Damayanti, and Etain.

Like the story of Urvaśī, that of the Celtic Etain must be pieced together from different sources. The part of the narrative most relevant to a study of swan maidens tells how Etain came to have two husbands, Midir and Eochaid, and thus to belong both to this and the otherworld. Midir, denizen of the supernatural realm, demands to have the most beautiful maiden in Ireland, Etain. But Midir's first wife, Fumach, skilled in magic, acts out her rage by turning Etain into a series of nonhuman beings, the last a fly that is swallowed by a mortal woman. Thus is Etain reborn, and eventually she marries Eochaid. Meanwhile, however, Midir plots to get Etain back. In one version of the story he kidnaps her; in another, Eochaid loses Etain at a chess game played with Midir. At first Eochaid wins the game, and, gaining confidence, agrees to any stake Midir asks. Midir demands a kiss from Etain, but although her husband agrees, he sets a distant date and secures Etain in a locked palace surrounded by armed men. Despite her husband's precautions, Etain disappears with Midir, and like the Orpheus characters of folklore, Eochaid searches for his wife until (in one version of the story) he reaches the abode of Midir, where Etain is surrounded by many identical-looking women from whom he must identify her. When he mistakenly picks out Etain's daughter (this variation on a widespread narrative motif is reminiscent of the Odette/Odile duality), he must renew his efforts to win back his wife.[7]

The story is replete with popular folklore themes and resembles such narratives as the Scandinavian ballad, "The Power of the Harp," and the romance, Sir Orfeo, of which Etain's story is held by some to be a source.[8] The question here, however, is whether Etain can really be thought of as making a choice between her two husbands, or whether she is—as swan maiden—but the passive object of a struggle that can scarcely be perceived as the working out of any inner conflict.

That Etain is a swan maiden has been recognized in studies of Celtic folklore.[9] Her tale is consistently linked to another, "The Dream of Oengus," in which the swan maiden, succubus, and nightmare themes converge. A beautiful woman appears to Oengus in a dream, that is, as "a maiden near him at the top of his bed." Then a "whole year [elapsed] to him and she [went on] to visit him in his bed so that he fell in love." But Oengus cannot take her from her father, Ethal Anbual, who explains that she is under a spell he cannot control, which causes her to appear in the "shape of a bird every day of a year; the other year in human shape." Oengus finds his beloved surrounded by 150 swan maidens, and the two of them, in the shape of swans, return to his kingdom. Similarly, as Midir carries Etain away from her mortal husband, Eochaid, "two white swans were seen, flying towards the fairy-hill."[10] That in one story the swans are flying toward the world, and in the other away from it, speaks to the dichotomy at the heart of the swan maiden pattern.

When Midir confronts Eochaid over which of them has the higher claim to Etain, they play their game of chess to resolve the stand-off. The gamble in which Etain is the stakes provides another link to swan maiden stories. As noted in an earlier chapter, in some versions of the Jason and Medea story the male folklore actor loses at cards and must seek out the ogre to repay the debt. It is the ogre's daughter, frequently a swan maiden, who performs the tasks that save his life. In Celtic folklore, a comparable story involves a motif known as the "geasa-game," and in Irish tales it often involves a man who meets "one of the Swan-Maidens, who challenges him to a game of cards and puts geasa upon him to find her palace."[11] In "The Wooing of Etain" the gambling motif combines with others from the folklore surrounding swan maidens

—Eochaid's search for the fairy world to which his lost wife has been taken, and perhaps even his need to dig up fairy mounds to find her, a feat comparable to the arduous tasks set many folklore husbands in search of their missing wives.

Gambling provides an important motif in the similar tale of Nala and Damayanti, which appears in the *Mahabharata*.[12] Nala, "brave, handsome, virtuous, skilled in arms and the management of horses, but addicted to gambling" loses to his brother his palace, kingdom, clothing, and other personal possessions; but in contrast to the Pandava brother who gambled away Draupadi, Nala refuses to wager his wife, Damayanti, to risk sacrificing her to his brother's passion. Damayanti returns her husband's love by accompanying him in exile into the wilderness.

But Damayanti had already faced an equally great danger. Just as Etain's beauty had made her the object of Midir's desire, so has Damayanti's loveliness brought her to the attention of Indra. In the meantime Nala has also heard of her renowned beauty (significantly, by an intermediary in the form of a swan), and Damayanti dares to choose him over a divine spouse. The gods do not retaliate at once; like the Gandharvas who want Urvaśī back, they bide their time. Nala and Damayanti live happily for many years and have two children, until Nala plays the fateful game with his brother, who in the human world reenacts the passion and threat of the gods. And as was true in the story of Purūravas and Urvaśī, Nala's error (in this case, gambling serves the function of the broken taboo motif) supplies the irate gods with their opportunity to move against the mortal pair. The ensuing catastrophe can thus be located in the dynamics of human relations and actions rather than any simplistically conceived of intervention of supernatural agencies.

Their status as mortal women about whom hover the images of the fairy wife provides the stories of Etain and Damayanti with an ambiguity that is underscored by juxtaposing the stories of the two women. Midir had been Etain's first husband, and thus her "complicated history of previous existences"[13] roots her in the otherworld. Like the seal maiden whose primary allegiance is to the bull seal who claims her, or the archetypal swan maiden described by Lessa, Etain lives in this world as a temporary guest and never seems quite to belong in it. In contrast, Damayanti's allegiance to Nala—symbolically, to the human world— seems unambivalent, and only by appearing as mortals can the gods hope to trick and thus conquer her. But in contrast to Alcmena, who is unwittingly unfaithful to her husband, Amphytrion, when Zeus appears disguised as her spouse, and other folklore characters on whom a demon lover uses this strategy, Damayanti is not fooled. A comparison has been drawn between Damayanti and Eochaid, forming another example of the strong woman and weak man. Eochaid cannot on his own select Etain from the group of women who look exactly like her. When, in contrast, the Hindu gods seek to trick Damayanti by appearing in number looking just like Nala and by forcing her to pick one of their group as a husband, she is able to choose Nala for precisely those qualities that made him human, "from the fact that he cast a shadow and that he perspired and blinked, all of which the gods do not do."[14]

The question of why beings from the otherworld require human consorts has already been asked. Christianity explains that these otherworldly beings are hellish demons, and their evil consists in their need to corrupt the as yet uncorrupted. A story is told of an eleventh-century woman beloved by a demon, who does not return the "affection of the incubus and instead took a human husband." The demon retaliates by causing the husband seven years of impotence, but because the woman perseveres in loving her husband, the spell is broken. Still, the incubus does not give up, continuing to assault the woman in her bed, until, with the help of the Virgin Mary, the wife is able to rid herself of the demon.[15] Religious meanings often reduce the complexity of folklore themes, just as positivistic thought can relegate such themes to tales spun for children. Jean Giraudoux, who in his play *Ondine* ironically portrays a woman on trial for her life for no other charge than being a mermaid, also created Ondine's obverse, the mortal Alcmena, who does not have sufficient imagination to prefer Zeus to Amphytrion.[16]

The Amphytrion motif also shows up in the *Dravidian Nights*, a story being told of how a woman acts against her own self-interest by discarding the medicine that would bring her unfaithful husband under her control. It is swallowed instead by a serpent who takes her husband's form and becomes her lover, not to corrupt her nor to be disenchanted by her, but rather to stand in for her lawful spouse until he is returned to her. The wife is ultimately rewarded not only for her commitment to her husband but, again, for displaying proper feminine obedience throughout her ordeal.[17] And in a Himalayan tale, an adulteress keeps a tryst with her lover only to encounter a man who appears to be her husband, making the best of the compromising situation by giving herself to the supposedly lawful spouse. But in the firelight she becomes aware that she has mated with a demon and repents, regretting her infidelity. Commentary on this story has it that the people who told it did not take adultery too seriously unless it was persistent or—perhaps more important—unless the woman preferred her lover to her husband.[18]

A preference for a human lover is the basis of a story that again tells how Indra is displeased because his subject Bakawali has absented herself from his revels: "caught in the net of love by a man, and, intoxicated with this passion, she is constantly with him and has no longer any dislike for his race." Enraged, Indra orders a group of fairies to bring Bakwali back to him. Her mortal mate, disoriented by the loss of her, wanders aimlessly in the wilderness, one day falling asleep near a pond where fairies are accustomed to bathe. Without being themselves trapped in the world, these swan maidens help him find and win back Bakwali.[19] These antithetical groups of fairies also help define the tension in the story of Etain, a folklore mortal who is also a fairy bride: not clearly preferring either human or supernatural mate, she is instead caught in what has been described as an infinite circle of loss and recovery[20] that prefigures the essential conflict in the swan maiden narrative.

It is a conflict depicted in an Italian story related by Calvino. An unfaithful woman is drowned by her husband and becomes a siren. "What with so many comforts and celebrations, the wife's days flew by in joy. But the memory of her husband would often return to haunt her and make her sad." At the same time, her husband is drawn by the sirens' song to fling himself into the water, where he is rescued by his former wife. Together they outwit the temptresses whose company she had erringly joined.[21] In effect, both have exorcised their demons, although, typically, the story implies that the wife bears the greater burden of the social contract to which they are now equally pledged.

Both the demons within as well as their external projections must be subdued, and where the demon is not integrated into human society, it must be outwitted or destroyed. For in much folklore, animal and otherworldly lovers are not lovely humans in disguise, but are, to the contrary, devils camouflaged as beautiful-seeming persons. The Tahltans tell a frog prince type story that hinges on this premise. A young girl who has just "finished the training that girls undergo at puberty" kicks a toad out of the road. But then she elopes with a handsome man, not realizing that he is the reptile in human form. Her father-in-law encourages her to visit her parents, and her father asks her "not to go back with Toad, but to stay with them." When she agrees, her animal husband leaves her and her people experience a plague of toads that will not disperse until the "girl returned to the Toad chief's house." The tale concludes with the explanation that this is why women are afraid of toads, but in fact the story, while not entirely coherent, suggests more widespread significance.[22]

The young woman is buffeted about by the men in her life: her father, her animal husband, and his father, whose reasons for sending her back home are unclear. Her kicking the toad out of her doorway after she had completed puberty tends to confirm Bettelheim's interpretation of the tale group to which this story belongs. Overcoming her revulsion to the toad symbolizes the young woman's acceptance of adult sexuality; in this story, however, her father's attempts to hold on to her make it difficult for any transference of loyalty from father to husband to take place, and the husband must coerce her into returning to him. At the same time, it is the woman's actions that have brought a plague on her people, and her elopement with a beast she does not recognize beneath the fair exterior of a handsome man suggests that some fantasized union has made it difficult for her to adapt to a socially sanctioned marriage and that her people suffer from her disorientation. It is possible to argue that the story, as told, reflects a narrator who has combined diverse strains in the animal groom stories in an inconsistent—again, even incoherent—fashion so that the toad husband is both disguised demon and rightful spouse. But it is also arguable that the tensions within the entire animal groom cycle, part of which involves the confusion between animal/human and animal/demon, are reflected in the tale—the very confusion reinforcing the story's themes and the woman's plight.

In Japanese folktales, a supernatural mate is often "an animal and must be killed so that the bride can return to normal society,"[23] interest centering on how the wife can escape rather than disenchant him. For example, a father promises his daughter to a monkey, and she, not docile but cunning, more like Lady Isabel than Belle Rose, asks for an earthen jar with lots of needles. As the wedded couple cross a narrow bridge, it requires only a "bare touch" of the bride's hand for the animal to fall into the stream, "carried away with the jar of needles still on his back."[24] But the widespread Japanese serpent bridegroom tales prove more ambiguous than stories about how resolute human beings may outwit evil forces, for often humans cannot easily decide "whether the serpent is an honorable deity or an evil spirit."[25] In a typical version, when a young woman becomes pregnant, her suspicious mother elicits from her daughter the admission that she is courted at night by a mysterious lover. At her mother's instruction, the daughter thrusts a needle into her lover's coat collar, and following the thread she arrives at a big rock cavern where she finds a dying serpent with a needle in its throat.[26]

In Japan, even honorable deities cannot be merely adopted into a human world, and thus the woman who enters into a union with one appears to have placed herself outside the boundaries of her people. And if, like Lohengrin's Elsa or Zeus's Semele, she seeks knowledge of her mysterious lover, it would appear to be because of some misguided notion that disparate worlds can be united. A particularly striking rendering of such an error can be found in an eighth-century Japanese tale in which the wife of a deity "who appeared before his wife only at night" demands to see him. He agrees that her desire is reasonable and instructs her to examine her comb case the next morning. In it she discovers a pretty little snake, significantly as long as the band on her underclothes. But her lover has been shamed by the discovery, and when he leaves her, she commits suicide by thrusting a chopstick into her "private parts,"[27] a death that points to the uncontrolled passion that, perhaps, had first led her to mate with a snake, and then, more certainly, had resulted in her willful demand for knowledge of him.

The Eskimos, who believe that ghosts have human figures and can inhabit the human realm without being seen, tell similar tales, among them an account of how an Inuit woman marries one of the invisible ones. He is a good husband, but the woman cannot bear the thought that she has never seen the one she is married to. At last she can contain herself no longer, and one day, sitting in their house together, she thrusts a knife in there where she knows he must be sitting. And her desire is fulfilled. A handsome young man falls on the floor and remains there, dead and stiff. And now it is too late for her to regret the loss of a good husband.[28] These tales do not merely point to Psyche's rebellion against her passive role but also suggest that she has at the same time begun to accept the light of common day, being a romantic who thinks, however, that if she can comprehend the world in which she lives, she can also unite the mundane and the extraordinary.

For even if the otherworldly suitor is not a malevolent demon, he is dangerous to the extent that he provides the focal point for woman's resistance to culture. The Zuñi, who believe that union with the supernaturals prepares a mortal for ordinary marriage, also reveal the other side of the psychological coin: the woman who marries a Kachina may not always be able to return to her own people (adapt to her society) if the otherworld proves unsatisfactory. "That is the reason that a [Zuñi] girl, when she sees a nice looking Kachina, does not want him for her husband."[29] The Cheyenne similarly tell how a woman is dismayed to discover that her mysterious lover is a dog, and how she beats him until he breaks loose from her. But when maternal feelings for the pups she bears inspire her to find their father, she is barred from both her own and his world, remaining in a perpetually liminal state.[30]

Norway, rich in tales of supernatural lovers, tells many stories of the *huldre* folk, who seek salvation in human mates but who also can be dangerous to the mortals who must be rescued from them. Many stories tell how a *seter* girl becomes the desired object of the *huldre* man, and these are particularly telling because the economic structure of Norwegian society places the young woman in a particularly vulnerable position as she lives alone in a mountain hut, tending cattle, making cheese, or weaving, living a marginal existence part of each year, outside the confines of the organized social life of her village. She may, as Holbek points out, enjoy her freedom and the company of other women. But the stories also suggest that the *huldre* men prey on the *seter* women because so much of their time is spent without the protection of human men.

Christiansen relates several *huldre* stories, and it is possible to discern in his collection alone a significantly varied narrative pattern. One folktale tells how a young woman unwittingly finds herself about to marry the *huldre,* and how she must be rescued by her mortal fiancé, that is, brought once more within the bounds of patriarchal society.[31] But the Norwegian woman's independence may also help her develop strengths not evidenced by some of her folklore sisters. When one of the Norwegian women is "taken," that is, stolen by the fairies when a child, she enjoys her life with them and yet does not feel as if she is in the "right company." It is "as if something were nagging her," making it impossible for her to marry one of the *huldre* men. In striking contrast, another "Girl Who Was Taken" is glad that the village has failed in its efforts to get her back; indeed, she finds an advantage what other female folklore characters find their undoing, that her would-be human male rescuers cease their efforts on her behalf (in this case, ringing church bells) just short of the point when they would have succeeded: she "would have come home" but not been able to "live as well off as if it was Christmas all the time."

From the vastness of the Norwegian folktale tradition emerge these multiple variations on the same theme. The stories make it clear that it is not easy to reject the good life in the otherworld, yet a surprising number of folklore women do so, and they are joined by those *huldre* women who accept baptism to become ordinary women. The widespread narratives explore all the possible outcomes of the story. One folktale relates how a cotter's wife had used magic herbs to ward off the advances of an otherworldly suitor, and when her own life becomes hard and she and her husband have trouble making ends meet, she is taunted by her demon lover: "You could have chosen me, you could! Then you wouldn't have had to toil and struggle the way you're doing now!" Her lot is hardly likely to impress young women with the dangers of taking demon lovers, and a more effective model might be the young woman of another story, who outwits her *huldre* suitor and later marries a man from her own parish, having lots of children. In general, the story says, "all went well with her."[32]

Women determined to outwit demon suitors recognize that whatever the allure of the supernatural, it is somehow contrary to human nature. In a Gaelic tale, a maiden transported to the otherworld is informed that she will have to remain there as the fairy chief's wife unless she can get her own chosen mortal lover to marry her before the year is up. She is "so eager to get away" from the demon lover that she accedes to the conditions of her escape even though she expects the subsequent difficulty she faces in fulfilling her bargain.[33] A suggestion of Christian saintliness hovers about a Micmac tale in which a young woman suspects that the dog who fawns on her is an evil spirit and shuns him. Then she dreams that "a man would come to pluck her white flowers" and similarly spurns a fine-looking gentleman, for which she is transported to heaven.[34] Not too many folklore heroines are martyred or sainted for their efforts to evade demon lovers, but many do suffer, even die. The maiden in an African tale "spat blood because she had been running so long" from the monster who pursues her, but she recovers and remains under the protection of an uncle.[35]

A less happy fate awaits the married woman in a Musquakie story: pursued by a demon, she "ran till she fell down," continuing to fight with her unwelcome suitor until morning, when she arrives home but nonetheless dies. Perhaps she provides a cautionary example of the difficulty of outwitting a demon suitor without the support of the male-dominated culture exemplified in, for example, the African uncle. For the Musquakie tale begins much as book 9 of Milton's *Paradise Lost* does, with domestic discord provoked by the woman who wants to strike out on her own. "There was a woman got mad at her husband when they were out hunting plums," and she leaves him to return home alone.[36] The contrast between the African and North American tales reveals once again a thematically double-edged sword: women who outwit their demon lovers are notable for being strong and resolute; but such resoluteness may be subversive of the essential necessity of living under the rule (often, euphemistically, the protection) of men. Again, the extent to which they can ever really *choose* the direction of their lives remains doubtful.

Holbek points out that the majority of human beings lack genuine, meaningful choices about how they live their lives, and that this is particularly true of the folk for whom the narratives under discussion here were intended. But they are also the group from whom these stories emerge. Choice may, in fact, constitute for the folk the ultimate human fantasy: that they do not experience volition does not mean they cannot imagine an existence in which they do. *Not* choosing may be the obverse of such a dream. Some contemporary and unsympathetic commentators on woman's quest for liberation have accused the modern feminist of childishly wanting to have it all, of wanting, that is, not to have to make decisions about how to live life, decisions about—for example—whether successful career or motherhood should be a first priority (this subject will be returned to shortly). From an existentialist point of view, to be able to evade choice constitutes the ultimate evasion of the human condition. It is arguable that some folklore narrators understood this. The folk as well as the privileged had always to make moral choices. And, as has been argued all along in this book, some narrators prove more psychologically astute than others and are capable of pursuing the wider implications of human choice. In any event, *choice* as a folklore motif imbues many narratives with their themes.

That Etain has a choice in the matter of whether Midir or Eochaid will possess her, but that her choice is also severely limited by her position as Eochaid's wife, is thematically embedded in her folklore and its analogues, as well as in the literary renditions of her story, such as that of James Stephens in *The Feast of Lugnasa*. When Midir comes to reclaim Etain, he sings to her of the wonderland he comes from, an earthly paradise to fulfill the heart's desires. But she is not swayed by this enticement and spurns him—"I will not give up the king of Ireland for thee, a man who knows not his own clan nor his kindred"—content with the mundane and familiar and proud of her worldly status. But at this point her autonomy is challenged, for Midir asks if she will follow him if Eochaid should command it. "I would come in such case," she replies.[37]

When Stephens wrote his version of Etain's story, he appears to have been haunted by the image of a noble Celtic woman who might not so readily obey her husband. For his narrator, Queen Maeve, contextualizes her story of Etain with comments and questions about woman's role: whether women or poets could participate in war and have a "part in the common security of their land" was becoming "an angrily debated question." Stephens's concerns were hardly feminist, however. During the nineteenth century, writers frequently made a symbolic equation between the writer who chooses art over the active life and the human who chooses a supernatural over a mortal lover. If Stephens thus identified with Etain, he would have had strong motive to insist that she choose her fate freely rather than be a passive stake in a wager between men. Thus, in contrast to her folkloristic model, Stephens's Etain elicits from Eochaid the agreement that if she does not agree to go with Midir, "he cannot accept" Midir's wager.

At the same time, Stephens's making of Etain a symbolic point of reference for the (male) artist—on whom the rhetorical demands of art make claims that can neither be wholly accepted nor wholly denied—keeps his Etain in her paradoxical place, both of the world and not of it. For unlike the muse whom many writers thought should not be forced into the service of the mundane world, Etain "was Midir's wife; and his claim to her was not and could not be abrogated by any heavenly or earthly law, or by any interplanetary event or accident." And from this cosmic perspective, and within Stephens's concern with the artist's plight, the feminist implications of his work recede into the background. Etain is once again forced into passivity, in effect denied a chance to participate in her fate.[38]

Choice as a theme in folklore can be found in animal groom tales whenever the Psyche character is asked whether she would prefer her husband to be an animal by day or by night, Beach arguing that this narrative device is the source for Chaucer's knight's offering to his loathly bride the power to decide what kind of wife she will be,[39] thus inverting the conventional relationship of obedient wife to masterful husband. A similar choice is offered by a loathly lady to Gawain in *Sir Gawain and Dame Ragnell*. The argument has been made that when such female folklore characters demand sovereignty in marriage, they are really asking for equality and respect. But this interpretation is hard to sustain: as the feminist critic who makes the argument admits, what his loathly wife tells Gawain is that women want sovereignty; what the story actually reveals is that what she most desires is Sir Gawain.[40]

From folklore to modern polemics, no issue appears as problematic as woman's ability to make choices in patriarchal society. For those sympathetic to women's dissatisfaction, women either have no choice, have been encouraged to abandon choice in the name of misguided femininity, or face at best Hobson's choice. Antagonists of modern feminism argue, however, that a woman's liberation ideology masks woman's attempt to evade choice. Either side might find support in a crucial passage from *The Bell Jar*, by Sylvia Plath, a poet who in her juvenalia described the experience of "Looking into the Eyes of a Demon Lover,"[41] and of seeing her *own* transformation from frog to Venus. The novel is, however, pessimistic about such happy metamorphoses, as Plath's persona pictures her life as a fig tree from which she may pick but one fig. From each branch "a wonderful future beckoned and winked." One fig offered "a husband and a happy home with children," while another appealed to the "famous poet" *or* "brilliant professor" *or* "amazing editor." Other figs offered still other choices: travel to distant lands *or* exposure to new cultures *or* quasi–demon "lovers with queer names and offbeat professions." Faced with the necessity of selecting only one fig from among such riches, Plath's heroine imagines herself sitting "in the crotch of this fig tree, starving to death, just because I couldn't make up my mind which of these figs I would choose"—her imagery making it clear that her predicament is a gender-based one. In her paralysis, she watches the fruit rot and die: "one by one, they plopped to the ground at my feet."[42]

Again, the questions remains of what can be said about the swan maidens who choose husband, domestic role, and children over the supposed advantages of the otherworld, for while these are a minority, they do exist. Some of these have already been met with, such as the mysterious housekeeper who, like some of the swan maidens described by Lessa, seeks out the human world; or the Medea figure who helps a young man perform superhuman tasks on condition that he will take her back with him to his world.[43] Sometimes the sorceress–swan maiden seeks baptism and thus salvation, and her motives for assuming the mundane are essentially rooted in self-interest. But there is another folktale group in which swan maidens appear, that of the man envied by a powerful person for his beautiful swan maiden wife, who, in a Finnish version, for example, acts solely out of love for her husband and supplies the magical help necessary for the husband to defeat his rival.[44]

Is hers really a choice or the not-so-subtle coercion of a culture that grants her sovereignty with one hand and, with the other, warns her that she then may not have her Gawain? Swan maiden tales sometimes confirm the argument that if man gives woman a genuine choice, she may indeed choose him. A possible example is "Toria the Goatherd," in which Toria is enticed by the swan maidens to swim with them, but immediately returns the stolen garments of one of these, whose acceptance of him as a human husband is expressed in ambiguous terms:

Seeing such a fair and noble creature before him, for very bashfulness he could not open his mouth to ask her to be his wife; so he simply said, "Now you may go." But she replied, "No, I will not return; my sisters by this time will have gone home; I will stay with you, and be your wife."[45]

Similarly, in a Roman story, a variation on the animal groom story, a maiden is assured by a loathsome man that "whether you will be my wife or not depends on you. It is for you to say whether you will or not." But the story contains the usual catch-22 predicament. Only the *free* consent of a maiden also free to dissent will restore the monster to his earlier handsome form and his former status as king.[46] Once again, he regains the privileges that come from ruling his kingdom; but her freedom of choice is limited precisely at that moment she chooses to become a wife.

That a woman might indeed perish when her choice is in effect not a choice is a theme found in a story popular in Greece, Turkey, and Armenia, best described by one of its titles, "The Girl with Two Husbands." It tells how a young woman nurtures (that is, civilizes) a serpent child and then marries him. At some point in a story that combines several folklore themes, but not always coherently, her serpent husband turns demon, and she must flee him to save her life. During her hapless wanderings, she is rescued by another man whose wife she becomes. Now, like Etain, she is a woman with two husbands. When her animal husband reappears, she must choose between the two men.[47] In an Armenian version, the woman recognizes her dependency on man and calculates whether she can hope to combine love with an essentially unromantic material necessity: "When she gets thirsty she will ask for water from the man she really loves."[48] In a Turkish variant, she chooses the otherworld, which she apparently equates with love, telling her mortal husband that although they have two children, "Black-eyed Snake possesses my heart."[49]

That preoccupations with problems of the "self" are not solely an upper-class privilege[50] but are intrinsic to the folk's fantasy life is as an argument sustained by the conflict in a Greek version of the two husbands story. A judge determines that the woman and her two spouses must climb a mountain, one husband carrying a jug of water, the other a baby. Whether the woman asks for water or for the child will determine whom she belongs to.[51] That her conflict is virtually unresolvable is the point of another Greek variant, in which the wife "stood between" her two husbands, the one she had made a man but who has thus remained dependent on his mother-wife, and the one who had subsequently rescued her, on whom she may rely. Unable to decide, she dies.[52]

Despite the expanded options available to modern women in many parts of the world, there are those who argue that the essential narrownesses of woman's choices has remained virtually unchanged. This female dilemma has been blamed by some on the very structure of the nuclear family, which may depend for its existence on woman's accepting her traditional role. It would seem, however, paradoxical to argue that the swan maiden tale forms a commentary on the nuclear family, since the societies that retained and told the tale (which means, most societies) differ according to how family groups are defined and organized as well as according to the value systems that emerge from such organization. But attention has recently been paid to the very prevalence in folktales of the nuclear family, and its symbolism has elicited significant discussion.

Max Lüthi has contended that since "each action of a man [and woman] is also an argument of this man [and woman] with himself [herself], it seems . . . that one cannot deny the supposition that the family in the folktale is a symbolic representation of the total personality."[53] Doniger has made a similar point about the five Pandava brothers in the *Mahabharata*.[54] And Fischer has argued that many psychoanalytic critics have "interpreted political references in tales as disguised and inflated references to the nuclear family":

Community hierarchical organization may be reflected in turn both in the nuclear family structure and in the internal psychological structure of the individuals who have an important internal conflict between resentment of demands for service to authority and desire to submit to authority to avoid punishment and to gain security and praise by voluntary association with traditionally legitimate force. Dégh's remark that the community constitutes a condensed society and that the individual constitutes a condensed community is also applicable here.[55]

It is the internal psychological structure of the individual that concerns Bettelheim, who also addresses the nuclear family symbolism in fairy tales, which he considers allegories in whose characters are reflected id, ego, and superego. He argues that readers of fairy tales become familiar with their true selves, with the inner workings of their own minds, by integrating "discordant tendencies" after they "project them into separate figures."[56]

But for Fischer the process is more dialectical, since internal dynamics are constantly mirrored by external structures, by the society that does not easily relinquish autonomy of thought or action to an individual but that also cannot fully control feelings. Some folktales, therefore, "may at times be maladaptive from the point of view of the individual, although adaptive from the point of view of maintaining the existing social structure."[57] It is this very relationship of the nuclear family to the wider environment in which it is established as well as to the individual psyche it reflects that supplies the thematic tension to *A Doll House*. In his use of the swan maiden story, Ibsen is both true to his folklore sources and, typical of how he transforms them, original in the way he inverts narrative motifs in order both to give them new meaning and also to illuminate their original significance. The swan maiden tale may supply Fischer's argument with its paradigmatic example, because its subject *is* the nuclear family (sometimes in conflict with a member of an extended family); because the family conflict reflects internal strife while, at the same time, internal strife leads to the alteration of the family structure. And, finally, the swan maiden tale is certainly about adaptation and maladaptation. Thus Ibsen's invention of a character whose *choice* it is to disrupt her home and family paradoxically places her among those fairy wives who elect to remain attached to human husband and children. For Nora elucidates the final act of the typical swan maiden, who appears in the context of Ibsen's play not only essentially hebephrenic—as Lessa would have it—but also impulse ridden; and it is the folklore swan maiden who supplies a context for evaluating Nora's decision, which, sudden as it may be, relies so little on impulse.

It is not, that is, contradictory to conclude a chapter about swan maidens who elect to live in the human word and remain with husbands and children even when escape is available to them with an analysis of what leads Nora to slam the famous door on her family and on her conventional life. No demon lover awaits her beyond that door; no fantasies of the otherworld instigate her to act as she does. To the contrary, by conceiving of her as living in a doll house, Ibsen has, again, inverted the pattern of the narrative on which she draws: Nora leaves behind the symbolically unreal existence of the only world she has ever known in order to seek reality.

The argument for *A Doll House* as a modern dramatization of the swan maiden tale rests on both contextual and internal evidence. When Ibsen referred to his later plays, he asked his audience to read them as a group, beginning with *A Doll House*.[58] In these late plays can be found not only images derived from swan maidens but also the other folklore characters that have traditionally been attached to the runaway fairy wife: demon lovers, animal brides and grooms, and other forms of wild man and wild woman. The seal maiden informs both *Rosmersholm*, in which Rebecca West returns to her native element by suicidally plunging into a body of water, and *The Lady from the Sea*, in which Ellida Wangel finally repudiates her demon lover in favor of an ordinary mortal husband. In Ibsen's last play, *When We Dead Awaken,* the unworldly Irene wears a robe made of swan feathers, and the swan knight, Lohengrin, becomes a symbolic character in a drama of mismating.[59] But it is in *A Doll House* that Ibsen not only draws heavily on folklore, but actually appears to write a dramatization of a folktale.

Nora is a symbolically captured bride who becomes transformed when a missing dancing dress is recovered by her maid, and, taking charge for once of her own clothing, Nora leaves her husband rather than continue to live under his despotic rule. Although she would have taken her children with her had she been given that opportunity and, implicitly, had she a way to care for them, the pain of leaving them behind does not deter her from leaving her husband. In this way too, then, she reenacts the swan maiden's story.

Had Torvald Helmer been a less despotic husband, had he not failed to live up to what Elaine Hoffman Baruch describes as his wife's "image of him," then Nora might never have come to realize that she is virtually a captive living under the protective custody of a man whose economic control over her is both literal and symbolic, but who, as Baruch notes, shelters her not too much, but, ultimately, not enough.[60] The imagery of the play sustains such a reading. Nora is described by her husband not only as a bird wife, his little lark, but also as his squirrel, an animal whose association with rodents evokes the more unpleasant aspects of the animal bride whose husband recoils from and rejects her as soon as she deviates from his expectations of a wife. And just as the animal wife hopes her husband will not discover the truth about what she really is, so Nora, who has not yet enough knowledge of herself even to evaluate the danger she faces, also hopes that her husband will not discover her guilty secret, that she had once forged his name on a check and lied to him about the money she acquired, all this done to obtain for him the vacation rest he had needed to overcome a threatening illness. Naively she expects him to be pleased by her actions on his behalf, just as mysterious housekeepers might expect gratitude for the good they do but are instead, like Nora, repudiated because of some evil their husbands impute to them.

Act 2 begins with the finding of the costume that Nora will wear to a party at which she will—like other swan maidens—dance for the delight and enhanced status of her husband. Her maid's line, "Well, at last I found the box with the masquerade clothes," parallels the initial loss and final discovery of the swan maiden's magic coverings, which are implied in the idea of a masquerade, of that which is outside of ordinary life. In act 3, both stage directions and lines persistently refer to Nora's changing of clothes as who—she or her husband—is actually in control of what she wears becomes an issue. And in another inversion of Ibsen's folklore motifs, Nora leaves her house not in the dancing dress that signals her eventual separation from the life woman lives from day to day, not in a masquerade garment that implies a flight to an unreal world, but in her everyday clothing. She sets out not to flee the real world but to learn about it and about those activities from which women were as yet essentially excluded.

Again, Nora does not yet know in act 1 that she is a captive bride, and with a certain smugness as well as sympathy she contrasts her love for Helmer with the necessity out of which her friend, the now-widowed Kristine Linde had wed. It is only in act 3 that she realizes that she had been handed from father to husband and that she actually exercised no choice at all when she became Nora Torvald. What the folklore swan maiden realizes at the beginning of her marriage is what Nora discovers only at the end of hers. And Torvald's faint hope that he may yet persuade his now-lost wife to return to him suggests Ibsen's fidelity to the narrative pattern on which he has drawn. A Doll House concludes as the swan maiden story sometimes ends, with the husband's intention to follow and win back his runaway wife. To know the folklore is to realize how little hope for such an outcome is held out by Ibsen. But in drawing on the failed quest motif, Ibsen has also revealed, as Baruch notes, that the doll house has imprisoned Helmer Torvald as well as his wife.[61] Nora's husband is already another failed Orpheus.

That Nora actually changes not in act 3 but in act 2 when she changes her clothing has been argued by Stanley Cavell in—ironically—a book about movie comedies of remarriage.[62] In folklore, the swan maiden who recovers her dancing dress and uses it as her means of permanently exiting her marriage can be found in Japan and Turkey, for example. In contrast, seal maidens must doff their animal skins to dance and disport themselves as human beings. Whatever Ibsen's specific sources for the missing dancing dress might be (Scandinavian swan maidens do not recover such garments, but rather find their stolen animal coverings), a tale from Iceland contrasts the revelry a woman free of her husband's rule might experience in the otherworld with the celebrations some swan maidens must flee to escape ties to human husbands.

"Una, the Elfwoman" tells of a character who, like the mysterious housekeeper, voluntarily enters the mortal world, laboring so arduously at farm work that she is offered a permanent place in the household she miraculously appears in. But she periodically attires herself in a dancing dress she carefully hides on the farm and returns in this magic garment to the otherworld to enjoy the festivities there. On one such occasion she is followed by a man who has no relationship to her other than that they work on the same farm; he is not even threatened by harm from her as was the Icelandic farmhand who followed Hild, Queen of the Elves, to her supernatural revels.[63] Rather, in seeking to learn Una's secret, her pursuer seems merely to exercise the prerogatives of men in patriarchal systems, who deem themselves the moral guardians of wayward women. But when this man discovers Una's secret, he and the farm lose the benefits of her hard work, for she disappears.

The space in this folktale is divided not only between this and the otherworld, but also between areas of this world that Una must distinguish and move among in order to live with mortals and yet retain the freedom periodically to escape from culture. There is the farmhouse itself where she will not store the chest in which she keeps her dancing dress. There is also the church to which she steadfastly refuses to go—that patriarchal institution that Helmer Torvald will unsuccessfully invoke to keep Nora in her place. And there is nature itself: not the cultivated nature of the farm, which already depicts the triumph of culture, but raw nature, the swamp through which Una sinks in her dancing dress in order to enter the otherworld.[64]

In *A Doll House*, the otherworldly revels have been preempted by society: the party that Nora and Helmer attend takes place, if not inside a farmhouse, then in its equivalent, a home that represents a social and familial structure (of which a doll house is not only a miniature but in Ibsen's play a parody). And Nora's dancing dress is, significantly, mislaid (not hidden), existing neither within the secure boundaries of the doll house nor definitively outside of it. When Nora dances the tarantella, her performance, moreover, involves another irony. Folk culture itself has become marginal, trotted out for entertainment when the occasion demands. In Nora's tarantella, the tarantula for which the dance has been named has effectively become domesticated: to invoke Garnett's novella, Sylvia the fox wife has been tamed.

As a folk dance, the tarantella is, to begin with, a means by which the folk mediated between nature and culture. The origins of the dance have to do with the belief that its lively movements are an antidote to the spider's bite and the illness that follows it. But to dance the tarantella at the kind of party to which Helmer takes his wife is to move still further from nature. But this, perhaps, is Ibsen's point. His Nora is a descendent of the swan maidens. The donning of her dancing dress has brought about the turning point in her life. But whereas the swan maiden, like Una the elfwoman, can be conceived of as escaping culture entirely, Nora neither experiences nor desires such implied regression to nature or the supernatural. She leaves her doll house and, like Una, repudiates the church to which Torvald appeals in a futile attempt to stop her, but not because she is fleeing the real world.

Indeed, it is arguable that as Nora moves toward culture, her husband regresses to the unnatural, his erotic life being rendered perverse, evoking the obscene acts performed by incubi and other malign demon lovers. For Torvald cannot enjoy his wife sexually without imagining each time he makes love to her that it is the first time, the idea of deflowering a virgin being necessary to his enjoyment, the capturing and recapturing of his little bird constituting a pleasure that is essentially autoerotic. When he and Nora leave the party, he describes how

when we leave and I place the shawl over those fine young rounded shoulders— *over that wonderfully curving neck*—then I pretend that you're my young bride, that we're just coming from the wedding, that for the first time I'm bringing you into my house—that for the first time I'm alone with you—completely alone with you, your trembling young beauty! All this evening I've longed for nothing but you. When I saw you turn and sway in the tarantella—my blood was pounding till I couldn't stand it—that's why I brought you down here so early.

As Torvald describes how he places Nora's shawl over her wonderfully curving (swanlike) neck *(denne vidunderlige nakkeboyning)* and takes her for, in his fantasy, the first time, his little speech is reminiscent of the Icelandic seal maiden tale, in which the man who has stolen the sealskin must cover the naked young woman with some clothing before he takes her to his home for the first time. The bitterly weeping and captured seal maiden is echoed in Ibsen's play when Nora repulses her husband: "Go away, Torvald! Leave me alone. I don't want all this." But the force that underlies Helmer's verbalization of his fantasies, again more autoerotic than aimed at enticing his wife, emerges from a comparison of the passage from Ibsen with what may well have been one of the playwright's sources, the capture by Hasan of Basorah of his swan maiden in the *Arabian Nights:*

Passion got the mastery of his reason and he had not patience to endure from her. So springing up from his hiding-place, he rushed upon her and laying hold of her by the hair dragged her to him and carried her down to the basement of the palace and set her in his own chamber, *where he threw over her a silken cloak* and left her weeping and biting her hands.[65]

Both Hasan and Helmer are portrayed in the throes of uncontrollable desire; both carry their captured swan maidens to some symbolically hidden and subterranean place despite the women's resistance; both use force, one brutal force, the other gentle physical pressure masked by a coercively seductive language; and both cover the resistant women with shawls or cloaks.

The silken cloak belongs to Hasan, not the swan maiden, as the human clothing the seal maiden wears belongs to the man who has entrapped her. As noted earlier, the swan maiden's garment is her exit from the human world, and human clothing her tie to it.[66] Insofar as all of Nora's possessions belong to Helmer, they remain in his control, so that in his anger at Nora after learning her secret, he revokes her so-called privileges and commands, "Take off the shawl. I said, take it off!" But as Nora's resolve to leave Helmer gathers force, her control over her own clothing increases. As she walks into another room and Helmer asks what she is doing, she says she is taking off her costume. Almost puzzled, he notes that she has changed her dress, and she agrees: the power between them has shifted. Significantly then, when Nora finally exits, bidding her husband goodbye and admitting that as a doll, she is no use to her family, the stage direction say that *she* "throws her shawl about her."

Ibsen's Nora has, of course, become a feminist goddess, although, as Baruch argues, she hardly deserves that much credit, since it is her "disillusionment over Torvald" rather than idealism or political conviction "that provides the soil out of which Nora's feminism grows."[67] Yet, her swan maiden ancestresses suggest that Nora's is an incipient feminism that awaits its chance to emerge just as the swan maiden endures her earthly life until a chance to escape offers itself. But to establish Nora's folklore origins is not sufficient to resolve the ambiguities of her character or of her actions. Yet few story groups illustrate as profoundly as the swan maiden narratives the importance of—to use contemporary slang—"getting it together." The swan maiden's flight from home and family can, indeed, illustrate one of the most pressing questions some branches of psychology have been asking themselves about their relation to ethics. Just as some folklorists have addressed the implications of the nuclear family as a symbol in fairy tales, as a structure that may hold together or may disintegrate, so many psychologists are concerned with the ethical dimensions of the "integration" and "fragmentation" of the human personality.

As Stephen Toulmin has argued, the cohesive or fragmented personality points to matters concerning the "ability (or inability) to perceive clearly and realistically, the proper relationship" between one's own needs, wishes, hopes, fears, plans, intentions, and so forth and "those of other agents, with whom [one has] to deal, and on whom [one is] practically and/or emotionally dependent." Integration thus involves being *morally* autonomous and moving in a *moral* sphere of action, treating "all other agents as ends in themselves, never as means only." [68] That gender plays a part in one's ability to become a morally autonomous being, however, is not part of Toulmin's argument.

As a moral agent who is only beginning to understand what it is to be one, Ibsen's Nora outraged his contemporary audience and continues to fascinate and perplex today those not entirely comfortable with her final action. As is true in the swan maiden tale and in the Child ballad of the demon lover, the problem is not that Nora leaves Helmer but that she seemingly abandons her children. But here a comparison between Nora and her swan maiden sisters can lead to the realization that Nora makes an authentically ethical decision when she exits her doll house. The breakdown of the marriage between the swan maiden and her mortal husband, the symbolic extension of this collapse to the nuclear family and to society at large, speaks to an essential absence of psychic integration on the part of the folklore actors. Lacking a true sense of agency, both swan maiden and her captor husband vie for power, and even so-called happy endings speak to the essentially dismal compromises (usually on the wife's part) that must be made for the pair to remain together. In contrast, Nora distinguishes between freedom and responsibility based on the laws of patriarchy, and the genuine freedom on which all true agency must rest: "Listen, Torvald—I've heard that when a wife deserts her husband's house just as I'm doing, then the law frees him from all responsibility. In any case, I'm freeing you from being responsible. Don't feel yourself bound, any more than I will. There has to be absolute freedom for us both."

There are few scenes in drama as powerful as Torvald Helmer's taunt that his wife thinks and talks like a child and her reasoned and calm response, itself a sign of inner cohesion, that he neither thinks nor talks like the kind of man she would wish to be joined to. Reality, not fantasy, is what Nora acts on. In asking for absolute freedom, she is not requesting entry into the amoral world of the swan maiden, but is insisting on living according to a more profound ethics than her husband's so-called morality grants her. The facts that she must lose her children when she abandons her husband and that she comes to realize that she has been a playmate rather than an effective mother to her offspring are part of Nora's tragedy, not her shame.

Which is to argue neither that Nora was right to leave her children nor that she was wrong when she failed to sacrifice herself for them, but only to claim that in the context of the swan maiden tale, which depicts fantasies not only of a pleasurable but also of an amoral existence, Ibsen's play depicts not only a moral dilemma but also a genuinely ethical act. But to compare his work with his sources is to confront the implications of what has happened to a disappearing folklore tradition. Old narratives are dusted off occasionally for entertainment, much as Nora's dress is mended so that she might dance the tarantella; or surviving bits of folklore are relegated to archives whose very existence speaks to the demise of a living culture. The question of whether Nora should or should not have left Helmer's house cannot be answered in this book. Ibsen appears to have thought she should have, but drawing on folklore sources allowed him to infuse *A Doll House* with its persistent ambiguities. Baruch appears correct in her argument that Nora rejects Helmer almost as thoroughly as he rejects her, but it is not a power struggle that she engages in. Nora's attachment to Helmer may have been based on an illusion of romantic love, but there is little illusion in her repudiation of him. Yet it seems that Nora will not even allow her Orpheus his chance to fail in an attempt to win her back.

In light of how Ibsen came to conceive of this play, it is difficult not to conclude that problems arise when folk narratives no longer bridge the gap between reality and fantasy, supplying a shared outlet for tensions and emotions that once made the swan maiden a ubiquitous folklore character. The modern world, in which the swan maiden story is hardly known but is so frequently acted out, must confront a greater problem than did past ages—in which telling stories about runaway wives substituted for wives running away.

# Notes

## Preface

1. Dorson, "Print and American Folktales": 207. Relations between the fields have improved, but Holbek describes a persistent problem when he writes on Hans Christian Andersen's use of folklore: "I, as a folklorist, am not sufficiently schooled in literary criticism and the literary critics who have written on the subject know too little about folklore": 177.

2. Since the work by Dégh and Vázsonyi, there can be no facile distinction between legends as narratives that relate events believed to be true and fairy tales as narratives understood by narrators and audience to be fiction. Genre will be discussed again in the next chapter.

3. Hatto 332.

4. Claire Farrer invokes the concept of woman as "other" to help define a *woman's* folklore: xiii.

5. Taggart also notes that narrators are not able to interpret their own stories, "because their metaphorical meaning is often unconscious or subconscious," and that storytellers "prefer to reflect on themselves" through "the safety of fantasy": *Enchanted Maidens* 9. Crapanzano consistently warns against interpreting demon invasion and possession in terms of Western ideas of subjectivity. I am persuaded that folklore narrators could not explain their narratives in terms of, for example, Western psychoanalysis; but they seem aware that some people are more likely than others to be the objects of demonic invasion.

6. See Bascom, particularly 290–91; Bascom also quotes from Ruth Benedict on this subject: 288; also see Dundes, ed., *Study of Folklore*: 277–78; Fischer, "Sociopsychological Analysis": particularly 257.

7. I will discuss Bynum's theories further in the next chapter. Most important studies of folk or fairy tales concede that interpretation should not rest too heavily on a single version. See Bettelheim 91; Darnton 18.

8. Thompson, *The Folktale*: 92.

9. Betty Friedan relates that an article in *McCall's* and the readers' response to it ("The Mother Who Ran Away," July 1956) was one of the inspira-

tions for *The Feminine Mystique:* 50. Also see Robbins and Robbins. This runaway mother, however, was suffering from psychological amnesia. It would take two more decades for magazines like *McCall's* to report (without negative judgments) on women who consciously decided to flee. See, for example, the August 1977 issue of *Family Circle* and its cover story on "Why Mommies Run Away"; for a report on such flight as a virtual domestic epidemic in the United States, see Brenton 122; Casady 42. That contemporary swan maidens will command significant female attention is evidenced by one of the most popular soap operas in Brazil, an analysis of which confines an "existential crisis," the "notion of 'self,' " to the middle class: Leal and Oliven 90. Folklore reveals the universality of human fantasies that would later be defined as a quest for selfhood; one might distinguish, however, between societies in which women have some opportunity to act out such fantasies and those in which they can only unconsciously and vicariously experience them through the medium of story. Sklar notes with satisfaction in *Runaway Wives* that if "there is a single thread that weaves through these women's stories, it is their attempt to *live out* their fantasies rather than relegating them to some corner of their minds": 26.

10. *Women, Androgynes, and Other Mythical Beasts* 211.

11. Comparably, in *Ibsen's Forsaken Merman* I argue that the opposition between the real and supernatural worlds involves not a two- but a four-way split, each realm being itself divided into positive and negative attributes: Jacobsen and Leavy 19–21.

12. *La Belle Dame sans Merci* 119–21.

13. As later chapters will reveal, swan maidens appear in other tale types: for example, 313 and 465, and even in Type 425 stories. Stories of the immortal man and the immortal woman not only coexist but also overlap.

14. A. L. Miller 60. In his study of Cupid and Psyche, Swahn declares his intention to do a comparable work on Type 400 tales but has not done so. In any event, he is one of those folklorists who most vehemently rejects the literary interpretation of folklore.

15. Newell, for example, notes only that "the change in the sex of the suitor is a transition not uncommon in folk-tales": "Sources of Shakespeare's *Tempest*" 249–50. Lang (*Custom and Myth:* 75) and Ralston ("Beauty and the Beast": 993, 1003) merely remark on such transitions without attention to gender.

16. Holbek contends that the success or failure to win back the supernatural spouse often has to do with genre: "In [the] legends the emphasis is on the irremediable difference between 'our' world and 'theirs'; [the legends] nearly always end tragically" (personal correspondence). Hartland contends that only in fairy tales and dreams can the impossible be achieved: 283–85. And it is true that in legend and myth—for example, the stories of Elsa and Lohengrin and Zeus and Semele—the woman cannot recover her supernatural spouse or mate. Christiansen notes in his monograph on

the swan maiden that "Holmström examined both folktale and legend, and of his list of variants only twelve entries are folktales proper": *Studies in Irish* 134 n.2.

17. Lundell 154–55. Holbek suggests (in his marginal notes to this study) that Aarne and Thompson were probably placing the searching husband of Tale Type 400 in the tradition of medieval romance, which involves questers. But even if this were so, the invocation of a long-established literary tradition only intensifies the ironic failure of so many husbands in Type 400 tales.

18. Maria Tatar rightly takes Bettelheim to task for neglecting frog princesses (42–43), but even she does not mention how often they must remain frogs. This neglect is, moreover, another affirmation of Estés's contention that the wild woman (of which the frog princess is a variant) is an endangered species: 3.

19. There is more than one ending to the ballet and sometimes the prince and Odette are left standing on stage, presumably to live happily ever after once the curtain falls. I have never been persuaded or left satisfied by these versions. I will discuss the so-called happy endings to swan maiden tales in chapters 6, 7, and 8. For the swan maiden sources of Tchaikovsky's ballet, see Beaumont.

CHAPTER 1 *Introduction*

1. A statement by Lord Acton about one of his teachers, quoted in Carr 14. A book is not supposed to be perfect, writes Duerr in a prefatory explanation of why in the translated edition of *Dreamtime* he did not avail himself of an opportunity to revise his book and accommodate criticism of it.

2. Introductory notes to the five-volume Caedmon record set of the Child ballads: 5.

3. See Swahn for a list of impossible tasks: 29.

4. Apuleius 263.

5. Delarue 111.

6. "More about Folklore and Literature" 12.

7. McCulloch 285 n.3.

8. *Interpretation of Fairy Tales* 7.

9. "Nordic Research" 156.

10. In contrast to most historians, Darnton contends that "folktales are historical documents": 13.

11. See preface, n.6.

12. Fischer, "The Position of Men and Women." Comparably, Taggart claims that perceptions of women as sexually voracious and incompetent (i.e., susceptible to demon lovers) are inversely proportional to the relative importance of their roles in a society: "Men's Changing Image of Women."

13. Kapferer supplies significant insight into this subject.

14. Dégh is quoted by Stern: 9; Dundes, *Interpreting Folklore:* 6–7. Coffin has told me he thinks this definition of the "folk" is too loose.
15. With, of course, qualifications about specific cultural distinctions. See the introductions to F. de Caro, Weigle, and Jordan and Kalcik, which assume a specifically *woman's* folklore.
16. Roiphe 18.
17. Bynum 35.
18. See, for example, Howe's and Hirschfeld's analysis of the theme of female otherness in the Panamanian star girl tale.
19. Bynum 24–25.
20. Dundes, *Interpreting Folklore:* ix.
21. This biographical information is not included in her book and was gleaned from such reference works as *Who's Who among English and European Authors.*
22. All paraphrases and quotations will be from Stevens's introduction and notes.
23. Fine 87.
24. Noel 8–9.
25. Abrahams, "Personal Power": 28.
26. Mathias 4, 5, 39–60; the story is "The Twelve Doves on the Mountain of the Sun": 192–209. On genre and the swan maiden tale, see preface; n.31 below; chapter 2.
27. Quoted by Ben-Amos: xii.
28. Dégh and Vázsonyi 93, 109.
29. *Vanishing Hitchhiker* xii, 2.
30. *Tales of Sex and Violence* 10.
31. *Studies in Irish and Scandinavian Folktales* 134.
32. This is Richard Dorson's way of describing the debate among folklorists over the universalist and culture-specific approaches: *Folklore Research* 1.
33. *Childhood of Fiction* 1.
34. Hartland 320. See chapter 7 concerning analogous changes in the Orpheus and Euridice story.
35. *The Folktale* 5.
36. Mathias 4.
37. Dorson, "Foreword": vii.
38. See preface, n.1 above.
39. On the subject of "Fakelore," see Coffin in Ranke, et al.; the term refers to pseudo-folklore or literary imitations of folklore, but, from the purist point of view, can extend to folklore collections perceived to be contaminated.
40. I have made this case before; see Jacobsen and Leavy xii–xiii.
41. *Interpretation of Fairy Tales* 24.
42. Callan 98.
43. *Folktales and Society* 91; also see Swahn 437–38.
44. Benedict 1: xxiii, xli–xlii.
45. *Problems of the Feminine* 1–4.

46. See, for example, Denton 21.
47. Spender 12.
48. Bengis 61.
49. *The Telling of Stories* 167. Also see his *Interpretation of Fairy Tales* 154–57.
50. McCulloch v–vi.
51. Dracott x.
52. *Tales from the Arab Tribes* 110–30; also see *Told in the Market Place* 150.
53. See n.56 below.
54. "The Thorn-seller"; "The Crystal Ship."
55. Jameson 17.
56. Glassie 10.
57. "Mohammed and Dawia" 165.
58. Lecture at Baruch College, 1987.
59. Bynum 102.
60. Suleiman, "Introduction": 37–38.
61. Personal conversation.
62. Jameson 16.
63. Chase vii.
64. Calvino xix, xxi.

CHAPTER 2 *Urvaśī and the Swan Maidens*

1. Cross defends the swan as a designation for the entire group: "The Celtic Elements": 36.
2. Wratislaw 290–91; Aarne and Thompson (Type 409) 137.
3. Hartland 255.
4. Seaton 126; also see Penzer 2:245.
5. See, for example, Natalia Bessmertnova's performance with the Bolshoi Ballet, available on videotape (Kultur Video).
6. DuBois-DeSaulle 221–28.
7. *Women, Androgynes, and Other Mythical Beasts* 180.
8. While most scholars consider Urvaśī a swan maiden, there are some dissenters. Compare Seaton (125) with Wright (527) and Hatto (346).
9. Penzer 2:248; in his commentary on the story, Wilson writes, "The love of Purūravas for his bride increased every day of its duration, and the affection of Urvaśī augmented equally in fervour, she never called to recollection residence amongst the immortals": 6–7.
10. Karnik and Desai 27.
11. All quotations are from Doniger's translation and edition.
12. All quotations are from Wilson's edition. In her edition of the *Rig Veda*, Doniger compares the two main versions of the story: 252.
13. Wright 533.
14. My figure of speech is coincidentally allusive. Men play cards, chess, or

dice in a contest in which a woman is the stake; or a gambler who loses a game and consequently faces danger (a variation on *Sir Gawain and the Green Knight*) relies on a swan maiden to rescue him, sometimes from her ogre father (a variation on the Jason and Medea theme). See chapters 6, 8. There are also stories in which the genders are reversed and the woman plays with the man and wins the game. See, for example, Doniger, *When God Has Lipstick on His Collar*: 9. Sometimes the swan maiden herself challenges her would-be lover to a game; Christiansen, *Studies in Irish*: 140. For commentary on the gaming motif, see Clouston, *A Group of Eastern Romances*: 522–31.

15.  Kosambi 54.
16.  Lessa 142.
17.  Thomson 167.
18.  The story of Wayland the Smith is Holmström's point of departure for his study of the swan maiden tale.
19.  Krappe, "The Valkyries": 66; MacCulloch does not equate them: *Eddic* 160–61.
20.  Lessa 160.
21.  Bynum 103, 78–79, 97.
22.  Lüthi, *The European Folktale*: 4–10.
23.  Dorson, *Folk Legends of Japan*: 227.
24.  Croker 187; also see Jacobsen and Leavy for a discussion of seal maiden stories: 10–20.
25.  Lawson 135.
26.  The swan maiden tale is usually held to belong to Tale Type 400, "The Quest for the Lost Wife." For discussions that assume the husband is the story's focus of interest, see Thompson, *The Folktale*: 88, 91; Holmström 136; Hartland 283.
27.  Cross, "Celtic Elements": 616–17.
28.  MacCulloch, *Eddic*: 258–59.
29.  Hall 197–201.
30.  Pakrasi 105.
31.  Dorson, *Folktales Told around the World*: 262.
32.  Anesaki 257–58.
33.  Parker, *More Australian Legendary Tales*: 41.
34.  Sibree 203.
35.  Dwyer 74–75.
36.  Burton, *Arabian Nights*: 8:42.
37.  Skinner, "Iowa": 402.
38.  Chapman, *Ten'a*: 11.
39.  Lermontov 275.
40.  Ralston, *Tibetan Tales*: 56.
41.  See Spender 113–14; Kolbenschlag 51.
42.  Leland 301.
43.  Kolbenschlag 51–52.

44. See preface, n.6 above.
45. E. Ardener 151–52.
46. Coxwell 22.
47. For further discussion of the swan maiden's mother-in-law, see chapter 7.
48. Leland 301.
49. Simpson, *Icelandic:* 101.
50. Dorson, *Folk Legends of Japan:* 226.
51. Keightley 169. Also see Maxfield and Millington 2:96.
52. Croker 181.
53. Sibree 204.
54. Keightley 410.
55. Emerson 61.
56. Dunlop 34.
57. Pakrasi 74.
58. Dempster 61.
59. Lessa 131, 143.
60. Rabuzzi 103.
61. E. Ardener 65, 66.
62. See, for example, Lifton 68.
63. Hartland 283; also see Holmström 97.
64. Thomson 162.
65. Yates 57.
66. Dorson, *Folk Legends of Japan:* 226.
67. H. Rink 146.
68. MacRitchie 4.
69. Zobarskas 59.
70. Simpson, *Icelandic:* 101.
71. Ha 59.
72. Maxfield and Millington 2:96.
73. Dorson, *Folktales Told around the World:* 263, 266.
74. Garnett, *Women of Turkey:* 2:353.
75. Croker 184–85.
76. Rhys, *Celtic Folklore:* 1:45.
77. Dempster 165.
78. Mathews 78.
79. Newell, "Lady Featherflight": 58–59.
80. Sastri and Natesa 82.
81. Friedan, *It Changed My Life:* 340.
82. See preface, n.9.
83. Friedan, *It Changed My Life:* 341.
84. Croker 187.
85. On this point Taggart and I significantly disagree (see my introduction and chapter 6). Faced with variations of Tale Type 313 in which the female character performs the arduous tasks the man cannot complete, Taggart explains her superior strength: "the heroine has supernatural power,

which represents the power of a woman's love for a man": *Enchanted Maidens:* 183. In general Taggart argues that woman can better than man sustain the "emotional bond in marriage": *Enchanted Maidens:* 164. Compare Taggart with Lundell: 153–54; and Simpson, "Be Bold."

86. Kakar and Ross 9.
87. Kinsley 62.
88. See, for example, Im Thurn 381–82; Yearsley 187; Brett 29.
89. Jagendorf 87–88.
90. Holmström 97.
91. Hartland 320, 319.
92. Codrington 172.
93. Swanton 192.
94. Dixon, *Oceanic:* 209.
95. Simpson, *Icelandic:* 101.
96. MacRitchie 3.
97. H. Rink 146.
98. Biggs 69–77.
99. Ha 62.
100. Grey, *Polynesian:* 42–57.
101. Lessa 130.
102. Finlay 90.
103. Burrows 80.
104. Lessa 38, 121.
105. Hatt 95.
106. Garnett, *Women of Turkey:* 354–55.
107. Leland 144.
108. M. Owen 91.
109. Howard 322.
110. MacRitchie 4.
111. Lawson 138–39.
112. Lim 44.
113. Hatt 95.
114. Garnett, *Women of Turkey:* 299–300.
115. I found no examples of Scandinavian tales in which a dancing dress substitutes for the swan's feather robe (or some other animal skin). Holbek says he does not know of any. See chapter 8 for a discussion of a dancing dress in another story type found in Scandinavia. Ibsen, of course, knew other than Scandinavian versions of the swan maiden tale, for he lived for years outside of Norway.
116. Another example of how a feature of the swan maiden tale has been acted out in recent times comes from Brenton's account of a woman who suddenly decides she does not want to be a hostess at a party given by her husband and suddenly withdraws their joint savings from the bank, leaving both him and their children: 130.

CHAPTER 3  *The Devil's Bride*

1. Craigie 232.
2. Croker 187.
3. MacGregor 113–14.
4. See Jacobsen and Leavy for my analysis of these patterns in the seal maiden tale: 10–21.
5. *Rig Veda* 276, 271; also see my chapter 8.
6. Deane and Shaw 108–9.
7. R. Smith, *South Carolina Ballads:* 77; Davis, *Traditional Ballads of Virginia:* 439.
8. Burrison supplies a comprehensive history of the ballad; also see Gardner-Medwin. All citations to British versions are to Child.
9. Coffin, *British Traditional Ballad:* 138. Coffin cautions against making too much of titles. True, ballad collectors are more likely than singers to be concerned with them. But there is a significant body of commentary on the titles of Child 243. See nn.10, 34 below. My research on Child 243 was based on the 1963 edition of Coffin. Interested readers will find many more versions provided in the Supplement to the 1977 edition—as well as further commentary.
10. Burrison 279; Brewster 136; Lomax 170.
11. Davis, *More Traditional Ballads:* 286, 289.
12. Flanders and Olney 132.
13. Davis, *Traditional Ballads:* 488.
14. Coffin, *British Traditional Ballad:* 139.
15. Davis, *More Traditional Ballads:* 282.
16. Barbour 210.
17. Davis, *Traditional Ballads:* 443.
18. Cox 148.
19. High 17.
20. Belden 297; R. Smith 154.
21. Coffin, *British Traditional Ballad:* 9–11.
22. Barry, "Traditional Ballads in New England": 209.
23. See Gardner-Medwin for a discussion of sea imagery in Child 243.
24. Barry, "Some Aspects of Folk-Song": 274.
25. Barry, *British Ballads from Maine:* 305.
26. Davis, *Traditional Ballads:* 451, 454.
27. Flanders, *Garland:* 81.
28. Barry, *British Ballads:* 309.
29. Barry, "Traditional Ballads": 209.
30. M. C. Dean, for example: 55–56.
31. Davis, *More Traditional Ballads:* 276. Coffin notes that it is rare for her to miss her husband: *British Traditional Ballad* 139.
32. See Skolnik. While she does not say she regrets her decision to end her

marriage, her description of her situation compared to her husband's reveals that women who try to discover more satisfactory ways to live than marriage has supplied must confront the reality that in many ways it remains a man's world.

33. Henry, "Still More Ballads": 23.
34. Davis, *More Traditional Ballads*: 270. In *Traditional Ballads of Virginia*, Davis cites a singular version entitled "The House Carpenter's Wife," which he calls "a slightly more appropriate title": 439. Most commentators on Child 243, however, note the persistence of "The House Carpenter" as a title. See n.9 above.
35. Cox 144, 142.
36. For discussion of "The Gypsie Laddie" (Child 200), closely related to Child 243, see Coffin, *British Traditional Ballad*: 120. Whether the borrowing from Child 200 for Child 243 merely involves what Coffin reminds me are floating lyrics is questionable. The two ballads are so thematically similar that it is difficult to think the borrowing of stanzas is arbitrary. Child A voices concern for fatherless children; it is not illogical to extend this concern to motherless ones, especially because how men are to care for their children is a concern reflected in many folktales (see my chapter 7). "The Gypsie Laddie" has also been studied as a variation on the the Orpheus theme, thus supplying another link between demon lover and Orpheus narratives; see Knoblock and chapter 7 below.
37. Cox 143.
38. Davis, *Traditional Ballads*: 465.
39. Cox 142.
40. R. Smith 152–53.
41. Sharp and Karpeles 249–50.
42. Henry, "Still More Ballads": 23.
43. Hubbard and Robertson 49.
44. Barry, *British Ballads*: 306.
45. Davis, *Traditional Ballads*: 446.
46. Gilbert 36.
47. Luther 17. In an essay on Shirley Jackson's story "The Tooth," Pascal cites but virtually dismisses Child 243 as Jackson's source, making the frequently invidious distinction between the complexity of literature and the simplicity of folklore: "some readers might be tempted to regard ["The Tooth"] as a sort of Freudian version of the morality tale contained in the old ballad": 138.
48. Lomax 169–70.
49. Owens, *Texas Folk Songs*: 56.
50. Person 212–37.
51. See in particular *La Belle Dame sans Merci*.
52. *The Lottery*: 191, 28. "The Demon Lover" was first published in *The Woman's Home Companion* in 1949, and there is perhaps no better way

to construct the life of the American housewife during that period than to examine the magazine's issue as a context for the story.

53. In *The Feminine Mystique,* Jackson is one of those women writers Friedan criticizes for not being sufficiently aware of the typical housewife's plight: 57. But that plight is precisely what Jackson persistently writes about in the stories based on Child 243.

54. "Got a Letter from Jimmy," *The Lottery:* 289.

55. *Come Along with Me* 142.

56. *The Lottery* 270–71.

57. *Come Along with Me* 59–65.

58. Arnott 67.

59. Christiansen, *Folktales of Norway:* 133. This story will be cited again in chapter 8.

60. Godwin 278.

61. Greer 290.

62. Matalene 585.

63. Ginzburg 5–6, 300, 307, and 1–9 for a useful survey of scholarship in which he presents his own position; Duerr 45–46, 125.

64. For my discussion of the wild man and wild woman, see chapter 11 of Jacobsen and Leavy, *Ibsen's Forsaken Merman.*

65. Remy 56.

66. Klaits 76–77.

67. Kapferer 108.

68. Monter, *Witchcraft in France:* 124.

69. Lindow 14.

70. Kinsley 203.

71. Groome 188–97.

72. Prince 59.

73. Monter, *Witchcraft in France:* 200.

74. *The Fairies in English Tradition* 140–41.

75. Michelet 310, 24.

76. Webster 49, 64; also see Addy 70.

77. See Briggs concerning the difficulty of distinguishing between witch and fairy: *Fairies in English Tradition* 67; also consult C. Grant Loomis; and J. P. Gray.

78. Monter, *Witchcraft in France:* 124.

79. See Midelfort 184–85; Garrett 465–66; Sebald 191–92.

80. Straparola 89.

81. Robe 79–81.

82. See, for example, Christiansen, *Migratory Legends:* 53.

83. Aarne and Thompson Type 306.

84. Pourrat 183–90.

85. Much speculation exists on this subject; see Kapferer for a thorough survey of the arguments as well as his own analysis: 95–99.

86.  Jones and Kropf 278–87, 416–17.
87.  Baudis 179–81.
88.  Monter, "Pedestal": 133; Midelfort 184–85.
89.  Ortutay 339; also see Dégh, *Folktales of Hungary* 46–57.
90.  Underwood 330.
91.  Baroja 256.
92.  Groome 98.
93.  Monter, *Witchcraft in France:* 124.
94.  Garrett 466.
95.  Conway 2: 101 n.1.
96.  Cooke 126.
97.  Dobie 66–67.
98.  Boas, *Folk-Tales of the Salishan:* 30–31.
99.  Dorsey and Kroeber, *Arapaho:* 209.
100. Ranke 42, 44, 45.
101. Fansler 214.
102. Henderson and Calvert, *Old Tyrol:* 36.
103. Hunt 234–39.
104. Luzel 258–59.
105. Jacobsen and Leavy 72.
106. Calvino 26.
107. Simpson, *Icelandic:* 35–40.
108. Moore 168–70.
109. Kapferer's arguments are frequently gender related. See Victor Turner's forward to Kapferer's book for a more generally theoretical comparison between actions in the world and in the cosmos.
110. Noel 11–12.
111. Dobie 159–60.
112. Emerson 61; Hartland 110.
113. Schorer 19.
114. Thompson, "The Star Husband Tale": 96. This thorough study of the star husband tale follows the method of the Finnish school, Thompson tracing the dispersion of the story and supplying very little interpretation.
115. For discussion of how native lore merged with European, see Thompson's study of "European Tales among North American Indians."
116. Curtis 9:166.
117. Boas, *Folk-Tales of the Salishan:* 31.
118. Kroeber, "Wishosk Myths": 124.
119. Prince 57–76.
120. Lee 71.
121. Young, "Fifth Analysis": 399.
122. Dorsey, *Caddo:* 29.
123. Parsons, "Micmac": 65.
124. Howe and Hirschfeld 321.
125. Wissler and Duvall 58–61.

126. Teit, "The Shuswap": 687. Hall may provide a gloss on this story when he notes that if a "daughter would not marry and add a provider to the family, as well as extending the kinship ties of the family's members, then she was a burden": 318.
127. McClintock 492.
128. Kerceval 199.
129. Haeberlin 375, 373.
130. Lowie, "Ethnographic Notes on the Washo": 350–51.
131. Reichard 283–84.
132. Schorer 17–18. A star woman tale popular in South America tells of an ugly and despised man who longs to marry a bright star, becoming handsome and successful when his wish is granted. His supernatural wife takes him to the sky world where he dies of the cold: Maria Leach 2: 1080–82. In contrast, the surviving wives of star men exercise ingenuity in escaping the otherworld and returning to earth. The star woman story, however, confirms Holbek's point that the tragic conclusion to many legends is the result of a human crossing the forbidden boundary into the supernatural realm. As Keats's Lamia tells her lover, finer spirits cannot breathe in human climes, whereas Keats's Endymion comes to realize that the mortal man who bent his "appetite beyond his natural sphere" would starve and die.
133. Jones and Michelson, "Ojibwa Tales": 151, 455.
134. Dorsey, Traditions of the Arikara: 56.
135. Teit, "Tahltan Tales": 247.
136. Dixon, Maidu Texts: 183.
137. Kroeber, "The Patwin": 306.
138. Humphreys 97.
139. Boas, Bella Bella Tales: 107.
140. Skinner, "Notes on the Eastern Cree": 113.
141. Sapir 302–3.
142. See Thompson, "European Tales."

CHAPTER 4 *The Animal Groom*

1. Lang, Custom and Myth: 64–65; also see Liebrecht.
2. Dorson, Folktales Told around the World: 230.
3. Dorson notes that Swahn's eleven hundred versions are only a fraction of available versions: Folktales Told around the World 230. Megas, for example, compares Swahn's thirty-five Greek versions against his own knowledge of 379: 226.
4. Massignon xxxi; also see Swahn, particularly 18–20, 374. Swahn excludes such stories as the Japanese serpent groom tales because they do not hinge on the search motif. In contrast, Seki's study of the serpent groom makes no such distinction: "Spool of Thread" 267. Also consult

T. F. Crane 1, for a description of the different narrative patterns that belong to the Cupid and Psyche tale. Also see entry on "Amor and Psyche" in Ranke et al. 1: 465–73.

5. Not that folklorists have failed to note the complementarity. See Lang, *Custom and Myth:* 85; MacCulloch, *Childhood of Fiction:* 325, 347; Ralston, "Beauty and the Beast": 1003; Swahn 210, 17 n.2, 384; Jameson 101. But to my knowledge, no single and systematic study of the animal bride exists.

6. Swahn 200; also see Aarne and Thompson on Tale Type 425.

7. Lieberman 392–93; also see Edwards's study.

8. That is what Swahn considers them.

9. Dawkins, *Modern Greek Folktales:* 55.

10. Espinosa, *Spanish Folk-Tales:* 194–95. Perhaps the audience would be assumed to know the so-called introductory elements so that they were dispensed with as unnecessary.

11. See chapter 8.

12. See Liebrecht.

13. See Seki, "Spool of Thread": particularly 284; Dorson, "Introduction" to Seki's *Folktales of Japan:* xiii–xiv.

14. Lang, *Custom and Myth:* 82–84; MacCulloch, *Childhood of Fiction:* 347; Swahn (who does not quite put it that way) 210; Beach 3:27–29.

15. Ralston, "Beauty and the Beast": 993.

16. Ralston, *Russian Folk Tales:* 116; also see Zobarskas 1–14: Swahn 210.

17. Curtis 9:166.

18. Schoolcraft, *Indian Legends:* 31–33. The inherent identification of the aggressive hunter with his animal prey will be one of the subjects of chapter 6.

19. H. Parker 345–55.

20. Bompas 59; also see 212–214.

21. Stevens 45–57.

22. This is a variant of the bird lover tales that are, for example, a source for Marie de France's *Lay of Yonec.* Supernatural lovers who assume a bird's shape are a significant subgroup of Tale Type 425 (although designated Type 432). They have obvious connections to swan maidens and swan knights.

23. See chapter 2.

24. See Frey 22–23. The Grimm's story of "The Six Swans" is a good example.

25. Fitzgerald 187–88; Seaton 125–26.

26. Fitzgerald 187–90.

27. See Edwards's contrary argument (which in any event depends on Apuleius's version): 10–11.

28. Dawkins, *Modern Greek Folktales:* 55.

29. Calvino xxix.

30. Neumann, *Amor and Psyche:* 108–11, 120–21, 129–32.

31. Lang, *Custom and Myth:* 75.

32. Whiting 20.
33. "Spool of Thread" 279–80.
34. Bernstein 145–46.
35. Kinsley 97, 113–14.
36. Nicoloff 33.
37. Bernard and Slaveikoff 66–67.
38. Nicoloff 33.
39. Bernard and Slaveikoff 158.
40. Nicoloff 62.
41. M. Martin, *Basutoland:* 84, 169.
42. Romilly 102.
43. Griffis 176.
44. Bourhill 212–23.
45. Delarue 178–79.
46. This is a summary of Beach's argument.
47. Parsons, *Folk-Lore of the Antilles:* 444.
48. Bettelheim 279. Ernest Jones had already offered the same interpretation: 70.
49. Bettelheim 285.
50. See, for example, Darnton: 15.
51. Grimm 501.
52. Calvino 508–14. For another significant example and its interpretation, see Holbek n.139 below).
53. Bettelheim 283–84.
54. Jacottet, *Études:* 78–80.
55. Hall 279–81.
56. Swanton, "Ethnology of the Haida": 230.
57. Bettelheim 284.
58. Dawkins, *Modern Greek Folktales:* 63.
59. Barnouw 210–13.
60. Halliwell-Phillips 44.
61. Nicoloff 89–90.
62. Roussel 348–51.
63. Megas 65–70.
64. Paton 501.
65. Dasent 24.
66. Sastri and Natesa 57.
67. Noy 163.
68. For example, Megas 59.
69. El Fasi and Dermenghen 116–22.
70. Busk, *Roman:* 117–18.
71. This is the only pattern Bettelheim finds significant.
72. J. F. Campbell 1:208–13.
73. Chase 57.
74. Artin Pacha 92.

75. Swahn 437–38; also see Dégh, *Folktales and Society:* 91.
76. Holbek's *Interpretation of Fairy Tales* treats as very significant the narrator's gender: see 154–57.
77. Calvino xxiii.
78. Dorson, *Folktales Told around the World:* 230–37.
79. Fansler 303.
80. Swahn 20, 17 n.2, 384.
81. See preface, n.15 above.
82. Lang, *Custom and Myth:* 75.
83. Ogle 129.
84. Johnston 322.
85. Cross, "Celtic Origin of the Lay of Yonec": 454.
86. Cross, "Celtic Elements": 33–34, 58.
87. For general surveys of the legend, see L. H. Loomis; Frey, particularly 123. For folklore references see Jaffray 7–8, and his chapter on the swan children story.
88. Frey 48–49, 60–62.
89. Chilli 98–108. Kinsley describes a myth that can be read as a variation on the animal groom tale in which the loathly groom is an "untouchable" and his previously unsuspecting bride commits suicide: 200.
90. Frey 70–75.
91. Grant 72.
92. Frey 123.
93. Swahn 241.
94. MacCulloch, *Childhood of Fiction:* 340. His speculations have to do with an animal bride story, but are applicable to animal groom tales insofar as he contemplates the meaning of the prohibition.
95. Harding 302–3.
96. For a list of taboos see Swahn 27; he contends that no taboo predominates: 241–42.
97. See chapter 6.
98. El Fasi 225–40. See 240–47 for discussion of the Cupid and Psyche motif.
99. Basile Night 5, Story 4.
100. Chilli 108.
101. See n.89 above.
102. Lang, *Olive Fairy Book:* 252. Also see Chilli: 98–108.
103. See n.99 above.
104. Megas 57–65.
105. Dracott 15–19.
106. Eells 133–34.
107. Jones and Kropf 285.
108. Webster 171.
109. Afanas'ev 200.
110. Dawkins, *Forty-Five Stories:* 115–23.

111. Busk, *Roman Legends:* 101.
112. Massignon 141; also see 272.
113. Paton 115.
114. Webster 38–41.
115. Addy 2–4.
116. Schneller 63–65; my translation.
117. Calvino 12–14.
118. Buchan 33–34.
119. Grimm 400.
120. Artin Pacha 87–101.
121. Lang, *Custom and Myth:* 81.
122. d'Aulnoy 21.
123. Murphy 103–13.
124. Carnoy 137.
125. *Rig Veda* 254.
126. Jacobs 34.
127. Henderson and Calvert, *Spain:* 9–29.
128. Bettelheim 294–95: "If this were not a most ancient tale, one would be tempted to think that one of the messages inherent in fairy tales of this cycle is a most timely one": 294–95.
129. Maliver 110, 128, 140.
130. Cerquand 98.
131. Gardner, "Tagalog": 302–4.
132. MacDougall and Calder 2–15.
133. Leland 255–56.
134. Hampden 83.
135. Ortutay 94.
136. Hoogasian-Villa 139.
137. Andersen 255.
138. M. Campbell, *Cloudwalking:* 228–30.
139. Bain 193. See Holbek, *Interpretation of Fairy Tales,* for an analysis of a similar tale, "King Wivern": 457–98
140. Jordan, "The Vaginal Serpent": 36.
141. Borrow 157.
142. Jordan, "A Note about Folklore and Literature": 64. That the story may depict gynecological problems as well, see my book *To Blight with Plague:* 170.
143. Cushing 93–103.
144. Prior 1:263–68.
145. Hall 279–81.
146. Lüthi, *European Folktale:* 70.
147. T. F. Crane 322.
148. Calvino 83.
149. Fuchs 52–58; see also Ennis 99–101.
150. Dorsey, *Traditions of the Arikara:* 153–54.

151. Venkataswami 133–34.
152. Kúnos 71.
153. Jacottet, *Études:* 78–80, 69–70.
154. Goddard 234–35.
155. Mills 317–18.
156. Boas, *Bella Bella Tales:* 67–69. See Thompson, *Tales of the North American Indians,* for other versions of this widespread story.
157. Hoogasian-Villa 410–11.
158. Jordan, "Vaginal Serpent": 35.
159. Hole 55.
160. Jameson 101.
161. For connections between Eskimo culture and swan maiden tale, see Kleivan.
162. Ennis 99–101.
163. Curtin, *Seneca:* 86–90.
164. Abrahams, *African Folktales:* 336–37.
165. Hill-Tout 347–52.
166. Teit, "Tahltan Tales": 340–41.
167. Abrahams, *Afro-American Folktales* 108–10.
168. Abrahams, *African Folktales:* 337, 341.
169. See Taggart, "Men's Changing"; also see Howe and Hirschfeld; and J. L. Fischer, "The Position of Men and Women."
170. Opler, *Myths and Tales of the Jicarilla Apache:* 373.
171. Curtis 9:121–25.
172. Boas, "The Eskimo of Baffin Land": 327–28.
173. Kroeber, "Tales of the Smith Sound Eskimo": 168.
174. Adamson 96–99.
175. Farrand 127–28.
176. Teit, "Mythology of the Thompson Indians": 354–55.
177. Wissler and Duvall 107–8.
178. Adamson 328–29.
179. Teit, "Kaska": 463.
180. Boas, "Eskimo of Baffin Land": 223.
181. Leland 266, 273–74.
182. Morice 11.
183. Boas, *Folktales of the Salishan:* 53.
184. Boas, "Eskimo of Baffin Land": 222–26.
185. Teit, "Tahltan Tales": 242.
186. Jones and Michelson 407, 45; Knox 401–3.
187. Skinner and Satterlee 305.
188. Morice 4.
189. Leland 278.
190. Skinner, "Eastern Cree and Northern Saulteaux": 168–73.
191. Curtin, *Seneca Indian Myths:* 102–4.
192. Skinner, "Notes on the Eastern Cree and the Northern Saulteaux": 168.

193. Curtin, *Seneca Indian Myths:* 181.
194. Jones and Michelson 407.
195. Dorsey, *Traditions of the Caddo:* 66–67.
196. For example, Jones and Michelson 405–13; Morice 4–22. See Thompson, *Tales of the North American Indians,* for more versions.
197. Jones, *Nightmare:* 69–70; also see Willis 128–29.
198. Kinsey 502.
199. Bernheimer 53. These little girls appear as the symbolic antithesis of the wild woman, whom Bernheimer admits has a well-developed mythology but about whom he has relatively little to say. See Schmölders; Estés.
200. Neumann, *Great Mother:* 278–79.
201. Straparola 58–65.
202. Kúnos 188–97.
203. Sastri and Natesa 54–79.
204. Pourrat 223–24.
205. Hsieh 74.
206. Ekrem 58.
207. Ralston, "Beauty and the Beast": 994; italics added.
208. Hertslet 55–65.
209. Coxwell 206–9.
210. Hoogasian-Villa 228.
211. "The Story of Long Snake" 1:105.
212. Benedict 1:126–30. Holbek suggests that this is another depiction of exogamous marriages (personal correspondence).
213. Barchilon 28.
214. Stevens 20–26.
215. Cosquin, *Contes Populaires:* 215.
216. Megas 60.
217. Basile 2:114.
218. Postma 71–77.
219. Hertslet 55.
220. Finnegan 117–24.
221. Postma 58–70.
222. Kolbenschlag 206, 163, 159.
223. Hsieh 56–57. Holmström cites what he calls a male swan maiden: 9.
224. Fansler 179–81.
225. Sastri and Natesa 1–18.
226. Seki, *Folktales of Japan:* 90–92.
227. O'Sullivan 116–30.
228. Mullen 137–65.
229. Henderson and Calvert, *Wonder Tales of Ancient Spain:* 22.
230. d'Aulnoy 237.

CHAPTER 5 Swan Maiden and Incubus

1. See Kiessling on the difficulty of separating the wild hairy man of the woods from the incubus: 34.
2. Benjamin Walker 1:372.
3. Masters calls them the "blood-sucking Hindu incubi": 184; Doniger refers to their ambivalent nature as a "mediating group between gods and demons": *Origins of Evil* 118–19; also see her *Tales of Sex and Violence* 86–87; and Crim et al., 271.
4. On the subject of the incubus in literature, see Kiessling.
5. MacCulloch, *Eddic:* 288–89; Sebald 66.
6. For further discussion of incubus beliefs, see my essay on "Faith's Incubus."
7. Masters, *Eros and Evil:* 31.
8. Dégh, *Folktales of Hungary:* 385–87, 354.
9. Kittredge, *Witchcraft:* 117; also see N. Cohn, "Myth": 11.
10. Craigie 272.
11. Tillhagen 318; on the connection of the swan maiden and the nightmare, see Holmström 89; MacCulloch, *Eddic:* 289; Hartland 279.
12. Tillhagen 326.
13. Jones and Kropf 364.
14. Craigie 273.
15. Tillhagen 319; also see Lindow 181–82.
16. Doniger, *Women, Androgynes, and Other Mythical Beasts:* 212.
17. Wardrop 168–71.
18. On the relationship between Urvaśī and the mare see Doniger, *Women, Androgynes, and Other Mythical Beasts:* 181; Holmström 118; and the last chapter of Lecouteux.
19. Doniger, *Women, Androgynes, and Other Mythical Beasts:* 203; on etymology see Shulman 12; E. Jones 243.
20. Kelly 240–41; Shulman 20.
21. E. Jones 85; MacCulloch, *Eddic:* 288.
22. Doniger, *Women, Androgynes, and Other Mythical Beasts:* 203.
23. Boas, *Salishan:* 53.
24. Simpson, *Icelandic:* 43–51.
25. Baudis 191–92.
26. G. Douglas 228–30.
27. Espinosa, *Spanish:* 215.
28. Craigie 275.
29. Doniger, *Women, Androgynes, and Other Mythical Beasts:* 83, 127.
30. Tillhagen 318.
31. Zilboorg 73.
32. C. G. Loomis 77.
33. Coffin, *Female Hero:* 131; see also Bernheimer 100.
34. Fiske 92.
35. Bernheimer 100.

36. Masters, *Eros and Evil:* xvii–xviii; see also Bernheimer 101.
37. F. Carpenter 26–29.
38. N. Cohn, *Europe's Inner Demons:* 22.
39. Kiessling 21–22; also see E. Jones 237; Hays 148.
40. Zilboorg 78.
41. Mack 9.
42. Masters, *Eros and Evil:* 146.
43. Shumaker 79.
44. R. H. Robbins 490; also see my chapter 3.
45. Lea 1:159–60.
46. Waller 68; E. Jones claims women outnumber men in incubus visitations: 84.
47. See Hersen.
48. Freeman 318, 334.
49. See Masters, *Eros and Evil*; R. H. Robbins.
50. R. H. Robbins 490.
51. Craigie 270–71; also see MacCulloch, *Eddic:* 289–90.
52. Freeman 318.
53. Hole 55.
54. Shulman 12.
55. Fiske 79.
56. Kelly 238–39.
57. Fiske 91.
58. Kelly 239.
59. Randolph 154.
60. Ruel 345.
61. Michelet 44–45.
62. See Guazzo 33; Remy 47; Scot 57; Sinistrari 204.
63. E. Jones 183.
64. Cowan 55–64.
65. Sprenger and Kramer 47.
66. See Leavy, "Faith's Incubus."
67. Dyer, "Dreams": 697; E. Jones 65.
68. See Devi; Brody.
69. Godwin, "A Sorrowful Woman": 192.
70. Holmström 92.
71. de la Saussaye 294; Kiessling 1, 14.
72. Swahn 412.
73. Shulman 11.
74. For contemporary dream theory see Goleman; also see Hillman and Roscher xii–xiii.
75. E. Jones 59–60.
76. Dyer, "Dreams": 706.
77. Coxwell 80.
78. Coxwell 724–25.

79. Htin Aung 127.
80. Coelho 178.
81. Dorsey, "Wichita": 298.
82. Dorsey, *Caddo:* 76–77.
83. Dixon, *Maidu:* 197–201.
84. Freeman 322.
85. Bettelheim's argument: 58.
86. Crapanzano, "Saints": 158. The personal versus the communal nature of dream interpretation and of ideas concerning spirit visitation is too broad a subject to receive adequate attention here. Crapanzano has repeatedly warned against substituting for the idiom of other cultures the Western idiom of subjective experience and psychological interpretation; see, for example, "Saints" 145, 150; "Mohammed" 141, 163. I. M. Lewis touches on the matter of personal responsibility and spirit possession: 293. And Freeman notes that among the Ibans, the incubus allows the dreamer to divest himself in part of personal responsibility for the "nocturnal erotic experience," thus "lessening the guilt and shame associated with her illicit libidinal impulses, both conscious and unconscious": 339. But Obeyesekere points out that spirits supply personal symbols and thus the "individual exercises an option or choice in selecting a spirit from a known cultural category": 115. There seems, however, to be no necessary contradiction between a group's allowing its afflicted (possessed) an exit from their difficulty by diminishing shame and guilt, and the group's understanding that spirits may not arbitrarily choose their victims. The doubleness of dreams is central to Kruger's analysis of medieval dream theory; he describes the concept of a central "ground, where divinely-inspired and internally-stimulated dreams coexist," and "purely external dreams can . . . be moderated by internally-generated material": 26, 45. Also see Kruger's discussion of demonic dreams: 44–53. To the problem of subjective dream experience versus the supposedly "hard facts of waking life" Doniger has devoted an entire book, *Dreams, Illusion, and Other Realities*. See, in particular, chapter 1.
87. M. Douglas xxvi–xxvii.
88. Benedict 1:xxiv.
89. See Hufford on the visitation of "old hag," dreams, and folklore traditions.
90. Crapanzano, "Mohammed": 142–43; "Saints" 158.
91. Amado 534–35, 546.
92. D. Patai 124, 138.
93. Hillman and Roscher xxiii.
94. E. Jones 45, 47, 85.
95. Bernheimer 101.
96. Masters, *Eros and Evil:* 6–7. Also see nn.97–101 below.
97. Rad 110; Vawter 25; Williams 22–25.
98. Williams 22.

99.   This is a Christian interpretation of Genesis 6: Williams 34.
100.  Craigie 93; see Christiansen's account of how Norwegians believe their fairy folk are descended from Lilith; *Folktales of Norway* 89–91.
101.  Vawter 25.
102.  The Sinistrari text can be found in Clymer and at the end of Masters, *Eros and Evil.*
103.  This is the essence of Clymer's commentary on Genesis: 11–13.
104.  Clymer, particularly 11, 15, 17.
105.  Scott's concern for the transmutation of folklore into demonology is central to my essay on Scott and Hawthorne: "Faith's Incubus."
106.  Nodier xiii, 1–2.
107.  Nodier, particularly 6, 15–16, 59.
108.  Stutley 90.
109.  Fox 293.
110.  MacCulloch, *Eddic:* 205.
111.  Holmberg 159–60.
112.  Carol Gilligan's emphasis on the "self" in her study of gender and identity mitigates against the totally *natural* concept of woman's development, but does not really resolve the dilemma of how to reconcile caring for "self" with caring for others—the central conflict of the runaway mother. If anything, Gilligan's use of the abortion issue evades some of the problem, because to abort the fetus is to bypass the need to choose between the needs of a living child and the realization of selfhood, as Ibsen's Nora had to choose (Gilligan cites *A Doll House*). One of the problems of this interesting book is that it is caught between a "natural" Freudian model for male and female development, and the feminist stance that a woman is usually but does not necessarily have to be the first caretaker in a child's life, the implication being that a male caretaker would impact differently on how the child would develop a superego, in which case the Freudian model appears compromised.
113.  See Greer on the runaway wife: 320–21.
114.  Hillman and Roscher xix.
115.  Busk, *Roman:* 315–17.
116.  Lessa 126.
117.  Pakrasi 74.
118.  Rhŷs, *Celtic Folklore:* 1:11.
119.  Kittredge, *Witchcraft:* 116; R. S. Loomis 126.
120.  Quoted in Denham, 2:42.
121.  Hamilton 25, 27.
122.  E. Jones 121.
123.  For analyses of Kleist's story consistent with this chapter's interest in the incubus and related folklore, see the work of D. Cohn; Dyer; Ellis; also see Heibling 151 n.1.
124.  Ausubel 593.
125.  Bamberger 142–43.

126. Graves and Patai 65; see Rivlin and Barbara Walker for feminist interpretations of Lilith.
127. Markale 181.
128. "Lilith," *Encyclopedia Judaica:* 247.
129. Rudwin 96.
130. Roscher 80–81.
131. "Lilith," *Encyclopedia Judaica:* 247; *Jewish Encyclopedia* 88.
132. Rudwin 98.
133. Weigle 255.
134. Robe 108–9; Barakat 270.
135. For discussion of La Llorona as mythical White Lady and for further references, see Jacobsen and Leavy 280–84.
136. Robe 114.
137. Barakat 291.
138. Kearny 203.
139. Conway 2:99–100.
140. Jordan in Jordan and Kalčik: 37.
141. Elaine K. Miller, *Mexican Folk Narrative:* 107.
142. Lessa 151–52.
143. Morgan 213–14, 243.
144. Boswell 10.
145. Craigie 267; see also Tillhagen 321.
146. For summary see Löseth vi.
147. Ravenel 153–56.
148. R. S. Crane 61.
149. Campbell and McKay 93.
150. Ravenel 158.
151. Meyer 164.
152. Hartland 117.
153. Hartland 93–94; see also Jacobsen and Leavy on the changeling motif: 238–55.
154. Holmberg 166.
155. Keightley 355–56.
156. Evans-Wentz 182.
157. Gruffydd 17.
158. Evans-Wentz 136, 198, 491.
159. Sklar 21, 44.
160. Kolbenschlag 170.
161. For an analysis of the film in terms of real parent-child relationships, see Robin Wood.
162. See G. Wills, et al.
163. Oates 38, 51, 128, 158, 290, 301.
164. See Friedrich for a study of the split between the maternal and the erotic in Western Europe, particularly 187–88.
165. Addams 64–65, 68.

CHAPTER 6  *The Animal Bride*

1. I am using Edward G. Fichtner's translation for me of the Helgi story from the *Hromundar Saga Gripssonar*. Also see Seaton; Masters, *Forbidden Sexual Behavior:* 91.
2. "Polly Von," *Peter, Paul, and Mary: Blowing in the Wind.* Warner Brothers Recordings, 1963.
3. Abrahams, *Afro-American Folktales:* 112–13.
4. Doniger, *Tales of Sex:* 97.
5. Jameson 90.
6. See discussion of the loathly lady theme later in this chapter.
7. Swire 265–67.
8. Christiansen, *Studies in Irish:* 132–33. Holbek argues that the two versions may have at least as much to do with genre (legend as opposed to fairy tale) as theme (personal correspondence).
9. Thompson, *One Hundred Tales:* 81.
10. Thorpe 158–68.
11. Sellers 133–49.
12. Hoogasian-Villa 180–89.
13. Ralston, *Tibetan Tales:* 44–74.
14. Sibunruang 65.
15. Biggs 69–78.
16. Thorpe 168.
17. Ishiwara 41. Swahn comments on the demand for a happy ending to Cupid and Psyche type tales: 411.
18. Craigie 231.
19. Beck 214.
20. Lessa 143.
21. Luzel 294.
22. Jegerlehner 157.
23. Ha 58.
24. Jameson 94.
25. Hatt 99, 101.
26. Bernheimer 34.
27. Jameson 92–93.
28. Conway 2:100.
29. Fiske 101.
30. Rhys, "Welsh Fairy Tales": 99.
31. Boas, "The Central Eskimo": 615–18.
32. Pakrasi 95–111.
33. Day 198.
34. Dirr 47–50.
35. Wardrop 15–21.
36. Megas 50–51.
37. Curtin, *Seneca Indian Myths:* 452–56.

38. Teit, "Traditions of the Lillooet": 309–10.
39. Boas and Hunt 122–23.
40. E. A. Smith 103–4.
41. Turner, "Ethnology of the Ungava District": 11:264.
42. Golder 87–90.
43. Cross, "The Celtic Elements": 624. See Condren for an important feminist discussion of this tale: 31–33.
44. Holmström 152.
45. Delarue 110.
46. Calvino 43–44.
47. Pourrat 27.
48. Christiansen calls Type 313 the Jason and Medea type tale: "A Gaelic Fairytale" 107. Also see Aarne and Thompson 106; Thompson, *The Folktale:* 280.
49. Khatchatrianz 32–42.
50. Webster 120–30.
51. Busk, *Hofer:* 367.
52. Massignon 89–92.
53. Mechling 95–97.
54. Delarue 10–19.
55. For example, see Dobie 61–66; Paredes 78–88; and Taggart.
56. Wratislaw 9–18.
57. Curtin, *Myths of Ireland:* 32–49.
58. Dorsey, *Traditions of the Skidi Pawnee:* 284–93.
59. Busk, *Hofer:* 370.
60. Wake 284–87.
61. Mijatovich 45.
62. Wheeler 142–44.
63. Webster 121.
64. Grimm 781–90.
65. Vernaleken 278.
66. Bourhill and Drake 244.
67. Delarue 110.
68. Busk, *Hofer* 356–57.
69. Pyle 232.
70. Britten 321.
71. Christiansen, *Folktales of Norway:* 218. Lundell notes the anomoly of categorizing stories such as "Mastermaid" under the rubrik of "Girl as Helper in Hero's Tasks": 153. The story group has also been studied recently by Simpson: "Be Bold."
72. Randolph 5.
73. J. F. Campbell 1:51.
74. Pourrat 29.
75. Wheeler 352–55.

76. Sastri and Natesa 80–119.
77. Massignon 56.
78. Christiansen, *Folktales of Norway:* 227.
79. Kent 108.
80. Grimm 430.
81. Busk, *Hofer:*148.
82. Wheeler 124–26.
83. Stokes 6.
84. L. Garnett, *Greek Folk Poesy:* 2:19.
85. Andrews 287–94.
86. Pedroso 9–13.
87. Wratislaw 70–71.
88. T. F. Crane 340.
89. Stokes 142–43.
90. See Croce for an interesting reading of the relationship of Odette to Odile.
91. The racist implications of an equation of blackness with loathliness or evil are obvious. Croce's review (see previous note) concerns Baryshnikov's attempt to eliminate racist elements in the ballet by dressing *all* the swans in white; and Croce notes that only in the 1930s did it become traditional to present Odile as a black swan: until then the imposter was dressed in red or gold which have their own symbolic if not racist meanings). Black swans do appear in nature as striking counterparts to white ones, but, of course, they bear no taints of foulness or sin. As Holbek points out, although folktales may not be intentionally racist, they often perpetuate damaging stereotypes, and he comprehends the resentment they may evoke.
92. Kent 41.
93. Dasent 155.
94. Ranke 60.
95. Bompas 461–64.
96. Woolsey 70–77.
97. For example, Wheeler 194–95; Paredes 92–95.
98. Delarue 133.
99. Walker and Uysal 66.
100. Stokes 73–84.
101. Boulenger 21.
102. Paredes 92–93.
103. L. Garnett, *Greek Folk Poesy:* 2:20.
104. Ranke 59–61.
105. Berne 8.
106. Obeyesekere 38–42.
107. See Beach, chapter 2: 46–47; Roussel 341–44; Kittredge, "Arthur and Gorlogon": 187–88; MacCulloch, *Childhood of Fiction:* 326; Dawkins, *Modern Greek:* 89–95. Beach notes that blackness is a typical attribute

of the loathly lady: chapter 11: 5. In general, however, the iconography of the black man has received more scholarly attention than that of the black woman. For an important exception, see Gilman's essay.

108. Dawkins, *Forty-Five Stories:* 205.
109. Massignon 111–13.
110. Dawkins, *Forty-Five Stories:* 207–12.
111. Kent 41–45.
112. Calvino 392.
113. Bernheimer 374; also see 33–37, 157–58. For an analysis of the wild woman archetype replete with narrative illustrations, see Estés. Regrettably, her book appeared too late for me to make more than passing reference to it.
114. Carpenter, "The Loathly Lady": 49.
115. Bernheimer 34.
116. Teit, "The Shuswap": 715–18.
117. Mayer 32–34.
118. J. F. Campbell, *Popular Tales:* 3:421–40.
119. See R. P. Miller on the Wife of Bath.
120. Bin Gorion 3:1056–66.
121. Shenhar 113.
122. Lang, *Custom and Myth:* 76–80.
123. Skinner and Satterlee 381–82.
124. Curtin, *Myths of the Modocs:* 219–27.
125. Dorsey, *Traditions of the Skidi Pawnee:* 294–95.
126. Craigie 168–69; also see Jacobsen and Leavy for a discussion of the *huldre* woman (as a source for *Hedda Gabler*): 211–24.
127. Russ 88–94.
128. Lowie, "The Crow": 205–6.
129. Opler, *Myths and Tales of the Jicarilla Apache:* 254–56.
130. Dorsey, *Traditions of the Caddo:* 73–76.
131. Marriott and Rachlin 161–65.
132. Cross, "The Celtic Elements": 619–20.
133. Lüthi, *European Folktale:* 9.
134. Kapferer 104.
135. Cowan 153–64.
136. Walker and Uysal 110–11.
137. Grimm 635.
138. Briggs, *The Vanishing People:* 108–9.
139. Carmichael 17.
140. Howe and Hirschfeld 296.
141. Dawkins, *Modern Greek Folktales:* 99–103.
142. Drummond 848; italics added.
143. Ralston, "Beauty and the Beast": 1003; italics added.
144. Dozon 95–96.
145. Foster 148. See Darnton on the mutilation of the cat people: 92–93.

146. Garnett 4, 5, 40–41.
147. The text of Verga's story is supplied by Lucente. See his analysis of "La Lupa," one that touches on the other folklore characters associated with the female demon, werewolf, and so forth.
148. Kapferer has his own theories concerning why women are conceived of as particularly subject to demon invasion, surveying the previous theories of other major scholars: 95–99. For an interesting approach to this subject, see Monique Schneider.
149. Ebon 73–74; Kraemer 65, 68.
150. Messing 1125.
151. Pedroso 113–15.
152. Related by Bernheimer: 37.
153. Bourhill and Drake 208.
154. Lorimer 291–92.
155. Landtman 444.
156. Teit, "Mythology of the Thompson Indians": 339; also see Leavy on the relationship of the poison damsel legend to such folklore: *To Blight with Plague* 168–70.
157. Cushing 162.
158. Leland 268.
159. Marriott and Rachlan 162.
160. For example, Teit, "Tahltan Tales": 340.
161. Jones and Michelson 399.
162. Barnouw 195.
163. Jenks 33–35.
164. Beach, chapter 12, 44–45.
165. See Schofield for a study of the fearful kiss motif and for a comprehensive list of variants: *Studies:* 200–201.
166. See Leavy, "Faith's Incubus": 286–87; also see O'Sullivan 273.
167. See Leavy, *La Belle Dame sans Merci:* 35.
168. Henderson and Calvert, *Wonder Tales of Alsace-Lorraine:* 13–16.
169. Woolsey 46–48.
170. Grimm 425–30; Kent 102–9; M. Campbell, *Cloudwalking:* 151–55.
171. Markale 92, 108, 197; Lecouteux 56.
172. See Leavy, *La Belle Dame sans Merci,* for a discussion of the Melusine motif: 19, 277 n.20.
173. For an extensive study of Japanese serpent lore, see De Visser; Krappe links the Melusine legend to fox lore: "Far Eastern" 146–47.
174. Seki, *Folktales of Japan:* 80.
175. Jameson 94–96.
176. Dorson, *Folk Legends of Japan:* 133–34.
177. In *The Great Mother* Neumann depicts what he calls the "Lady of the Beasts," who represents a stage in the "development leading from the group psyche to ego-consciousness and individuality": 268–76.
178. De Visser 303.

179. See n.126 above.
180. In Cross, "The Celtic Elements in the Lay of Lanval": 622.
181. See Leavy, n.126 above.
182. Eisner 129.
183. This is Beach's argument; also see Eisner 12.
184. Jegerlehner 54–61.
185. Thompson, *Tales:* 150–52, for example.
186. Dorsey, *Traditions of the Skidi Pawnee:* 284–93.
187. Teit, "Traditions of the Lillooet": 329–31.
188. Stack and Lyall 64.
189. Lowie, "Shoshonean Tales": 33–36.
190. Du Bois 153.
191. Simms 289–290.
192. Opler, *Myths and Legends of the Lipan Apache:* 66.

CHAPTER 7 *Orpheus's Quest*

1. Hartland 283.
2. Lundell 154–55.
3. *Rig Veda* 253. Later in this chapter, I will relate such desertion to what men may perceive as the early abandonment of them by mothers who recognize a cultural imperative to separate from their sons and thereby help them be men. For encouragement to look at the swan maiden story from a man's point of view, I appreciate the advice of a friend and psychiatrist, Lawrence Friedman.
4. Allen 108, 111.
5. Hultkrantz 176–77.
6. Briggs, "The Fairies and the Realms of the Dead": 81.
7. Hultkrantz 92; also see 91, 93.
8. Wang 13.
9. Bernheimer 134.
10. Christiansen, "Some Notes on the Fairies": 111.
11. For similarities between the realms, see "Fairy," in Maria Leach: 1:363.
12. Hultkrantz notes that despite the blissful character of these realms of the dead, Indians "considered even the happy lands of the dead to suffer from serious defects as compared with the land of the living": 93.
13. Hultkrantz 176–77; Warden vii.
14. Hultkrantz 21, 17.
15. Kroeber, "Indian Myths of South Central California": 216–18.
16. Hultkrantz 174–75, 123–24.
17. For a list of taboos, see Hultkrantz 131–36.
18. Graves 1:128. Graves's view has been challenged; see Leavy, "Faith's Incubus": 302.
19. Markale 150–52.
20. *Mahabharata* 15.

21.  Friedman, *Orpheus in the Middle Ages:* 26; also see Donovan 163.
22.  Hultkrantz 199.
23.  Bernheimer 132–35.
24.  Friedman, *Orpheus in the Middle Ages:* 180–87.
25.  Dorsey, *Skidi Pawnee:* 297–99.
26.  This story is discussed in chapter 2.
27.  Hatt 69.
28.  E. Robbins 3.
29.  Anderson 25–27, 43.
30.  Friedman, *Orpheus in the Middle Ages:* 1.
31.  Sastri and Natesa 85; also see 148–49.
32.  See Davidson and Phelps 23.
33.  Simpson, *Icelandic:* 51.
34.  See Jacobsen's discussion in Jacobsen and Leavy 59–61.
35.  Benjamin Walker 1:371–72.
36.  Dixon, *Oceanic:* 72–74, 78–79.
37.  Briggs, *Vanishing:* 2:372–75.
38.  Foster 197–98.
39.  Briggs, *Vanishing:* 111–12; also see Leavy, "Faith's Incubus," for discussion of this story: 287.
40.  Craigie 150–51; also see Leavy, "Faith's Incubus": 287.
41.  Henderson and Calvert, *Alsace:* 229–32.
42.  Doniger, *Women, Androgynes, and Other Mythical Beasts:* 182.
43.  Harney 37–50.
44.  See Jacobsen and Leavy 216–19.
45.  Zipes, *Breaking the Magic Spell:* 170.
46.  Thornhill 15–48.
47.  Kincaid 75–91.
48.  McCulloch 283–304.
49.  Dorsey, *Pawnee:* 126–37.
50.  See Hultkrantz 20; Holbek, *Interpretation of Fairy Tales:* 163.
51.  Dorsey, *Pawnee:* 129.
52.  Dorsey, *Wichita:* 306–10.
53.  Erdoes and Ortiz 462–63.
54.  Jacobsen informs me that recent anthropological studies of polygamy are unlikely to extoll its advantages for a woman, and some research on my part indicates that contemporary scholars are focusing on the disfunctional aspects of polygamy.
55.  For the connection of "Mudjikiwis" to the Orpheus story, see Hultkrantz 174–75.
56.  Jones and Michelson 372–75; Skinner, "Plains Ojibwa": 293–95.
57.  Skinner, "Plains Cree": 353–61.
58.  See Kakar and Ross 53–54, 198–99.
59.  Erdoes and Ortiz 447–51.
60.  Clark 11–12.

61. Parsons, "Pueblo-Indian": 253–55.
62. Hertslet 43–54.
63. Grinnell, *Blackfoot:* 127–31.
64. Cushing 16–17.
65. Speck 144–46.
66. Kroeber, "Smith Sound Eskimos": 170–72.
67. Gros Louis 251.
68. Clouston, *A Group of Eastern Romances:* 320–21.
69. Eisner 80.
70. Anderson, "Orpheus": 36; for his commentary on Vergil, see 30–31.
71. These accounts have been chosen in part because in their imagery, the authors reflect a folklore tradition of which they are probably unaware.
72. A. Martin 272–74; Martin first published his plaint in the *New York Times,* June 25, 1973: C33.
73. Koffend 86–104.
74. Goldberg, *Hazards:* 10–13.
75. The parallels between psychiatrists and folklore figures represented by witch doctors and wise men were the subject of my lecture to the Seminars in the Behavioral Sciences of the Department of Psychiatry, New York Hospital, Payne Whitney Clinic: "Orpheus and the Psychiatrists": November 1987.
76. Scott, *Letters on Witchcraft:* 140.
77. Lessa 123.
78. Grinnell, *Pawnee:* 129–31.
79. Maxfield and Millington 96.
80. E. A. Smith 103–4.
81. Dixon, *Oceanic:* 9:110.
82. McCulloch 298–99.
83. Hynam 41–55.
84. Masters, *Eros and Evil:* 102–3. Masters writes often with tongue-in-cheek irony, but this ludicrous idea concerning such naive men appears to have actually aroused the skepticism of some Renaissance thinkers and to have made some contribution to the end of witch hunting.
85. Metzger 36.
86. Linforth 14, 20.
87. Ralston, "Beauty and the Beast": 1011–12.
88. Goldberg, *Hazards:*13.
89. See, for example, Fasteau: 199; Tavris and Offir 220. The advantages to man of woman's liberation by no means constitute an accepted premise. For a discussion of the sexual struggle between men and liberated women, see Gittelson 216–23. She interviewed a psychiatrist who claimed that although the "domineering, take-charge kind of wife has been around a long, long time," what is "new today is that, between her and her man, the bedroom's become the biggest field of conflict." To suggest that this site of conflict is not new is not to challenge what this doctor learns from his

patients so much as to argue that folklore reveals that the situation goes back at least as far as the story of Lilith. About a "new" impotence, Frosch, Ginsberg, and Shapiro note that although "sexually demanding women are no longer seen as bad, nor are they to be avoided," the breakdown of such mythologies has deprived men of a "culturally approved" refuge. Men must now confront their own neuroses and inhibitions: 319–25.

90. Tavris and Offir 156.
91. Von Gunther 33.
92. Sellers 137.
93. May, "Fantasy Differences": 42–45. May's argument is developed in *Sex and Fantasy*.
94. Freeman 339–40.
95. Giles 9–13.
96. Curčija-Prodanović 155–64.
97. For example, compare Boas, "The Eskimo of Baffin Land": 181–82, with Burrows 80.
98. Curčija-Prodanović 163.
99. Baudis 71–97. Many of these motifs also appear in "Fairy Elizabeth," a story that is virtually an anthology of the themes discussed in this chapter: Jones and Kropf 95–110, 362–73.
100. Thrum 43–48.

CHAPTER 8 *Etain's Two Husbands*

1. Lucas 6.
2. Karnik and Desai 28–29.
3. Rees and Rees 277; also see Doniger's commentary on the *Rig Veda:* 274 n.38.
4. "Hans Christian Andersen's Use of Folktales" 176.
5. For discussion of Lady Isabel and further sources, consult index in Jacobsen and Leavy.
6. For an example of the "Robber Bridegroom," see Grimm's *Fairy Tales*.
7. The tale is summarized in many places: I recommend Leahy; and Rees and Rees 271–78.
8. For connections between these narratives, see Kittredge, "Arthur and Gorlogon"; Severs; Bliss (who disputes the connection).
9. For example, see Christiansen, *Studies in Irish:* 150; Rees and Rees 278.
10. Dillon 53–57; and Muller 347–49. Also see Christiansen, *Studies in Irish:* 150.
11. Christiansen, *Studies in Irish:* 140, 150.
12. Benjamin Walker supplies a thorough summary: 2:113.
13. Rees and Rees 276. Fewer comparisons between Etain and Damayanti or between their stories exist than one would expect: see Rees and Rees (they also compare the story of Etain to that of Purūravas and Urvaśī): 271–78; MacCana 90.

14. Benjamin Walker 2:113.
15. Masters, *Eros and Evil:* 54.
16. See Leavy, *La Belle Dame San Merci:* 243–45.
17. Sastri and Natesa: see ninth story.
18. Gorer 464. I could cite many examples of demon lovers who appear disguised as a woman's lawful fiancé or husband; see as an example Craigie 241.
19. Clouston, *A Group of Eastern Romances:* 316–21; see his notes for a discussion of the gambling motif: 522–31.
20. Gertrude Schoepperle Loomis: 428.
21. Calvino 455–58.
22. Teit, "Tahltan Tales": 340–41.
23. Seki, *Folktales:* 167.
24. Yanagida 52.
25. Seki, "Spool of Thread": 284.
26. See chapter 4 for a discussion of the Japanese serpent bridegroom tale.
27. Seki, "Spool of Thread": 276.
28. Rasmussen 245–46.
29. Benedict 1:166.
30. Kroeber, "Cheyenne": 181–82.
31. For discussions of the *seter* girl and of *huldres,* and for other sources, consult index, Jacobsen and Leavy.
32. These stories are well represented in Christiansen, *Folktales of Norway:* 61–66, 77–78, 113–66. See also n.31 above.
33. MacDougall and Calder 133–41.
34. Rand 150–53.
35. Fuchs 17–19.
36. M. Owen 89.
37. Leahy 27.
38. Stephens's work constitutes a novella in which the "Wooing of Etain" is but one story element; see especially 188, 237, 247–50, 276.
39. Beach, chapter 7.
40. Heyneman 18–19.
41. *Collected Poems* 325.
42. *The Bell Jar* 84–85.
43. See my chapters 2 and 6.
44. Bowman and Bianco 105–16; this swan maiden pattern is found in Tale Type 465.
45. Cole 10–12.
46. Busk, *Roman Legends:* 108.
47. Dawkins, *Modern Greek Folktales:* 70–80.
48. Surmelian 166–72.
49. Kúnos 188–97.
50. Leal and Oliven 90.
51. Dawkins, *Forty-Five Stories:* 387–88; also see notes: 388–93.

52. See n. 47 above.

53. Lüthi in Ben-Amos 20.

54. Lecture on the *Mahabharata* at the Asia Society, New York, October 31, 1987.

55. Fischer, "Sociopsychological Analysis": 246.

56. Bettelheim 75n., 97.

57. Fischer, "Sociopsychological Analysis": 257.

58. Many critics, for example Baruch, adopt Rolf Fjelde's translation of Ibsen's Norwegian text into *Doll House* rather than *Doll's House*, because as Baruch notes, both Nora and Helmer are imprisoned in it. My own reading is consistent with such views but rests on a somewhat different premise: I see the doll house as an image of a play or unreal world, in this sense an analogue of supernatural otherworlds.

59. See discussions in Jacobsen and Leavy. In that book I did not follow Ibsen's urging that his late plays be read as a group beginning with *A Doll House*. I began instead three plays later with *Rosmersholm*. Folklore themes in the previous two plays, *Ghosts* and *An Enemy of the People*, were subsequently discussed in my book *To Blight with Plague*. The analysis here of *A Doll House* allows me to feel that finally, if in reverse order, I have responded to Ibsen's design.

60. Baruch 378.

61. Baruch 377; see n.58 above.

62. Cavell 22–24.

63. See chapter 5 for the story of Hild, the equestrian fairy who rides mortal men to their death.

64. Una's story is told in Booss 617–19, xvi. Booss notes that all of her Icelandic tales were taken from a translation of Jón Arnason's *Icelandic Legends*. But so far as I have been able to ascertain, Una's story was not included in the Danish translation of Arnason published in Ibsen's time. Thus I do not argue for direct influence, although I do not discount the possibility that Ibsen encountered the story.

65. Burton 8:42.

66. See chapter 2. Duerr cites Diderot in a quotation widely applicable to swan maiden tales, that one "should wear the coat of the country he visits and save the one of the country from where he comes": 32.

67. Baruch 378.

68. Toulmin 308–9, 314–15.

# Bibliography

Aarne, Antti, and Stith Thompson. *The Types of the Folktale.* 2d rev. ed. Helsinki: Suomalainen Tiedeakatemia, 1961.

Abrahams, Roger D. *Afro-American Folktales: Stories from Black Traditions in the New World.* New York: Pantheon, 1985.

———. *African Folktales: Traditional Stories of the Black World.* New York: Pantheon, 1983.

———. "Personal Power and Social Restraint in the Definition of Folklore." In *Toward New Perspectives in Folklore,* ed. Américo Paredes Americo and Richard Bauman. Austin: University of Texas Press, 1972. 16–30.

Adamson, Thelma. *Folk-Tales of the Coast Salish.* New York: American Folk-Lore Society, 1934.

Addams, Jane. "The Devil Baby at Hull House." *Atlantic Classics.* 2d series. Boston: Atlantic Monthly Press, 1918.

Addy, Sidney O. *Household Tales: With Other Traditional Remains.* London: Nutt, 1895.

Afanas'ev, Aleksandr. *Russian Fairy Tales.* Trans. Norbert Guterman. New York: Pantheon, 1973.

Allen, Dorena. "Orpheus and Orfeo: The Dead and the Taken." *Medium Aevum* 33 (1964): 102–11.

Amado, Jorge. *Dona Flor and Her Two Husbands: A Moral and Amorous Tale.* Trans. Harriet de Onis. New York: Knopf, 1969.

Andersen, Johannes C. *Myths and Legends of the Polynesians.* London: Harrap, 1928.

Anderson, W. S. "The Orpheus of Virgil and Ovid: *Flebile nescio quid.*" In Warden: 25–50.

Andrews, James B. *Contes ligures: Traditions de la rivière.* Paris: Leroux, 1892.

Anesaki, Masaharu. *Japanese.* Vol. 8 of *The Mythology of All Races,* ed. Louis Herbert Gray.

Apuleius, Lucius. *The Golden Ass: Being the Metamorphoses of Lucius Apuleius.* Trans. W. Adlington [1566]. Cambridge, Mass.: Harvard University Press, 1958. Loeb Classical Library.

Ardener, Edwin. "Belief and the Problem of Women." In *The Interpretation of*

*Ritual: Essays in Honour of I. A. Richards,* ed. J. S. La Fontaine. London: Tavistock, 1972. 135–58.

Arnott, Kathleen. *African Fairy Tales.* London: Muller, 1967.

Artin Pacha, S. E. Yacoub. *Contes populaires inédits de la vallée du Nil.* Paris: Maisonneuve, 1895.

d'Aulnoy, Marie Catherine (Countess). *Fairy Tales.* Trans. James R. Planche. London: Routledge, 1855.

Ausubel, Nathan. *A Treasury of Jewish Folklore.* New York: Crown, 1948.

Bain, R. Nisbet. *Cossasck Fairy Tales and Folk-Tales.* London: Bullen, 1902.

Bamberger, Bernard J. *Fallen Angels.* Philadelphia: Jewish Publication Society of America, 1952.

Barakat, Robert A. "Aztec Motifs in 'La Llorona.' " *Southern Folklore Quarterly* 29 (1965): 288–96.

Barbour, Frances M. "Some Fusions in Missouri Ballads." *Journal of American Folklore* 49 (1936): 207–14.

Barchilon, Jacques. "Beauty and the Beast." *Psychoanalysis and the Psychoanalytic Review* 46 (1959): 19–29.

Barnouw, Victor. *Wisconsin Chippewa Myths and Tales: And Their Relation to Chippewa Life.* Madison: University of Wisconsin Press, 1977.

Baroja, Julio C. *The World of Witches.* Trans. O. N. V. Glendinning. Chicago: University of Chicago Press, 1964.

Barry, Phillips. *British Ballads from Maine.* New Haven: Yale University Press, 1929.

———. "Some Aspects of Folk-Song." *Journal of American Folklore* 25 (1912): 274–83.

———. "Traditional Ballads in New England, II." *Journal of American Folklore* 18 (1905): 191–214.

Baruch, Elaine Hoffman. "Ibsen's *Doll House:* A Myth for Our Time." *Yale Review* 69 (1980): 374–87.

Bascom, William R. "Four Functions of Folklore." In Dundes, *The Study of Folklore:* 279–98.

Basile, Giambattista. *Pentamerone.* Trans. N. M. Penzer. 2 vols. London: Lane, 1932.

Baudis, Josef. *Czech Folk Tales.* London: Allen & Unwin, 1917.

Beach, Joseph Warren. "The Loathly Lady." Ph.D. diss., Harvard University, 1907.

Beaumont, Cyril W. *The Ballet Called Swan Lake.* London: Beaumont, 1952.

Beck, Horace. *Folklore and the Sea.* Middletown, Conn.: Wesleyan University Press, 1973.

Belden, H. M. "Old-Country Ballads in Missouri, II." *Journal of American Folklore* 19 (1906): 281–99.

Ben-Amos, Dan. "Introduction." *Folklore Genres.* Ed. Dan Ben-Amos. Austin: University of Texas Press, 1976. ix–xlv.

Benedict, Ruth. *Zuñi Mythology.* 2 vols. New York: Columbia University Press, 1935.

Bengis, Ingrid. *Combat in the Erogenous Zone.* New York: Knopf, 1973.

Bernard, Henry, and Pencho Slaveikoff. *The Shade of the Balkans: Being a Collection of Bulgarian Folksongs and Proverbs.* London: Nutt, 1904.

Berne, Eric. "The Mythology of Dark and Fair: Psychiatric Use of Folklore." *Journal of American Folklore* 72 (1959): 1–13.

Bernheimer, Richard. *Wild Men in the Middle Ages: a Study in Art, Sentiment, and Demonology.* Cambridge: Harvard University Press, 1952.

Bernstein, Gail Lee. *Haruko's World: A Japanese Farm Woman and Her Community.* Stanford, Calif.: Stanford University Press, 1983.

Bettelheim, Bruno. *Uses of Enchantment: The Meaning and Importance of Fairy Tales.* New York: Knopf, 1976.

"The Bewitched King." *South African Journal of Folklore* 1 (1879): 103–9.

Biggs, Maude Ashurst. *Polish Fairy Tales.* Trans. from A. J. Glinski. London: Lane, 1920.

Bin Gorion, Micha J. *Mimekor Yisrael: Classical Jewish Folktales.* 3 vols. Bloomington: Indiana University Press, 1976.

Bliss, A. J., ed. *Sir Orfeo.* Oxford: Clarendon, 1966.

Boas, Franz. *Bella Bella Tales.* New York: American Folk-Lore Society, 1932.

———. *Folk-Tales of the Salishan and Sahaptin Tribes.* Lancaster, Penn.: American Folk-Lore Society, 1917.

———. "Mythology and Folk-Tales of the North American Indians." *Journal of American Folklore* 27 (1914): 374–410.

———. *Kwakiutl Tales.* 1910; rpt. New York: AMS, 1969.

———. "Chinook Texts." *Bulletin of the Bureau of American Ethnology* 20 (1894): 1–278.

———. "The Eskimo of Baffin Land and Hudson Bay." *Bulletin of the American Museum of Natural History* 15 (1901): 1–370.

———. "The Central Eskimo." *Report of the Bureau of American Ethnology* 6 (1884–85): 401–675.

Boas, Franz, and George Hunt. "Kwakiutl Texts." *Memoirs of the American Museum of Natural History* 5 (1902): 1–270.

Bompas, Cecil H. *Folklore of the Santal Parganas* [Northeast India]. London: Nutt, 1909.

Booss, Claire. *Scandinavian Folk and Fairy Tales.* New York: Avenal, 1984.

Borrow, George. *The Songs of Scandinavia and Other Poems and Ballads.* Vols. 7–9 of *The Works of George Borrow.* London: Constable, 1923.

Boswell, John Eastburn. "*Expositio* and *Oblatio:* The Abandonment of Children and the Ancient and Medieval Family." *American Historical Review* 89 (1984): 10–33.

Bottigheimer, Ruth B. *Fairy Tales and Society: Illusion, Allusion, and Paradigm.* Philadelphia: University of Pennsylvania Press, 1986.

Boulenger, Jacques. *Les contes de ma cuisinière* [Tales from Corfu]. Paris: Gallimard, 1935.

Bourhill, E. J., and J. B. Drake. *Fairy Tales from South Africa.* London: Macmillan, 1908.

Bowman, James Cloyd, and Margery Bianco. *Tales from a Finnish Tupa*. Chicago: Whitman, 1936.

Brenton, Myron. *The Runaways: Children, Husbands, Wives, and Parents*. Boston: Little, Brown, 1978.

Brett, Rev. William Henry. *Legends and Myths: Of the Aboriginal Indians of British Guiana*. London: Gardner, [ca. 1880].

Breul, Karl, ed. *Sir Gowther*. Jena: Wilhelm Gronau, 1886.

Brewster, Paul G. *Ballads and Songs of Indiana*. Bloomington: Indiana University Press, 1940.

Briggs, Katherine. *The Vanishing People: Fairy Lore and Legends*. New York: Pantheon, 1978.

———. "The Fairies and the Realms of the Dead." *Folklore* 81 (1970): 81–96.

———. *The Fairies in English Tradition and Literature*. Chicago: University of Chicago Press, 1967.

Britten, James. "Irish Folk-Tales." *Folk-Lore Journal* 1 (1883): 316–24.

Brody, Jane E. "Health Vitality and Sex: Books for Women." *New York Times*, June 25, 1984, B9.

Brunvand, Jan H. *The Vanishing Hitchhiker: American Urban Legends and Their Meanings*. New York: Norton, 1981.

Buchan, Peter. *Ancient Scottish Tales*. Peterhead: 1908.

Burrison, John. " 'James Harris' in Britain since Child." *Journal of American Folklore* 80 (1967): 271–84.

Burrows, Elisabeth. "Eskimo Tales." *Journal of American Folklore* 39 (1926): 79–87.

Burston, Daniel. "Myth, Religion, and Mother Right: Bachofen's Influence on Psychoanalytic Theory." *Contemporary Psychoanalysis* 22 (1986): 666–87.

Burton, Richard. *The Book of the Thousand Nights and a Night*. 10 vols. Benares: Kamashastra Society, 1885.

Busk, Rachel H. *Roman Legends: A Collection of the Fables and Folk-Lore of Rome*. Boston: Estes & Lauriat, 1877.

———. *Sagas from the Far East; or, Kalmouk and Mongolian Traditionary Tales*. London: Griffith & Farran, 1873.

———. *Household Stories from the Land of Hofer; or, Popular Myths of Tirol*. London: Griffith & Farran, 1871.

Bynum, David E. *The Daemon in the Wood: A Study of Oral Narrative Patterns*. Cambridge, Mass.: Harvard University Press, 1978.

Callan, Hilary. "The Premise of Dedication: Notes towards an Ethnography of Diplomats' Wives." In *Perceiving Women*, ed. Shirley Ardener. London: Malaby, 1975. 87–104.

Calvino, Italo. *Italian Folktales*. Trans. George Martin. New York: Harcourt, Brace, Jovanovich, 1980.

Campbell, C. G. *Told in the Market Place* [Iraq]. London: Benn, 1954.

———. *Tales from the Arab Tribes: A Collection of the Stories Told by the Arab Tribes of the Lower Euphrates*. New York: Macmillan, 1950.

Campbell, John F. *Popular Tales of the West Highlands: Orally Collected.* 4 vols. 1890; rpt. Detroit: Singing Tree, 1969.

Campbell, John F., and John G. McKay. *More West Highland Tales.* Edinburgh: [Scottish Anthropological and Folklore Society] Oliver and Boyd, 1940.

Campbell, Marie. *Tales from the Cloud Walking Country.* Bloomington: Indiana University Press, 1958.

Carmichael, Alexander. *Carmina Gadelica: Hymns and Incantations.* Edinburgh: Oliver and Boyd, 1941.

Carnoy, E. Henry, and J. Nicolaïdes. *Traditions populaires de l'Asie Mineure.* Paris: 1889.

Carpenter, Ann. "The Loathly Lady in Texas Lore." *Journal of the American Studies Association of Texas* 5 (1974): 48–53.

Carpenter, Frances. *Tales of a Basque Grandmother.* Garden City, N.Y.: Doubleday, Doran, 1930.

Carr, Edward Hallett. *What Is History?* New York: Knopf, 1963.

Casady, Margie. "Runaway Wives: 'Husbands Don't Pick Up the Danger Signals Their Wives Want Out.' " *Psychology Today*, May 1975, 42.

Cavell, Stanley. *Pursuits of Happiness: The Hollywood Comedy of Remarriage.* Cambridge, Mass.: Harvard University Press, 1981.

Cerquand, J. F. *Légendes et récits populaires du pays basque.* Pau: Ribaut, 1875.

Chapman, John W. *Ten'a Texts and Tales from Anvik, Alaska.* 1914; rpt. New York: AMS, 1974.

Chase, Richard. *Grandfather Tales.* Boston: Houghton Mifflin, 1948.

Child, Francis J. *The English and Scottish Popular Ballads.* 5 vols. Boston: 1882–1898.

Chilli, Shaikh. *Folk-Tales of Hindustan.* Bahadurganji, Allahabad: Panini Office, 1913.

Christiansen, Reidar T. "Some Notes on the Fairies and the Fairy Faith." *Bealoides* 39–41 (1971–73): 95–111.

———. *Folktales of Norway.* Trans. Pat Shaw Iversen. Chicago: University of Chicago Press, 1964.

———. *Studies in Irish and Scandinavian Folktales.* Copenhagen: Rosenkilde and Bagger, 1959.

———. *The Migratory Legends: A Proposed List of Types with a Systematic Catalogue of the Norwegian Variants.* Helsinki: Suomalainen Tiedeakatemia Academia Scientiarum Fennica, 1958.

———. "A Gaelic Fairytale in Norway." *Bealoideas* 1 (1927): 107–14.

Clark, Kate McCosh. *Maori Tales and Legends.* London: Nutt, 1896.

Clouston, William Alexander. *A Group of Eastern Romances and Stories: From the Persian, Tamil, and Urdu.* Privately printed, 1889.

———. *Popular Tales and Fictions: Their Migrations and Transformations.* 2 vols. London: Blackwood, 1887.

Clymer, Reuben Swinburne. *The Divine Mystery.* Allentown, Penn.: Philosophical, [ca. 1910].

Codrington, R. H. *The Melanesians: Studies in Their Anthropology and Folk-Lore.* 1891; rpt. New Haven: HRAF, 1957.

Coelho, Francisco Adolpho. *Tales of Old Lusitania: From the Folk-Lore of Portugal.* Trans. Henriqueta Monteiro. London: Sonnenschein, 1885.

Coffin, Tristram P. *The Female Hero in Folklore and Legend.* New York: Seabury, 1975.

———. *The British Traditional Ballad in North America.* Rev. ed. with a Supplement by Roger deV. Renwick. Austin: University of Texas Press, 1977.

Cohn, Dorrit. "Kleist's 'Marquise von O . . . ': The Problem of Knowledge." *Monatshefte* 67 (1975): 129–44.

Cohn, Norman. *Europe's Inner Demons: An Enquiry Inspired by the Great Witch-Hunt.* New York: Basic, 1975.

———. "The Myth of Satan and His Human Servants." In M. Douglas: 3–16.

Cole, F. T. "Santhali Folklore." *Indian Antiquary* (1875): 10–12.

Condren, Mary. *The Serpent and the Goddess: Women, Religion, and Power in Celtic Ireland.* San Francisco: Harper & Row, 1989.

Conway, Moncore Daniel. *Demonology and Devil-Lore.* 2 vols. New York: Holt, 1879.

Cooke, Elizabeth Johnston. "English Folk-Tales in America." *Journal of American Folklore* 12 (1899): 126–30.

Cosquin, Emmanuel. *Contes populaires de Lorraine.* 2 vols. Paris: 1886.

Cowan, James. *Fairy Folk Tales of the Maori.* Auckland: Whitcomb & Tombs, 1925.

Cox, John Harrington. *Folk Songs of the South: Collected under the Auspices of the West Virginia Folk-Lore Society.* Cambridge, Mass.: Harvard University Press, 1925.

Coxwell, C. Fillingham. *Siberian and Other Folk Tales: Primitive Literature of the Empire of the Tsars.* London: Daniel, 1925.

Craigie, William A. *Scandinavian Folk-Lore: Illustrations of the Traditional Beliefs of the Northern Peoples.* 1896; rpt. Detroit: Singing Tree, 1970.

Crane, Ronald S. "An Irish Analogue of the Legend of Robert the Devil." *Romanic Review* 5 (1914): 55–67.

Crane, Thomas Frederick. *Italian Popular Tales.* 1885; rpt. Detroit: Singing Tree, 1968.

Crapanzano, Vincent. "Mohammed and Dawia: Possession in Morocco." In *Case Studies in Spirit Possession,* ed. Vincent Crapanzano and Vivian Garrison. New York: Wiley, 1976. 141–76.

———. "Saints, Jnun, and Dreams: An Essay in Moroccan Ethnopsychology." *Psychiatry* 38 (1975): 144–59.

Crim, Keith, et al. "Gandharvas." *Abingdon Dictionary of Living Religions.* Nashville, Tenn.: Abingdon, 1981.

Croce, Arlene. "The Story of O" [Mikhail Baryshnikov's production of *Swan Lake*]. *New Yorker,* May 29, 1989, 105–7.

Croker, Thomas Crofton. *Fairy Legends of the South of Ireland.* London: Tegg, 1862.

Cross, Tom Peete. "The Celtic Elements in the Lays of Lanval and Graelent." *Modern Philology* 12 (1915): 585–646.

———. "The Celtic Origin of the Lay of Yonec." *Revue Celtique* 31 (1910): 413–47.

Culhane, John. "The Cases of the Runaway Wives." *New York Times Magazine*, June 10, 1973, 87.

Curčija-Prodanović, Nada. *Yugoslav Folk-Tales*. London: Oxford University Press, 1957.

Curtin, Jeremiah. *Seneca Indian Myths*. New York: Dutton, 1923.

———. *Myths of the Modocs*. 1912; rpt. New York: Blom, 1971.

———. *Myths and Folk-Lore of Ireland*. 1890; rpt. Detroit: Singing Tree, 1968.

Curtis, Edward S. *The North American Indian*. 20 vols. Ed. Frederick Webb Hodge. Seattle: E. S. Curtis; Cambridge, Mass.: Harvard University Press, 1907–30.

Cushing, Frank Hamilton. *Zuñi Folk Tales*. 1931; rpt. Tucson: University of Arizona Press, 1986.

Darnton, Robert. *The Great Cat Massacre: And Other Episodes in French Cultural History*. New York: Basic, 1984.

Dasent, George W. *Popular Tales from the Norse*. London: 1907.

Davidson, Sarah, and Eleanor Phelps. "Folk Tales from New Goa, India." *Journal of American Folklore* 50 (1937): 1–51.

Davis, Arthur K. *More Traditional Ballads of Virginia*. Chapel Hill: University of North Carolina Press, 1960.

———. *Traditional Ballads of Virginia*. 1929; rpt. Charlottesville: University Press of Virginia, 1969.

Dawkins, Richard M. *More Greek Folktales*. 1955; rpt. Westport, Conn.: Greenwood, 1974.

———. *Modern Greek Folktales*. Oxford: Clarendon, 1953.

———. *Forty-Five Stories from the Dodekanese*. Cambridge, England: Cambridge University Press, 1950.

Day, Lal Behari [Lalaavihari De]. *Folk-Tales of Bengal*. London: 1885.

Dean, Michael C. *The Flying Cloud, and One Hundred and Fifty Other Old Time Songs and Ballads*. Virginia, Minn.: Quickprint, 1922.

Deane, Tony, and Tony Shaw. *The Folklore of Cornwall*. London: Batsford, 1975.

De Caro, Francis A. *Women and Folklore: A Bibliographic Survey*. Westport, Conn.: Greenwood, 1983.

De Caro, Rosan Jordan. See Jordan, Rosan.

Dégh, Linda. *Folktales and Society: Story-Telling in a Hungarian Peasant Community*. Bloomington: Indiana University Press, 1969.

———. *Folktales of Hungary*. Trans. Judith Halasz. Chicago: University of Chicago Press, 1965.

Dégh, Linda, and Andrew Vázsonyi. "Legend and Belief." In Ben-Amos: 93–123.

Delarue, Paul. *The Borzoi Books of French Folk Tales*. New York: Knopf, 1956.

Delarue, Paul, and Marie-Louise Teneze. *Le conte populaire français*. Vol. 2. Paris: Maisonneuve & Larose, 1964.

Dempster, Miss. "The Folk-Lore of Sutherlandshire." *Folk-Lore Journal* 6 (1988): 149–89.

Denham, Michael Aislabie. *The Denham Tracts: A Collection of Folklore*. Ed. James Hardy. 2 vols. London: Folklore Society, 1892–95.

Denton, W. "Introduction." In Mijatovich: 1–22.

Devi, Shovana. *The Orient Pearls: Indian Folk-Lore*. London, 1915.

De Visser, M. W. "The Snake in Japanese Superstitition." *Mitteilungen des Seminars für Orientalische Sprachen an der Königlichen Friedrich-Wilhelms-Universität zu Berlin* 14 (1911): 267–322.

Dillon, Myles. *Early Irish Literature*. Chicago: University of Chicago Press, 1948.

Dirr, Adolf. *Caucasian Folk-Tales*. Trans. Lucy Menzies. New York: Dutton, 1925.

Dixon, Roland B. *Oceanic*. Vol. 9 of *The Mythology of All Races,* ed. Louis Herbert Gray.

———. *Maidu Texts*. Leyden: Brill, 1912.

Dobie, J. Frank. *Puro Mexicano*. Austin: Texas Folk-Lore Society, 1935.

Doniger, Wendy. *When God Has Lipstick on His Collar: Theological Implications of Divine Adultery*. The Kathryn Fraser Mackay Memorial Lecture Series, September 23, 1991. Ogdensburg, N.Y.: Ryan, 1991.

———. *Tales of Sex and Violence: Folklore, Sacrifice, and Danger in the Jaiminiya Brahmana*. Chicago: University of Chicago Press, 1985.

———. *Dreams, Illusion, and Other Realities*. Chicago: University of Chicago Press, 1984.

———. *Women, Androgynes, and Other Mythical Beasts*. Chicago: University of Chicago Press, 1980.

———. *The Origins of Evil in Hindu Mythology*. Berkeley: University of California Press, 1976.

———, transl. and ed. *Hindu Myths: A Sourcebook*. Harmondsworth: Penguin, 1986.

———, transl. and ed. *The Rig Veda: An Anthology*. Harmondsworth: Penguin, 1986.

Donovan, Mortimer J. "Herodis the Auchinleck *Sir Orfeo*." *Medium Aevum* 27 (1958): 162–65.

Dorsey, George A. *The Pawnee: Mythology* (Part I). Washington, D.C.: Carnegie Institution of Washington, 1906.

———. *Mythology of the Wichita*. Washington, D.C.: Carnegie Institution of Washington, 1904.

———. *Traditions of the Arikara*. Washington, D.C.: Carnegie Institution of Washington, 1904.

———. *Traditions of the Caddo*. Washington, D.C.: Carnegie Institution of Washington, 1904.

——. *Traditions of the Skidi Pawnee.* 1904; rpt. New York: Kraus, 1969.

Dorsey, George A., and Alfred L. Kroeber. *Traditions of the Arapaho: Collected under the Auspices of the Field Columbian Museum and of the American Museum of Natural History.* Chicago: 1903.

Dorson, Richard M. *Folktales Told around the World.* Chicago: University of Chicago Press, 1975.

——. "Foreword." In O'Sullivan v–xxxii.

——. *Folk Legends of Japan.* Rutland, Vt.: Tuttle, 1962.

——. *Folklore Research around the World: A North American Point of View.* Bloomington: Indiana University Press, 1961.

——. "Print and American Folk Tales." *Western Folklore* 4 (1945): 207–15.

Douglas, George B. *Scottish Fairy and Folk Tales.* New York: Burt, [ca. 1903].

Douglas, Mary, ed. *Witchcraft: Confessions and Accusations.* London: Tavistock, 1970.

Dozon, Auguste. *Contes Albanais.* Paris: Leroux, 1881.

Dracott, Alice Elizabeth. *Simla Village Tales; or, Folk Tales from the Himalayas.* London: Murray, 1906.

Drummond, Lee. "Structure and Process in the Interpretation of South American Myth: The Arawak Dog Spirit People." *American Anthropologist* 79 (1977): 842–68.

Du Bois, Constance Goddard. "The Religion of the Luiseño Indians of Southern California." *University of California Publications in American Archeology and Ethnology* 8 (1908): 68–186.

DuBois-Desaulle, Gaston. *Bestiality: An Historical, Medical, Legal, and Literary Study.* New York: privately printed at Panurge Press, 1933.

Duerr, Hans Peter. *Dreamtime: Concerning the Boundary between Wilderness and Civilization.* Trans. Felicitas Goodman. Oxford: Blackwell, 1985.

Dundes, Alan. *Interpreting Folklore.* Bloomington: Indiana University Press, 1980.

——. "The Study of Folklore in Literature and Culture: Identification and Interpretation." *Journal of American Folklore* 78 (1965): 136–42

——, ed. *The Study of Folklore.* Englewood Cliffs, N.J.: Prentice-Hall, 1965.

Dunlop, W. "Australian Folk-Lore Stories." *Journal of the Royal Anthropological Institute of Great Britain and Ireland* 28 (1899): 22–34.

Dwyer, Daisy Hilse. *Images and Self-Images: Male and Female in Morocco.* New York: Columbia University Press, 1978.

Dyer, T. F. Thiselton. "Dreams and Their Folk-Lore." *Gentleman's Magazine* 253 (1882): 696–707.

——. "Nightmare." *Gentleman's Magazine* 252 (1882): 79–88.

Ebon, Martin. *The Devil's Bride.* New York: Harper & Row, 1974.

Eddy, Mary O. *Ballads and Songs from Ohio.* New York: Augustin, 1939.

Edwards, Lee R. *Psyche as Hero: Female Heroism and Fictional Form.* Middletown, Conn.: Wesleyan University Press, 1984.

Eells, Elsie Spicer. *Tales of Enchantment from Spain* 1920; rpt. New York: Dodd, Mead, 1950.

Eisner, Sigmund. *A Tale of Wonder: A Source Study of the Wife of Bath's Tale.* Ireland: English, 1957.

Ekrem, Selma. *Turkish Fairy Tales.* Princeton, N.J.: Van Nostrand, 1964.

El Fasi, Mohammad, and Emile Dermenghem. *Nouveaux contes fasis.* Paris: Reider, 1928.

————. *Contes fasis.* 1926; rpt. Paris: Presses Universitaires de France, 1976.

Ellis, John M. *Henrich von Kleist: Studies in the Character and Meaning of His Writings.* Chapel Hill: University of North Carolina Press, 1979.

Emerson, Ellen Russell. *Indian Myths; or, Legends, Traditions, and Symbols of the Aborigines of America.* 1884; rpt. Minneapolis, Minn.: Ross & Haines, 1965.

Ennis, Merlin. *Umbundu: Folk Tales from Angola.* Boston: Beacon, 1962.

Erdoes, Richard, and Alfonso Ortiz. *American Indian Myths and Legends.* New York: Pantheon, 1984.

Espinosa, José Manuel. *Spanish Folk-Tales from New Mexico.* New York: American Folk-Lore Society, 1937.

Estés, Clarissa Pinkola. *Women Who Run with the Wolves: Myths and Stories of the Wild Woman Archetype.* New York: Ballantine, 1992.

Evans-Wentz, Walter Y. *The Fairy-Faith in Celtic Countries.* University Books, 1966.

Fansler, Dean S. *Filipino Popular Tales.* 1921; rpt. Hatboro, Penn.: Folklore Association, 1965.

Farrand, Livingston. *Traditions of the Quinault Indians: Memoirs of the American Museum of Natural History* 4 (1902): 77–132.

Farrer, Claire R. *Women and Folklore.* Austin: University of Texas Press, 1975.

Fasteau, Marc Feigen. *The Male Machine.* New York: McGraw-Hill, 1974.

Fine, Elizabeth C. *The Folklore Text: From Performance to Print.* Bloomington: Indiana University Press, 1984.

Finlay, Winifred. *Folk Tales from Moor and Mountain.* New York: Roy, 1969.

Finnegan, Ruth. *Limba Stories and Story-Telling.* Oxford: Clarendon, 1967.

Fischer, J. L. "The Sociopsychological Analysis of Folktales." *Current Anthropology* 4 (1963): 235–95.

————. "Folktales, Social Structure, and Environment in Two Polynesian Outliers." *Journal of the Polynesian Society* 67 (1958): 11–36.

————. "The Position of Men and Women in Truk and Ponape: A Comparative Analysis of Kinship Terminology and Folktales." *Journal of American Folklore* 69 (1956): 55–62.

Fiske, John. *Myths and Mythmakers: Old Tales and Superstitions Interpreted by Comparative Mythology.* Boston: Houghton, Mifflin, 1888.

Fitzgerald, David. "Popular Tales of Ireland." *Revue Celtique* 4 (1879–80): 171–200.

Flanders, Helen H. *Garland of Green Mountain Song.* Northfield, Vt.: Commission for Conservation of Vermont Traditions, 1934.

Flanders, Helen H., et al. *Ancient Ballads Traditionally Sung in New England.* Vol. 3. Philadelphia: University of Pennsylvania Press, 1963.

Flanders, Helen H., and Marguerite Olney. *Ballads Migrant in New England.* New York: Farrar, Straus, & Young, 1953.

Foster, James R. *Lovers, Mates, and Strange Bedfellows: Old World Folktales.* New York: Harper, 1960.

Fox, William Sherwood. *Greek and Roman.* Vol. 1 of *The Mythology of All Races.* Ed. Louis Herbert Gray.

Freeman, Derek. "Shaman and Incubus." *The Psychoanalytic Study of Society.* Ed. W. Muensterberger and S. Axelrod. New York: International Universities Press, 1967.

Frere, Mary. *Old Deccan Days; or, Hindoo Fairy Legends.* London: Murray, 1868.

Frey, Anna Louise. *The Swan-Knight Legend: Its Background, Early Development, and Treatment in the German Poems.* Nashville, Tenn.: George Peabody College for Teachers, 1931.

Friedan, Betty. *It Changed My Life: Writings on the Women's Movement.* New York: Random House, 1976.

———. *The Feminine Mystique.* New York: Norton, 1963.

Friedman, John B. *Orpheus in the Middle Ages.* Cambridge, Mass.: Harvard University Press, 1970.

———. "Eurydice, Heurodis, and the Noon-Day Demon." *Speculum* 1 (1966): 22–29.

Friedrich, Paul. *The Meaning of Aphrodite.* Chicago: University of Chicago Press, 1979.

Frosch, William A., George L. Ginsberg, and Theodore Shapiro. "Social Factors in Symptom Choice: The New Dynamics of Impotence." In *On Sexuality: Psychoanalytic Observations,* ed. T. B. Karasu and C. W. Socarides. New York: International Universities Press, 1979. 317–25.

Fuchs, Peter. *African Decameron: Folk Tales from Central Africa.* Trans. Robert Meister. New York: Obolensky, 1963.

Gardner, Fletcher. "Tagalog Folk-Tales." *Journal of American Folklore* 20 (1907): 300–310.

Gardner-Medwin, Alisoun. "The Ancestry of 'The House-Carpenter': A Study of the Family History of the American Forms of Child 243." *Journal of American Folklore* 84 (1971): 414–27.

Garnett, David. *Lady into Fox.* New York: Knopf, 1923.

Garnett, Lucy. *Greek Folk Poesy: Annotated Translations from the Whole Cycle of Romaic Folk-Verse and Folk-Prose.* 2 vols. London: Nutt, 1896.

———. *The Women of Turkey and Their Folk-Lore.* 2 vols. London: Nutt, 1890.

Garrett, Clarke. "Women and Witches: Patterns of Analysis." *Signs* 3 (1977): 461–70.

Gaster, M., ed. and trans. *Rumanian Bird and Beast Stories.* London: Sidgwick and Jackson, 1915.

Gilbert, Douglas. *Lost Chords: The Diverting Story of American Popular Songs.* Garden City, N.Y.: Doubleday, Doran, 1942.

Giles, Herbert A. *Strange Stories from a Chinese Studio* [P'u, Sung-Ling, 1640–1715]. 4th ed. rev. Shanghai: Kelly and Walsh, 1926.

Gilligan, Carol. *In a Different Voice: Psychological Theory and Women's Development.* Cambridge, Mass.: Harvard University Press, 1982.

Gilman, Sander L. "The Hottentot and the Prostitute: Toward an Iconography of Female Sexuality." *Difference and Pathology: Stereotypes of Sexuality, Race, and Madness.* Ithaca, N.Y.: Cornell University Press, 1985. 76–108.

Ginzburg, Carlo. *Ecstasies: Deciphering the Witches' Sabbath.* Trans. Raymond Rosenthal. New York: Pantheon, 1991.

Gittelson, Natalie. *Dominus: A Woman Looks at Men's Lives.* New York: Farrar, Straus, Giroux, 1978.

Glassie, Henry. *Irish Folktales.* New York: Pantheon, 1985.

Goddard, Pliny Earle. "Kato Texts." *University of California Publications in American Archaeology and Ethnology* 5 (1907–10): 67–238.

Godwin, Gail. *Violet Clay.* New York: Knopf, 1978.

———. "A Sorrowful Woman." In *In the Looking Glass,* ed. Nancy Dean and Myra Stark. New York: Putnam's, 1977. 167–73.

Goldberg, Herb. *The New Male: From Self-Destruction to Self-Care.* New York: Morrow, 1979.

———. *The Hazards of Being Male: Surviving the Myth of Masculine Privilege.* New York: Signet, 1977.

Golder, F. A. "Tales from Kodiak Island, II." *Journal of American Folklore* 16 (1903): 85–103.

Goleman, Daniel. "Do Dreams Really Contain Important Secret Meaning?" *New York Times,* July 10, 1984, C1, C12.

Gorer, Geoffrey. *Himalayan Village: An Account of the Lepchas of Sikkim.* 2d ed. London: Nelson, 1967.

Grant, Mary A. *Folktale and Hero-Tale Motifs in the Odes of Pindar.* Lawrenceville: University of Kansas Press, 1967.

Graves, Robert. *The Greek Myths.* 2 vols. Baltimore: Penguin, 1964.

Graves, Robert, and Raphael Patai. *Hebrew Myths: The Book of Genesis.* New York: Doubleday, 1964.

Gray, J. Patrick. "The Universality of the Female Witch." *International Journal of Women's Studies* 2 (1979): 541–50.

Gray, Louis Herbert, ed. *The Mythology of All Races.* 13 vols. Boston: Marshall Jones, 1916–32.

Greer, Germaine. *The Female Eunuch.* New York: McGraw-Hill, 1970.

Grey, Sir George. *Polynesian Mythology: And Ancient Traditional History of the Maori as Told by Their Priests and Chiefs.* 1854; rpt. London: Whitcome & Tombs, 1956.

Griffis, William Elliot. *Korean Fairy Tales.* London: Harrap, 1923.

Grimm, Jacob, and Wilhelm Grimm. *The Complete Grimm's Fairy Tales.* Trans. Margaret Hunt; Rev. James Stern. New York: Pantheon, 1972.

Grinnell, George B. *Blackfoot Lodge Tales: The Story of a Prairie People.* Lincoln: University of Nebraska Press, 1962.

————. *Pawnee Hero Stories and Folk-Tales.* 1889; rpt. Lincoln: University of Nebraska Press, 1961.

Groome, Francis H. *Gypsy Folk Tales.* London: Hurst & Blackett, 1899.

Gros Louis, Kenneth R. "The Significance of Sir Orfeo's Self-Exile." *Review of English Studies* 18 (1967): 245–52.

Gruffydd, W. J. *Folklore and Myth in the Mabinogian: A Lecture.* 1958; rpt. Cardiff: University of Wales Press, 1961.

Guazzo, Francesco Maria. *Compendium Maleficarum.* Trans. Montague Summers. Secaucus, N.J.: University Books, 1974.

Ha, Tae Hung. *Folk Tales of Old Korea.* Seoul: Yonsei University Press, 1962.

Haeberlin, Hermann. "Mythology of Puget Sound." *Journal of American Folklore* 37 (1924): 371–438.

Hall, Edwin S. *Eskimo Storyteller: Folktales from Noataki, Alaska.* Knoxville: University of Tennessee Press, 1975.

Halliwell-Phillips, James Orchard. *Popular Rhymes and Nursery Tales.* London: Smith, 1849.

Hamilton, Mary. *Incubation; or, The Cure of Disease in Pagan Temples and Christian Churches.* London: Henderson, 1906.

Hampden, John. *The Gypsy Fiddle: And Other Tales Told by the Gypsies.* New York: World Publishing, 1969.

Harding, Susan. "Women and Words in a Spanish Village." In *Toward an Anthropology of Women,* ed. Rayna Reiter. New York: Monthly Review, 1975. 283–308.

Harney, W. E. *Tales from the Aborigines.* London: Hale, 1959.

Hartland, Edwin S. *The Science of Fairy Tales: An Inquiry into Fairy Mythology.* 1891; rpt. Detroit: Singing Tree, 1968.

Hastings, James, ed. *Encyclopedia of Religion and Ethics.* 13 vols. New York: Scribner's, 1925–32.

Hatt, Gudmund. *Asiatic Influences in American Folklore.* Copenhagen: Kommission Has Esnar Munksgaard, 1949.

Hatto, A. T. "The Swan Maiden: A Folk-Tale of North Eurasian Origin." *Bulletin of the School of Oriental and African Studies* [University of London] 24 (1961): 326–52.

Hays, H. R. *The Dangerous Sex: The Myth of Feminine Evil.* New York: Putnam's, 1964.

Heibling, Robert E. See Kleist, Henrich von.

Henderson, Bernard, and C. V. Calvert. *Wonder Tales of Alsace-Lorraine.* London: Allan, 1925.

————. *Wonder Tales of Old Tyrol.* London: Allan, 1925.

————. *Wonder Tales of Ancient Spain.* London: Allan, 1924.

Henry, Mellinger E. *Folk-Songs from the Southern Highlands.* New York: Augustin, 1938.

Henry, Mellinger E. "Still More Ballads and Folk-Songs from the Southern Highlands." *Journal of American Folklore* 45 (1932): 1–176.

————. "Ballads and Songs of the Southern Highlands." *Journal of American Folklore* 42 (1929): 254–300.

Hersen, Michael. "Personality Characteristics of Nightmare Sufferers." *Journal of Nervous Mental Disease* 153 (1971): 27–31.

Hertslet, Jessie. *Bantu Folk Tales.* Cape Town: African Bookman, 1946.

Heyneman, Martha. "Sir Gawain and Woman's Liberation." *Journal of Our Time* 1 (1977): 15–20.

High, Fred. *Old, Old Folksongs.* Berryville, Ark.: n.d.

Hillman, James, and Wilhelm Heinrich Roscher. *Pan and the Nightmare: Two Essays* ["*Ephialtes: A Pathological-Mythological Treatise on the Nightmare in Classical Antiquity Together with an Essay on Pan*"]. Zurich: Spring, 1972.

Hill-Tout, Charles. *British North America.* Vol. 1, *The Far West: The Home of the Salish and the Déné.* London: Constable, 1907.

————. "Ethnological Report on the Stseelis and Sk'aulito Tribes of the Halokmelem Division of the Salish of British Columbia." *Journal of the Anthropological Institutes of Great Britain and Ireland* 34 (1904): 311–76.

Holbek, Bengt. "Hans Christian Andersen's Use of Folktales." In *The Telling of Stories: Approaches to a Traditional Craft: A Symposium,* ed. Morton Nojgaard, et al. Odense: Odense University Press, 1988. 165–82.

————. *The Interpretation of Fairy Tales.* Helsinki: Suomalainen Tiedeakatemia, 1987.

————. "Nordic Research in Popular Prose Narrative." In *Trends in Nordic Traditional Research,* ed. Lauri Honko. Helsinki: Suomalainen Kirjallisuuden Seura, 1983. 145–62.

Hole, Christina. *A Mirror of Witchcraft.* London: Chatto and Windus, 1957.

Holmberg, Uno. *Finno-Ugric.* Vol. 4 of *The Mythology of All Races.* Ed. Louis Herbert Gray.

Holmström, Helge. *Studier over svanjungfrumotivet.* Malmo: 1919.

Hoogasian-Villa, Susie. *One Hundred Armenian Tales: And Their Folkloristic Relevance.* Detroit: Wayne State University Press, 1966.

Horsley, Richard A. "Who Were the Witches? The Social Roles of the Accused in the European Witch Trials." *Journal of Interdisciplinary History* 9 (1979): 689–715.

Howard, Jane. *A Different Woman.* New York: Dutton, 1973.

Howe, James, and Lawrence Hirschfeld. "The Star Girls' Descent: A Myth about Men, Women, Matrilocality, and Singing." *Journal of American Folklore* 94 (1981): 292–322.

Hsieh, Tehyi. *Chinese Village Folk Tales.* Boston: Humphries, 1948.

Htin Aung, U. *Burmese Folk-Tales.* Calcutta: Oxford University Press, 1948.

Hubbard, Lester A., and LeRoy J. Robertson. "Traditional Ballads from Utah." *Journal of American Folklore* 64 (1951): 37–53.

Hufford, David J. *The Terror That Comes in the Night.* Philadelphia: University of Pennsylvania Press, 1982.

Hultkrantz, Ake. *The North American Indian Orpheus Tradition: A Contribution to Comparative Religion.* Stockholm: Statens Etnografiska Museum, 1957.

Humphreys, Clarence B. *The Southern New Hebrides: An Ethnological Record.* Cambridge, England: Cambridge University Press, 1926.

Hunt, Robert. *Popular Romances of the West of England.* London: Camden, [ca. 1871].

Hynam, F. Ethel. *The Secrets of the Night, and Other Esthonian Tales.* London: Stock, 1899.

Ibsen, Henrik. *A Doll House.* In *Henrik Ibsen: The Complete Major Prose Plays.* Trans. Rolf Fjelde. New York: Farrar, Straus, Giroux, 1978.

Im Thurn, Everard F. *Among the Indians of Guiana: Being Sketches Chiefly Anthropologic from the Interior of British Guiana.* London: Paul, Trench, 1883.

Ishiwara, Yasuyo. "The Celestial Wife in Japanese Folk Tales." *University of Manila Journal of East Asiatic Studies* 5 (1956): 35–41.

"I Was a Runaway Wife." *Good Housekeeping,* May 1976, 16, 25–26, 28, 30.

Jackson, Shirley. *Come Along with Me: Part of a Novel, Sixteen Stories, and Three Lectures.* Ed. Stanley Edgar Hyman. New York: Viking, 1968.

———. *The Lottery; or, The Adventures of James Harris.* 1959; rpt. Cambridge, Mass.: Bentley, 1980.

Jacobs, Joseph. *More English Fairy Tales.* London: Nutt, 1894.

Jacobsen, Per Schelde, and Barbara Fass Leavy. *Ibsen's Forsaken Merman: Folklore in the Late Plays.* New York: New York University Press, 1988.

Jacottet, Edouard. *Études sur les langues du Haut-Zambèze.* Vol. 3, *Textes Louyi: Contes, légendes, etc.* Paris: 1901.

Jaffray, Robert. *The Two Knights of the Swan.* New York: Putnam's, 1910.

Jagendorf, N. M., and R. S. Boggs. *The King of the Mountains: A Treasury of Latin American Folk Stories.* New York: Vanguard, 1960.

Jameson, Raymond D. *Three Lectures on Chinese Folklore.* Peiping, China: San Yu, 1932.

Jegerlehner, Johannes. *Alp Legends.* Trans. I. M. Whitworth. Manchester: Sherratt & Hughes, 1926.

Jenks, Albert E. "The Bear Maiden: An Ojibwa Folk-Tale from Lac Courte Oreille Reservation, Wisconsin." *Journal of American Folklore* 15 (1902): 33–35.

Johnston, Oliver M. "Sources of the Lay of Yonec." *PMLA* 20 (1905): 322–38.

Jones, Ernest. *Nightmares, Witches, and Devils.* New York: Norton, 1931.

Jones, W. Henry, and Lewis L. Kropf. *Folk-Tales of the Magyars.* London: Stock, 1889.

Jones, William, and Truman Michelson. "Ojibwa Tales from the North Shore of Lake Superior." *Journal of American Folklore* 29 (1916): 368–91.

Jordan, Rosan A. "The Vaginal Serpent and Other Themes from Mexican-American Women's Lore." In Jordan and Kalcik: 26–44.

————. "A Note about Folklore and Literature." *Journal of American Folklore* 86 (1973): 62–65.

Jordan, Rosan A., and Susan J. Kalčik. *Women's Folklore: Women's Culture*. Philadelphia: University of Pennsylvania Press, 1985.

Kakar, Sudhir, and John Munder Ross. *Tales of Love, Sex, and Danger*. New York: Blackwell, 1987.

Kapferer, Bruce. *A Celebration of Demons*. Bloomington: Indiana University Press, 1983.

Karnik, H. R., and S. G. Desai, eds. and trans. *The Vikramorvastyam of Kalidasa*. Bombay: Booksellers', 1959.

Kearny, Michael. "La Llorona as a Social Symbol." *Western Folklore* 28 (1969): 199–206.

Keightley, Thomas. *The Fairy Mythology: Illustrative of the Romance and Superstition of Various Countries*. 1850; rpt. New York: AMS, 1968.

Kelly, Walter. *Curiosities of Indo-European Tradition and Folklore*. 1863; rpt. Detroit: Singing Tree, 1969.

Kennedy, Peter, and Alan Lomax. *The Folk Songs of Britain* [introductory notes to 5 vol. record set]. New York: Caedmon Records, 1961.

Kent, Margery. *Fairy Tales from Turkey*. London: Routledge & Kegan Paul, 1946.

Kerceval, George Truman, "An Otoe and an Omaha Tale." *Journal of American Folklore* 6 (1893): 199–204.

Khatchatrianz, I. *Armenian Folk Tales*. Trans. N. W. Orloff. Philadelphia: Colonial, 1946.

Kieckhefer, R. *European Witch Trials, Their Foundation in Popular and Learned Culture*. London: Routledge & Kegan Paul, 1976.

Kiessling, Nicolas. *The Incubus in English Literature: Provenance and Progeny*. Pullman: Washington State University Press, 1977.

Kincaid, C. A. *Tales of Old Sind*. London: Oxford University Press, 1922.

Kinsey, Alfred C. *Sexual Behavior in the Human Female*. Philadelphia: Saunders, 1953.

Kinsley, David. *Hindu Goddesses: Visions of the Divine Feminine in the Hindu Religous Tradition*. Berkeley: University of California Press, 1986.

Kirtley, Basil F. " 'La Llorona' and Related Themes." *Western Folklore* 19 (1960): 155–68.

Kittredge, George L. *Witchcraft in Old and New England*. 1929; rpt. New York: Russell & Russell, 1956.

————. "Arthur and Gorlogon." [*Harvard*] *Studies and Notes in Philology and Literature* 8 (1903): 149–275.

Klaits, Joseph. *Servants of Satan: The Age of the Witch Hunts*. Bloomington: Indiana University Press, 1985.

Kleist, Henrich von. *The Major Works of Henrich von Kleist*. Ed. Robert E. Heibling. New York: New Direction, 1975.

Kleivan, Inge. "The Swan Maiden Myth among the Eskimo." *Acta Arctica* 13 (1962): 15–49.

Knoblock, Judith Ann. " 'The Gypsy Laddie' (Child 200): An Unrecognized Child of Medieval Romance." *Western Folklore* 19 (1960): 35–45.

Knox, Robert H. "A Blackfoot Version of the Serpent Lover." *Journal of American Folklore* 36 (1923): 401–3.

Koffend, John B. *A Letter to My Wife*. New York: Saturday Review Press, 1972.

Kolbenschlag, Madonna. *Kiss Sleeping Beauty Good-Bye*. Garden City, N.Y.: Doubleday, 1979.

Koritschoner, H. "Ngoma y Sheitan." *Journal of the Royal Anthropological Institute* (1936).

Kosambi, D. D. *Myth and Reality: Studies in the Formation of Indian Culture.* Bombay: Popular Prakashan, 1962.

Kraemer, Ross S. "Ecstasy and Possession: Women of Ancient Greece and the Cult of Dionysus." In *Unspoken Worlds,* ed. Nancy A. Falk and Rita M. Gross. San Francisco: Harper & Row.

Krappe, Alexander H. "Far Eastern Fox Lore." *California Folklore Quarterly* 3 (1944): 124–47.

———. "Scandinavian Seal Lore." *Scandinavian Studies and Notes* 18 (1944): 156–62.

———. "The Valkyries." *Modern Language Review* 21 (1926): 55–73.

Kroeber, Alfred L. "The Patwin and Their Neighbors." *University of California Publications in American Archeology and Ethnology* 29 (1932): 253–428.

———. "Gross Ventre Myths and Tales." *Anthropological Papers of the American Museum of Natural History* 1 (1907): 55–139.

———. "Indian Myths of South Central California." *University of California Publications in American Archaeology and Ethnology* 4 (1906–07).

———. "Wishosk Myths." *Journal of American Folklore* 18 (1905): 85–107.

———. "Ute Tales." *Journal of American Folklore* 14 (1901): 252–85.

———. "Cheyenne Tales." *Journal of American Folklore* 13 (1900): 181–82.

———. "Tales of the Smith Sound Eskimo." *Journal of American Folklore* 12 (1899): 166–82.

Kruger, Steven F. *Dreaming in the Middle Ages.* Cambridge, England: Cambridge University Press, 1992.

Kúnos, Ignácz. *Forty-Four Turkish Fairy Tales.* London: Harrap, 1913.

Landtman, Gunnar. *The Folk-tales of Kiwai Papuans.* Helsinki: Finnish Society of Literature, 1917.

Lang, Andrew. *The Olive Fairy Book.* 1907; rpt. New York: Dover, 1968.

———. *Custom and Myth.* 2d ed. rev. London: Longmans, Green, 1885.

Lawson, John Cuthbert. *Modern Greek Folklore and Ancient Greek Religions: A Study in Survivals.* 1910; rpt. New York: New York University Press, 1964.

Lea, Henry Charles. *Materials toward a History of Witchcraft.* 3 vols. New York: Yoseloff, 1957.

Leach, MacEdward. "Fairy." In Maria Leach: 1:363–65.

Leach, Maria, ed. *Funk and Wagnalls Standard Dictionary of Folklore, Mythology, and Legend.* 2 vols. New York: Funk and Wagnalls, 1949.

Leahy, A. H. *The Heroic Romances of Ireland*. London: Nutt, 1905.

Leal, Ondina Fachel, and Ruben George Oliven. "Class Interpretations of a Soap Opera Narrative: The Case of the Brazilian *Novela*, 'Summer Sun.'" *Theory, Culture, and Society* 5 (1988): 81–99.

Leavy, Barbara Fass. *To Blight with Plague: Studies in a Literary Theme*. New York: New York University Press, 1992.

———. "Faith's Incubus: The Influence of Sir Walter Scott's Folklore on 'Young Goodman Brown.'" *Dickens Studies Annual* 18 (1989): 277–308.

———. *La Belle Dame sans Merci and the Aesthetics of Romanticism*. Detroit: Wayne State University Press, 1974.

Lecouteux, Claude. *Melusine et le chevalier au cygne*. Paris: Payot, 1982.

Lee, Frank H. *Folk Tales of All Nations*. New York: McCann, 1930.

Leland, Charles G. *The Algonquin Legends of New England*. Boston: Houghton, Mifflin, 1884.

Lermontov, Mikhail. "The Sea Princess." In *Major Poetical Works*. Trans. Anatoly Liberman. Minneapolis: University of Minnesota Press, 1983.

Lessa, William A. *Tales from Ulithi Atoll: A Comparative Study in Oceanic Folklore*. Berkeley: University of California Press, 1961.

Lewis, I. M. "Structural Approach to Witchcraft and Spirit Possession." In Mary Douglas, ed.: 293–310.

Lieberman, Marcia R. "Some Day My Prince Will Come: Female Acculturation through the Fairy Tale." *College English* 34 (1972): 383–95.

Liebrecht, Felix L. "Amor und Psyche—Zeus und Semele—Purūravas und Urvaci." *Zeitschrift für vergleichende Sprachforschung* 18 (1869): 56–66.

Lifton, Robert J. "Woman as Knower: Some Psychohistorical Perspectives." In *The Woman in America*, ed. Robert J. Lifton. Boston: Houghton, Mifflin, 1965. 27–51.

"Lilith." *Encyclopedia Judaica*. 16 vols. New York: Macmillan, 1972.

———. *Jewish Encyclopedia*. Ed. Isidore Singer. 12 vols. New York: Funk and Wagnalls, 1916.

Lim, Sian-tek. *Folk Tales from China*. New York: Day, 1944.

Lindow, John. *Swedish Legends and Folktales*. Berkeley: University of California Press, 1978.

Linforth, Ivan M. *The Arts of Orpheus*. Berkeley: University of California Press, 1941.

Lomax, Alan. *The Folk Songs of North America: In the English Language*. Garden City, N.Y.: Doubleday, 1960.

Loomis, C. Grant. *White Magic: An Introduction to the Folklore of Christian Legend*. Cambridge, Mass.: Medaeval Academy of America, 1948.

Loomis, Gertrude Schoepperle. *Tristan and Isolt: A Study of the Sources of the Romance*. 2 vols. New York: Franklin, 1960.

Loomis, Laura A. Hibbard. *Medaeval Romance in England: A Study of the Sources and Analogues of the Non-Cyclic Metrical Romances*. 1924; rpt. of rev. ed., New York: Franklin, 1960.

Loomis, Roger S. *Celtic Myth and Arthurian Romance*. New York: Columbia University Press, 1927.

Lorimer, D. L. R., and E. O. Lorimer. *Persian Tales: Written Down for the First Time in the Original Kermani and Bakhtiari*. London: Macmillan, 1919.

Löseth, E. *Robert le Diable: Roman d'aventures*. 1903; rpt. New York: Johnson Reprint, 1968.

Lowie, Robert H. "Ethnographic Notes on the Washo." *University of California Publications in American Archaeology and Ethnography* 36 (1939): 301–52.

———. "Shoshonean Tales." *Journal of American Folklore* 37 (1924): 1–242.

———. "Myths and Traditions of the Crow." *Anthropological Papers of the American Museum of Natural History* 25 (1918): 1–308.

Lucas, Peter J. "An Interpretation of *Sir Orfeo*." *Leeds Studies in English* 6 (1972): 1–9.

Lucente, Gregory L. "The Ideology of Form in 'La Lupa.' " *The Narrative of Realism and Myth: Verga, Lawrence, Faulkner, Pavese*. [Includes text of Verga's "La Lupa."] Baltimore: Johns Hopkins University Press, 1981. 54–94.

Lundell, Torborg. "Gender-Related Biases in the Type and Motif Indexes of Aarne and Thompson." In Bottigheimer: 149–63.

Luther, Frank. *Americans and Their Songs*. New York: Harper, 1942.

Lüthi, Max. *The European Folktale: Form and Nature*. Trans. John D. Niles. Philadelphia: Institute for the Study of Human Issues, 1982.

———. "Aspects of the Märchen and the Legend." In Ben-Amos: 17–33.

Luzel, F. M. *Contes populaires de Basse-Bretagne*. 2 vols. Paris: Maisonneuve & Leclerc, 1887.

MacCana, Proinsias. *Celtic Mythology*. New York: Bedrick, 1985.

McClintock, Walter. *The Old North Trail: Life, Legends, and Religion of the Blackfeet Indians*. 1910; rpt. Lincoln: University of Nebraska Press, 1968.

MacCulloch, John A. "Changeling." *Encyclopedia of Religion and Ethics*, ed. James Hastings: 3:359–63.

———. *Eddic*. Vol. 11 of *The Mythology of All Races*. Ed. Louis Herbert Gray.

———. *The Childhood of Fiction: A Study of Folk Tales and Primitive Thought*. London: Murray, 1905.

McCulloch, William. *Bengali Household Tales*. London: Hodder and Stoughton, 1912.

MacDougall, James, and George Calder. *Folk Tales and Fairy Lore in Gaelic and English*. Edinburgh: Grant, 1910.

MacGregor, Alasdair A. *The Peat-Fire Flame: Folk-Tales and Traditions of the Highlands and Islands*. Edinburgh: Moray, 1937.

Mack, John E. *Nightmares and Human Conflict*. Boston: Little, Brown, 1970.

MacRitchie, David. *The Testimony of Tradition*. London: Kegan Paul, Trench, Trübner, 1890.

*The Mahabharata of Vyasa Krishna Dwaipayana: Selections from the Adi Parva and the Sambha Parva*. New York: Philosophical Library, 1952.

Maliver, Bruce L. *The Encounter Game*. New York: Stein and Day, 1973.

Markale, Jean. *Melusine: Ou l'androgyne*. Paris: Retz, 1983.

Marriott, Alice, and Carol K. Rachlin. *American Indian Mythology*. New York: Crowell, 1968.

Martin, Albert. *One Man, Hurt*. New York: Macmillan, 1975.

Martin, Minnie. *Basutoland: Its Legends and Customs*. London: Nichols, 1903.

Massignon, Geneviève. *Folktales of France*. Trans. Jacqueline Hyland. Chicago: University of Chicago Press, 1968.

Masters, R. E. L. *Eros and Evil: The Sexual Pathology of Witchcraft*. Baltimore, Md.: Penguin, 1974.

————. *Forbidden Sexual Behavior and Morality: An Objective Re-Examination of Perverse Sex Practices in Different Cultures*. New York: Julian, 1962.

Matalene, Carolyn. "Women as Witches." *International Journal of Women's Studies* 1 (1978): 573–87.

Mathews, Cornelius. *Hiawatha and Other Legends of the Wigwams of the Red American Indians*. London: Sonnenschein, 1882.

Mathias, Elizabeth. *Italian Folktales in America*. Detroit: Wayne State University Press, 1985.

Maxfield, Berton L., and W. H. Millington. "Visayan Folk-Tales, II." *Journal of American Folklore* 20 (1907): 97–112.

————. "Visayan Folk-Tales, I." *JAFL* 19 (1906): 89–103.

May, Robert. *Sex and Fantasy*. New York: Norton, 1980.

————. "Fantasy Differences in Men and Women." *Psychology Today*, April 1968, 42–45, 69.

Mayer, Fanny Hagin. *Ancient Tales in Modern Japan: An Anthology of Japanese Folk Tales*. Bloomington: Indiana University Press, 1985.

Mechling, W. H. "Malecite Tales." *Geological Survey of Canada, Anthropological Series*. 49 (1914): vi–133.

Megas, Georgios A. *Folktales of Greece*. Trans. Helen Colaclides. Chicago: University of Chicago Press, 1970.

Messing, Simon D. "Group Therapy and Social Status in the Zar Cult of Ethiopia." *American Anthropologist* 60 (1958): 1120–26.

Metzger, Berta. *Tales Told in Korea*. New York: Stokes, 1932.

Meyer, Paul. "L'enfant voué au diable: Rédaction en vers." *Romania* 33 (1904): 162–78.

Michelet, Jules. *Satanism and Witchcraft: A Study in Medieval Superstition*. 1939; rpt. New York: Citadel, 1971.

Midelfort, H. C. Erik. *Witch-Hunting in Southwestern Germany, 1562–1684*. Stanford, Calif.: Stanford University Press, 1972.

Mijatovich, Elodie L. *Serbian Folklore*. 2d ed. London: 1899.

Miller, Alan L. "The Swan-Maiden Revisited: Religous Significance of 'Divine-Wife': Folktales with Special Reference to Japan." *Asian Folklore Studies* 46 (1987): 55–86.

Miller, Elaine K. *Mexican Folk Narrative from the Los Angeles Area*. Austin: University of Texas Press, 1973.

Miller, Robert P. "The Wife of Bath's Tale and Medaeval Exempla." *Journal of English Language History* 32 (1965): 442–56.

Mills, James Philip. *The Ao Nagas.* London: Macmillan, 1926.

Mitchell, Mary. *Birth of a Legend* [Lohengrin]. London: Methuen, 1956.

Monter, E. William. "The Pedestal and the Stake: Courtly Love and Witchcraft." In *Becoming Visible: Women in European History,* ed. Renate Bridenthal and Claudia Koonz. Boston: Houghton Mifflin, 1977. 119–36.

———. *Witchcraft in France and Switzerland: The Borderlands during the Revolution.* Ithaca: Cornell University Press, 1976.

Moore, George. "Julia Cahill's Curse." In *The Untilled Field.* 1903; rpt. Freeport, N.Y.: Books for Libraries Press, 1970.

Morgan, Elaine. *The Descent of Woman.* New York: Stein & Day, 1972.

Morice, Rev. Father. "Three Carrier Myths." *Transactions of the Canadian Institute* 5 (1898): 2–36.

Mullen, Pat. *Irish Tales.* London: Faber & Faber, 1938.

Müller, Eduard. "Two Irish Tales." *Revue Celtique* 3 (1876–78): 342–60.

Mulley, Jane. "Danish Popular Tales." *Folk-Lore Record* 3 (1881): 201–36.

Murphy, Gerard. *Tales from Ireland.* Dublin: Browne & Nolan, 1947.

Neumann, Erich. *The Great Mother: An Analysis of the Archetype.* Trans. Ralph Manheim. 1963; rpt. Princeton, N.J.: Princeton University Press, 1970.

———. *Amor and Psyche: The Psychic Development of the Feminine, A Commentary on the Tale by Apuleius.* Trans. Ralph Manheim. New York: Pantheon, 1956.

Newell, William W. "Sources of Shakespeare's *Tempest.*" *Journal of American Folklore* 16 (1903): 234–57.

———. "Lady Featherflight: An English Folktale." *Journal of American Folklore* 6 (1893): 54–62.

Nicoloff, Assen. *Bulgarian Folklore.* Cleveland: Assen Nicoloff, 1975.

Nodier, Charles. *Trilby: The Fairy of Argyle.* Trans. Nathan Haskell Dole. Boston: Estes & Lauriat, 1895.

Noel, Sybille. *The Magic Bird of Chomo-Lung-Ma: Tales of Mount Everest, the Turquoise Peak.* Garden City, N.Y.: Doubleday, Doran, 1931.

Noy, Dov, ed. *Folktales of Israel.* Trans. Gene Baharav. Chicago: University of Chicago Press, 1963.

Oates, Joyce Carol. *Marriages and Infidelities.* New York: Vanguard, 1972.

Obeyesekere, Gananath. *Medusa's Hair: An Essay on Personal Symbols and Religious Experience.* Chicago: University of Chicago Press, 1981.

O'Flaherty, Wendy Doniger. See Doniger, Wendy.

Ogle, M. B. "Some Theories of Irish Literary Influence and the Lay of Yonec." *Romanic Review* 10 (1919): 123–48.

Opler, Morris E. *Myths and Legends of the Lipan Apache Indians.* New York: American Folklore Society, 1940.

Opler, Morris E. *Myths and Tales of the Jicarilla Apache Indians.* New York: American Folk-Lore Society, 1938.

Ortutay, Gyula. *Hungarian Folk Tales*. Budapest: Kossuth, 1962.

O'Sullivan, Sean, ed. and trans. *Folktales of Ireland*. Chicago: University of Chicago Press, 1966.

Owen, Mary Alicia. *Folk-Lore of the Musquakie Indians of North America*. London: Nutt, 1904.

Owens, William A. *Texas Folk Songs*. Austin: Texas Folklore Society, 1950.

Pakrasi, Mira. *Folk Tales of Assam*. Delhi: Sterling, 1969.

Paredes, Américo, ed. and trans. *Folktales of Mexico*. Chicago: University of Chicago Press, 1970.

Parker, H. *Village Folk-Tales of Ceylon*. 3 vols. London: Luxac, 1910–14.

Parker, K. Langloh. *More Australian Legendary Tales*. London: Nutt, 1898.

Parsons, Elsie Clews. *Folk-Lore of the Antilles*. Vol. 2. New York: American Folk-Lore Society, 1936.

———. "Micmac Folk-Lore." *Journal of American Folklore* 38 (1925): 55–133.

———. "Pueblo-Indian Folk-Tales, Probably of Spanish Provenience." *Journal of American Folklore* 31 (1918): 245–55

Pascal, Richard. " 'Farther than Samarkind': The Escape Theme in Shirley Jackson's 'The Tooth.' " *Studies in Short Fiction* 19 (1982): 133–39.

Patai, Daphne. *Myth and Ideology in Contemporary Brazilian Fiction*. Rutherford: Fairleigh Dickinson University Press, 1983.

Patai, Raphael. "Lilith." *Journal of American Folklore* 77 (1964): 295–314.

Paton, William R. "Folktales from the Aegean, 2." *Folk-Lore* 11 (1900): 113–19.

———."Folktales from the Greek Islands." *Folk-Lore* 10 (1899): 495–502.

Pedroso, Consiglieri. *Portuguese Folk-Tales*. Trans. Henriqueta Monteiro. 1882; rpt. New York: Blom, 1969.

Penzer, N. M. *The Ocean of Story*. 10 vols. London: Sawyer, 1923.

Person, Ethel Spector. *Dreams of Love and Fateful Encounters: The Power of Romantic Passion*. New York: Norton, 1988.

Plath, Sylvia. *The Collected Poems*. Ed. Ted Hughes. New York: Harper & Row, 1981.

———. *The Bell Jar*. New York: Harper & Row, 1971.

Postma, Minnie. *Tales from the Basotho*. Trans. Susie McDermid. Austin: University of Texas Press, 1974.

Pourrat, Henri. *A Treasury of French Tales*. London: Allen & Unwin, 1953.

Prince, J. Dyneley. *Passamaquoddy Texts*. New York: Stechert, 1921.

Prior, R. C. A. *Ancient Danish Ballads*. 3 vols. London: 1860.

Pyle, Howard. *The Wonder Clock*. New York: Harper, 1915.

Rabuzzi, Kathryn Allen. *The Sacred and the Feminine: Toward a Theology of Housework*. New York: Seabury, 1982.

Rad, Gerhard von. *Genesis: A Commentary*. Philadelphia: Westminster, 1961.

Ralston, W. R. Shedden. *Tibetan Tales: Translated from the Tibetan of the Kah-Gyur by F. Anton von Schiefner*. London: Routledge, 1926.

———. "Beauty and the Beast." *Nineteenth Century* 4 (1878): 990–1012.

———. *Russian Folk Tales*. London: Smith, Elder, 1873.

Rand, Silas T. *Legends of the Micmacs.* 1894; rpt. New York: Longmans, Green, 1971.

Randolph, Vance. *The Devil's Pretty Daughter: And Other Ozark Folk Tales.* New York: Columbia University Press, 1955.

Ranke, Kurt, ed. *Folktales of Germany.* Trans. Lotte Baumann. Chicago: University of Chicago Press, 1968.

Ranke, Kurt, Hermann Bausinger, et al., eds. *Enzyklopadie des Märchen.* 7 vols. [to date]. New York: de Gruyter, 1977–.

Rasmussen, Knud. *The Netsilik Eskimos: Social Life and Spiritual Culture.* Copenhagen: Gyldendalske Bofhandel, Nordisk Verlang, 1931.

Ravenel, Florence Leftwich. "*Tydorel* and *Sir Gowther.*" *PMLA* 20 (1905): 152–77.

Reed, Toni. *Demon-Lovers and Their Victims in British Fiction.* Lexington, Ky.: University Press of Kentucky, 1988.

Rees, Alwyn, and Brinley Rees. *Celtic Heritage: Ancient Tradition in Ireland and Wales.* London: Thames & Hudson, 1961.

Reichard, Gladys A. "Literary Types and Dissemination of Myths." *Journal of American Folklore* 34 (1921): 269–307.

Remy, Nicholas. *Demonolatry.* Trans. E. A. Ashwin. Secaucus, N.J.: University Books, 1974.

Rhŷs, John. *Celtic Folklore: Welsh and Manx.* 2 vols. Oxford: Clarendon, 1901:

———. "Welsh Fairy Tales." *Y Cymmrodor: Magazine of the Honourable Society of Cymmrodorion* 5 (1882): 49–143.

Rink, Henrik. *Tales and Traditions of the Eskimos.* 1875; rpt. Montreal: McGill-Queen's University Press, 1974.

Rink, Signe. "The Girl and the Dogs: An Eskimo Folk-Tale with Comments." *American Anthropologist* 11 (1898): 181–87.

Rivlin, Lily. "Lilith." *Ms.* 1 (1972): 92–97, 114–15.

Robbins, Emmet. "Famous Orpheus." In Warden: 3–23.

Robbins, Jahn, and June Robbins. "The Mother Who Ran Away." *McCall's,* July 1956, 48, 105–8, 112.

Robbins, Rossell Hope. *The Encyclopedia of Witchcraft and Demonology.* New York: Crown, 1959.

Robe, Stanley L. *Mexican Tales and Legends from Veracruz.* Berkeley: University of California Publications, Folklore Studies, 1971.

Roiphe, Anne Richardson. *Up the Sandbox!* New York: Simon & Schuster, 1970.

Romilly, H. H. *From My Verandah in New Guinea.* London: Nutt, 1889.

Roscher, Wilhelm Henrich. See Hillman and Roscher.

Rose, H. J. *A Handbook of Greek Mythology.* New York: Dutton, 1959.

Roussel, Louis. *Contes de Mycono.* Léopol: Societé Savante des Sciences et des Lettres, 1929.

Rudwin, Maximilian. *The Devil in Legend and Literature.* 1931; rpt. New York: AMS, 1970.

Ruel, Malcolm. "Were-Animals and the Introverted Witch." *Witchcraft: Confessions and Accusations.* In Mary Douglas: 333–50.

Russ, Joanna. "Russalka or the Seacoast of Bohemia." In Zipes, *Don't Bet on the Prince:* 88–94.

Russell, W. M. S. "More about Folklore and Literature." *Folklore* 94 (1983): 3–32.

Sapir, Edward. *Wishram Texts.* Leyden: Brill, 1909.

Sastri, Pandit, and S. M. Natesa. *Dravidian Nights: Being a Translation of Madanakamarajankadai.* Madras: Excelsior, 1886.

de la Saussaye, P. D. Chantepie. *Religon of the Teutons.* Trans. B. J. Vous. Boston: Ginn, 1902.

Schaafsma, Karen. "The Demon Lover: Lilith and the Hero in Modern Fantasy." *Extrapolation* 28 (1987): 52–61.

Schmölders, Claudia. *Die Wilde Frau: Mythische Geschichten zum Staunen, Fürchten, und Begehren.* Köln: Diederichs, 1984.

Schneider, Monique. *De l'exorcisme à la psychanalyse: Le féminin expurgé.* Paris: Retz, 1979.

Schneller, Christian. *Märchen und Sagen aus Walschtirol.* Insbruck: Wagner, 1867.

Schofield, William H. "The Lays of Graelent and Lanval, and the Story of Wayland." *PMLA* 15 (1900): 121–79.

———. *Studies on the Libeaus Desconus.* Boston: Ginn, 1895.

Schoolcraft, Henry R. *Indian Legends: from Algic Researches.* 1956; rpt. Westport, Conn.: Greenwood, 1974.

———. *Myth of Hiawatha.* Philadelphia: 1856.

Schorer, C. E. "Indian Tales of C. C. Trowbridge: *The Star Woman.*" *Midwest Folklore* 12 (1962): 17–24.

Scot, Reginald. *The Discovery of Witchcraft.* Carbondale: Southern Illinois University Press, 1964.

Scott, Sir Walter. *Letters on Witchcraft and Demonology.* New York: Gordon, 1974.

———. "Introduction to the Tale of Tamlane." *Minstrelsy of the Scottish Border.* London: Harrap, 1931.

Seaton, Mary E. "Swan Maidens." *Encyclopedia of Religion and Ethics,* ed. James Hastings: 12:125–26.

Sebald, Hans. *Witchcraft: The Heritage of a Heresy.* New York: Elsevier, 1978.

Seki, Keigo. *Folktales of Japan.* Trans. Robert J. Adams. Chicago: University of Chicago Press, 1963.

———. "The Spool of Thread: A Subtype of the Japanese Serpent-Bridegroom Tale." In *Studies in Japanese Folklore,* ed. Richard M. Dorson. Bloomington: Indiana University Press, 1963. 267–88.

Seklemian, A. G. *The Golden Maiden: And Other Folk Tales and Fairy Stories Told in Armenia.* Cleveland: Helman-Taylor, 1898.

Sellers, Charles. *Tales from the Lands of Nuts and Grapes: Spanish and Portuguese Folklore.* London: Field & Tuer, 1888.

Severs, J. B. "Antecedents of Sir Orfeo." In *Studies in Medieval Literature: In Honor of Albert Croll Baugh*, ed. MacEdward Leach. Philadelphia: University of Pennsylvania Press, 1966. 187–207.

Sharp, Cecil, and Maud Karpeles. *English Folk Songs from the Southern Appalachians*. London: Oxford University Press, 1932.

Shenhar, Aliza. "The Woman with the Animal Face." In *Fields of Offerings: Studies in Honor of Raphael Patai*, ed. Victor D. Sanua. London: Associated University Press, 1983. 111–27.

Shulman, Sandra. *Nightmare*. London: David & Charles, 1979.

Shumaker, Wayne. *The Occult Sciences in the Renaissance: A Study in Intellectual Patterns*. Berkeley: University of California Press, 1972.

Sibree, James, Jr. "The Oratory, Songs, Legends, and Folk-Tales of the Malagasy [part 3]." *Folk-Lore Journal* 1 (1883): 201–43.

Sibunruang, Jit-Kasem. *Siamese Folktales*. Bangkok: M. Gomiero, 1954.

Simms, S. C. "Traditions of the Crows." *Field Museum of Natural History: Anthropological Series* 6 (1903): 289–90.

Simpson, Jacqueline. " 'Be Bold, but Not Too Bold': Female Courage in Some British and Scandinavian Legends." *Folklore* 102 (1991): 16–30.

———. *Icelandic Folktales and Legends*. London: Batsford, 1972.

Sinistrari, Ludovico M. *Demoniality*. Printed in full in Masters, *Eros and Evil*.

Skinner, Alanson. "Traditions of the Iowa Indians." *Journal of American Folklore* 38 (1925): 425–506.

———. "Plains Ojibwa Tales." *Journal of American Folklore* 32 (1919): 293–95.

———. "Plains Cree Tales." *Journal of American Folklore* 29 (1916): 353–61.

———. "Notes on the Eastern Cree and Northern Saulteaux." *Anthropological Papers of the American Museum of Natural History* 9 (1912): 1–177.

Skinner, Alanson, and John V. Satterlee. "Folklore of the Menomini Indians." *Anthropological Papers of the American Museum of Natural History* 13 (1915): 249–53, 305–11, 381–82.

Sklar, Anna. *Runaway Wives*. New York: Coward, McCann & Geoghegan, 1976.

Skolnik, Jennifer. "Notes of a Recycled Housewife." *New York Magazine*, May 22, 1972, 36–40.

Smith, Erminnie A. "Myths of the Iroquois." *Report of the Bureau of American Ethnology* 2 (1880–81): 49–116.

Smith, Reed. *South Carolina Ballads: With a Study of the Traditional Ballad To-Day*. Cambridge, Mass.: Harvard University Press, 1928.

Speck, Frank G. "Myths and Folk-Lore of the Timiskaming Algonquin and Timagami Ojibwa." *Geological Survey of Canada, Anthropological Series* 9 (1915): 48.

Spender, Dale. *Man-Made Language*. London: Routledge & Kegan Paul, 1980.

Sprenger, Jakob, and Heinrich Kramer. *Malleus Maleficarum*. Trans. Montague Summers. 1928; rpt. New York: Blom, 1970.

Spring, Ian. "Orfeo and Orpheus: Notes on a Shetland Ballad." *Lore and Language* 3 (1984): 41–52.

Stack, Edward, and Charles Lyall. *The Mikirs.* London: Nutt, 1908.

Steere, Edward. *Swahili Tales.* London: 1870.

Stephens, James. *Land of Youth.* New York: Macmillan, 1924.

Stern, Stephen. "Studies in Folklore and Ethnicity." *Studies in Folklore and Ethnicity,* ed. Larry Danielson. Los Angeles: California Folklore Society, 1978. 7–32.

Stevens, E. S. [Lady Drower]. *Folk-Tales of 'Iraq: Set Down and Translated from the Vernacular.* London: Oxford University Press, 1931.

Stokes, Maive S. H. *Indian Fairy Tales.* London: 1880.

Stone, Kay F. "The Misuses of Enchantment: Controversies on the Significance of Fairy Tales." In Jordan and Kalčik: 125–45.

"The Story of Long Snake." *South African Journal of Folklore* 1 (1879): 7–9.

Straparola, Giovanni Francesco. *The Nights of Straparola.* Trans. W. G. Waters. 2 vols. London: Lawrence & Bullen, 1894.

Stutley, Margaret, and James Stutley. *Harper's Dictionary of Hinduism.* New York: Harper & Row, 1977.

Suleiman, Susan R. "Introduction: Varieties of Audience-Oriented Criticism." In Susan R. Suleiman and Inge Crossman, *The Reader in the Text: Essays on Audience and Interpretation.* Princeton: Princeton University Press, 1980. 3–45.

Surmelian, Leon. *Apples of Immortality: Folktales of Armenia.* Berkeley: University of California Press, 1968.

Swahn, Jan O. *The Tale of Cupid and Psyche.* Lund: Gleerup, 1955.

Swanton, John R. "Contributions to the Ethnology of the Haida." *Memoirs of the American Museum of Natural History* 8 (1905–9): 1–300.

Swire, Otta F. *The Highlands and Their Legends.* Edinburgh: Oliver & Boyd, 1963.

Taggart, James M. *Enchanted Maidens: Gender Relations in Spanish Folktales of Courtship and Marriage.* Princeton, N.J.: Princeton University Press, 1990.

———. "Men's Changing Image of Women in Nahuat Oral Tradition." *American Ethnologist* 6 (1979): 723–42.

Tatar, Maria. *The Hard Facts of the Grimms' Fairy Tales.* Princeton, N.J.: Princeton University Press, 1987.

Tavris, Carol, and Carole Offir. *The Longest War: Sex Differences in Perspective.* New York: Harcourt, Brace, Jovanovich, 1977.

Teit, James A. "Tahltan Tales" Part 3. *Journal of American Folklore* 34 (1921): 336–56.

———. "Kaska Tales." *Journal of American Folklore* 30 (1917): 427–73.

———. "Mythology of the Thompson Indians." *Memoirs of the American Museum of Natural History* 12 (1912): 199–416.

———. "Traditions of the Lillooet Indians of British Columbia." *Journal of American Folklore* 25 (1912): 287–371.

―――. "The Shuswap." *Memoirs of the American Museum of Natural History* 4 (1900–9): 443–790.

Thompson, Stith. *Motif Index of Folk-Literature: A Classification*. Rev. ed. Bloomington: Indiana University Press, 1966.

―――. "The Star Husband Tale." *Studia Septentrionalia* 4 (1953): 93–163.

―――. *The Folktale*. New York: Dryden, 1951.

―――. *Tales of the North American Indians*. Cambridge, Mass.: Harvard University Press, 1929.

―――. "European Tales among the North American Indians: A Study in the Migration of Folk-Tales." *Colorado College Publication: Language Series* 2 (1919): 319–471.

―――, ed. *One Hundred Favorite Folktales*. Bloomington: Indiana University Press, 1968.

Thomson, David. *The People of the Sea: A Journey in Search of the Seal Legend*. London: Barrie & Rockliff, 1965.

Thornhill, Mark. *Indian Fairy Tales*. London: Hatchards, 1889.

Thorpe, Benjamin. *Yule-Tide Stories: A Collection of Scandinavian and North German Popular Tales and Traditions*. London: Bohn, 1853.

Thrum, Thomas G. *Hawaiian Folk Tales*. Chicago: McClurg, 1912.

Tillhagen, Carl H. "The Conception of the Nightmare in Sweden." In *Humaniora: Essays in Literature, Folklore, Bibliography, Honoring Archer Taylor*, ed. Wayland D. Hand and Gustave O. Arlt. Locust Valley, N.Y.: Augustin, 1960. 317–29.

Toulmin, Stephen E. "Self-Knowledge and Knowledge of the Self." In *The Self: Psychological and Philosophical Issues*, ed. Theodore Mischel. Totowa, N.J.: Rowman & Littlefield, 1977. 291–317.

Turner, Lucien M. "Ethnology of the Ungava District, Hudson Bay Territory." *Report of the Bureau of American Ethnology* 11 (1889–90): 264–350.

Underwood, Mary Grace. "Courted by the Devil: A Perthshire Folk-Tale." *Folk-Lore* 22 (1911): 330–31.

Updike, John. Review of *Italian Folktales*, by Italo Calvino. *New Yorker*, Feb. 23, 1981, 120–26.

Vawter, Bruce. *On Genesis: A New Reading*. New York: Doubleday, 1977.

Venkataswami, M. N. "Folklore in the Central Provinces." *Indian Antiquary* 31 (1902): 133–34, 447–54.

Verga, Giovanni. See Lucente.

Vernaleken, Theodor. *In the Land of Marvels: Folk-Tales from Austria and Bohemia*. London: Sennenschein, 1889.

von Franz, Marie-Louise. *Problems of the Feminine in Fairytales*. Zurich: Spring, 1972.

von Gunther, Maria A. *Tales and Legends of the Tyrol*. London: Chapman & Hall, 1874.

von Sydow, C. W. *Selected Papers on Folklore: Published on the Occasion of His Seventieth Birthday*. Copenhagen: Rosenkilde & Bagger, 1948.

Wake, C. Staniland. "Ananci Stories." *Folk-Lore Journal* 1 (1883): 280–92.

Walker, Barbara G., ed. *The Woman's Encyclopedia of Myths and Secrets*. San Francisco: Harper & Row, 1983.

Walker, Benjamin. *The Hindu World: An Encyclopedic Survey of Hinduism*. 2 vols. New York: Praeger, 1968.

Walker, Warren S., and Ahgmet E. Uysal. *Tales Alive in Turkey*. Cambridge, Mass.: Harvard University Press, 1966.

Waller, John. *A Treatise on the Incubus or Night-Mare*. London: Cox, 1816.

Wang, Chi-Chen. *Traditional Chinese Tales*. New York: Columbia University Press, 1944.

Warden, John. *Orpheus: The Metamorphoses of a Myth*. Toronto: University of Toronto Press, 1982.

Wardrop, Marjorie S. *Georgian Folk Tales* [from the Caucasus]. London: Nutt, 1894.

Webster, Wentworth. *Basque Legends*. London: de Farran, 1887.

Weigle, Marta. *Spiders and Spinsters: Women and Mythology*. Albuquerque: University of New Mexico Press, 1982.

Wheeler, Howard T. *Tales from Jalisco, Mexico*. Philadelphia: Folk-Lore Society, 1943.

White, Hayden. "The Forms of Wildness: Archaeology of an Idea." In *The Wild Man Within: An Image in Western Thought from the Renaissance to Romanticism*, ed. Edward Dudley and Maximillian E. Novak. Pittsburgh: University of Pittsburgh Press, 1972. 3–38.

Whiting, Henry. *Sannillac: A Poem*. Boston: 1831.

Williams, Norman Powell. *The Ideas of the Fall and of Original Sin: A Historical and Critical Study*. London: Longmans, Green, 1927.

Willis, Roy. *Man and Beast*. New York: Basic, 1974.

Wills, Garry, et al. "Do Americans Suddenly Hate Kids?" *Esquire*, March 1974, 80–95.

Wilson, Horace Hayman, ed. and trans. *Works*. 12 vols. Vols. 6–10, *Vishnu Purana*. London: Trubner, 1861–77.

Wissler, Clark. *Star Legends among the American Indians*. New York: American Museum of Natural History, 1936.

Wissler, Clark, and D. C. Duvall. "Mythology of the Blackfoot Indians." *Anthropological Papers of the American Museum of Natural History* 2 (1908–9): 1–164.

Wood, Robin. "The Return of the Repressed." *Film Comment* 14 (1978): 24–32.

Woolsey, Gamel. *Spanish Fairy Tales*. 2d ed. London: Carrington, 1946.

Wratislaw, A. H. *Sixty Folk-Tales from Exclusively Slavonic Sources*. London: Stock, 1889.

Wright, J. C. "Purūravas and Urvaśī." *Bulletin of the School of Oriental and African Studies* [London] 30 (1957): 526–47.

Yanagida, Kunio. *Japanese Folk Tales*. Trans. Fanny Hagin Mayer. Tokyo: Tokyo News Service, 1954.

Yates, Dora E. *A Book of Gypsy Folk-Tales*. London: Phoenix House, 1948.

Yearsley, Macleod. *The Folklore of Fairy-Tales*. 1924; rpt. Detroit: Singing Tree, 1968.

Young, Frank W. "A Fifth Analysis of the Star Husband Tale." *Ethnology* 9 (1970): 389–413.

Zilboorg, Gregory. *The Medical Man and the Witch during the Renaissance*. Baltimore: Johns Hopkins Press, 1935.

Zipes, Jack. *Breaking the Magic Spell: Radical Theories of Folk and Fairy Tales*. Austin: University of Texas Press, 1979.

———, ed. *Don't Bet on the Prince: Contemporary Feminist Fairy Tales in North America and England*. New York: Methuen, 1986.

Zobarskas, Stepas. *Lithuanian Folk Tales*. Brooklyn, N.Y.: Rickard, 1958.